REFORMING ROME

Reforming Rome

Karl Barth and Vatican II

Donald W. Norwood

WILLIAM B. EERDMANS PUBLISHING COMPANY
GRAND RAPIDS, MICHIGAN / CAMBRIDGE, U.K.

Published 2015 by

Wm. B. Eerdmans Publishing Co.

2140 Oak Industrial Drive N.E., Grand Rapids, Michigan 49505 /

P.O. Box 163, Cambridge CB3 9PU U.K.

Printed in the United States of America

21 20 19 18 17 16 15   7 6 5 4 3 2 1

Library of Congress Cataloging-in-Publication Data

Norwood, Donald W., 1940-
    Reforming Rome: Karl Barth And Vatican II / Donald W. Norwood.
       pages   cm
    Includes bibliographical references and index.
    ISBN 978-0-8028-7210-4 (pbk.: alk. paper)
    1. Vatican Council (2nd : 1962-1965 : Basilica di San Pietro in Vaticano)
    2. Church renewal. 3. Barth, Karl, 1886-1968 — Influence.   I. Title.

BX8301962 .N626   2015
262′.52 — dc23
                                            2014039160

www.eerdmans.com

To

Nathaniel Micklem
John Marsh
George Caird
Norman Goodall

Contents

FOREWORD, *by Baroness Helena Kennedy*   xii

ACKNOWLEDGMENTS   xiv

ABBREVIATIONS   xvi

Introduction   xvii

1. Why Rome? Why Reform? Why Barth?   1

Why Rome?   1

Why Reform?   6

Reform and the Scandal of Sexual Abuse   9

Why Barth?   11

Why Only Barth?   13

Barth as a "Catholic" and Ecumenical Theologian
for the Whole Church   15

Ecumenical and Polemical   18

How Can One Who Is Not a Roman Catholic Assist
the Reform of Rome?   23

2. Reforming Rome: Continuing the Reformation   25

Reformation and Reunion, Barth and Congar   25

Catholic Challenges to Be More "Catholic"   29

Straight Talking and Dialogue   32

The Reformers and Their Hopes for a Free Reforming Council   35

Vatican II: The Council the Reformers Hoped For?   39

What Influence Did Barth and the Observers Have?   42

Specific Influences   46

Examples of the Observers' Influence   47

   Scripture   47

   Tradition   47

   Church   48

   Roman Catholic Ecumenism and the
      World Council of Churches   48

   Israel and the Jews Today   53

   Human Rights   53

   East/West Conflict and Communism   54

   Mary Co-Redeemer and Mother of the Church?   55

Is the Reformation Over?   55

3. **Responding to Vatican II, Part 1**   57

The Surprise Announcement   57

Barth's Excitement and Cautious Expectations   59

Barth's Summing Up of Main Issues at Vatican II   61

Dei Verbum   62

   Scripture and Tradition   64

   Hierarchy of Truths   65

   Tradition and Magisterium   66

Lumen Gentium   70

Vatican Documents about the Church   71

   People of God and/or Body of Christ   72

   Body of Christ, Head of the Body   74

   People of God and Vox Populi   77

   Subsistit in   78

   Eucharist Makes the Church?   80

   Local Church and/or Universal Church   81

   Authority beyond the Local Church   83

4. **Responding to Vatican II, Part 2**   85

Barth as Questioner   85

Humanae Vitae and the Challenge to Papal Authority   86

Papacy as a Question for All Christians   88

Can Only a Pope Get Things Done and Speak for All Christians?   90

How Does Barth Contribute to the Debate? Barth on Pope and Polity   91

Papal Infallibility?   94

Is the Pope Successor of Peter?   97

Irreformable Dogmas?   99

What More Did Barth Say about Hierarchy and Apostolic Succession?   102

Does It Matter to God How the Church Is Ordered?   104

What about the Hierarchy?   106

What about the Laity?   108

The Ministry of the Community: Is Barth's Radically Different Approach to Questions of Ministry Ecumenically Helpful?   110

Responding to Vatican II's Unfinished Agenda: Laity, Community of Women and Men?   113

Collegiality?   115

Collegial Theology   116

5. **Reforming or Converting Karl Barth: Roman Catholic Critics**   118

Dialogue Is Two-Way   118

Converted Critics   121

Is Barth Sufficiently "Catholic"?   122

Six Fundamental Roman Catholic Criticisms of Barth   124

Misunderstandings or Valid Criticisms?   125

Provisional Ecclesiology   126

Criticisms of Barth: Ecclesial Mediation   127

Baptism and Sacraments 128

Human Cooperation in Salvation 135

Church as Event and Institution 138

The Work of the Holy Spirit in the Church 143

The Church Universal 145

The Question of Woman, a Question Addressed
to Barth *and* Rome 146

Vatican II and Women 146

Women Arguing with Barth 149

*Moving on from Barth: Post–Vatican II Partnership of
Barth Scholars and Feminists* 158

Can Barth, with the Help of His Critics, Women and Men,
Help Reform Rome? 163

6. **Differences That Still Divide?** 165

After Vatican II, Are There Still Differences That Divide? 165

Justification by Faith 167

Natural Knowledge of God and the *Analogia Entis* 177

Mary and Joseph, Immaculate Conception, and the
Assumption of the Blessed Virgin 182

Hierarchy of Truths 192

7. **The Rediscovery of Unity** 197

Unity in Theory and Practice: Vatican II as an
Example of Unity 198

Jewish Comment: The Joy of Acceptance 200

Pope John XXIII's Vision 201

The Council Was an "Event" 202

The Restoration of Unity, an Event Not of Our Making 204

Saying Yes, "placet," to God's Will 205

Praying Together 206

Responding to the Word 208

Receptive Ecumenism 211

The Ecumenical Gift Exchange   213

Catholic Learning   215

Universal Catholicity   216

Pastoral Council   217

Subsidiarity   219

Conciliar Consensus and Discerning Truth through Debate   220

Does Barth Have Anything to Add to Discussions
    about Bishops?   220

Mission, Ecumenism, or an Interfaith Issue?
    The Jewish Question   222

Concluding Comment   230

Postscript: Joy and Peace and a New Pope   231

Bibliography   233

INDEX OF NAMES   258

INDEX OF SUBJECTS   262

Foreword

As a Catholic child in Glasgow at the time of the Second Vatican Council, the full meaning of the event passed over my head. That is not to say I was unaware of this significant happening. Catholicism was at the very heart of our family life, and at home, church, and school we were made deeply aware that something important was taking place in Rome and that it was auguring great change in the Church. My parents were enthusiasts for Pope John XXIII and welcomed his modernizing instincts. As dwellers in a city cruelly divided by sectarianism, they were very ready and willing to embrace ecumenism. They had watched families fall apart over inter-faith marriage and seen friends barred from mass and communion because they had married out. My parents and teachers were hoping for real change, imagining this was an opportunity to melt the hostilities of Protestants, who were just as hard line as their Catholic neighbors and, being the Scottish establishment, were able to discriminate against Catholics in jobs and services.

The Council was to address relations between the Catholic Church and the modern world, and while today it may not seem to have gone very far in that direction, at the time the changes seemed very significant to everyone in my community. Suddenly the mass was different; the priest no longer spoke in Latin. He faced the congregation, and the parishioners were more active participants. Prayers were revised, and some very unattractive references to other religions were abandoned. It was made clear that Jews were no more responsible for the death of Christ than Christians. There was recognition that disparate faiths had a common belief in God, and there was a swing away from biblical literalism. The theological conception that the Church was the eternal home of the saved and that outside the Church there was no salvation was suddenly questioned. The by-word was that Church principles should align human experience to the life of Christ.

Nuns threw off their traditional garb, and the clergy were more willing to speak out in favor of civil rights and trade unionism and against the Vietnam war. In retrospect, it seems to me that the post-war, post-Holocaust spirit of respecting human rights and the dignity of all humanity was infecting Rome too.

In his book, my dear friend, Reverend Dr. Donald Norwood, describes the role that was played by the observers and guests from other Christian denominations who attended the Council. They were all widely respected theologians, and amongst those invited was Karl Barth, who is at the center of Donald's work. Barth was too ill to attend but had visited the Pope and published his own book commenting on the outcome of the Council reports. Here Donald expands upon that work and helps us see events in their full historical and theological context.

Vatican II was a significant step of change for the Catholic Church, but many feel there is a need for a new Council to respond to some of the challenges facing our contemporary world. The Church has opposed war and is a vocal champion of the poor. It has been highly critical of the morality that permits the growing divide between rich and poor, but it has remained rigid in its stance on women priests, celibacy, sexuality, and other profoundly human matters.

This is a book about Barth, who was clearly an extraordinary man. But so too is Donald Norwood, and his book is a refreshing look at the important ways in which Christianity needs reform.

BARONESS HELENA KENNEDY
Principal of Mansfield College
Oxford, UK

Acknowledgments

This book is dedicated to four ecumenical pioneers who, in their last years, were members of our United Reformed Church congregation and Ecumenical Parish in Oxford: Nathaniel Micklem, John Marsh, George Caird, and Norman Goodall. As their student and later minister, I learned more from them than they from me. What I hope to share is their ecumenical inspiration.

Just before the War, Nat Micklem and John Marsh undertook a dangerous mission of support to persecuted Christian leaders, Roman Catholic and Protestant, in Hitler's Germany. John Marsh and Norman Goodall were active in the first Assemblies of the World Council of Churches. All three knew Karl Barth. George Caird was an observer at Vatican II. After the Council, Norman Goodall was one of the first Protestants to be invited to give lectures in Rome. None lived to see the day when the college they served with such distinction as principals and alumni would be led by a distinguished Roman Catholic laywoman, Baroness Helena Kennedy, current Principal of Mansfield College, Oxford, and staunch advocate of human rights.

Participation in a wide range of Ecumenical Assemblies and Conferences has meant that I have never been short of expert advice and encouragement in studying the main themes covered in this book. Books come to life when you meet their authors. Through being the reporter for Churches Together in England at World Council of Churches events since the Faith and Order Conference at Santiago de Compostela in 1993, I have met with many of its key leaders like Tom Best, Lukas Vischer, Konrad Raiser, and Mary Tanner. Bill Rusch and Norman A. Hjelm helpfully commented on earlier drafts of this book. In 2007-2008 we spent a year working with younger students at the World Council of Churches Ecumenical Institute at Bossey, near Calvin's Geneva. Friend Paul Murray's initiative with Conferences at Durham on "Receptive Ecumenism and the Call to Catholic Learning" revived the excitement I once felt when I first heard about Vatican II. There are many Roman Catholics who long for renewal, reform, and the restoration of unity. Along with Paul Murray, I mention Cecily Boulding, Nicholas Harvey, Fergus Kerr, Paul Lakeland, Nicholas Lash, Annemarie Mayer, Margaret O'Gara, and Mark Woodruff. My seminar paper on "Non-Roman Catholic Observers at Vatican II," delivered at a Vatican II Jubilee Conference in Leeds in 2012, received helpful comments from Mathijs Lamberigts from Leuven, one of the authors of *The History of Vatican II*. Professor Mary Grey preached at my Induction in Bournemouth in 1995 while my closest colleague when reporting on WCC events has been Fr. Thaddée Barnas of *Irénikon* and the monastery at Chevetogne, forever famous for the ecumenical links first forged by Dom Lambert Beauduin.

Every sermon I ever preach owes something to Barth, and over the years my understanding has been enriched by Barth scholars and friends like Paul Avis, Nigel Biggar, David Clough, David Ford, Tim Gorringe, Garrett Green, Tom Greggs, Colin Gunton, Dan Hardy, Bruce McCormack, Paul Nimmo, and Tom Torrance. All are or were involved with me in the Society for the Study of Theology, where every year we are delighted to discover more seminar papers being offered on Barth than on any other theologian. The same is probably true of books. Like many other Barth scholars, I have visited Karl Barth's home in Basel and received much help and encouragement from the Director of the Karl Barth Archive, Hans-Anton Drewes.

I am especially indebted to William B. Eerdmans Jr. and his staff for publishing this work (and many other books on Barth), and to editors Linda Bieze and Jenny Hoffman and all who have helped improve the original drafts.

Living and working in Oxford most of my life as student, minister, and teacher has been and remains an enormous privilege. It grants me access to one of the best libraries in the world and one of the best bookshops. But study even in a university city can often be a lonely pursuit, and without the support of my lovely wife, Margaret, I could not write another word.

DONALD W. NORWOOD,
Oxford

Abbreviations

BEM   *Baptism Eucharist and Ministry,* WCC Faith and Order Document

CD   Karl Barth *Church Dogmatics*

ET   English Translation

F&O   Faith and Order Commission of World Council of Churches

JWG   Joint Working Group between the Roman Catholic Church and World Council of Churches

WCC   World Council of Churches

Vatican II Documents

All Vatican II documents are known by the first two words in the original Latin text:

DH   Dignitatis Humanae, Religious Freedom

DV   Dei Verbum, Word of God and Tradition

GS   Gaudium et Spes, Church in World

LG   Lumen Gentium, the Church

NA   Nostra Aetate, Church and Other Religions

SC   Sacrosanctum Concilium, the Liturgy

UR   Unitatis Redintegratio, Church Unity

Introduction

Karl Barth was among a select group of non–Roman Catholic observers and special guests who were invited to the Second Vatican Council (1962-65) to assist the reform, renewal, or, as it was described, the *aggiornamento* of the Roman Catholic Church. Ill health prevented his attendance but with the help of his Roman Catholic friend, Hans Küng, one of the *periti*, experts at the Council, he kept himself informed about all its deliberations and a year after it ended made his own visit to Rome, armed with carefully prepared questions and comments on key documents of the Council. He became one of the first Protestant theologians ever to have an hour-long discussion with the pope. Bishop Otto Dibelius of Berlin had met with Pius XII in 1955 but the conversation only lasted a few minutes and some of that was about the weather!

Rome's invitation to Barth was testimony to the high regard Roman Catholics had for one who can justly be regarded as one of the greatest theologians of the twentieth century. Other observers were invited to represent their own denomination or confessional group. So Lukas Vischer as Director of the Faith and Order Commission of the World Council of Churches represented the World Council. George Caird of Oxford represented the International Congregational Council, Albert Outler Methodists, Krysten Skydsgaard the Lutheran World Federation, John R. H. Moorman the Anglican Communion. These men (no women) and their colleagues of other traditions were each highly respected in their own churches and were commissioned to represent their church's views and to report back. Barth was invited in his own right. Often a strong critic of Rome but never just of Rome, he became *the* non–Roman Catholic theologian who was most respected in Rome. Pope Pius XII is said to have described Barth as the greatest theologian since Thomas Aquinas — praise indeed since the great thirteenth-century theologian continues to be highly regarded in and beyond Rome. Barth's Roman Catholic friends and colleagues included Erich Przywara from his days when both were teachers at Münster and Hans Küng who wrote his doctoral dissertation on Barth and Justification, and Hans Urs von Balthasar, his colleague in Basel, author of what is still regarded as one of the best books on Barth. Yves Congar invited Barth to share in lectures and seminars with him in Paris in the 1930s. Barth often commented that he was better understood in Rome than he was in his own Reformed Church circles. But the main point here is that even where Roman Catholics strongly disagreed with some of Barth's theology, they held him in deep respect. That is why even the pope wanted to talk with him. So did Ratzinger, Rahner, and Congar, and a number of other distinguished Roman Catholic theologians whom he met in Rome.

The observers were not simply observers. They had meetings, formal and informal, with the bishops and the *periti* who included theologians like Congar, Küng, Rahner, and Ratzinger. They were asked for their views on the different schema and gave them boldly. Though only the Roman Catholic bishops could debate and decide, the non-Catholic observers came to feel they were part of the council and sometimes it was their views that carried the day. This had never happened before. Protestants were invited to the Council of Trent but felt it too risky to attend — remember what happened to John Hus at Constance in 1415. Despite assurances of safe conduct, he was burned at the stake. They were also not sure they would be given a fair hearing. They were not invited to the First Vatican Council but urged to repent and return to Rome. Vatican II offered a generous invitation — come and help us! It delivered no anathemas or condemnations. Rome showed that the invitations were genuine when she committed herself irrevocably to join in the ecumenical movement, a commitment that was further endorsed in Pope John Paul's ecumenical encyclical, *Ut Unum Sint* in 1995. Prior to Vatican II, Rome had banished or silenced her more ecumenically minded theologians and ordered them to take no part in ecumenical conferences. Many of them were now reinstated and consulted. This Council was prepared to listen and learn, even from Rome's critics.

The convictions and sometimes disagreements expressed by the observers can be read in their own accounts and also in the "official" five-volume *History of Vatican II*. Barth published his own short report in his *Ad Limina Apostolorum: An Appraisal of Vatican II*. It was read and studied by Roman Catholic colleagues, among them Cardinal Joseph Ratzinger, later Pope Benedict XVI.

Barth's account is very brief and needs to be amplified. This is what I attempt to do, drawing on the whole range of his numerous theological writings. It is also one-sided in that he promised not to report Pope Paul VI's responses or those of other theologians he met with in Rome. Apart from a lighthearted remark that the pope promised to pray for him that in his old age he might be given further enlightenment about the Virgin Mary and about Joseph, Barth kept his promise. In the early days of the Council, Barth believed and accepted that the Council's prime objective was the Roman Catholic Church's own internal renewal. If as part of this process Rome became more ecumenical, that was a bonus, not the main intention. He therefore counseled some of his friends in the World Council of Churches not to expect too much from Rome and was among those who were delighted when the Council exceeded their own or his more modest expectations. Indeed, it became something of an embarrassment that Rome might turn out to be more reformed than the Reformed! After the Council, Barth quickly discovered that the subject universities and congregations were most interested in was Vatican II's ecumenical significance. In many of the speeches and interviews he gave in his final years, 1965-68, church unity was what caught most people's attention. What had Barth to say about Rome and Reunion?

As I say, Barth's brief but lively account is one-sided. We are left with his questions, not with the answers.[1] Some of the answers we can glean from closer study of the Council documents and debates, debates that were sometimes quite contentious. Other responses we can guess at but in an informed way, based on what Roman Catholic theologians criticize in Barth. And just as the Council is still being studied nearly fifty years after it ended, so Barth research is alive and flourishing nearly fifty years after his death in December 1968. This is as it should be. In Barth's own view there is no past in the church. Aquinas and Anselm, Luther and Calvin are still with us. So is Pope John XXIII who convened the Council in 1959 and Congar and Barth who commented on it.

Barth was about to retire when the Council began, but his interest in Rome goes back in earnest to his days when he was a young Protestant professor in a predominantly Roman Catholic city and university in Germany in the 1920s. Before that when a pastor in a Swiss village at Safenvil he had oc-

---

1. One brief Roman Catholic response is the essay by Philip J. Rosato SJ, "*Ad Limina Apostolorum* in Retrospect: The Reaction of Karl Barth to Vatican II," in *Karl Barth Centenary Essays*, ed. S. W. Sykes (Cambridge: Cambridge University Press, 1989), pp. 87-114.

casional discussions with a Roman Catholic priest in a nearby village, something not so common in days when Catholics and Protestants rarely met. Not to be ignored is his lifelong love of Mozart, the Catholic composer he much preferred to the Protestant Bach, and the warm appreciation he expressed in his final years for his Roman Catholic doctor and nurse and the numerous unnamed priests who ministered to him through radio broadcasts, as did Protestant pastors on Sundays, when he was too ill to go to church.

When Barth criticized Rome as he often did, his positive intention was to aid her reform. In this I see Barth as continuing the Reformation. The sixteenth-century Reformers, Luther, Calvin, Zwingli, were all Roman Catholics. It was not their intention to separate from Rome and form new churches. "Protestantism" was an unintended consequence of the failure to reform the whole church as it then was, at least as far as the West was concerned. Barth longed for the day when the label "Protestant" no longer applied. He also preferred the word "catholic" to ecumenical. He wanted to be part of a reformed catholic church. This was also Calvin's wish. As a Reformed professor, Barth was expected to lecture on Calvin and on Zwingli and the Reformed Confessions. As he did so, he soon discovered one could not make sense of their aims without studying the Roman Catholic Church they were originally part of. What were they trying to reform? Trent was not the free, reforming Council the Reformers hoped for. Vatican II nearly was. This is another reason why Barth got so excited about a Council the Reformers could only dream of but never lived to see. And none of the Reformers ever met the pope. Barth did.

I mentioned earlier that Barth was about to retire when the Council began. I was tempted to add that he was therefore quite old. Age is a relative factor and easily exaggerated. Barth was in fact five years younger than Pope John XXIII who convened the Council and five years younger than Cardinal Bea who became the first Secretary for Christian Unity at the Vatican and as such extended the invitation to Barth. Pope John XXIII and Bea were both born in 1881. Barth was born in 1886. What all three had in common in addition to their profound Christian faith was the experience of living through two world wars, the rise of fascism and anti-Semitism in Germany and Italy, and the failure of the churches, Roman Catholic and Protestant, to relate the gospel to the desperate needs of the modern world. Rome had withdrawn from the modern world and locked herself away in a fortress. Liberal Protestants like those who had supported the German Kaiser's war aims had betrayed and compromised the faith. There was and is dire need for a real *aggiornamento* rooted in the gospel. One Protestant theologian's vast though incomplete *Church Dogmatics* were seen and can still be seen as an ecumenical, or as Barth would say, "catholic," resource for such a task.

This study is partly historical but mainly theological. It is about the whole Christian Church. Rome is the most universal of all churches. She manages to hold together half the world's Christians. But she also alienates the other half — for a whole variety of different reasons that Vatican II and its heirs sought to resolve. The Council changed the atmosphere in which we meet. Though progress has been slow, there is no going back, especially if you believe with Barth that we must deal with our divisions as we deal with sin, "our own and others," and are helped by God to do just that. It is Christ's prayer that all may be one, not just for our own sakes, but that the world may believe.

CHAPTER ONE

Why Rome? Why Reform? Why Barth?

In this chapter I ask a number of obvious questions whose answers are not so obvious: Why Rome, why reform, why Barth? I hope in this way to take nothing for granted but to look more carefully for reasons and explanations as to how one Protestant theologian of a previous century should still be of great interest to those of us who long for a better and more united church in the twenty-first. And even here we cannot take concern for church reform and church unity for granted, as there are always those who will tell us that other things are far more important or that mutual tolerance is as far as we need go, in which case we do not need to worry too much about reform. So first Rome, meaning of course the Roman Catholic Church.

Why Rome?

It is especially important for those of us who are not Roman Catholics to accept as a fact that half the world's Christians are Roman Catholic. Christians account for one-third of the world's people, that is, for some two billion when world population stood at six billion. One billion are Roman Catholics, united across national frontiers by common allegiance to the Bishop of Rome. In many countries almost all the Christian population is Roman Catholic. This applies to every country in Latin America and in Europe to Austria, Belgium, France, Ireland, Italy, Luxembourg, Malta, Poland, Spain, and Portugal. Even in those lands that we most associate with the Protestant Reformation of the sixteenth century, Germany and Switzerland, Christian allegiance is almost equally divided between Roman Catholics and Protestants. In Switzerland the largest single tradition is the Roman Catholic

Church. In the United States and Canada there are whole states/provinces that are predominantly Roman Catholic. Great Britain is constitutionally a Protestant country where the reigning monarch is the titular head of the Church of England, but it is often pointed out that on a given Sunday more Christians would be found at Mass than at services in parish churches, and Catholic archbishops like Basil Hume have been as highly respected as any other Christian leader. As for the rest of the world, the Protestant-Catholic divide partly reflects the strength of different European missionary agencies in the nineteenth century or earlier. Ninety percent of people in the Philippines are Christian, the most predominantly Christian country in Asia and mainly Roman Catholic. Their strength is reflected in their role in the recent political liberation of the country from dictatorial rule. Angola and the Congo are predominantly Roman Catholic. Other countries in Africa have large Roman Catholic populations. Here, and indeed in most of the world outside Europe and the United States and Canada, the church is growing so much that most Christians now live in the so-called global south. This then leaves those countries that are easily labeled Orthodox — Greece, Russia, and countries once part of the USSR. There the Greek or Russian Orthodox churches embrace most citizens.

Those who want to go into more detail about the shape of what is sometimes called "the New Christendom" will learn much from the various books by Philip Jenkins[1] and others. They offer a healthy reminder to those of us who live in "secular" countries that religion, not least the Christian faith, remains a major influence in people's lives and world affairs, and, as I noted, in most parts of the world the church is growing.[2] My own research here was also informed by the World Council of Churches' prayer book, *In God's Hands: Common Prayer for the World.*[3] It enables Christian congregations everywhere to pray for every country in the world, week by week, and in an informed sort of way, not just for places that are unfortunate enough to be headline news and not just for churches in their own tradition. As a resource, it also reminds us there are many countries in which there are no member churches of the World Council. The *oikumene,* or whole inhabited world of

1. Philip Jenkins, *The Next Christendom: The Coming of Global Christianity* (Oxford: Oxford University Press, 2007); *God's Continent: Christianity, Islam and Europe's Religious Crisis* (Oxford: Oxford University Press, 2007).

2. Wesley Granberg-Michaelson, *From Times Square to Timbuktu* (Grand Rapids: Eerdmans, 2013), pleads with people in all churches to respond to these facts, for too few are doing so.

3. Hugh McCullum and Terry MacArthur, *In God's Hands* (Geneva: WCC, 2006).

the Greek New Testament as in Matthew 24:14, is bigger than the ecumenical movement of the World Council of Churches. The WCC currently includes some 349 member churches in 120 of the 204 or so different countries round the world. There are no countries in which there are no Christian churches. There are very few countries in which there is no Roman Catholic congregation. Everyone, everywhere lives in a Roman Catholic diocese. Rome is the most geographically universal of all Christian churches. Its leadership until most recently was predominantly European,[4] but one of the things that made the Second Vatican Council such a historic event was its global reach. It brought together 2,500 bishops from every continent. In March 2013 her cardinals elected the first "global pope," Francis I from Argentina. No other church can match the claim to have the whole world as her parish. John Wesley once made this claim for his own ministry as his right to preach anywhere. A similar claim to Rome's is made for Pentecostalism by the sociologist David Martin in *Pentecostalism: The World Their Parish*. The growth of Pentecostalism in the twentieth century has been phenomenal. But here we are talking about a movement and association of Pentecostal-type churches rather than a single institution.[5] The only institution that is more universal is the United Nations. Yet even this secular organization looks for leaders with what we may call a catholic and global vision and has found them, more often than not, in the Christian churches. All eight Secretary Generals to date have been religious men and all except U Thant have been Christian, and two of them Roman Catholic. U Thant was a Buddhist.

A second answer to the question "why Rome?" is that for Christians in the West, Rome or the medieval church is the mother of us all. The Protestant Reformation resulted in a break from Rome. All the Reformers were Roman Catholics. The divisions were the unintended consequence of failures to agree on the reform of Rome, failures for which it is now officially recognized that "people on both sides were to blame."[6] Subsequent subdivisions have aggravated our disunity and complicated the picture. In England churches like my own, the United Reformed Church, composed of Congregation-

---

4. Granberg-Michaelson, *From Times Square*, p. 11: "The balance of power in the college of cardinals among the 115 who entered the conclave in March 2013 to elect a new pope remained decisively in the global North. . . . This made the election of Pope Francis from Argentina all the more remarkable."

5. David Martin, *Pentecostalism: The World Their Parish* (Oxford: Blackwell, 2002). Martin sees Pentecostalism as the heir of Methodism.

6. Pope John Paul II's encyclical letter *Ut Unum Sint* 1995, para. 11; *Unitatis Redintegratio*, para. 3.

alists and Presbyterians and Churches of Christ, are often categorized as "Nonconformists" because their ancestors would not conform to the Act of Uniformity of 1662 and the Established Church of England. The founders of Methodism were and remained Anglicans. Hence the separate existence of the Methodist Church is the result of disagreement with the Church of England. Nonetheless, it remains true that prior to the sixteenth century, all of us in Great Britain belonged to what we now call the Roman Catholic Church. There was no other church to belong to. Hence the expression "the medieval church is the mother of us all."

A third point follows from this: Rome was and is *the* debating partner with whom we non–Roman Catholics in the West have to deal. Other dialogues are of course important, not least with the Orthodox and with Pentecostals, and there are numerous examples of such.[7] Historically the main argument for the Orthodox is with Rome and the division dated at 1054. Rome accepts that she is closer to the Orthodox than to the communities that emerged from the sixteenth-century Reformation. The Pentecostals pose a challenge to all churches and raise a whole lot of issues that I cannot deal with in this book except to mention in passing that Vatican II was hailed as a New Pentecost, while critics of Karl Barth say he should say more about the Holy Spirit. They ask, "Whatever happened to the Spirit in his theology?" In much of Latin America, Pentecostal churches are growing at the expense of the Roman Catholic Church and this despite the influence of Roman Catholic "liberation theologians." It's a cause of some bewilderment, but the fact is summed up in the comment: "The Church turned to the poor but the poor turned to the Pentecostals." Why? Perhaps because reforms in the Catholic Church did not go far enough and allow for "grassroots" participation.

The ecumenical and Lutheran theologian Robert Jenson argues that there are "only two functioning divides in modern ecumenical dialogues." The first is between East and West. The second is between Catholic and Protestant. The second observation is supported by the Reformed theologian and brother of the Taizé Community, Max Thurian, and based on his long experience of editing the responses to the multilateral convergence text, *Baptism, Eucharist and Ministry.* When it came to final decisions about what to say in a given paragraph, the fault line always lay between those who were more

---

7. Reports of key dialogues are now included in three volumes of *Growth in Agreement,* published by the Faith and Order Commission of the World Council of Churches, 1984, 2000, and 2007.

"catholic" and those who were more "protestant."[8] As an example, I cite the response of the Baptist Union of Great Britain and Ireland. They complain that the whole manner in which the eucharist is described is more "catholic" than scriptural and might say the same about what they call "the heavy insistence on the 'threefold order'" of ministry.[9] As Baptists, they would claim to be "scriptural." Another Lutheran theologian, Paul Tillich, once contrasted the "Protestant principle" with the "Catholic substance."[10] A similar but more personal contrast was made by Louis Bouyer. He began life as a Protestant, and served for a time as a pastor, and then became a Roman Catholic but retained his appreciation for Protestantism as "a genuinely spiritual movement stemming from the teachings of the Gospel." He continued to admire its spirit but rejected its forms, hence the English title of his French book *Du Protestantisme à l'Église* is presented as *The Spirit and Forms of Protestantism*. The book was described by the Roman Catholic journal *The Tablet* as "of immense significance for Christian unity" and added that it "will be to many a revelation of the importance of the Ecumenical Movement."[11] This was stated in the 1963 edition just as the Vatican Council was itself coming to terms with the Ecumenical Movement. As with Jenson and Tillich, Bouyer, who was then a priest and professor in Paris, saw the fundamental divide as that between Catholics and Protestants and their respective allies. Barth, as we shall see, had other ideas about when the most serious division occurred but in an early lecture in 1928 saw Rome as the chief challenger and spoke of "Roman Catholicism: A Question to the Protestant Church."[12] His work in the Roman Catholic city and university of Münster and his studies of the Reformers had forced this question on him. Unlike too many Protestants, Barth was prepared to listen to Rome even if he may not always have heard what Rome was trying to say.

8. Robert W. Jenson, *Unbaptized God: The Basic Flaw in Ecumenical Theology* (Minneapolis: Fortress Press, 1992), pp. 9-10. Max Thurian, cited from an article in 1985. Thurian edited the Responses to *Baptism, Eucharist and Ministry.*

9. Max Thurian, ed., *Churches Respond to BEM*, vol. 1 (Geneva: WCC, 1986), pp. 76-77.

10. Paul Tillich; ET James Luther Adams, *The Protestant Era* (London: Nisbet, 1951); Ronald Modras, *Paul Tillich's Theology of the Church* (Detroit: Wayne State University, 1976), with a Foreword by Hans Küng.

11. Louis Bouyer (1954), Fontana edition (London: Collins, 1963), p. 13, and commendations on back cover.

12. Karl Barth, "Roman Catholicism: A Question to the Protestant Church," in ET Louise Pettibone Smith, *Theology and Church: Shorter Writings 1920-1928* (New York: Harper & Row, 1962), pp. 307-33.

Why Reform?

Why reform? At different times the answer has been painfully obvious but at other times the mere mention of reform was enough to get a Roman Catholic theologian into trouble. The Holy Office would not allow Yves Congar's epoch-making book *True and False Reform in the Church*[13] to be reprinted or translated, and Congar himself was banished and prevented from writing for a time. But in the providence of God the future Pope John XXIII read the book and asked himself: "A reform of the Church; is such a thing really possible?"[14] Traditionalists would ask "is such a thing really necessary?"

At the end of the fourteenth century it was obvious the church needed reforming. In the Great Schism, which began in 1378 and was not resolved until 1415, there were at first two rival claimants to the Papacy, one in Rome and the other at Avignon and later a third elected at Pisa. The Council of Constance was convened to deal with the crisis. The conviction had been growing that the only way to reform the church and the papacy was to call a Council. There was talk of the need to reform the church "in head and members." It was said then, and is still being said today, that too much power is centralized in Rome.

If, as Roman Catholics claim, Peter was the first bishop of Rome though not officially listed as the first pope, he too needed reforming. The Gospels make no secret of this. Later in a famous incident at Antioch, Paul would confront Peter "to his face" because, in Paul's view, Peter was clearly in the wrong in giving in to the so-called Judaizers and not sharing table fellowship with Gentiles. James Dunn in his careful commentary on *Galatians* thinks that Paul failed to convince Peter; otherwise he would have said so, for the issue of Jewish Christian–Gentile Christian and Jewish-Christian relationships was so important for him.[15] Thus the Antioch incident may not be such a good precedent for any who would wish to reform the papacy! The story would continue to be aired, however, whenever there was discussion of infallibility. Peter and his successors might be wrong.

In popular accounts, Luther's reformation was prompted by a Dominican friar named Tetzel who in a flamboyant manner sold indulgences or

---

13. Yves Congar (1950), new translation by Paul Philibert, *True and False Reform in the Church* (Collegeville, MN: Liturgical Press, 2011).

14. See Paul Philibert, "Translator's Introduction," p. xi.

15. James D. G. Dunn, *The Epistle to the Galatians* (London: A. & C. Black, 1993), with reference to Galatians 2:11-15. For Peter's side in the argument, see Martin Hengel, ET Thomas H. Trapp, *Saint Peter: The Underestimated Apostle* (Grand Rapids: Eerdmans, 2010), pp. 52-64.

pardons for the building of St. Peter's in Rome. He may have declared "the moment the money tinkles in the collecting box, a soul flies out of purgatory." On 31 October 1517 Martin Luther fastened to the door of the castle church at Wittenberg a placard inscribed with "Ninety-five Theses upon Indulgences." The reformation of the church had officially begun.

Whether all that happened thereafter was a "reformation" is understandably disputed today and was so at the time. The Second Vatican Council's Decree on Ecumenism speaks rather cautiously of "the events which are usually referred to as 'the Reformation.'"[16] Important for this study is to ask whether Barth should be understood as an heir of the Reformation, inheriting a vocation to contribute to the reform of Rome.

Partly for historical reasons associated with conciliarism and the Reformation, "reform" remains a controversial issue for many, though not all, Roman Catholics. As noted earlier, Pope John XXIII's gut reaction to Congar's book on reform was to ask "is such a thing possible?" Possibly to calm the fears of traditionalists who would automatically reject all talk of "reform," he chose to speak of the Council's work as *aggiornamento*, a lovely Italian word that tends to be translated according to the whims of the Council's interpreters! He would be pleased to read in a Council document published after his death and quoted by John Paul II in *Ut Unum Sint* (1995) that "Christ summons the Church, as she goes her pilgrim way, to that continual reformation of which she always has need."[17] To such an admission, churches in the Reformed tradition would respond with a cheer, *Semper reformanda; ecclesia reformata sed semper reformanda!* I cannot resist adding that in the first edition of *Vraie et Fausse Réforme,* Congar was rather critical of this slogan and also of Karl Barth.[18]

Like many slogans, it is repeated by many of us in the Reformed churches without our realizing it was not something the sixteenth-century Reformers actually taught! For some of us, its origins only came to light through dialogue with Roman Catholics, through the French-speaking conversations conducted by the Groupe des Dombes and published in their best-known document, *The Conversion of the Churches.* We learned there that the pietist Jodocus von Lodenstein was probably the first to coin the phrase and did so in 1675.[19]

---

16. *Unitatis Redintegratio* 13.

17. *Unitatis Redintegratio* 6; *Ut Unum Sint* 16.

18. Yves Congar, *Vraie et Fausse Réforme dans l'Église* (Paris: Éditions du Cerf, 1950), p. 461.

19. Groupe des Dombes (1991), ET James Greig, *For the Conversion of the Churches* (Ge-

In this study I try to allow the Vatican II "reformers" to set the agenda. This is what Barth himself was doing in his visit to Rome. He was responding to documents agreed by the Council. Rome's repeated commitment to the restoration or recovery of unity with other Christian churches and communities positively invites us to continue in dialogue and debate on issues already raised in the council and some that have arisen since. Pope John Paul II, thirty years after the Council, asked "Church leaders and their theologians" for help in being pope.[20] We can listen to many Roman Catholics who think too much depends on Rome, too many decisions are taken in Rome. The church is overcentralized. Can this be reformed? Can non–Roman Catholics offer the help they were asked for at the Council and in the pope's encyclical?

The Council did not debate controversial issues like contraception or priestly celibacy. Human sexuality was not on its agenda, but a whole range of issues connected with sexuality and gender have to be confronted because they confront the Roman Catholic Church and, of course, other churches. Here too, various statements and encyclicals issued by Rome since Vatican II demonstrate the need and the demands for reform. Respected theologians like Karl Rahner and Nicholas Lash are no longer convinced by standard arguments against the ordination of women. Rahner commended a 1969 study, *Priestertum der Frau,* which begins with this appeal:

> The ordination of women is a lively issue for many churches and a potentially explosive one in ecumenical circles. A way must be found to open discussion between the Protestant and Catholic traditions in which each will be willing to take the other's position seriously and to open its own to honest and searching study.[21]

I shall explore this issue more fully in a chapter on the "Reform of Karl Barth." Many feminists in all our churches have expressed disappointment that more help is not offered by Barth though he did support the ordination

---

neva: WCC, 1993), p. 95, note 57: "Contrary to the commonly accepted view the expression seems not to go back to the sixteenth-century Protestant Reformers but to the Pietist Jodocus von Lodenstein (1620-77)." See also John P. Bradbury, *Perpetually Reforming: A Theology of Church Reform and Renewal* (London: Bloomsbury T. & T. Clark, 2013).

20. *Ut Unum Sint,* 1995, paras. 95-96.

21. Karl Rahner, "Women and the Priesthood," in *Theological Investigations* XX (London: Darton, Longman & Todd, 1981), pp. 35-50; Haye Van der Meer, ET Arlene and Leonard Swidler, *Women Priests in the Catholic Church: A Theological-Historical Investigation* (Philadelphia: Temple University Press, 1973), p. vii.

of women and votes for women in a country that remained until recently hesitant on both issues.

Nicholas Lash, Hans Küng, Peter Hebblethwaite, and many more find the case for obligatory clerical celibacy less and less convincing. Some, including Lash and Hebblethwaite, had to leave the priesthood because they also had a vocation to marry. Even the Orthodox allow priests to marry, though bishops must be celibate. If Rome will allow such matters to be debated, then Barth and his "successors" can join in. At present there remains an embargo on further discussion but other questions can no longer be silenced.

Reform and the Scandal of Sexual Abuse

Today, any general survey of the church in society by Roman Catholic theologians will comment on sexual abuse by the clergy. An American commentator describes it as "the gravest crisis in the history of the Catholic Church in the United States." Another refers to "the fury unleashed by *The Boston Globe*" in January 2002 in its treatment of the issue.[22] Clergy abuse is a scandal that might be blamed on a few errant priests. Offenders can be found in other churches and other professions, including doctors and police. It is the scale of abuse by Catholic priests and the fact they were priests that has been truly shocking. In the United States alone 10,667 victims were reported and 4,397 priests were accused between 1950 and 2002. In Ireland, the Netherlands, and elsewhere this has been headline news. The offense has been aggravated by the way in which bishops and those in authority have failed to deal with offenders. Claims for compensation seemed like bankrupting various dioceses in the United States and elsewhere. The church often appears to be more concerned about her own reputation than the hurts inflicted on her victims by clergy who were in a position of trust. So today, if we are asking "why reform?" the answer is painfully obvious. Catholic theologian Paul Lakeland in the *Liberation of the Laity* (2007) includes a chapter on "An Accountable Church" and begins by stating that church leaders have failed to address the crisis of abuse adequately: "A crisis of sexual abuse has become a much deeper

---

22. See articles by James Martin SJ and Thomas P. Doyle OP in Mary Gail Frawley-O'Dea and Virginia Goldner, eds., *Predator Priests, Silenced Victims* (London: Analytic Press, 2007), pp. 139, 155.

crisis of leadership."[23] Another study by a Franciscan[24] who became head of his order gives a detailed account of how he and others faced up to the crisis and tried to minister to the victims and those who abused them. A sad fact is that the scandal of abuse has come to light just as the level of abuse is decreasing. Incidents are being reported that happened thirty or more years ago.

One reason why they are being reported is because the Roman Catholic laity has become less docile. This is in part a consequence of Vatican II and the "liberation of the laity" that Lakeland writes about. Joseph Chinnici describes the period 1952-1980 as one of "public invisibility." Bishops covered up the reports they were receiving. Predator priests were moved on to a different parish. It was taken for granted by the Catholic laity that a holy church was led by holy men. According to Thomas Doyle OP, the cover-up of clergy abuse could not have happened without the acquiescence of the laity who often believed that cooperation with the bishops in such cover-ups was helping the church. He adds: "Catholic victims, conditioned by their religious indoctrination, looked at their priest-abuser with a mixture of awe and fear."[25] He is also highly critical of the way Pope John Paul II in 1993 "set a tone with this first pronouncement about the crisis and effectively disowned any institutional responsibility" for what was happening.[26]

Revelations of abuse created for many a crisis of faith, faith in God, faith in the church. They also opened up wide-ranging discussions on questions that went far beyond the immediate offense. Who has authority in the church? Who has the power?[27] And is there a need to review matters like compulsory celibacy, which after all has not always been compulsory and which maybe is better regarded as a charism that some women and men freely accept but should never be an obligation imposed on all clergy? And is a church that, like most churches receives most of its support from women, dominated by men who discriminate against women? Such questions, which

23. Paul Lakeland, *Liberation of the Laity* (New York: Continuum, 2003), p. 257.

24. Joseph Chinnici OFM, *When Values Collide: The Catholic Church, Sexual Abuse, and the Challenges of Leadership* (Maryknoll, NY: Orbis, 2010), pp. 15-16, 20, 87.

25. The British scandal in 2012 surrounding the once very popular TV presenter and charities fundraiser, Jimmy Savile, as a prolific sexual predator illustrates that the problem of misplaced respect and trust is not peculiar to priests. People assumed Savile was too nice a man to do such things, and victims went unheeded, all 450 of them, until after his death.

26. Frawley-O'Dea and Goldner, eds., *Predator Priests, Silenced Victims*, p. 155.

27. Linda Hogan of the Irish School of Ecumenics, "The Clerical Sexual Abuse Scandal," *Theological Studies* 72, no. 1 (March 2011): 170-86.

were deliberately kept off the agenda of Vatican II, are now very much on the agenda whenever the Roman Catholic laity and some of their theologians have a voice.

Reform in the Roman Catholic Church? "Is this possible?" asked a much-respected pope. The response today is not only that it is essential, but that we need each other's help. Through the ecumenical movement we have become mutually accountable. We can no longer spot the speck in our brother or sister's eye and ignore the plank in our own and have no desire to do so. All churches are in desperate need of reform, but some find this easier to admit than others and for theological reasons that need to be respected.

In commending the Reformed theologian Karl Barth as a reformer of the whole church catholic, I will often pause to reflect how much we all owe to Roman Catholic reformers like Congar. His ecumenical commitment led him to see the need for reform and to be open to the counsels of non–Roman Catholics. He constantly urged us all to be patient but also expectant, and to persist in prayer. He was sometimes badly treated by his own church but he did not give up. His recently translated *Journal of the Council* engages our sympathy for a Christian with a real vocation to unity who needed a great deal of reassurance that he was actually doing any good or making any progress. Barth, too, might be more vulnerable to criticism than he sometimes appeared. Like Congar, he was often misunderstood by his own church and by his own country, but then we were warned "a prophet is not without honor except in his home town" (Mark 6:4).[28]

Why Barth?

A brief answer has already been given in my opening summary. According to Pope Pius XII, Barth was the greatest theologian since Thomas Aquinas. This judgment is often quoted, but according to my Dominican colleague Fergus Kerr, nobody seems to know where and when the pope said this. Suffice to say, it remains repeatable because perfectly plausible. Nor was Pius the only pope to appreciate Barth. It was obvious to Barth on his visit to Rome that Pope Paul VI had read some of his books. And when Pope

28. Frank Jehle; ET Richard and Martha Burnett, *Ever Against the Stream: The Politics of Karl Barth* (Grand Rapids: Eerdmans, 2002). Jehle begins by noting that when Barth died in December 1968 not one member of the Federal Government honored its most famous citizen at his funeral in Basel Cathedral because the government had often found his views, especially in wartime, uncomfortably controversial.

John Paul II died, another Oxford Dominican said at a Requiem Mass that one of his influences was Barth. Pope Benedict in his Commentary on Vatican II acknowledges Barth's influence on documents about Divine Revelation and the Church in the Modern World. Unlike the sixteenth-century Reformers who were confronted by popes who were for the most part theologically illiterate and inaccessible, Barth would have been able to have a serious theological discussion with Pius XII and his successors and did so with Paul VI and with Joseph Ratzinger, once a theology professor in Germany, later Pope Benedict XVI.

A sad consequence of the bitterness created by the Reformation, Counter-Reformation, and Wars of Religion was that for nearly four hundred years thereafter, Anglican and Protestant theologians rarely met with their counterparts from Rome. There were notable exceptions, like the correspondence between the famous French bishop John Jacques Bossuet (1627-1704) and the even more famous Lutheran philosopher, Gottfried Leibniz (1646-1716), aided by the bishop's reservations about the Council of Trent and about papal intransigence and interference, and Leibniz's commitment to Christian reunion. Barth envied the Reformers their face-to-face confrontation with their opponents and this comment is quoted by one of his contemporary Roman Catholic interpreters, Hans Urs von Balthasar:

> In the sixteenth and seventeenth centuries Catholics and Protestants still looked at each other in the eye — angrily, but in the eye. They talked with each other sharply and harshly; but they really talked. We today, however, weary of the long conflict and perhaps also weary of this kind of Christian seriousness, look past each other all along the line, and talk past each other in unfruitful and ineffective fashion about the deep mystery which certainly concerns us equally on this side and on that. Still oftener we stand opposite each other in complete detachment.[29]

I like this quotation so much that I will repeat it in the chapter on the Reformation! This is Barth in a lecture at Münster in 1927 in which he was pleased to note that Catholics and Protestants could both now talk about the church and know they were talking about the same subject. After Trent, divisions hardened and, as I have noted, interconfessional conversations were almost nonexistent for the next four hundred years. The unofficial or

29. Karl Barth, "The Concept of the Church" (1927), in ET Louise Pettibone Smith, *Theology and Church* (New York: Harper & Row, 1962), p. 72; Hans Urs von Balthasar (1951); ET Edward T. Oakes SJ, *The Theology of Karl Barth* (San Francisco: Ignatius Press, 1992), p. 6.

semi-official Malines Conversations between Anglicans and Roman Catholics between 1921 and 1926 had pioneered the way.[30] Barth was also a pioneer in holding joint seminars with a Roman Catholic colleague, Erich Przywara, on the concept of analogy and related topics at Münster at this time.[31] Later such dialogues and indeed friendships would continue with Robert Grosche, Yves Congar, Hans Küng, and his Basel colleague Hans Urs von Balthasar. Küng and von Balthasar became well known, among other reasons, for their scholarly studies of Barth and in this are joined by other Roman Catholic theologians like Henri Bouillard and Jérôme Hamer. Hamer is listed as one of the "driving forces" at Vatican II.[32]

Why Only Barth?

I have searched around for other Protestant theologians who engaged in controversy with Rome but in a constructive manner, not in the style of the Protestant Truth Society or the veteran Ian Paisley in his early days — he has mellowed since — where Rome is still the Antichrist or whore of Babylon. Paul Tillich is notable for seeking to define the Protestant Principle over against Rome, and some studies compare his way of doing theology with Thomas Aquinas.[33] Throughout his *Systematic Theology*[34] there are frequent comparisons made between Protestant and Roman Catholic and also Orthodox theology. Where there are criticisms of Rome, they are much gentler than those found in Barth. Unlike Barth, Tillich tends to make sweeping comments about Roman Catholicism whereas Barth engages with specific authors and is averse to generalizations as far too abstract. It is also the case that now in the twenty-first century much more scholarly attention by theologians of all traditions is devoted to Barth than to his contemporary Paul Tillich. They were both born in the same year, 1886. Tillich's influence seems to have faded with his death in 1965 whereas interest in Barth and possibly his influence still flourishes nearly fifty years after his death in 1968

---

30. John A. Dick, *The Malines Conversations Revisited* (Leuven: Peeters, 1989).

31. Amy Marga, *Karl Barth's Dialogue with Catholicism in Göttingen and Münster* (Tübingen: Mohr-Siebeck, 2010); Benjamin Dahlke, *Karl Barth, Catholic Renewal and Vatican II* (London: Bloomsbury T. & T. Clark, 2012) for German Roman Catholic engagement with Barth.

32. *History of Vatican II*, vol. 2, p. 493.

33. Paul Tillich, *The Protestant Era*, ET James Luther Adams (London: Nisbet, 1951); Ronald Modras, *Paul Tillich's Theology of the Church* (Detroit: Wayne State University, 1976).

34. Paul Tillich, *Systematic Theology*, vols. I-III (Welwyn, UK: James Nisbet, 1953-64).

and could have another revival when we consider his impact on Vatican II, 1962-65 in its Jubilee celebrations.

The best answer to the question "why Barth?" is given by Hans Urs von Balthasar:

> We must choose Barth for our partner because in him Protestantism has found *for the first time* its most completely consistent representative. He embodies a Protestantism that can only be reached by going back to its roots, its deepest sources: to Calvin and Luther. . . .
>
> We have in Barth, then, two crucial features: the most thorough and penetrating display of the Protestant view and the closest rapprochement with the Catholic.[35]

He goes on to say that a Roman Catholic can read through hundreds of pages of Barth's *Church Dogmatics* or his book on Anselm without having any objections to raise and even on occasion to find in Barth a corrective or "dash of spice lending piquancy to the Catholic dough." Not surprisingly, Barth was quite pleased with von Balthasar's account, not only because of the obvious compliments but because I think Barth should be seen as a "catholic" theologian, in the fullest sense of the word, as one hoping to write theology for the whole church, not just a small part of it like his own Reformed tradition. His great expositor and leading English translator, Thomas Torrance, once remarked "that if anyone in our day is to be honoured as *Doctor Ecclesiae Universalis,* it must surely be Karl Barth."[36] The claim still holds twenty and more years after it was uttered, especially if we also learn from Barth to see earlier theologians as our contemporaries. My colleague Colin Gunton appreciated this point when shortly before his own sudden death he wrote: "The culture which mattered to Barth is that of the communion of saints," and he quoted this extract from Barth's *Protestant Theology in the Nineteenth Century:*

> Bearing and being borne by each other, asking and being asked, having to take mutual responsibility for and among the sinners gathered together in Christ. . . . Augustine, Thomas Aquinas, Luther, Schleiermacher and all the rest are not dead but living. They still speak and demand a hearing

35. Balthasar, *The Theology of Karl Barth,* pp. 22-23; George Hunsinger, "Baptised into Christ's Death: Karl Barth and the Future of Roman Catholic Theology" (1997), in *Disruptive Grace: Studies in the Theology of Karl Barth* (Grand Rapids: Eerdmans, 2000), pp. 253-78, 255.

36. Thomas F. Torrance, *Karl Barth: Biblical and Evangelical Theologian* (Edinburgh: T. & T. Clark, 1990), p. 164.

as living voices, as surely as we know that we and they belong together in the Church.[37]

He also pleaded that we should also listen to those once branded as "heretics":

> The theology of any period must be strong and free enough to give a calm, attentive and open hearing not only to the voices of the Church Fathers, not only to favourite voices but to all the voices of the past. God is the Lord of the Church. He is also the Lord of theology. We cannot anticipate which of our fellow-workers from the past are welcome in our own work and which are not.[38]

So for more conservative Roman Catholics or liberal Protestants, and any tempted to dismiss Barth, the short answer to the question Why listen to Barth? is that Barth is still speaking to us. Listen to what he has to say before you disagree with him!

Barth as a "Catholic" and Ecumenical Theologian for the Whole Church

One way of honoring fellow theologians of all eras is to respect their good intentions even if we disagree with the way they carried them out. Barth should be respected by all because he set out to write theology for all, not just for his own Reformed confessions. In his first teaching post at Göttingen in 1921 he was appointed to teach "Reformed Dogmatics" but declined to do so. Why? Why refuse to do what he was appointed to do? He was appointed as the first Honorary Professor of Reformed Theology in a predominantly Lutheran University. Johann Heilmann, pastor of a Reformed congregation in Göttingen, felt the need for such a professorship. He said he had no wish to "conjure up any confessional narrowness" but he did feel that the Lord had given the Reformed certain charismata that were now in danger of being "unused, forgotten and scorned. Reformed Protestantism has a calling and should fulfil it to the blessing of German Christianity."[39] He therefore

---

37. Colin E. Gunton, "Introduction" in Karl Barth, *Protestant Theology in the Nineteenth Century,* new edition (London: SCM, 2001), pp. xvii-xviii, quotation from chapter 1, p. 3.

38. *Protestant Theology,* p. 3.

39. Heilmann's letter is in the Karl Barth Archives and is quoted in the Preface to Dar-

invited his Reformed pastoral colleague who had established his academic credentials by his Commentaries on Romans to be the first incumbent of this new teaching post. Barth accepted but with one major reservation. If theology is about God and about expounding the Word of God, can there be such a thing as "Reformed Theology"? This reservation and the ensuing argument Barth had with the Faculty about his title suggests that from the start of his teaching career Barth intended to do theology for the whole church, not just elucidate and defend his own tradition. In support, he cited John Calvin. He, too, did not set out to write "Reformed Dogmatics," but offered *Institutes of the Christian Religion* and Commentaries on almost every book of the Bible for all Bible readers. In the first and all subsequent editions, Calvin included a Prefatory Address to King Francis I of France in which he argued that, despite all accusations to the contrary, all he, Calvin, and his colleagues sought to do was to expound "the common cause of all believers, that of Christ himself."[40]

It could also be argued that just as Calvin intended his exposition of the Christian faith to be of benefit to all Christians — which is one reason that his *Institutes* was published in Latin as well as in French and later of course translated into countless other languages, Heilmann's larger vision was that Barth's lectureship should be, as he said, for "the blessing of German Christianity." He might have added "Catholic and Protestant," but perhaps in 1921 that was expecting too much. It was not, I shall argue, too much to expect from Karl Barth. He did not want to be a spokesman for Reformed concerns but to be "a watchman in the service of the entire church."[41]

At Göttingen Barth did indeed lecture on "Reformed," or should we say Catholic theologians, Calvin and Zwingli. He also lectured on the Heidelberg Catechism and the Theology of the Reformed Confessions but he also planned lectures on books of the Bible such as the Letter to the Ephesians, the Letter to the Hebrews and James, books that we now see as addressed to all Christians of all confessions.

Barth set out to be a catholic theologian. Was he also an "ecumenical theologian"? The question has often been asked.[42] He was not like his

---

rell and Judith J. Guder's translation of Karl Barth, *The Theology of the Reformed Confessions* (Louisville: Westminster John Knox, 2002), p. vii.

40. John Calvin (1559), John T. McNeill, ed., *Institutes of the Christian Religion* (Philadelphia: Westminster Press, 1960), Prefatory Address, p. 11.

41. H. Vorländer cited by Darrell and Judith Guder's Preface to *Theology of the Reformed Confessions*, p. 18.

42. Adolf Keller, *Karl Barth and Christian Unity* (London: Lutterworth, 1931); J. K. S. Reid,

Reformed colleague Willem Visser 't Hooft, the first General Secretary of the World Council of Churches, constantly engaged with different church leaders in the work of such a council. Nor was he like another Reformed colleague, Lesslie Newbigin, active in the formation of a United Church, the United Church of South India, in which this Presbyterian minister became one its first bishops. Newbigin in his *Autobiography* recalls an incident where Barth is sitting in the garden of the World Council's Ecumenical Institute at Bossey, struggling with a mass of documents from different churches. Newbigin senses that Barth seems ill at ease. "You look as if you are in trouble," he says to Barth. Barth agreed: "I am. This is a task for some great ecumenical theologian." Someone perhaps like Newbigin himself![43] But why not Barth?

Barth was and is a great ecumenical theologian. He may have lacked the ecumenical diplomacy and patience of people like Rome's foremost ecumenical leader, Yves Congar, or the Anglican bishop Oliver Tomkins, but it is unfair to Barth to write off some notable occasions when he was directly engaged in ecumenical negotiations. Foremost is his work in drafting the final statements in the Barmen Declaration of the Confessing Church for a Synod consisting of Lutheran, Reformed, and United representatives. This was one of the key documents that provided churches in Germany with a theological basis for their opposition to Hitler. It has often been cited since, most notably in the churches' struggle against apartheid in South Africa.[44] He was not directly involved in either the Life and Work Conference or the Faith and Order Conferences of 1937 but he prepared a key lecture for the latter, *The Church and the Churches*.[45] The distinguished Lutheran ecumenical leader William Rusch, in his Foreword to a new edition, says it ranks as "one of the classic ecumenical texts of the twentieth century." The two assemblies of 1937 paved the way for the formation of the World Council of Churches but its inauguration was then delayed by the outbreak of war. When it convened, Barth gave the keynote address at the First Assembly of the World Council of Churches at Amsterdam in 1948. He was active with a group of twenty-five distinguished theologians in preparing a statement for

"Karl Barth and Ecumenical Affairs," in *Theology Beyond Christendom: Essays on the Centenary of the Birth of Karl Barth*, ed. John Thompson (Eugene, OR: Pickwick, 1986), pp. 303-30.

43. Lesslie Newbigin, *Unfinished Agenda: An Autobiography* (London: SPCK, 1985), p. 140.

44. Charles Villa-Vicencio, ed., *On Reading Karl Barth in South Africa* (Grand Rapids: Eerdmans, 1988).

45. Karl Barth, *The Church and the Churches* (1936), new edition, William G. Rusch, ed. (Grand Rapids: Eerdmans, 2005).

the next Assembly at Evanston in 1954. In the course of one of their meetings Newbigin commented that "Barth was at his most polemical."[46]

Ecumenical and Polemical

Is being polemical always a fault, especially for an ecumenical theologian? Roman Catholic theologian John Yocum thinks not.[47] This view is supported by another recent study, Benjamin Dahlke's *Karl Barth, Catholic Renewal and Vatican II*, the first major study of Roman Catholic reaction to Barth prior to the Council. In the 1930s when at Münster, Barth and a Roman Catholic priest friend, Robert Grosche, revived what at the Reformation was called "Controversial Theology." Grosche and Barth both belonged to a lively theological discussion circle, and to engage more people in the arguments, Grosche started the journal *Catholica* in 1932. Dahlke explains that in the 1930s polemical theology was seen as "in no way opposed to the ecumenical movement and in fact could be understood as making its own contribution to the unity of the Church."[48] Vatican observer Douglas Horton took with him the Puritan William Ames's replies to the Controversial Theology of Cardinal Bellarmine and found it helpful background reading to Council debates![49] Barth wholeheartedly supported the aims of *Catholica* and said so in *Church Dogmatics* I/2:

> We meet a theological adversary in a manlier and more worthy way, the more it is recognised on both sides that in this clash ultimate things are at stake, not merely fortuitous inclinations and disinclinations, not merely things in which one side or the other could think differently, but is prevented only by the laziness or arrogance of the flesh. We may go even further. In theological conflict, the opponents are still together in Christ and therefore still within the Church when it is clear they are separated in Christ and that they contend, not about the respective rights of their

46. Lesslie Newbigin, *Autobiography*, p. 131.

47. John Yocum, *Ecclesial Mediation in Karl Barth* (Aldershot, UK: Ashgate, 2004).

48. Benjamin Dahlke, *Karl Barth: Catholic Renewal and Vatican II* (London: T. & T. Clark, 2012), p. 50.

49. Theodore Louis Trost, *Douglas Horton and the Ecumenical Impulse in American Religion* (Cambridge, MA: Harvard University Press, 2002), p. 226. Horton introduced Barth to many English-speaking readers with his translation of *The Word of God and the Word of Man* (London: Hodder & Stoughton, 1928).

Churches, or tendencies within their Churches, or only their own personal opinions, but about the right of the Church against heresy, which makes the dispute necessary. At this point we may refer expressly to the *Vierteljahrschrift für Kontroverstheologie,* published since 1932 by Robert Grosche under the title *Catholica.*[50]

For Evanston as with Barmen, big issues were at stake. Barmen was about giving the church a theology strong enough to resist Hitler. The argument in the group of twenty-five was about "the Hope of Israel." The group failed to convince the Assembly at Evanston. As at Barmen, the churches had still to see Israel and the Jewish people as ecumenical partners, fellow members of the People of God. Barth like Calvin before him had little time for the "polite ecumenism" that is prepared to soft pedal on key convictions for the sake of peace. He always regretted that Barmen had not spoken up for the Jews. And in retrospect, if not at the time, do we not admire most those who have the courage of sound convictions and are prepared to go, as Barth often said, "against the stream"?

It was because Barth was recognized by Roman Catholic theologians as in the broadest sense "catholic" and ecumenically committed to the visible unity of the church that he was invited to the Second Vatican Council. And it was because of such ecumenical involvement that Barth devoted a large part of his last years talking about the Council that he truly regarded as a God-given event. The last thing he wrote was an address for the Week of Prayer for Christian Unity in January 1969. Barth died in December 1968 and his address and work for church unity remained unfinished.

Barth was sometimes criticized by Visser 't Hooft and others for not being sufficiently positive about the ecumenical movement, especially in its early days. Again, it would be a mistake to assume that criticism is negative. Barth's prime conviction was that church unity is far too important to be left to a movement. It must engage the churches. Looking back, Visser 't Hooft offered this balanced tribute to Barth:

> He could be terribly intransigent and sometimes quite unfair in his criticisms of what he called "the ecumenical circus" and I would then protest strongly. But it was really a blessing that during the formative period of the ecumenical movement there was a man who was asking us fundamental questions and calling us back to the central truths. I have therefore said

50. Karl Barth, *Church Dogmatics* I/2, p. 826; Dahlke, *Karl Barth: Catholic Renewal and Vatican II,* p. 51.

more than once that without Karl Barth the movement would not have had the spiritual substance which it did receive.[51]

In letters he wrote to various colleagues in the last years of his life, Barth was obviously sensitive to the charge that he was not ecumenical. The very brief note in the *Dictionary of the Ecumenical Movement* is rather dismissive: "As a leading theologian, Barth had a decisive influence on the course of Protestantism in the 20th century, but remained a critical challenger of the ecumenical movement."[52] He remained critical but positively so as in such comments as these. In a letter to a former doctoral student, Professor Grover Foley of Texas in 1963, Barth comments: "Have you followed the proceedings at Vatican II? The pope's summons to Christological concentration was remarkable. We heard nothing like it either at Amsterdam, Evanston or New Delhi."[53] Barth might have read Foley's article, "The Catholic Critics of Karl Barth," which appeared in 1961.[54] In an earlier letter (1962), to Charles West of Princeton, who had invited Barth to contribute an article in a Festschrift for Visser 't Hooft, first General Secretary of the World Council of Churches, Barth declined to do so on the grounds that "[s]ince I have now become a marginal figure in ecumenical circles — and theology in general is more tolerated than really listened to in them — is it really necessary that you should have a contribution from me?"[55] To his 1936 criticism that church unity is far too important a matter to be left to a movement is added the plea that it is also far too basic to be left to ecclesiastical administrators or bureaucrats. As a critical comment it still needs to be heeded. If taken as a sweeping condemnation of the search for unity it is manifestly unfair. Vatican II would make good use of its theologians, a point that Visser 't Hooft wholeheartedly affirmed in his last book, *The Magistri and the Magisterium.*[56]

---

51. W. A. Visser 't Hooft, *Memoirs* (Geneva: WCC, 1973), p. 37. For more detail see Thomas Herwig, *Karl Barth und die Ökumenische Bewegung, Das Gespräch zwischen Karl Barth und Willem Adolf Visser 't Hooft auf der Grundlage ihres Briefwechsels 1930-1968* (Neukirchener: Neukirchener Verlag, 1998).

52. Nicholas Lossky et al., eds., *Dictionary of the Ecumenical Movement*, 2nd ed. (Geneva: WCC, 2002), note by Ans J. Van der Bent.

53. Karl Barth, *Letters 1961-1968* (Edinburgh: T. & T. Clark, 1981), Letter 134, p. 145.

54. Gregor Foley, "The Catholic Critics of Karl Barth," *Scottish Journal of Theology* 14 (2 June 1961): 136-55.

55. *Letters*, Letter 30, p. 38; Charles C. West, *The Sufficiency of God: Essays in Honour of W. A. Visser 't Hooft* (London: SCM, 1963).

56. W. A. Visser 't Hooft (1986), *Teachers and the Teaching Authorities* (Geneva: WCC, 2000), p. 77.

The first three assemblies of the World Council to which Barth refers did engage some of the best non–Roman Catholic theologians of that era, including Barth for Amsterdam (1948) and preparations for Evanston (1954). And the World Council of Churches' Faith and Order Commission could then claim to be — even as yet in the absence of Roman Catholic participation — the most comprehensive theological forum in the world. The Faith and Order document on *Christ and the Church*[57] (1963) was the work of highly respected American theologians like Norman Pittenger, Nels Ferré, Floyd Filson, Georges Florovsky, Paul Minear, and Richard Niebuhr; among the European theologians were Anders Nygren, Geoffrey Lampe, Beasley Murray, Oscar Cullmann, John Marsh, Gordon Rupp, Edmund Schlink, Gustav Wingren, and not least Thomas Torrance, the professor who translated much of Barth's *Dogmatics* into English and who at one point was destined to be Barth's successor at Basel. And even at this early stage, 1963, there had been a high-level theological debate between Raymond Brown, on the way to becoming one of Rome's foremost New Testament scholars, and the Lutheran New Testament scholar Ernst Käsemann on "Unity and Diversity in the New Testament," which is still worth reading fifty years after the event.[58] The fact that Barth applauds Pope Paul VI's "christological concentration" in his speech at the opening of the second session of Vatican II, 29 September 1963, simply confirms his judgment that often he was now better understood and followed in Rome in his own christological concentration, the centering of all theology and ecclesiology on God's revelation of himself in Christ, than he was in more Protestant circles.

Barth jumped to his own defense but in a lighthearted sort of way by assuring his ecumenical critics that for some time he had been engaged in an ecumenical movement of his own. He meant by this, as he explained to an author of a book about the end of the Counter-Reformation, that "I for my part have been an ecumenist on my own responsibility from my own particular position," in other words, not as a spokesman for the Reformed or the Swiss Protestant Federation but simply as a theologian who was ecumenically committed. In a radio interview, Barth explained further:

> I did not have time to devote to the ecumenical movement. I had other
> things to do. But then the Vatican Council came and showed me how in

57. Fourth World Conference on Faith and Order, Montreal, 12-26 July 1963, Faith and Order Paper 38, *Report on Christ and the Church* (Geneva: WCC, 1963), pp. 34, 62.

58. P. C. Rodger and L. Vischer, *The Fourth World Conference on Faith and Order,* Faith and Order Paper 42 (London: SCM, 1964), pp. 16-17. For a more recent study, see James D. G. Dunn, *Unity and Diversity in the New Testament* (London: SCM, 1977, 2nd ed. 1990).

a private way, with no commission from anyone, I might engage in a little ecumenical movement of my own. A very little one! This is why I went to Rome, visited Paul VI, and engaged in discussions with the Jesuits and Dominicans. It was all very stimulating and worthwhile. . . . Here on the Bruderholz we have good relations between the Reformed and Roman Catholic communions. And so I do a little here and there.[59]

And as evidence of this commitment he joked about a recent photograph of himself and Hans Küng together. As he told Hans Küng in 1966: "As is apparent in the fine photographs of you and me that you sent, it cannot really be said that I have no ecumenical concern."[60]

Barth was catholic and ecumenical. Let him have the last word on this controversy. It is indeed his final word. It comes from the last speech he ever prepared. He died before completing the address and a month before delivering it.

In December 1968 a Roman Catholic professor, J. Feiner, asked Barth to give the address during the Week of Prayer for Christian Unity in January 1969 to a meeting of Roman Catholic and Reformed Christians in the Paulusakademie in Zurich. The lecture is now available for us in the collection of his *Final Testimonies*. It is about looking forward in cheerful hope. We are addressed as "Dear Catholic and Reformed Fellow Christians," but then we are encouraged to drop such old descriptions of our divisions as he reminds his Roman Catholic listeners that "we are Catholic too." He prefers to speak of Petrine Catholic and Evangelical Catholic confessions. We are all Catholics. He continues:

> Listening to the past might be a beautiful idea, but it is not a churchly one either among you or us. On both sides the old to which the church turns back in true and authentic conversion is valid only as in and with and under it there takes place the new for which the church is starting out. . . . He, Jesus Christ, is the old and also the new. He it is who comes to the church and to whom the church goes. It is to him that it turns in its conversion. . . . God is not the God of the dead but of the living. All live to him.[61]

59. Interview on Swiss Radio 17 November 1968 in Karl Barth, *Final Testimonies* (Grand Rapids: Eerdmans, 1977), p. 27.

60. Karl Barth, Letter to Hans Küng 16 June 1966, *Letters 1961-1968* (Edinburgh T. & T. Clark, 1981), p. 209.

61. Karl Barth, "Starting Out, Turning Round, Confessing," ET Geoffrey W. Bromiley, *Final Testimonies* (Grand Rapids: Eerdmans, 1977), pp. 53-60.

The speech was never completed. Like the restoration of unity for which the Vatican Council prayed, it remains unfinished and still to be delivered. Barth is urging us to move on.

How Can One Who Is Not a Roman Catholic Assist the Reform of Rome?

A short answer might be "with great difficulty!" But a longer and more carefully considered reply is that for most of the twentieth century and, perhaps, still today it can be harder for a Roman Catholic theologian to promote reform. Rome resents dissent. Her bishops and theologians are expected to toe the line. Prior to Vatican II and continued in the long reign of Pope John Paul II and Cardinal Ratzinger, most of Rome's more radical and ecumenical theologians were at one time silenced or forced into exile. Yves Congar, author of pioneering Roman Catholic works on church unity such as *Chrétiens Désunis* and *Vraie et fausse réforme dans l'Église,* was censored for writing such works and for a time banished to Cambridge. Before that, Dom Lambert Beauduin (1873-1960), forever associated with the monastery at Chevetogne in Belgium, suffered exile because of his work for Anglican/Roman Catholic unity in the Malines Conversations (1925-26). His banishment lasted from 1928 to 1951. Barth's close friend and Swiss colleague Hans Küng publicly challenged the notion of infallibility and for this and other reasons was denounced in Rome and no longer permitted to teach as a Roman Catholic theologian at Tübingen, though he was able to continue teaching and writing as an ecumenical theologian in the same university.[62] Then there was the case of Leonardo Boff, which was graphically retold by the Baptist theologian Harvey Cox in *The Silencing of Leonardo Boff.*[63] One of Latin America's best-known liberation theologians, Boff was officially censured for books like *Church Charism and Power.* In the days of the Cold War, Rome acted like the KGB. Offenders were summoned to appear but not told what offense they had committed or given the right to reply. Dissent was not possible within the Roman Catholic communion. It could not be prevented outside. No one, not even Hitler, could silence Karl Barth! And as I have

---

62. Peter Hebblethwaite, *The New Inquisition? Schillebeeckx and Küng* (London: Collins, 1980); Hans Küng, ET John Bowden, *My Struggle for Freedom* (London: Continuum, 2003).

63. Harvey Cox, *The Silencing of Leonardo Boff: The Vatican and the Future of World Christianity* (Oak Park, IL: Meyer-Stone, 1988).

noted already, a lot of prominent Roman Catholics including four popes, Pius XII, Paul VI, John Paul II, and Benedict XVI, came to appreciate that this "separated brother" had a gospel to proclaim. They listened.

What is more, by the time of Vatican II Rome was actually asking non–Roman Catholic theologians like Barth to contribute to the process that Pope John called *aggiornamento.* Suspect theologians like Congar were reinstated and became *periti,* theological advisors at the Council, along with bright young scholars like Küng whose critical study in *Structures of the Church* (1963) and hopes for reunion in *The Council and Reunion* (1961) still passed the censor and had the official *Imprimatur* and *Nihil Obstat* to defend them as sound Catholic teaching. A very distinguished group of non–Roman Catholic participant observers and Roman Catholic experts were actually being asked to help Roman Catholic bishops from all over the world take counsel together in the processes of bringing the church up to date, being reformed and renewed and moved toward the restoration of unity. Only those "inside" the Roman Catholic Church, and indeed, only the hierarchy of the pope and the bishops could decide what teachings or "reforms" should be promulgated and hopefully implemented, but those "outside" were being asked for their opinions. They helped the Roman Catholic Church to change. They were also changed by the experience of Vatican II.

Next: Was Vatican II the reforming Council the Reformers asked for but never lived to see?

CHAPTER TWO

Reforming Rome: Continuing the Reformation

Reformation and Reunion, Barth and Congar

In Barth's lifetime Roman Catholics revised their understanding of the Reformation and Protestants wondered if "Counter-Reformation" was a fair description of Rome's response.[1] Prior to Vatican II, most of the heirs of the Reformation had given up on Rome, content like Senarclens[2] or Subilia[3] to list the points of difference that explained why Protestants must protest and defend the faith. But then as the Council began to make progress, some asked if this was indeed a Reformation and later if the Reformation was now over.[4] Had everything the Reformers hoped for been achieved? The World Council of Churches, encouraged by the good experience of Vatican II, contemplated "a genuinely universal council" that might speak for all Christians.[5] Less optimistically, some Roman Catholics

1. Roman Catholics had long been unhappy with this title. See John W. O'Malley, *Trent and All That: Renaming Catholicism in the Early Modern Era* (Cambridge, MA: Harvard University Press, 2000).

2. Jacques de Senarclens (1959), ET G. W. Bromiley, *Heirs of the Reformation* (London: SCM, 1963).

3. Vittorio Subilia (1962), ET Reginald Kissak, *The Problem of Catholicism* (London: SCM, 1964). Subilia, Dean of the Waldensian Faculty in Rome, was a Protestant observer at Vatican II, nominated by the World Alliance of Reformed Churches. He was described by Congar as "VERY anti-Catholic"; see Yves Congar, *My Journal of the Council,* p. 675, 13 November 1964.

4. See, for example, Mark A. Noll and Carolyn Nystrom, *Is the Reformation Over? An Evangelical Assessment of Contemporary Roman Catholicism* (Grand Rapids: Baker Academic, 2005).

5. WCC Uppsala Assembly (1968), "The Holy Spirit and the Catholicity of the Church"

saw an urgent need for a Vatican III because of the negative reactions to Vatican II.[6] And given the divided state of Protestantism, some questioned if the Reformation really was God's will because a better outcome might have been accomplished had the Reformers been more patient.[7] Lots of different people raised such questions and argued their case, but I can think of only two theologians who were at the center of these debates. One was the Dominican Yves Congar (1904-1995).[8] The other was, of course, Karl Barth (1886-1968).

Barth and Congar had this in common: they both believed, though in different ways, that reunion, or the restoration of unity, involves reformation. This would include correcting the unintended consequences of the sixteenth-century Reformation, the division of the one church of medieval Europe into a multiplicity of different churches. In his first major contribution to ecumenism, *Chrétiens Désunis*,[9] Congar welcomed the way in which Barth rejected all complacency about such divisions: "We have no right to explain the multiplicity of the Churches at all." He does not quote this passage from *The Church and the Churches* in full because he has his own argument to pursue. Barth had gone on to say:

> In fact, we have no right to explain the multiplicity of the churches at all. We have to deal with it as we deal with sin, our own and others, to recognise it as a fact, to understand it as the impossible thing which has intruded itself, as a guilt which we must take upon ourselves, without the power to liberate ourselves from it. We must not allow ourselves

---

(para. 19): "The members of the World Council of Churches, committed to each other, should work for the time when a genuinely universal council may once more speak for all Christians, and lead the way into the future," in *The Uppsala Report 1968*, ed. Norman Goodall (Geneva: WCC, 1968), p. 17. The resolution then became part of the program of the WCC Faith and Order Commission in which the Roman Catholic delegates are full members.

6. T. P. O'Mahony, *Why the Catholic Church Needs Vatican III* (Dublin: Columba Press, 2010).

7. A sympathetic answer was given by the Roman Catholic historian Joseph Lortz (1950), ET Otto Knab, *How the Reformation Came* (1955), 2nd ed. (New York: Herder & Herder, 1964).

8. See Paul D. Murray, "Expanding Catholicity through Ecumenicity in the Work of Yves Congar: *Ressourcement*, Receptive Ecumenism and Catholic Reform," in *Ressourcement: A Movement for Renewal in Twentieth Century Catholic Theology*, ed. Gabriel Flynn and Paul D. Murray (Oxford: Oxford University Press, 2012), pp. 457-81.

9. Yves Congar, *Chrétiens Désunis* (1937), ET M. A. Bousfield, *Divided Christendom: A Catholic Study of the Problem of Reunion* (London: Geoffrey Bles, 1939), p. 137.

to acquiesce in its reality; rather we must pray that it be forgiven and removed.[10]

Congar, at this stage, might claim that such divisiveness is only a Protestant problem. The church is one and she is the "Catholic Church." He therefore adds this critical comment on Barth: "But in common with members of the Ecumenical Movement he [Barth] explicitly rejects the idea that any existing Christian body is or can be, of itself, *the* Church, the visible Body of Christ."[11] Yet even here, Barth and Congar are not too far apart in their common concerns. Barth was writing a preparatory lecture for the Faith and Order Conference in Edinburgh (1937), which neither he nor Congar, though again for different reasons, were able to attend. Congar wanted to attend but Rome in *Mortalium Animos* (1928) had ruled out Roman Catholic involvement in the Ecumenical Movement and the ban would continue until after the announcement of the Council in 1959. Congar would also be refused permission to share in the first two Assemblies of the World Council of Churches at Amsterdam in 1948 and Evanston in 1954. Indeed, it was Congar who tried hard to negotiate with the local hierarchy and the Vatican about Roman Catholic observers at Amsterdam.[12]

Barth has his own strong reservations about "movements" for Christian unity and can therefore sympathize and does sympathize with Rome's reaction and said so in the 1936 lectures cited by Congar:

> From this point of view, I am not distressed by the well-known and widely regretted attitude of the Roman See towards union movements of the past and present. It was and is needful that someone somewhere should make a stand against the excessive claims of all church movements, and assert that the union of the churches is a thing which cannot be manufactured, but must be found and confessed, in subordination to that already accomplished oneness of the Church which is in Jesus Christ. It is in this sense that I understand the papal refusal

---

10. Karl Barth (1936), new edition with foreword by William G. Rusch, *The Church and the Churches* (Grand Rapids: Eerdmans, 2005), pp. 22-23.

11. Congar, *Divided Christendom*, p. 137.

12. Yves Congar, "La Question des Observateurs Catholiques à la Conférence d'Amsterdam" (1948), in *Die Einheit der Kirche. Festgabe Peter Meinhold*, ed. Lorenz Hein (Wiesbaden: Franz Steiner, 1977), pp. 241-54. Some forty Roman Catholics had expressed interest in attending Amsterdam. Congar drew up a list of those best qualified. He did not include himself.

to take a hand in the efforts which have been hitherto made towards union.[13]

The unity of the churches is far too important to be left to a movement. It must be a concern of the church and the churches. On this point Barth and Congar again come close to agreeing. Congar will say in his next major study of ecumenism, *True and False Reform in the Church,* that reforms and reformations can only avoid turning into sectarian divisions if they have a strong sense of the church. As the new translation and revised edition of his once controversial book has it: "The Whole Truth is grasped only in Communion with the whole Church."[14] He thinks Barth, or what he calls "the Barthian movement," appreciates this point:

> In the religious entities that arose out of the Reformation itself, renewal movements which did not turn into sects were those for which the church was considered a *given* and for which the goal was to revitalise the tradition. So in contemporary Protestantism, the Barthian movement or an initiative like the community of Taizé, and in Anglicanism in the nineteenth century, the Oxford movement, are examples of this. It is noteworthy — and I am not the first to make this remark — that if the revival movements of the sixteenth to the nineteenth centuries generally developed into sects, that is no longer the case today because of the clear revival of the idea of the church.[15]

And Barth, before he had even heard of Congar, had argued that the Reformers or certainly Calvin did have a strong idea of the church but this was something modern Protestantism, the heir of the Reformation, had lost. Protestants needed to listen to the question Rome is addressing to them. Hence Barth's lecture, given while he was a Professor at Münster, "Roman Catholicism: A Question to the Protestant Church."[16] In this section, I will concentrate on the various questions and challenges that the Reformers and

13. Karl Barth (1936), new edition, William G. Rusch, ed., *The Church and the Churches* (Grand Rapids: Eerdmans, 2005), p. 39.

14. Yves Congar (1950), ET (2nd ed. 1967) Paul Philibert OP, *True and False Reform in the Church* (Collegeville, MN: Liturgical Press, 2011), p. 229.

15. *True and False Reform,* p. 253. Congar's own reference is to C. T. Craig, "Report on the Study of the Church," in *The Nature of the Church: A Report of the American Theological Committee of Faith and Order* (Chicago: 1945).

16. Karl Barth, "Roman Catholicism: A Question to the Protestant Church" (1928), in ET Louise Pettibone Smith, *Theology and Church: Shorter Writings, 1920-1928* (New York: Harper & Row, 1962), pp. 307-33.

the Reformation presented to Barth and which he in turn addressed to his students and his contemporaries.

Catholic Challenges to Be More "Catholic"

Today's visitors to Germany are often surprised how much of the country is solidly Roman Catholic despite Martin Luther and Germany being the birthplace of the sixteenth-century Reformation. Barth could not ignore these facts when in 1925 he became a Professor in the predominantly Roman Catholic university of Münster.[17] And the more he immersed himself in the theology of Calvin and Zwingli and the Reformed Confessions, studies and lectures that he first gave in Lutheran Göttingen, the more he realized that you can only hear what the Reformers are saying if you note what they are opposing and better still, listen to their opponents.

Barth himself does not really do this listening in his *Theology of the Reformed Confessions,*[18] or at least not as much as we might wish. He does note that the Waldensians in Italy, being "on the frontline of the Reformed struggle," included in their Confession an index of supposed errors that Rome accused them of and he also contrasts the views of Reformed Christians in Poland with that of their Roman Catholic critics.[19] He does recognize that much that the Reformers thought was new was well known to Anselm, Peter Lombard, Alexander of Hales, Bonaventure, and Aquinas but it had somehow become obscured and forgotten.[20] The basic criticism of the "old church" in at least one of the Reformed confessions was that it sees "Catholicism as an attempt at self-help and it sees in this desire to help oneself an arrogance and a presumption" that is an insult to God who "desires to help."[21] A point he wishes to underline and finds in several of the Confessions is a strong belief in the church. There is a strong emphasis in the Westminster Confession on "the catholicity and universality of the visible church."[22] He describes Calvin in his Catechism as "a man of the church" and points out

---

17. Amy Marga, *Karl Barth's Dialogue with Catholicism in Göttingen and Münster* (Tübingen: Mohr Siebeck, 2010).

18. Karl Barth (1923), ET Darrell L. Guder and Judith J. Guder, *The Theology of the Reformed Confessions* (Louisville: Westminster John Knox Press, 2002).

19. *Reformed Confessions,* pp. 78, 126.

20. *Reformed Confessions,* p. 80.

21. *Reformed Confessions,* p. 72.

22. *Reformed Confessions,* p. 145.

that the church, as in the Apostles' Creed, is an object of our trust. "Catholic" means that there can "only be one Church of Christ." But Barth is also acutely aware that claims to be "catholic" are highly contentious: "The sharply anti-Roman aspect of the countenance of Reformed Christianity is a specifically Swiss legacy."[23] Those who might accuse Barth in his early days of being anti-Roman Catholic can blame this on his being Swiss and Reformed. He was born in Basel.

A different argument about being "Catholic" was once pursued by Calvin in his debate with Cardinal Sadolet. Barth deals briefly with this "Reformation Debate"[24] in his lectures on Calvin. He has great respect for Sadolet, as well he might. He describes him as "an extremely fine and sympathetic advocate," though in his thinking a scholar of the Middle Ages.[25] He was, as we can see now from later research, the sort of leader who would be in the reforming wing at Trent, alongside Contarini, whom Barth also admires, and Cardinal Pole, much loved by the English because he was the only Englishman who nearly became pope.[26]

Barth sums up Calvin's claims about the reform of the church: "We do not seek to erect a new church but specifically to set up again the oldest and true church that is now almost destroyed."[27] He does not have time or space to elaborate the point, which is a pity because Calvin's "Letter to Sadolet" offers one of the best replies to the charge that the Reformers were schismatics who cared little for the unity of the church. Sadolet had written to the citizens of Geneva, urging them to return to the Catholic fold. Calvin was persuaded to write the official reply. The gist of his argument is that it is Rome, not the reformed church in Geneva, that has departed from the faith and order of the one, holy, catholic, and apostolic faith. Here, in his own words, are some of the key points. Calvin tells Sadolet:

> You are mistaken in supposing that we desire to lead away the people
> from the method of worshipping God which the Catholic Church always

23. *Reformed Confessions*, pp. 103, 69.

24. For both sides of the argument see John C. Olin, ed., *John Calvin, Jacopo Sadoleto: A Reformation Debate* (Grand Rapids: Baker House, 1976).

25. Karl Barth (1922), ET Geoffrey W. Bromiley, *The Theology of John Calvin* (Grand Rapids: Eerdmans, 1995), pp. 402-3; Richard M. Douglas, *Jacopo Sadoleto, 1477-1547: Humanist and Reformer* (Cambridge, MA: Harvard University Press, 1959).

26. For a recent and excellent study of Trent see John O'Malley, *Trent: What Happened at the Council?* (Cambridge, MA: Belknap Harvard University Press, 2013).

27. *Theology of John Calvin*, p. 408.

observed. For you teach that all has been approved for fifteen hundred years or more by the uniform consent of the faithful, is by our rashness torn up and destroyed. . . . You know, Sadolet . . . that our agreement with antiquity is far closer than yours.[28]

But what arrogance, you will say, to boast that you alone are the church, and to deny it to all the rest of the world. We indeed, Sadolet, do not deny that those over which you preside are churches of Christ.[29]

One thing in particular made me [Calvin] averse to those new teachers [i.e., earlier Reformers], namely reverence for the Church. But when once I opened my ears and allowed myself to be taught, I perceived that this fear of derogating from the majesty of the Church was groundless. For they reminded me how great the difference is between schism from the Church, and studying to correct the faults by which the Church herself is contaminated.[30]

I cite these statements that Barth had obviously read in his studies of Calvin because they express Barth's own convictions about the church and church reform. What Barth laments is that too many of his Protestant contemporaries do not care enough about the church. For Barth, "the Reformation was the restoration of the Church." We are being questioned by the Roman Catholic Church, which believes that Christ is present in the church, as to whether "we are the Church, the reformed Church, but still — or again — the Church; or whether we stand on the foundation of the Reformation or on that of some intervening revolution?"[31] Do we believe that God has a special purpose for the church or do we not?

The very existence of the Roman Catholic Church and her certainty of her God-given mission posed these questions for Barth in 1928. They did not make him a Roman Catholic but they did strengthen his conviction that if there can only be one church, the one church must let herself be reformed, in obedience to God's gracious Word in Christ. Unknown to Barth and about

28. John Calvin, "Letter to Sadolet," in *Calvin: Theological Treatises,* ed. J. K. S. Reid (London: SCM, 1954), p. 231.

29. "Letter to Sadolet," p. 241. Such recognition is still not mutual. See *Dominus Jesus* (Congregation for the Doctrine of the Faith, 2000).

30. "Letter to Sadolet," 252.

31. "Roman Catholicism: A Question to the Protestant Church," pp. 315, 316.

the same time, 1930, Yves Congar had been meditating on Jesus' prayer in John 17 that all may be one and was finding a personal vocation for unity.[32] Barth was discovering a vocation to reform church teaching for the whole church, not just the Reformed. The two vocations would converge and meet at Vatican II and Barth and Congar would embrace one another in Rome as brothers in Christ, shortly after the Council ended. For them it was a reunion. They had met before.

Straight Talking and Dialogue

One thing Barth envied in the Reformation era was that in those days Catholics and Protestants actually spoke to each other! Post–Vatican II and after fifty years of intense dialogues and countless local conversations between Christians of different traditions, we take all this for granted. But even in the 1950s Roman Catholics in England were officially rebuked for saying the Lord's Prayer with their "heretical" neighbors. Prayer is vital for unity. Calvin had ended his letter to Sadolet with a beautiful prayer:

> The Lord grant, Sadolet, that you and all your party may at length perceive that the only true bond of ecclesiastical unity consists in this, that Christ the Lord, who has reconciled us to God the Father, gather us out of our present dispersion into the fellowship of his body, that so, through his one Word and Spirit, we may join together with one heart and soul.[33]

Is this a prayer all Christians could say "Amen" to? We might not have permission even to pray together, let alone debate together. By contrast, in the past we did talk. I quote again Barth's account:

> In the sixteenth and seventeenth centuries, Catholics and Protestants stared at each other grimly, but at least eyeball to eyeball. Then they talked to each other, sharply, harshly, but they really did speak. Whereas today, we have grown weary of the old quarrelling but perhaps also of the importance of the issues. Now all we see across the board are people who talk round the issues, looking past rather than at each other, standing around

32. Yves Congar (1964), ET Philip Loretz, *Dialogue between Christians* (London: Geoffrey Chapman, 1966), p. 3.

33. "Letter to Sadolet," p. 256.

without ever really confronting the great mystery that is the final point of all this hustle and bustle.[34]

As previously noted, this is quoted by Hans Urs von Balthasar in what is still regarded as one of the best Roman Catholic studies of Barth. Von Balthasar too felt challenged by it to engage in dialogue. The quotation comes originally from Barth's lecture, "The Concept of the Church," given in 1927 at the Catholic University of Münster. Granted there is a certain nostalgia for an era that did not always exist or was much harsher than here described — in Oxford I am daily reminded of the Protestant and Roman Catholic martyrs who were victims of their failures to agree — the fact remains that, with few exceptions, for the next four hundred years after the Council of Trent (1545-1563), Catholics, Protestants, Anglicans, and Orthodox rarely met and spoke with each other. Luther, Melanchthon, Zwingli, and Calvin could engage in public disputations and colloquies with people of the caliber of Erasmus, Eck and Cochlaeus, Sadolet and Contarini; in England, Thomas More and Reginald Pole. None of the Reformers ever met the pope, though given the caliber of all save Hadrian VI, or Paul III, the conversation would be limited despite a common language. Granted all this, such frank, "eyeball to eyeball" confrontations across confessional boundaries were by 1927 distant memories. Barth was saying there was no need for this. Catholics and Protestants could actually talk together about the church and know they were talking about the same subject. So why not talk together? Barth talked with Robert Grosche and Erich Przywara at Münster and later with his Swiss colleagues Hans Küng and Hans Urs von Balthasar. He joked about going to von Balthasar's "Lectures on Barth" to find out what Barth was saying! He had also met with Congar in Paris and in his final years would talk with Rahner, Ratzinger, and Pope Paul VI in Rome. No less important for him were the friends he found in Roman Catholic parishes in and around Basel.

Congar was possibly more aware than Barth that when we cease to talk with each other, potential truths become heresies, one-sided distortions of the truth. This is why Congar presses for *Dialogue between Christians* as in the book he published during the Council. His rule number one: "First of all, we must know one another."[35] At Vatican II he constantly sat with the observers but being so conscientious often regretted he had not spent more

---

34. Hans Urs von Balthasar (1951), ET Edward T. Oakes SJ, *The Theology of Karl Barth* (San Francisco: Communion Books, 1992), p. 6; Karl Barth, "The Concept of the Church" (1927), in *Theology and Church*, pp. 272-73.

35. *Dialogue between Christians*, p. 296.

time with them. He had also made the point noted earlier that "the whole truth is grasped only in communion with the whole Church."[36] Barth's style is more confrontational, or as John Yocum[37] would say, "polemical," but at least he engaged in serious debate with Rome and was respected for it, not least by popes and fellow Catholics and their theologians.

Congar could illustrate his thesis "that the whole truth is grasped only in communion with the whole Church" by the case of Martin Luther and the example of Barth himself. He regards Luther as an impatient reformer. He did not know how to hold back "when tempted by simple or abrupt solutions or by extremes of 'all or nothing.'"[38] Barth's fault too, in Congar's view, was that he worked too much on his own. As one man he "modified the theological map of Protestantism" but his almost exclusive emphasis on the sovereign causality of God without the capacity God gives us for "concausality with God," "renewed and reinforced in it an element of heresy which has been disastrous in its effects."[39]

Barth could think of different distortions that were a consequence of Rome's isolation from fellow Christians. It is surely significant that three of the major obstacles to reunion occurred before Rome's engagement in the ecumenical movement: the two Marian dogmas of 1854 and 1950 and the Declaration of Papal Infallibility in 1870. It is arguable that it was the presence of Protestant, Anglican, and Orthodox observers that discouraged the fathers at Vatican II from declaring Mary our Co-Redeemer. Their presence could not stop the pope calling Mary "Mother of the Church." That was a unilateral act, not supported by the Council. Congar too was not happy about it. Neither would Beauduin be. It would only make rapprochement with the Orthodox more difficult.[40] Pope Paul VI's action illustrates the point Congar was making about the need to discern truth *in communion*. With 2,500 bishops, expert theologians as *periti*, or observers there to give counsel together, it is hard to see why the pope on his own should say what the church believes. Popes don't need to argue but perhaps they should.[41]

---

36. *True and False Reform*, p. 229.

37. John Yocum, *Ecclesial Mediation in Karl Barth* (Aldershot, UK: Ashgate, 2004), p. xv.

38. *True and False Reform*, p. 269.

39. *Dialogue between Christians*, p. 12.

40. Mark Woodruff, "Arca Foederis, the Theotikos, Lambert Beauduin and the Church's Prayer for Unity," in *Ecumenical Prospects of Mary*, ed. Peter Marr (Plymouth, UK: Pilgrimage Trust, 2010), pp. 51-83, 81. Lambert Beauduin, pioneer of liturgical and ecumenical renewal, died in 1960, before the Council began.

41. Pope Paul VI could argue that many Roman Catholics, including many of the Council

The Reformers and Their Hopes for a Free Reforming Council

The Reformers hoped for a free, reforming Council where differences could be resolved through argument and open debate. All that happened was Trent, too little and too late. Four hundred years later came Vatican II. Was this the sort of Council the Reformers longed to see but never saw? In many ways, yes. I shall return to that question in a moment, but first more of the Reformation background to Vatican II.

Barth's lectures in the 1920s on Calvin, Zwingli, and the Reformed Confessions are obviously not to be regarded as the latest word in historical scholarship.[42] Their importance for this study is that they show where Barth is coming from. Roman Catholic historians were beginning to give a more balanced account of Luther, and Calvin would come to be described by Hans Scholl as *Calvinus Catholicus*.[43] Recent studies by Randall Zachman and others highlight "the remarkable fact a good deal of the best scholarship on Calvin has been done by Roman Catholics."[44] Calvin needs rescuing from his "friends," the Calvinists, said Reformed historian Heiko Oberman.[45] Zachman lists, among others, Alexandre Ganoczy, one-time student of Hans Küng. Barth told Küng that he had been reading Ganoczy's *Calvin und Vatikanum II*.[46] Zachman also mentions Kilian McDonnell who wrote about Calvin and the eucharist, and Fr. George Tavard who placed Calvin among the French Catholic Evangelicals. What all such studies are also doing is to remind us that Luther, Zwingli, and Calvin were themselves Catholics. Luther was a monk, Zwingli a priest, and Calvin destined and possibly or-

---

Fathers, though probably not the two-thirds majority Decrees required, agreed with him. See *History of Vatican II*, vol. 4, pp. 60-62, 445-48.

42. Barth was heavily dependent on secondary sources from the nineteenth century like Heinrich Heppe and Alexander Schweizer and, according to a recent thesis, read the Reformers through the eyes of such pietist students and sympathizers. See Ryan Glomsrud, *Karl Barth between Pietism and Orthodoxy* (unpublished Oxford DPhil, 2009).

43. Hans Scholl, *Calvinus Catholicus* (Basel: Habilitationsschrift, 1974).

44. Randall C. Zachman, ed., *John Calvin and Roman Catholicism* (Grand Rapids: Baker Academic, 2008), Introduction.

45. Heiko Oberman, *John Calvin and the Reformation of the Refugees* (Geneva: Droz, 2009), p. 11.

46. Karl Barth, Letter to Hans Küng, 27 June 1966, *Letters 1961-1968*, p. 241; Alexandre Ganoczy *Calvin und Vaticanum, II, Das Problem der Kollegialität* (Wiesbaden: Franz Steiner Verlag, 1965). Also *The Young Calvin* (1966) (Edinburgh: T. & T. Clark, 1987); *Calvin, Théologien de l'Église et du Ministère* (Paris: Éditions du Cerf, 1964); *Amt und Apostolizität . . . bei Calvin* (Wiesbaden: Franz Steiner, 1975).

dained in his youth for some dignified office in what we now call the Roman Catholic Church.

At the 500th anniversary celebrations in Geneva of Calvin's birth (1509), the Oxford church historian Diarmaid McCulloch argued very convincingly that Calvin would not like to be called a "Protestant." He demonstrated how important it was for Calvin to assure his contemporaries that he held the catholic faith, valued the tradition, and was not to be branded as sectarian along with the Anabaptist radicals of Münster. Convinced by his own arguments, McCulloch dared to suggest that Calvin should be regarded as "the Fifth Doctor of the [Latin] Church" in the succession of Ambrose, Jerome, Augustine, and Gregory.[47] Barth too would not wish to be labeled "Protestant" and would be deeply hurt by any suggestion that he did not hold "the catholic faith." He could qualify as a "sixth doctor"!

Such studies also show that the line between those who broke with Rome and those who remained obedient to hierarchical authority was often quite thin. Zachman gives this example from Tavard: Du Tillet was shocked when his friend John Calvin accepted a call to ministry in Geneva from the City Council and not from the bishop. (I am surprised that no one told Du Tillet that the bishop, who had once laid siege to the city, had now fled!) Calvin in turn was disappointed that his friend became a priest in the Roman Catholic Church after being so sympathetic to the reform. He saw this as a betrayal of the gospel. Calvin might also be puzzled to see whole sections of his writings quoted with approval, but without acknowledgment, by a contemporary Dominican critic, Pierre Doré, who could not help recognizing that much that this terrible "heretic" said was sound "catholic" teaching. He even quoted Calvin in support of more frequent communion.[48]

Barth, in his own way and in his own era, is entering into this exercise in historical revision where one attempts to see that there were good arguments on both sides. In his study of Calvin,[49] he says we should not treat the Middle Ages as Roman Catholics tended to treat Protestantism, as apostasy. Not all popes were diabolical and not all Reformers heavenly. Barth describes this sort of bias like this: "[T]he confessional antithesis was a tragedy in the 16th century and has now become a comedy" — which the learned editor and

47. Diarmaid McCulloch, "Calvin, Fifth Doctor of the Church," in *Calvin and His Influence*, ed. Irena Backhus and Philip Benedict (New York: Oxford University Press, 2011), pp. 33-45.

48. John Langlois, *A Catholic Response in Sixteenth Century France to Reformation Theology: The Works of Pierre Doré* (Lewiston, NY: Edwin Mellen Press, 2003), pp. 125-27, 222.

49. Karl Barth, *John Calvin*, pp. 18, 135.

translator Geoffrey Bromiley sees as a comment first made by Hegel and then by Karl Marx. Barth also sees the irony of our confessional divisions in the fact that John Calvin and Ignatius Loyola, the founder of the Jesuits, trained at the same College in Paris. Calvin left just as Loyola was entering. What a conversation they might have had, had Calvin stayed longer or Loyola arrived earlier!

Barth, as we know, did not agree with everything Calvin wrote nor warm to him as a person. At the 400th anniversary of Calvin's death (1564), Barth urged his audience to respect Calvin — "there is hardly a better teacher" — but added: "No one today should imagine that he would have been able to live in the Geneva ruled by Calvin with a good conscience, let alone with pleasure."[50] And with a deeper knowledge of church history than Barth was able to muster in a hurry, we can question some of Barth's assessments, not least on Calvin's hopes for a reforming Council: "Calvin's stance toward the idea that one could bring about the victory of the Reformation through a General Council, which both Luther and Melanchthon advocated, was never other than cold and skeptical,"[51] and he cites Calvin's comment in 1541 about the Colloquy at Regensburg: "What should one expect from such a society where among one hundred there is not one who could and will understand what the honour of God and the salvation of the church are?" Barth also notes Beza's comment that anyone who expected a proper ecumenical council could be likened to a council of pimps and prostitutes being asked to abolish public houses. Barth sees Calvin as giving up on Rome and resolved to establish Reformed churches. As we have seen, not all of us are convinced this was so.

Theodore Casteel made a detailed study of "Calvin and Trent."[52] Calvin initially favored a provincial council because he thought that Rome's talk of a general council was only a delaying tactic — as indeed he might since the Council desired by Luther in 1518 did not happen until 1545, and so only a year before Luther's death in 1546. Luther mocked this fact in 1541 in his sarcastic letter to one whom he called Hanswurst: "And what have you yourselves done that you now desire a council, now promising it, then again postponing it, and at other times refusing it?"[53] Calvin, like Luther, argued that councils should

---

50. Karl Barth, "Thoughts on the 400th Anniversary of Calvin's Death," in *Fragments Grave and Gay* (London: Collins, 1971), pp. 105-10.

51. Karl Barth, *Reformed Confessions*, pp. 10-11.

52. Theodore Casteel, "Calvin and Trent," *Harvard Theological Review* 63 (1970): 91-117.

53. Martin Luther, "Against Hanswurst," in *Luther's Works*, vol. 41 (Philadelphia: Fortress, 1966), p. 223.

be convened by the emperor as was the case with earlier councils like Nicea, not by the pope. He, too, was suspicious that a council convened by the pope would not be impartial. When at last it did meet at Trent he was critical of its membership. They were a hired crew of the pope's followers. It was not representative — only two bishops from his native France and both of them dull and unlearned. But he also applauded some of its decrees. He did not give up on hopes for a better Council, or for making Trent more ecumenical in its next sessions. In 1560 he renewed his plea for an ecumenical council just as the Council was in the process of being reconvened: "In order to put an end to the divisions which exist in Christianity, there is need to have a free and universal council." His criticisms, though harsh, are not necessarily partisan. French churchmen remained for the next two hundred years dubious about accepting or receiving Trent. Nor should Calvin's comments be taken as the rejection of the conciliar ideal. He was after all educated in Paris, which had been a center of conciliar theology. Ever since the Council of Constance in 1415, Paris upheld the view that a Council was above the Pope.[54] Calvin nurtured a tradition that to this day is strong on corporate decision making and inclined to be suspicious of personal leadership.

Protestants were invited to Trent. A few went but took no part in the debates. In retrospect we can understand why but regret the decision. Barth in *Church Dogmatics* IV/1[55] laments the fact that the fathers at Trent showed no sign of listening to the Reformers or even to Paul. The one person who did seem to understand their teaching on justification was Cardinal Caspar Contarini,[56] who had talked with the Protestants at Ratisbon in 1541. He died in 1542 before the Council opened. In Barth's view, his early death saved him from censure: "The Church was not willing to learn anything in this matter but only to continue unaltered and that is what it did." Hans Küng in his pioneering study, *Justification: The Doctrine of Karl Barth and a Catholic Reflection,* suggests that in the absence of dialogue, both sides offered only a one-sided perspective. Congar would agree: "[T]he whole truth is grasped only in communion with the whole church."[57]

54. J. H. Burns, *Conciliarism and Papalism* (Cambridge: Cambridge University Press, 1997), p. 285.

55. Karl Barth, *Church Dogmatics* IV/1, pp. 624-25. See also IV/3, p. 551.

56. Peter Matheson, *Cardinal Contarini of Regensburg* (Oxford: Clarendon Press, 1972), p. 37, notes that Contarini, Sadolet, Pole, and Fregosa were the Catholics in whom the Protestants had most confidence.

57. Yves Congar, *True and False Reform in the Church,* new edition and translation 2011, p. 229.

Vatican II: The Council the Reformers Hoped For?

The Reformers, of course, hoped for something better than Vatican II. They were Catholics whose only error, in their view, was that they believed the church must be reformed according to the Word of God and they demanded to be heard in a free and open Council. But compared with Trent, Vatican II was better by far than any of us, non–Roman Catholics or Roman Catholics, had come to expect. It met many of the Reformers' demands and even gestured reconciliation with the Orthodox East. These are some of its merits:

- Non–Roman Catholics were not only invited but made to feel part of the Council even though only the bishops could speak in the Council and vote on the documents. Most of the world's Christian communions welcomed the invitation and sent some of their best-informed and ecumenically minded people to offer their counsel whenever asked to do so. They even had meetings with the popes, John XXIII and Paul VI.
- The Council issued no anathemas. Pope John XXIII intended that it be a "Pastoral Council" and this is what it was. All can find help in all of the documents without having to agree with every paragraph. The Reformers were misguided to object that later councils sometimes contradicted earlier ones. Reforms might require changes. They accepted that Constantinople in 381 had slightly modified the Creed formulated at Nicea in 325. Many of the documents of Vatican II show signs of compromise. How otherwise can 2,500 bishops from such diverse cultures ever agree to anything? Ex-Anglican priest in Oxford, Cardinal Newman, shaped some of its thinking with his theory of "the development of doctrine."
- The Council was the most universal Council of the Christian Church that had ever been held, with over 2,500 bishops from almost every country in the world. Trent at most was attended by 200 bishops. The largest of the medieval councils never had more than 400 participants.
- It was influenced but not controlled by the popes, not even by the Curia, contrary to their wishes. We can now see from *The History of Vatican II* and from Congar's *Journal* that it did not work out as planned. There was no plan! The first session was almost chaotic, and *periti* like Congar felt they were wasting their time and might as well go home. So did some of the bishops. The traditionalists hoped the Council fathers would quickly rubber-stamp a whole host of documents that they had prepared and then depart. All they needed was their approval, not their opinions.

Joseph Ratzinger, one of the *periti* and the future pope Benedict XVI, commented:

> The preparatory commissions had undoubtedly worked hard. . . . Their diligence was somewhat distressing. Seventy schemas had been produced, enough to fill 2,000 pages of folio size. This was more than double the quantity of texts produced by all previous councils put together. . . . There was a certain discomforting feeling that the whole enterprise might come to nothing more than a mere rubber-stamping of decisions already made, thus impeding rather than fostering the renewal needed in the Catholic Church.[58]

The Council fathers found their feet, revised or rejected set schema, and with the help of the *periti* and the observers prepared new ones. The seventy schemas were reduced to seventeen that were discussed in detail. They insisted on having more say in the appointment of the commissions — many of whose members had been appointed by the pope. The commissions prepared each schema and no schema was accepted by the Council and could have the pope's approval without a two-thirds majority and ideally near unanimity. Instead of the Council being over in a few months or the equivalent of a university term of ten weeks, the fathers needed and were given four sessions in which to set about the renewal or *aggiornamento* of the Roman Catholic Church in the four years 1962-65. As with all Councils, the process of reception[59] takes longer and this, at least in theory, is where all the faithful, laity and priests, once represented in the Council by their bishops, still have a part to play. And so, too, do we who were represented by observers, appointed by our own communions, in my case by Professor George Caird, on behalf of what was then the International Congregational Council. If we Christians take no notice of what was once decided, the Council may be treated as though it had never been convened.

In fact, a lot of notice has been taken. Much has been received:

58. Joseph Ratzinger, *Theological Highlights of Vatican II* (New York, 1966), p. 5, quoted by Gerald P. Fogarty, "The Council Gets Underway," in *History of Vatican II*, vol. 2, pp. 2, 69. Ratzinger's point about the bulk of documents is illustrated by the two-volume *Decrees of the Ecumenical Councils*. Volume 1 covers eighteen Councils, volume 2 just three: Trent, Vatican I, and Vatican II.

59. William G. Rusch, *Ecumenical Reception: Its Challenge and Opportunity* (Grand Rapids: Eerdmans, 2007); Giuseppe Alberigo, Jean-Pierre Jossua, and Joseph A. Komonchak, ET Matthew O'Connell, *The Reception of Vatican II* (Tunbridge Wells, UK: Burns & Oates, 1987).

- The Mass in a local parish has been simplified thanks to the Council's first act, the reform of the Liturgy. The service is no longer in Latin. The Reformers would now find little to object to and would be delighted that their request for the use of the vernacular has at last been granted. More attention is paid to the reading of Scripture and, according to Karl Barth, who became in his last years an attentive listener to broadcast services, the preaching is better.[60] Sometimes it is hard to tell who is "Catholic" and who is "Protestant," but either may and often does preach the gospel.
- Renewed attention to the Scriptures, encouraged by *Dei Verbum,* has led to the use of a Common Lectionary in many different church traditions, with the bonus that congregations receive much more comprehensive teaching than when the choice of readings was at the mercy of the preacher's preferences. Many of the best Bible scholars are now Roman Catholics. In many countries we can even claim to have a common Bible. We can all appreciate the fact that the Reformers, Luther and Calvin, were great expositors and, in Luther's case, brilliant translators of the Bible. The *Luther Bible* is still in use and so too are many of *Calvin's Commentaries.* And how the Reformers would be thrilled to hear someone like Congar urge that when the Bible was enthroned at the center of the Council chamber, it should be allowed to speak and be responded to.[61] Often, this was all the Reformers asked.
- And without actually saying so, Vatican II demonstrated the value of Councils. Looking back to the centuries before the Reformation, we may all regret that councils were seen as enemies of the papacy and vice versa. As a result, both the councils and the popes failed to carry out the widespread appeals for the reform of the church "in head and members." The Fifth Lateran Council held on the eve of the Reformation set out to reform the church but failed to do so. Most popes underestimated the depth of the crisis. Councils, in theory, enable all voices to be heard. Vatican II gave a voice to many like Congar, De Lubac, Courtney Murray, and Rahner who had often been silenced. It listened to progressive bishops like Suenens and their opponents like Ottaviani. No one need pretend the process worked perfectly, and the question of papal power, so strongly asserted at Vatican I, remains unresolved. For Roman Catholics and many more, the conciliar movement, which Reformers before

---

60. Karl Barth, "Radio Sermons Catholic and Evangelical," in *Final Testimonies* (Grand Rapids: Eerdmans, 1977), pp. 43-49.

61. Congar, *Journal,* p. 87 at the Opening Ceremony, 11 October 1962.

and during the Reformation had supported, has proved its worth. Or, is this still a matter for heated debate about Vatican II in what Massimo Faggioli in a recent study describes as *The Battle for Meaning?*[62]

What Influence Did Barth and the Observers Have?

Trent would have been different and so would Vatican I if the Reformers and their heirs, and the Orthodox churches had been able to attend and participate. At Vatican II, the majority of the observers could be described as "heirs of the Reformation." Some could also be described as students of Barth. But even the Reformers in their absence aided the process of reform at Trent. Trent's great Roman Catholic historian, Hubert Jedin, generously concedes in a book contrasting Trent with Vatican II: "No one can dispute that the Tridentine reform of the Church came about under the pressure of the Reformation, and that the Catholic reform would have been unthinkable without the Protestant Reformation."[63]

What difference did the presence and active participation of observers make to Vatican II?

The consensus among Roman Catholic commentators is that their presence made an enormous difference. Cardinal Willebrands told Bishop John Moorman: "The presence of the observers here is very important. You have no idea how much they are influencing the work of the Council."[64] Joseph Komonchak, editor of the English-language edition of *History of Vatican II*, draws on the testimony of Congar, Alberigo, and Fouilloux, and no doubt others, to assert:

As things turned out, the decision to invite non Catholics as observers was one of the most important decisions made in the preparatory period, with consequences for the character the Council would assume and the work

---

62. Massimo Faggioli, *Vatican II: The Battle for Meaning* (New York: Paulist Press, 2012). Because of the shortage of priests, declining congregations — in some countries though far from all — and scandals of sexual abuse, it is easy to blame Vatican II for all that has happened since. But decline and scandals were evident long before the Council and, as in all social changes, there is never one simple cause.

63. Hubert Jedin (1964), ET N. D. Smith, *Crisis and Closure of the Council of Trent* (London: Sheed & Ward, 1967), p. 167.

64. John R. H. Moorman, "Observers and Guests of the Council," in *Vatican II by Those Who Were There*, ed. Alberic Stacpoole (London: Geoffrey Chapman, 1986), p. 166.

it would carry out that far surpassed the expectations of even the most optimistic. In more ways than one, their presence at the Council marked "the end of the Counter-Reformation."[65]

At the First Session, Congar is reported as saying, "I was on the verge of tears when I met the observers for the first time, here." He also notes that when some of the bishops referred to their presence, their remarks were greeted with loud applause. His assessment was that "[t]he presence of the [then] thirty-seven observers from the non–Roman Catholic Christian Communions is one of the most important elements in the conciliar situation."[66] And partly because of the warmth of their welcome and the way they were treated as honored guests with front seats in the Basilica, and partly because of the way the Council was developing ecumenically, there were in the end some 200 observers actively participating in the work of the Council.

Even so, one may wonder what impact even 200 non–Roman Catholics could have on decisions being made by 2,500 Roman Catholic bishops. They alone could speak and vote in the Assembly. Here we need to understand the dynamics of such a large assembly. Sociological studies of Vatican II help us do just that. John Coleman and Melissa Wilde set out to explain how the Curia, who presumed they had everything under control, were "stymied in their efforts to muffle reform." One intriguing explanation is offered by Coleman:

> An unspoken force at the Council, which fed into the progressives' sentiment pool and inhibited conservative strategies was the presence of Protestant observers. Where reforms were key to the ecumenical movement, positions congenial to mainline Protestants almost always won the day.[67]

Coleman was participating in a Conference about the extraordinary impact bishops and their *periti* from Belgium had at the Council. One graphic account sees the Belgium impetus for reform gaining a following as *The Rhine Flows into the Tiber* and church leaders along its banks go with the

65. Joseph A. Komonchak, "The Struggle for the Council during the Preparation of Vatican II, 1960-1962," in *History of Vatican II*, vol. 1, p. 326.

66. *History of Vatican II*, vol. 2, pp. 182, 178-79.

67. John A. Coleman, "Vatican II as a Social Movement," in D. Donnelly, M. Lamberigts, et al., *The Belgian Contribution to the Second Vatican Council* (Leuven: Peeters, 2008), pp. 5-28; Melissa J. Wilde, *Vatican II: A Sociological Analysis* (Princeton: Princeton University Press, 2007). Coleman is of course wrong to state that all the observers were Protestants. Some were Anglican or Orthodox.

flow.[68] The power of the few spokesmen for various groups is amply illustrated in Congar's *Journal* and its "Index of Names." Names like Alfredo Ottaviani, President of the Preparatory Theological Commission, Pericle Felici, later Secretary General of the Council, Cardinal Liénart from Lille, and the Belgians, Cardinal Suenens from Brussels, Émile de Smedt, Bishop of Bruges. And among the expert theologians, Lucien Cerfaux, Gustave Thils, and Gérard Philips, all from Louvain, are among not more than twelve bishops or experts whose names often occur on page after page. The list should include Congar, who was active in many of the key commissions and one of the most respected theologians in the Council. Most of the hard work in formulating documents was done in the Commissions and here the experts could give a lead. They in turn met with the observers and might be guided by their observations. None of this makes the actual assembly a mere cipher. Often confronted with conflicting arguments, the bishops had to exercise critical discernment. They could and did ask for whole schemas to be revised or rewritten. But in the end, the Council fathers had to make a straightforward "Yes/No" decision. Did they or did they not accept a document? In Council language, those in favor said *placet,* those against *non placet,* and those not sure, *placet iuxta modum.* Two-thirds had to agree for each document to be accepted and receive the pope's approval. In order to make such a "simple" response, complex issues had to be clarified into questions that pastorally minded bishops, who were not necessarily learned theologians, could understand and answer. This made the role of experts crucial for the Council and gave observers the scope to exercise their own expertise. They did this in formal meetings with the experts and leaders of commissions and in countless informal conversations during the course of the Council.

The highly visible presence of the observers meant that one of the questions the fathers had to ask and did ask, was: What might our "separated brethren" make of our decisions? The answer might be staring them in the face, "eyeball to eyeball," just as Barth said was the case in the Reformation debates of the sixteenth century. Moorman gives this example: The first draft of the schema on Scripture and Tradition spoke of "the inerrancy of the Scriptures, which were all written at the inspiration of the Holy Spirit, and therefore to be taken as absolutely free from error." One of the observers said to Moorman: "If they pass this, they will make themselves the laughingstock of the academic world." But they did *not* pass it. Cardinal Liénart of

68. Ralph Wiltgen, *The Rhine Flows into the Tiber* (Chumleigh, UK: Augustine Publishers, 1978).

Lille dismissed the document with his comment that what was being said is "offensive to our separated brethren in Christ, and harmful to the proper liberty required by any scientific procedure." Bishop de Smedt of Bruges said that the schema was against all that the church was doing with the other churches; if passed, "we shall be responsible for causing Vatican II to destroy a great, an immense hope."[69] But the *History of Vatican II* expresses surprise that Moorman himself was not sometimes more critical. In later talks about the Council, he has nothing to say about the pope's intervention in the so-called "Black Week," 14-21 November 1964.[70] This could be because high church Anglicans like Moorman found it much harder to be critical of Rome than Reformed theologians like Barth who were not craving for Rome's acceptance.

The observers were invited to be critical and were well equipped to be so. At the start of the Second Session in 1963, Cardinal Bea urged the observers "to grant us complete confidence and consequently to tell us frankly, everything you dislike, to share with us your positive criticisms, your suggestions, your desires."[71] And on their side, all the observers had been nominated by their respective World Communions because they had much to contribute to a wide range of ecumenical discussions. Many, like Lutheran scholars Oscar Cullmann and Kristen Skydsgaard; Reformed theologians Robert McAfee Brown, George Caird, Max Thurian, Douglas Horton, and Lukas Vischer; Orthodox theologians Archpriest Borovoy, Nikos Nissiotis, and Alexander Schmemann; and Methodist liberation theologian José Bonino from Argentina, were or would be deeply involved in the Faith and Order Commission of the World Council of Churches. Bishop John Moorman of Ripon was for twelve years a member of ARCIC, the Anglican Roman Catholic International Commission. Though none might presume to speak as spokesman for his own tradition, the fact that each was chosen by their World Communion meant that their "authority" was recognized beyond a particular denomination in one particular country. Collectively they could on occasion speak for that other half of the Christian world that is not Roman Catholic and so represent that fuller catholicity that the Council and Roman Catholic *periti* like Congar, Daniélou, Küng, Rahner, Schillebeeckx, and many more

69. John R. H. Moorman, "Observers and Guests at the Council," in *Vatican II by Those Who Were There*, pp. 165-66.

70. Riccardo Burigana and Giovanni Turbanti, "Preparing the Conclusion of the Council," in *History of Vatican II*, vol. 4, p. 462. But a different assessment is given in the previous chapter, p. 416 of Moorman's comment to Stransky.

71. Robert McAfee Brown, *Observer in Rome* (London: Methuen, 1964), p. xiii.

were seeking. Pope Paul VI, who, according to Congar, was good at making ecumenical gestures not always backed up by an ecumenical theology, is applauded by the American observer Robert McAfee Brown for telling the Curia in 1963: "We must welcome the criticisms which surround us with humility, with reflection, with recognition. Rome has no need to defend herself by being deaf to suggestions that come from honest voices, and all the less so, if the voices are those of friends and brothers."[72]

Specific Influences

It is of course hard to say. Footnotes to Council documents tend to restrict their references to Scripture, the fathers, earlier Councils, and papal encyclicals. They are not inclined to acknowledge debts to Martin Luther, John Calvin, or Barth's *Church Dogmatics*! In this respect, *Ut Unum Sint* marked a great advance, for in it Pope John Paul II publicly acknowledged the contributions of the World Council of Churches' Faith and Order Commission.[73] Vatican II was still inclined to be very cautious about giving praise to Protestants for fear of appearing to support their errors. Anglican scholars like Owen Chadwick resent the Council's reference to "the so-called Reformation" or in the official translation "events which are usually referred to as 'the Reformation,'" and Barth himself was critical of the way the same Decree on Ecumenism underplays the role of non–Roman Catholics in pioneering today's ecumenical movement: "Why is this initiative of the non-Catholic churches not explicitly recognised?"[74] Rome in retrospect seems less than generous to her separated brethren, let alone to her sisters.

But at their best, the non–Roman Catholic observers and Barth are not looking for compliments. What should delight us all is to see how they *contributed* to the reform, renewal, or *aggiornamento* of the Roman Catholic Church and helped us all respond more fully to our Lord's prayer that "all may be one, that the world may believe." These are some of their contributions. I shall return to some of them in more detail in later chapters about Barth's comments.

72. Brown, *Observer in Rome*, p. xiii.
73. *Ut Unum Sint* (1995) has some seventeen references to Faith and Order documents. Roman Catholics are now full members of the Faith and Order Commission.
74. *Unitatis Redintegratio* para. 13, 4; Karl Barth, *Ad Limina Apostolorum*, p. 30.

Examples of the Observers' Influence

Scripture

Lumen Gentium acknowledges that among those who "do not preserve the unity of communion under the successor of Peter" . . . "there are many who hold the sacred scripture in honour as the norm for believing and living." And the Decree on Ecumenism, *Unitatis Redintegratio,* admires the fact that: "Love and reverence, almost a cult, for holy scripture leads our brothers and sisters to a constant and expert study of the sacred text." The Council fathers wished to be even more generous and add: "Calling upon the Holy Spirit, they *find* God in the scriptures as speaking to them in Christ, the Word of God made flesh for us." This would have pleased John Calvin among others, for he always insisted that we needed the help of the Holy Spirit if we were to hear God speaking to us through the Bible. But, alas, the pope or his advisors, in that so-called "Black Week of Vatican II," and much to the distress of the observers and *periti* like Congar, insisted that we non–Roman Catholics "*seek* God in the scriptures." Rome is not so sure that we can find him without her help.[75]

Another *peritus,* Joseph Ratzinger, in his Commentary was more generous and also refreshingly honest about the way Roman Catholics sometimes use the Bible. He said that *Dei Verbum* owed much to the biblical theology of Karl Barth. He also admitted that the two Marian dogmas had exposed the fact that neither had a secure biblical basis and were therefore in need of much better exegetical support. The way in which the Bodily Assumption of the Blessed Virgin is "supported" by a strange assortment of texts proves his point.[76]

Tradition

During the Council an important Assembly of the WCC Faith and Order Commission was meeting in Montreal and taking a fresh look at "the Tra-

---

75. *Lumen Gentium* 15; *Unitatis Redintegratio* 21; *History of Vatican II,* vol. 4, pp. 406-17; Congar, *Journal,* pp. 689, 696.

76. Emery de Gaál, *The Theology of Pope Benedict XVI: The Christocentric Shift* (New York: Palgrave, 2010), p. 94; Joseph Ratzinger in Herbert Vorgrimler, ed., *Commentary on the Documents of Vatican II* (New York: Herder & Herder, 1968), vol. 3, p. 155.

dition and traditions."[77] Ideas were fed into Vatican II from an Assembly in which Roman Catholic biblical scholar Raymond Brown had played a major role. Congar had also been working on this theme, though, according to Barth scholar John Webster, with little understanding of Protestant attitudes. Webster refers to "the lengthy but curiously unperceptive treatments of Protestantism in Congar's *Tradition and Traditions*. Balthasar was not without reason for his dismay at the lack of deep and wide knowledge of classical and modern Protestantism on the part of his Catholic *confrères*."[78]

Church

Lumen Gentium's christological beginning, seeing Christ, rather than the church as "The Light of the World" was thoroughly Barthian and biblical. This was also the theme of the Third Assembly of the World Council of Churches that had just been held in New Delhi in 1961, "Jesus Christ, the Light of the World." It was the first time Roman Catholics had been permitted to accept the invitation to attend as observers. The first draft of the schema started with the church as hierarchy. Suenens is credited with the inversion of emphasis. Chapter 1 is about Christ, the Mystery of the Church; chapter 2, "The People of God"; chapter 3, "The Hierarchical Constitution of the Church." Barth, who thinks that at best there can only be "a flexible hierarchy" in the church, would be pleased, and so too would Calvin, as Roman Catholic scholars like Ganoczy were noting. Was Suenens responding to their influence or to a closer reading of the Bible under the inspiration of the Holy Spirit? Enough to say such a change has Barth's and the Reformers' support.

Roman Catholic Ecumenism and the World Council of Churches

Some inputs are easier to credit. The World Council was directly consulted about the Decree on Ecumenism and Lukas Vischer, the Director of the

77. Patrick C. Rodger and Lukas Vischer, eds., *The Fourth World Conference on Faith and Order: The Report from Montreal 1963* (London: SCM, 1964), pp. 50-60.

78. Yves Congar, *Tradition and Traditions: An Historical and a Theological Essay*, ET Michael Naseby and Thomas Rainborough (London: Burns & Oates, 1966); John Webster, "Ressourcement Theology and Protestantism," in *Ressourcement: A Movement for Renewal in Twentieth Century Catholic Theology*, ed. Gabriel Flynn and Paul D. Murray (Oxford: Oxford University Press, 2012), pp. 482-94, 483.

Faith and Order Commission, and once a student of Barth's in Basel, was one of the observers and often their spokesman. Vischer and Nikos Nissiotis, also a Barth student, then the Director of the WCC's Ecumenical Institute at Bossey, sent detailed reports to the WCC and so kept their colleagues in Geneva and in the Central Committee fully informed. A full account of ecumenical developments is given by the General Secretary of the WCC, Willem Visser 't Hooft, in his *Memoirs* as "The Ecumenical Mobilization of the Roman Catholic Church."[79]

Just as many non–Roman Catholics wanted to know what was envisaged when Pope John made the surprise announcement of an "Ecumenical Council," some Roman Catholics wanted to know what the World Council of Churches was. No one need be surprised that Yves Congar was at the heart of all attempts for mutual understanding. He had not been allowed to attend the First Assembly at Amsterdam in 1948 but was able to take part in an unofficial and confidential meeting in 1949 at the Istina Centre in Paris. Ten from the World Council met with ten Roman Catholic ecumenists, among them Congar. He was joined by Jean Daniélou SJ, Fr. Maurice Villain SM, and Fr. Jérôme Hamer OP, among others. Hamer wrote a doctoral thesis on Barth. He was later the Executive Secretary of the Vatican's Secretariat for Unity. Visser 't Hooft comments that "the discussions were exceedingly frank."

Some misunderstandings had to be cleared away. It was not true, for example, that "the council was dominated by Barthian theology, as others had declared." It was true, and stated earlier in these *Memoirs,* that Visser 't Hooft had enormous respect for Barth. He had read his *Epistle to the Romans* and "found it a terribly difficult book," but it convinced him that "[h]ere was a man who lived fully in the modern world . . . who had rediscovered the authority of the Word of God. This was a man who proclaimed the death of all the little, comfortable gods and spoke again of the living God of the Bible."[80] He often found Barth infuriating because of his critical attitude to the early ventures of the ecumenical movement, but the respect remained.

Congar explained that the 1928 encyclical, *Mortalium Animos,* placing an embargo on Roman Catholic involvement in the ecumenical movement, was no longer the last word. In Visser 't Hooft's summary: "Père Congar said that there were unchangeable elements in the church but also many elements

79. W. A. Visser 't Hooft, *Memoirs* (Geneva: WCC, 1973), pp. 319-39.

80. *Memoirs,* p. 16; Thomas Herwig, *Karl Barth und die Ökumenische Bewegung, das Gespräch zwischen Karl Barth und Willem Adolf Visser 't Hooft auf der Grundlage ihres Briefwechsels 1930-1968* (Neukirchener: Neukichener Verlag, 1998).

which could be reformed." (It is ironic that Congar should say this just as his book on *True and False Reform* was about to be banned!) The new Roman Catholic theology desired to go back to the original sources of the faith[81] and in so doing found much common ground with the Protestant biblical theology. Soon after this, the Holy Office issued a new "Instruction," which was indeed much more positive. The desire for unity was inspired by the Holy Spirit and therefore to be welcomed. Even so, says Visser 't Hooft, "[T]he proclamation in the same year of the doctrine of the bodily assumption of Mary made the impression that the Roman Catholic Church took no account of the convictions of the other Christian churches." Add to this the further complications about Roman Catholic participation in the next Assembly at Evanston, near Chicago in 1954, and we can see that right up to the eve of the Council, relationships between the two sides were often fraught.

Even at this early stage (1950), Congar had contributed an essay to the World Council of Churches Faith and Order study on Intercommunion explaining Rome's position in relation to that of Anglicanism.[82] He later wrote an essay for the Festschrift for Willem Visser 't Hooft, First General Secretary of the WCC, that was published in 1963, its title "Ecumenical Experience and Conversion: A Personal Testimony."[83] Without doubt, Congar was the most preeminent of all the Roman Catholics with whom the World Council chose to work, even though he was never Rome's official spokesman.

What eased the situation, as so often in the ecumenical journey, was Christian friendship.[84] In Britain such friendships between people of different Christian traditions were often forged in a common task. Future ecumenical leaders like Presbyterian Lesslie Newbigin and Anglican Oliver Tomkins came to know each other through the Student Christian Movement. But for Vatican II we should never underestimate the significance of the fact that *all* the participants had lived through the Second World War.

81. See Gabriel Flynn and Paul D. Murray, eds., *Ressourcement: A Movement for Renewal in Twentieth-Century Catholic Theology* (Oxford: Oxford University Press, 2012). The book is dedicated to Henri de Lubac and Yves Congar.

82. Yves Congar, "Amica Contestatio," in *Intercommunion*, ed. Donald Baillie and John Marsh (London: SCM, 1952), pp. 141-51. For some rather irritating reason, Congar assumes that Faith and Order was led by Anglicans when even the editors of the volume are both Reformed!

83. Yves Congar, "Ecumenical Experience and Conversion: A Personal Testimony," in *The Sufficiency of God: Essays in Honour of W. A. Visser 't Hooft*, ed. Robert C. Mackie and Charles C. West (London: SCM, 1963), pp. 71-87.

84. See Marc Boegner, *The Long Road to Unity* (London: Collins, 1970); Henri de Lubac, *Résistance Chrétienne à l'Antisémitisme, Souvenirs 1940-44* (Paris: Fayard, 1988), with numerous references to Boegner.

Some became friends, or, at least, understood each other better because of common resistance to Hitler. The French Roman Catholic theologian and expert at the Council, Henri de Lubac, had worked closely with Reformed leader and observer at the Council Marc Boegner in dangerous missions to save the lives of persecuted Jews. Congar had been a prisoner, Barth expelled from Germany. Ratzinger like others among his Protestant and Roman Catholic contemporaries was forced to belong to the Hitler Youth. The War made reconciliation after such conflicts a gospel imperative, often with agonized soul searching and the release that could only come through confession and reconciliation, as in the Stuttgart Declaration which Barth had urged Niemöller and the German churches to make in October 1945.[85] Only later, and perhaps through encounters at Vatican II, would we learn the full story of Roman Catholic resistance to Hitler. Only now, in my case, how Barth in Bonn may have been the inspiration behind a Roman Catholic tract published in Switzerland in 1934 and written by a young professor in Bonn, Alois Dempf, which began with this summons to his fellow Catholics to join the resistance to Hitler's tyranny:

> We German Catholics, too, have come to an hour of decision, like our Christian brothers, the Lutherans and Calvinists, who have already been facing this difficult decision for a year. However, not everyone is aware of it. Unfortunately those of us who have become clear-sighted must fear that we are in the minority, indeed that there may not be enough of us.[86]

Visser 't Hooft got on well with Johannes Willebrands. They spoke the same language and came from the same province of Holland. Their families and friends had suffered together in the War. Willebrands in turn arranged for a meeting with Cardinal Bea from Germany,[87] appointed by the new pope as head of the Secretariat for Unity. This turned out to be another breakthrough: "Cardinal Bea was one of those exceptional people who, even when you meet them for the first time, give you the feeling that you have known them for many years," said Visser 't Hooft.

---

85. James Bentley, *Martin Niemöller* (Oxford: Oxford University Press, 1984), pp. 175-78.

86. Klaus Scholder, *The Churches and the Third Reich, Volume Two: The Year of Disillusionment 1934, Barmen and Rome* (London: SCM, 1988), p. 175. Sadly, Scholder did not live to complete this history beyond 1934. But see also his "Eugenio Pacelli and Karl Barth," in *A Requiem for Hitler and Other New Perspectives on the German Church Struggle* (London: SCM, 1989), pp. 61-74. Pacelli became Pope Pius XII in 1939.

87. Jerome-Michael Vereb CP, *"Because He Was a German": Cardinal Bea and the Origins of Roman Catholic Engagement in the Ecumenical Movement* (Grand Rapids: Eerdmans, 2006).

The *Memoirs* go on to comment on the disappointment felt by the observers when Pope Paul VI altered some of the statements in the Decree on Ecumenism. "The first reaction of the non–Roman observers and even of a good many Roman Catholic ecumenists, was one of very great concern." But he goes on to say that the acceptance of the Decree, even with these alterations, created a new situation. There followed a meeting at the WCC in Geneva with Cardinal Bea and then the first meeting of the Joint Working Group between the WCC and the Roman Catholic Church in May 1965 even before the Council had come to an end, later that year.

There is one other comment in the *Memoirs* very relevant to my theme. Visser 't Hooft tells us that Barth several times tried to persuade him to attend the Council as an observer but that he felt he had too many other duties and should not get too directly involved in discussions with Rome.[88] We can make of that comment what we will. Aside from his own personal views, it is a fact that some member churches in the WCC were and perhaps still are suspicious of getting too close to Rome. This was one reason why Baptists did not send an observer to Vatican II.

What the *Memoirs* do not show is something we can glean from Hans Küng's early books about the Council and from the *History of Vatican II*. Rome's understanding of unity changed markedly even as the Council got under way. Even in Küng's account, the model is still that of "Return." Return to Rome, though to a Rome that is in the process of renewal or reform. The hope expressed is that the changes taking place will make Rome more attractive and welcoming to those outside. Pope John is quoted as saying: "Look, brothers, this is the Church of Christ. Come, here the way lies open for meeting and for homecoming; come, or take or resume, that place which is yours, which for many of you was your father's place."[89] It is a beautiful vision, not to be too easily dismissed, and I attempt to do it more justice in a final chapter. Furthermore, the original schema on unity ignored the Protestant and Anglican churches. It focused only on the divisions that had occurred in the eleventh century with the oriental churches.[90] By a complex process that included arguments about the status of the Unity Commission and who does what, the text came to include sections on Catholic

88. Visser 't Hooft, *Memoirs*, p. 335.

89. Hans Küng, *The Council and Reunion*, ET Cecily Hastings (London: Sheed & Ward, 1961), pp. x, 5-7.

90. The complex history has to be traced through all five volumes of the *History of Vatican II*, vol. 1, pp. 203-4; vol. 2, pp. 429-35; vol. 3, pp. 257-75; vol. 4, pp. 406-17, 473-76. Volume 5 deals with the follow-up in dialogues and the Joint Working Group.

Ecumenism *and* relations with the ecclesial bodies of the sixteenth-century Reformation. One can hardly imagine the observers, most of whom were Protestants and Anglicans, being satisfied with less.

Israel and the Jews Today

For some controversial issues, the difficulties were more easily shared. Barth complained later that the Jews were not included in the Decree on Ecumenism but he would know from his own experience how hard it had been for the World Council to face questions about Israel as God's people. Barth had been a member of an advisory group of some of the best known non–Roman Catholic theologians that prepared a statement for the WCC Evanston Assembly in 1954 on its theme, "Christ, the Hope of the World." He had persuaded his colleagues that the statement should include a section on "The Hope of Israel." The assembly itself did not agree and in the final report, a "Statement on the Hope of Israel" is only included as an appendix. It had to make it clear that "our concern in this issue is wholly biblical and is not to be confused with any political attitude toward the State of Israel."[91] The same potential confusion would afflict the Vatican Council ten years later. Barth was probably unaware of how much care the commissioners had taken to say the right thing in the right place without adding to the conflicts in the Middle East.

Human Rights

The WCC had been influential in making Human Rights the concern of the United Nations almost twenty years before Vatican II discussed the issue.[92] It was a subject many of the Council fathers found difficult because they had been taught that error has no rights and that those who were not Roman Catholics were by definition in error. Observers from North America who had been wrestling with the issue of "Civil Rights" had a big impact here.

91. *The Evanston Report* (London: SCM, 1955), pp. 70-79, 327-28.
92. John Nurser, *For All Peoples and All Nations: Christian Churches and Human Rights* (Geneva: WCC, 2005).

East/West Conflict and Communism

Some of the Council fathers wanted the Council to make a declaration against Communism. The issue was raised again in the last month of the Council but the pope and the mixed commission said there would be no express condemnation of Communism.[93] The World Council of Churches had confronted the same question at its first assembly in a famous debate between John Foster Dulles of the United States and Josef Hromádka of Czechoslovakia. Barth himself was accused of not being as opposed to Communism as he had been to Nazism.[94] The World Council was not going to be drawn into an East/West conflict, not only because there was truth on both sides but also because there were Christian churches on both sides of the Iron Curtain. Those guiding the debates at Vatican II made sure that this Council, too, did not become an instrument of the Capitalist West versus the Communist East. Barth wrote a postscript for Hromádka's "Gospel for Atheists" (1958). This essay stated:

> Yet there is no more tragic misunderstanding than the attitude that the Gospel and the Church of Jesus Christ are a frontier against atheism. . . . The Gospel of God's approach to man and of his presence in Jesus of Nazareth among the sinners, sick, wandering, needy, hungry and thirsty, and even among the doubting and those who flee from God, warn against every power front, against every attempt to mobilise the church in an alliance with a *"Weltanschauung,"* social-political, and cultural crusade against the so-called atheistic parties and the socialist-communist form of society.[95]

Just before the close, Hromádka, who was then President of the Christian Peace Conference, paid the Council an unofficial visit. He was, as one would expect, especially interested in the discussions that had taken place over *Gaudium et Spes*. He also had talks with Father Miano of the Secretariat for Nonbelievers.[96]

93. *History of Vatican II*, vol. 5, pp. 148-52, 406-8; A. Melloni, ed., *Vatican II in Moscow* (Leuven: Bibliotheek, 1997).

94. See Karl Barth, "The Church between East and West" (1949), in *Against the Stream* (London: SCM, 1954), pp. 125-46.

95. Josef Hromádka, "Gospel for Atheists" (1958), in *Christian Existence in Dialogue: Doing Theology in All Seasons* (Geneva: WCC, 1990), pp. 38-61, 38, 49.

96. *History of Vatican II*, vol. 5, p. 490.

It is not too much to claim that debates in the World Council and the views of people like Barth and Hromádka supported the majority in the Council who also did not wish to be drawn into an East/West conflict. But Barth was shocked when later during the Cuban Missile Crisis, his Czech friend Hromádka made it clear he supported the Soviet line.[97] *Semper reformanda!* Even the Reformed need reforming and Barth was never afraid to admit it!

Mary Co-Redeemer and Mother of the Church?

Mary was not an issue at the Reformation but she was at the center of deep divisions in the Council: What to say? And where to say it? In a vote on 29 October 1963, 1114 fathers wanted Mary to be included in the text on the church; 1074 said she should have a separate document.[98] Congar expressed fears of a "galloping mariology" that would like to see Mary hailed as Co-Redeemer and Mother of the Church. In the end the Council did not issue a separate statement on Mary but incorporated its thinking in *Lumen Gentium,* the document on the church. I would argue that the presence of observers and their comments helped tip the balance in favor of this more restrained approach. Those who were more ecumenically aware would also know how much damage had recently been done to ecumenical relations by Pius XII's unilateral declaration on the Bodily Assumption into Heaven of the Blessed Virgin Mary. They would also be upset that even during the Council another pope, Paul VI, had issued his own statement "declaring" Mary "Mother of the Church." Congar, too, was not happy about this, partly because he could not understand what it meant.[99]

Is the Reformation Over?

Barth was reluctant to describe Vatican II as a "Reformation,"[100] but even if it was, the reformation of the church is never over. *Semper reformanda,* once the slogan of the heirs of the Reformation, has become a program

---

97. Frank Jehle, ET Richard and Martha Burnett, *Ever Against the Stream: The Politics of Karl Barth, 1906-1968* (Grand Rapids: Eerdmans, 2002), p. 97.

98. Congar, *Journal,* 29 October 1963.

99. Congar, *Journal,* 22 November 1964.

100. Karl Barth, *Gespräche 1964-1968,* p. 540.

that is also accepted in Rome. As is stated in *Unitatis Redintegratio:* "In its pilgrimage on earth Christ summons the church to continual reformation, of which it is always in need, in so far as it is an institution of human beings here on earth."[101]

In the next chapters I shall examine in more detail some of the reforms carried out by Vatican II and Barth's comments on them.

101. *Unitatis Redintegratio* 6; *Ut Unum Sint* 16.

CHAPTER THREE

Responding to Vatican II, Part 1

This chapter will deal with Barth's response to two key documents of Vatican II: *Dei Verbum,* the Word of God and Revelation, and *Lumen Gentium,* about the Church and Christ, the Light of the World. But first a further comment about the actual calling of the Council and how Barth came to be invited and his initial assessments.

The Surprise Announcement

Pope John XXIII surprised the world and members of his own church when he announced that he was going to hold a Council. The idea had been mooted by his predecessor Pius XII but nothing came of it. Nobody need be surprised at that. Had not Vatican I declared that the pope was infallible, so what further need of councils? One need might be to complete the work of Vatican I because that Council was abruptly ended by the advent of the Franco-Prussian War and left with an unfinished agenda. But by all accounts good Pope John, as many of us in many churches have come to regard him, was simply inspired. He felt called to call a Council and this as pope he was entitled to do, though earlier ecumenical councils like Nicea had been convened by the Christian emperor, often with the intention to settle disputes and to keep the peace.

Pope John made his announcement on 25 January 1959. The day in January was already significant in church calendars. It marks the end of the Octave for Christian Unity that an American Episcopalian priest, later Roman Catholic, Paul Wattson inaugurated in 1908. January 18th celebrates the confession of Peter, January 25th the "conversion" of Paul. After prayer for the help of Mary and the protection of the saints — I am following Alberigo's account — Pope John explained why he was calling a Council. The Council would be for "the enlightenment, edification, and joy of the entire Christian people" and would offer "a renewed cordial invitation to the faithful of the separated churches to participate with us in the feast of grace and brotherhood, for which so many souls long in all parts of the world."[1]

As the pope's purpose became clearer it was Hans Küng who suggested to the Vatican that Karl Barth be one of the invited observers, and it was Küng who helped keep his friend well briefed and informed when it became clear that at this stage Barth was not fit enough to journey to Rome. When Barth did make the journey to the threshold of the apostles, as he described it, he impressed many of the bishops and theologians he met by his detailed knowledge of all the Council documents — not bad for a man born in 1886 who was then eighty. It was clear to all who met him or to all who have read the reports of his visit, that the Council, which had been in session in different stages from 1962 to 1965, had become a major event in his life. Much of this we can glean from his letters to Hans Küng, Oscar Cullmann, and others and from his own account in *Ad Limina Apostolorum,*[2] published soon after his return from Rome, and from his "Thoughts concerning Vatican II," which was printed in the early stages of the Council. There is also a comment on the Council in the Preface he wrote in Easter 1967 for the last part-volume of *Church Dogmatics,* IV/4 on baptism. Here is a great Christian contemplating his own demise but with his usual good humor, grace, and perception:

> I foresee that this book, which by my judgment will be my last major publication, will leave me in the theological and ecclesiastical isolation which has been my lot for almost fifty years. I am thus about to make a poor exit with it. So be it! The day will come when justice will be done to me in this matter too. I hazard the paradoxical conjecture that this will perhaps come about earlier, not on our side, but among Roman Catholic theologians who today are questioning almost everything — unless a new Pius IX blight the present hopes of blossom.[3]

1. Giuseppe Alberigo, "The Announcement of the Council," *History of Vatican II,* vol. 1, pp. 1-54, 15.

2. Karl Barth (1967), ET Keith R. Crim, *Ad Limina Apostolorum: An Appraisal of Vatican II* (Richmond, VA: John Knox Press, 1968). The book includes his "Thoughts on the Second Vatican Council," which was originally published in the World Council of Churches' *Ecumenical Review* 15, no. 4 (July 1963): 357-67.

3. Barth, *Church Dogmatics* IV/4, p. xii.

Barth's Excitement and Cautious Expectations

The reference to a Pius IX is significant. Though excited by the announcement of the Council, Barth was also cautious about how it might work out. We may remember that it was Pope Pius IX who summoned Vatican I to pronounce himself "Infallible"! He is also notorious for being reported as saying, in answer to the question "What is the Tradition? *I am* the Tradition," thus offering an ecclesiastical echo of Louis XIV's claim "l'état, c'est moi!" Barth saw this claim as typical of the age of absolutism, when Man assumed he had no one to answer to, not even God.[4]

Some Roman Catholics, notably scholars like Küng in his recently published *Memoirs* or Heinrich Fries in his sad little book, *Suffering from the Church*[5] or the book edited by Küng and Leonard Swidler in 1987, *The Church in Anguish: Has the Vatican Betrayed Vatican II?*[6] seem to suggest that Barth's last prediction could come true. Hopes of blossom have been blighted by much that has happened since the Council. But they remain convinced there is no turning back. This clearly is Barth's firm belief. Fries's book, first published in 1989, has the subtitle *Renewal or Restoration?* Twenty years later, the same question about Vatican II is still being fiercely debated in two very different accounts. Matthew Lamb and Matthew Levering both quote Pope Benedict XVI and assure us that it was about *Renewal within the Tradition.*[7] Their emphasis is on restoration and continuity. John W. O'Malley asks the question *What Happened at Vatican II?*[8] and is quite sure it was about renewal rather than restoration. Summarized in an earlier article,[9] he finds it hard to believe that 2,500 bishops would be summoned from 116 different countries, the most globally universal Christian Council that had ever been held, seventeen major documents debated and agreed to by two-

---

4. Karl Barth (1952), "Man in the Eighteenth Century," in *Protestant Theology in the Nineteenth Century,* new edition (London: SCM, 2001), p. 29.

5. Heinrich Fries (1989), ET Arlene Anderson Swidler and Leonard Swidler, *Suffering from the Church: Renewal or Restoration?* (Collegeville, MN: Liturgical Press, 1995).

6. Hans Küng and Leonard Swidler, *The Church in Anguish: Has the Vatican Betrayed Vatican II?* (San Francisco: Harper & Row, 1987); cf. George Lindbeck, "Crisis in American Catholicism" (1975).

7. Matthew L. Lamb and Matthew Levering, eds., *Vatican II: Renewal within Tradition* (Oxford: Oxford University Press, 2008).

8. John W. O'Malley, *What Happened at Vatican II?* (Cambridge, MA: Belknap Press, 2008).

9. John W. O'Malley, "Vatican II: Did Anything Happen?" *Theological Studies* 67 (March 2006): 3-33.

thirds majorities plus the pope, if all that really happened was more of the same "business as usual." He is convinced "the Council wanted something to happen" and much good did happen. A summary of conflicting assessments can be found, as noted earlier, in Massimo Faggioli's *Vatican II: The Battle for Meaning.*[10]

In this debate, no one with any real concern for the church of Christ can be neutral. Alberigo's history and the so-called Bologna School is accused of bias in favor of renewal, which is why I also think it important to consult Vorgrimler's *Commentary on the Documents of Vatican II,* which Cardinal Ratzinger, Karl Rahner, Josef Jungmann, and others helped to edit. I have also consulted Agostino Marchetto who is highly critical of Alberigo and offers an alternative history.[11] Barth went to Rome to find out for himself what was going on, well aware even then — in 1966 — of such a debate. This is his own account of inquiries he made prior to his visit:

> Since my spirits were beginning to revive through the goodness of God and the skill of my doctors, I wrote a letter to Rome. Were they inclined to receive me, as it were, *post festum,* so that I would acquire first hand information? It would be a purely private matter of instructing me in the way the decisions of the Council were understood and explained in the immediate vicinity of the centre of the Catholic Church. On this side of the Alps, present-day Catholic theology was not unknown to me through its literature and to some extent through its representatives. Now I wanted to become acquainted with it where it had long been operating, and from where, with conflicting and interrelated tendencies, it had now adopted for itself new standards and directions. The answer from Rome was friendly and cordial, as I had been sure it would be. The Secretariat for Christian Unity, to which I want to express my especial thanks, did everything needed to open the way for me.[12]

In a letter to Hans Küng shortly before the visit he was rather less restrained. He noted that in the Council documents, Mary was hailed as queen of the apostles, queen even of Peter and his college and the whole hierarchy. And did this make the lay apostolate superior to the hierarchy, in which case, long live Mariology! He had found the declaration on religious freedom "ab-

---

10. Massimo Faggioli, *Vatican II: The Battle for Meaning* (New York: Paulist Press, 2012).

11. Agostino Marchetto, ET Kenneth Whitehead, *The Second Vatican Council — a Counterpoint for History of the Council* (Scranton, PA: University of Scranton, 2010).

12. Barth, *Ad Limina Apostolorum,* p. 10.

solutely terrible" and asks why Küng, who was one of the expert theologians advising the Council, had done nothing to stop this "monstrosity." Then he added: "I have formulated some pertinent or impertinent questions on it which I will try to put to someone in Rome, though naturally not to His Holiness himself." In fact he was armed with questions and comments on all the documents he hoped he would have time to discuss, not just *Dignitatis Humanae*, which was agreed to in one of the last sessions of the Council in 1965.

Barth's Summing Up of Main Issues at Vatican II

Like Barth, we have not got time or space to discuss all the Council documents, nor do we need to. Barth was often asked by student groups and radio interviewers what really happened at Vatican II? What was most significant? In response, he invariably came up with two themes he regarded as most important: the rediscovery of the Word of God and the emphasis on Christ as Lord of the church. The two are closely related, as every student of Barth's careful comments on "the Word of God" can see. For, as Barth assured the students at the Ecumenical Institute at Bossey in 1967, "If Scripture is important then Jesus Christ becomes important."[13] His third point was about the laity and his fourth about unity, or Rome's new openness to other churches. Barth felt that this order of priorities reflected the chief intention of the Council. Yes, it was calling itself an "Ecumenical Council" and had gone out of its way to make non–Roman Catholic observers welcome and included; but its prime purpose, in Barth's understanding, was "the Church's own inner renewal," meaning the renewal of the Roman Catholic Church herself. Better ecumenical relations would be a consequence rather than a direct cause of what the Council was about. He made this point in the article the General Secretary of the World Council of Churches, Willem Visser 't Hooft, asked him to write for the *Ecumenical Review*[14] when the Council had only just begun its work. So Barth's comments here are on the Council's priorities: *Dei Verbum, Divine Revelation,* and then, *Lumen Gentium,* which, though mainly about the church, begins with Christ, the Light of the Nations, the Light of the World.

---

13. Karl Barth, *Gespräche 1964-1968* (Zürich: Theologischer Verlag, 1997), pp. 326-50, English text pp. 579-97. Meeting with students at Bossey, 23 January 1967.

14. Barth, "Thoughts on the Second Vatican Council" (1963), reprinted in *Ad Limina Apostolorum,* pp. 65-79.

Dei Verbum

Though he was not there to see it, Barth was deeply impressed with the account of how at the opening of the Council "the old book of the Gospels" was placed in the "direct line of vision of the bishops [and observers!] in St Peter's Cathedral."[15] This may have happened at previous councils but this time it was more than symbolic, or so, as we have noted, Congar hoped. The Council gathered round the Word of God and intended that its decisions should be in response to what God might say to them through the Scriptures. And toward the end of his life, when he could not always get to church, Barth felt the impact of this new emphasis on "the Word of God." He spent each Sunday listening to two sermons, one Protestant and the other Roman Catholic, on Swiss radio, and was delighted to discover how much more important and how much better preaching had become in all churches, but not least in the Church of Rome. Here are his comments:

> Among the Reformed some have been marked by prophetic power while among the Roman Catholics a series of fast sermons was characterized by mystical depth in the good sense. If I take closeness to the Bible and closeness to life as the decisive criteria for a good sermon, my impression is that with, of course, some regrettable exceptions, the preaching has been good — basic, edifying, and helpful. Only in a few cases have I turned off the set in disillusionment or annoyance. In comparison with the past I may even state, with all due reservations, that preaching is on the whole now better than it was. This is palpable on the Roman Catholic side. For other reasons it is so on the Reformed side too.[16]

This is praise indeed from a theologian who began life as a preacher, insisted on teaching homiletics to students in Bonn in the tense years 1932-33 when the state was trying to tell preachers what to say,[17] and who, in later years, preached "deliverance to the captives"[18] in Basel prison and who

---

15. Barth, "Thoughts on the Second Vatican Council," p. 68.

16. Karl Barth, *Final Testimonies*, ed. Eberhard Busch, trans. Geoffrey Bromiley (Grand Rapids: Eerdmans, 1977), pp. 43-44.

17. Angela Hancock, *Karl Barth's Emergency Homiletic, 1932-1933: A Summons to Prophetic Witness at the Dawn of the Third Reich* (Grand Rapids: Eerdmans, 2013).

18. Karl Barth, ET Marguerite Wieser, *Deliverance to the Captives* (London: SCM, 1961); ET A. T. Mackay, *The Call of God: New Sermons from Basel Prison* (London: SCM, 1967).

always hoped his theology would be absorbed and used by preachers. The detailed index volume to his *Church Dogmatics* honors his hope with its subtitle, *Aids for the Preacher.*[19]

Barth also welcomed the fact that he heard very little of what one might call "confessional" preaching on Swiss radio. "In the main," he said, "the serious and final focus on both sides is now on Jesus Christ. We should all be glad about this." Indeed! As he told the young students at Bossey, twenty years ago one could almost say that Roman Catholics were forbidden to read the Bible. Now the Council commands them: they *must* read the Bible! Barth sensed that "there is a clear tendency to make Scripture the real governing element in the Church, if I am right. And that is a renewal."[20] And if Barth was wrong in this assessment, he was inviting the Roman Catholics among the students to correct him. Also at Bossey at the time was the Greek Orthodox theologian Nikos Nissiotis, then the Director of Bossey. He had been an observer at Vatican II. No one disagreed. Barth asked if the students had been studying the Documents of Vatican II and the answer was they had. They would therefore know, for example, that *Dei Verbum* boldly states:

> This teaching function is not above the word of God but stands in its service, teaching nothing but what has been handed down, according as it devotedly listens, reverently preserves and faithfully transmits the word of God, by divine command and with the help of the Holy Spirit. (Chapter 2, paragraph 10)

The first line sounds great. It appears to express the symbolic act with which the Council began when the Gospels were placed at the center of the assembly and the whole Council acknowledged the authority of the Word of God. On the whole, Barth welcomed *Dei Verbum* but he spotted the "attack of weakness" in chapter 2: the Council could not make up its mind what it meant by "the word of God."

Readers of *Church Dogmatics* I/1 and I/2 will know that Barth makes a threefold distinction between:

---

19. Geoffrey W. Bromiley and Thomas F. Torrance, eds., *Church Dogmatics Index Volume with Aids for the Preacher* (Edinburgh: T. & T. Clark, 1977). The Index includes not only Bible texts but sections from *Church Dogmatics* appropriate for the Christian Year. All volumes of *Church Dogmatics* include a biblical index, and many pages in each are devoted to detailed biblical exposition.

20. Karl Barth, *Gespräche 1964-1968*, p. 582.

The Word of God Preached
The Word of God Written
The Word of God Revealed

The one Word of God is Christ as the God who reveals himself to us in Jesus. The Scriptures testify to this and human preachers through human words proclaim the gospel. So the three forms of the Word of God are a unity but they are not the same, and the priority belongs to Christ, the Word of God Revealed, the Word made flesh. At one point Barth even appeals to the Roman Catholic understanding of transubstantiation. Human words can be changed into the Word of God just as bread and wine can become for us the body and blood of Christ.[21]

Scripture and Tradition

The problem Barth has with Roman Catholic thinking about the Word of God and, much to his disappointment, even with one particular chapter in *Dei Verbum*, is that Scripture, Tradition, and the Teaching Authority of the Church's Magisterium are treated as though all three were on the same level and had the same authority. What he is criticizing can be seen in Pope Pius XI's encyclical *Mortalium Animos* (1928). This is the document in which the pope told the faithful not to get involved in all the "congresses and meetings" of the growing ecumenical movement. "Such efforts can meet with no kind of approval from Catholics" because their whole basis in faith was wrong. He therefore insisted:

> All true followers of Christ, therefore, will believe the dogma of the Immaculate Conception of the Mother of God with the same faith as they believe the mystery of the august Trinity, the infallibility of the Roman Pontiff in the sense defined by the Oecumenical Vatican Council, with the same faith as they believe the Incarnation of our Lord.[22]

Faced with such a demand, one can understand one of Barth's most outspoken, anti-Roman Catholic outbursts: "Roman Catholicism is a terrible

---

21. Barth, *Church Dogmatics* I/1, pp. 88-124, 89.
22. See Oliver Stratford Tomkins, "The Roman Catholic Church and the Ecumenical Movement 1910-1948," in Ruth Rouse and Stephen Charles Neill, *A History of the Ecumenical Movement*, vol. 1, 3rd ed. (Geneva: WCC, 1986), pp. 674-93, 682-83.

thing because it means the imprisonment of God himself! It claims to be the possessor of the Holy Spirit and revelation and Jesus Christ himself." Barth said this in the intimacy of a student gathering near his home in Basel. It is reported in Karl Barth's *Table Talk* by one of his students, John D. Godsey. It was uttered before Vatican II. It illustrates just how much has changed, on both sides — Barth's and Rome's![23]

Hierarchy of Truths

According to the 1928 encyclical, belief in the Trinity, papal dogmas about Mary and infallibility, and the biblical witness to the incarnation are all on the same level; each requires the same wholehearted assent. This encyclical was intended to discourage ecumenical engagement. It would certainly succeed! No non–Roman Catholic could accept such a "creed." But a remedy would be provided by Vatican II with its concept of "a hierarchy of truths." This is found in its Decree on Ecumenism, which positively encourages Roman Catholics to get involved in praying and working for reunion. Different truths are related in different ways to "the foundation of the Christian faith." Barth went to Rome to try and discover what Rome thought this foundation is. I reserve further comment on *Unitatis Redintegratio* and this particular paragraph 11 to a later chapter, but clearly it is as much concerned with the Scriptures and Revelation as with church unity.[24]

In his *Church Dogmatics* Barth does not deal with this particular encyclical, *Mortalium Animos,* but with another by the same pope in the same year, *Miserentisimus Redemptor* (1928), where Mary is hailed as the "Mediatrix of our reconciliation with God." Barth wants to know by what authority apart from that of the pope is Mary so proclaimed and he responds bluntly: "where Mary is venerated, where this whole doctrine with its corresponding devotions is current, there the Church of Christ is not." As I argued in the previous chapter, Vatican II became much more modest in its thinking about Mary, possibly under the influence of Barth and other Protestants. The bishops may also have listened with respect to the Orthodox, who despite their

---

23. John D. Godsey, ed., *Karl Barth Table Talk* (Edinburgh: Oliver & Boyd, 1963), p. 43.

24. In June 1984 Pope John Paul II visited the World Council of Churches offices in Geneva. General Secretary Willem Visser 't Hooft suggested that it would be useful to have a joint study on this concept. The pope agreed. Hence the Report of the Joint Working Group between the Roman Catholic Church and the World Council of Churches, *The Notion of "Hierarchy of Truths": An Ecumenical Interpretation* (Geneva: WCC, 1990).

own devotion to Mary are not happy about the way Rome tends to legislate devotion into dogma.

Papal pronouncements about Mary remain the strongest example of a very different view of how God's Word is proclaimed than that which Barth and most Protestants would accept. Indeed, according to Ratzinger's comments on *Dei Verbum*, it was the controversy over the papal dogmas about Mary and the difficulty of either justifying them and their "default of Biblical proof" or of appealing to long-held tradition that made it essential for the Roman Catholic Church to rethink Divine Revelation.[25]

Tradition and Magisterium

By the time of Vatican II Barth is much gentler and more sympathetic in his criticisms of Rome but some earlier concerns or "difficulties" remained unresolved. As an expression of sympathy Barth says:

> We must admit that the problems involved in the concepts "tradition" and "teaching office" exist on our side and cannot be ignored. As for the concept "tradition," did not the churches which arose in the Reformation in the sixteenth century appeal with one accord to the Councils of the first several centuries? And were we not justified in developing the traditions that became fixed in the various "confessions" [up to and including the Theological Declaration of Barmen in 1934] and also unwritten traditions? ... And did not Calvin exercise in the sixteenth century in Geneva, in all of French-speaking Protestantism, and even far beyond, a function not entirely unlike the office of Peter in Rome?[26]

Fair point! But Barth goes on to question "By what right" does Chapter 2 of *Dei Verbum* direct the Catholic Church to put Thomas à Kempis or Ignatius Loyola on the same level as Matthew as interpreters of the Evangelists? Or, by what right can the Protestant Christian give the same respect to Luther, Calvin, Zinzendorf, or Blumhardt as to the Apostle Paul? I wish he had also mentioned John Wesley, but we get the point![27]

25. Joseph Ratzinger, "Dogmatic Constitition on Divine Revelation, Origin and Background," in *Commentary on the Documents of Vatican II*, vol. 3, ed. Herbert Vorgrimler (New York/London: Herder & Herder/Burns & Oates, 1968), p. 155.

26. Karl Barth, "Conciliorum Tridentini et Vatican I Inhaerens Vestigiis," in *Ad Limina Apostolorum*, p. 49.

27. Barth, *Ad Limina Apostolorum*, p. 51.

On tradition, Barth is fully aware that prior to the Reformation there had been a constant debate in the church about the relative authority of tradition. We have to make up our minds: Is the church "resolved to ascribe direct absolute and material authority only to Holy Scripture and not to anything else, not even to itself? At this point we stand before one of the severest conflicts in its history." The issue "constitutes the frontier that separates the Catholic Church and the true, Evangelical Church, and which will inevitably separate them so long as both continue to be what they are." The church could not as a whole make up her mind about Scripture and Tradition, about customs or conventions and her own authority. This is true, says Barth, of many modern Protestants also. It was also true for the fathers at Trent. Barth notes that "[a]t the Council of Trent this decision was not made without difficulties and disputes." The balance of support during the preceding centuries favored the Tridentine theory of two sources of revelation, Scripture and Tradition. Hence the need for a strong resistance from the Reformers:

> The logic of the preceding developments was against them and their doubts and milder suggestions were necessarily opposed by a council which had made it its appointed task to fight the Reformation. If the Reformed decision was no novelty in the Church, neither was the Tridentine and we have to concede that the scales had long come down on the latter side. Had it been otherwise, the Reformation would not have had to be carried through in the painful but unavoidable form of a disruption.[28]

Barth is, of course, aware that infant baptism as practiced in most churches is part of a tradition that may have no clear warrant in Scripture. The same is true of any doctrine of the Trinity. Barth does not agree with infant baptism but not because it is not obviously biblical but because the custom allows us to become Christians in our sleep without necessarily giving our personal assent and commitment to Christ. He has no difficulty with the need for a Trinitarian faith, though you will not find in Barth a reference to the "triune God," which I think is a very ugly expression for God who makes himself personally known as Father, Son, and Holy Spirit. For these and other reasons, Barth's whole approach to Tradition and the need for a Teaching Magisterium became much more sympathetic. He is basically pleased with *Dei Verbum*. Except in the "dismal" chapter 2, it moves on from Trent and Vatican I:

---

28. Barth, *Church Dogmatics* I/2, pp. 546-48.

Important changes, even innovations, made from them show that the trend of the Constitution was in the direction of a doctrine which carefully [more carefully than we do] considers and includes the genuine problems of "tradition" and the "teaching office," a doctrine not of the *sole* authority but of the *supreme* authority of Holy Scripture for the Church and theology.[29]

Barth was aware that the authority of Tradition was and remains a contentious issue in the Roman Catholic Church. He would have realized this if he had been present at any of the debates. He therefore graciously concedes: "Complete clarity of formulation was thus not attained, nor could it be expected."[30] A Roman Catholic commentator, Enzo Bianchi, agrees.

In an article in *The Reception of Vatican II,* Bianchi rejoices that "[t]he word of God has been given back to the people who, as they listen to it, encounter the Lord and enter into communion with him. This is without qualification the greatest fruit of the Council." But it nearly did not happen. The schema on revelation went through a very wearisome journey, "the most wearisome of all at the Council." It was redrafted four times. The Council fathers appeared to be getting nowhere. The whole subject was almost dropped, but the pope, Paul VI, insisted the Council could not evade such a fundamental issue. Bianchi has to admit that "there was no in-depth resolution of the problem of the relationship between scripture and tradition, and that the very concept of tradition was not explained and set forth with sufficient clarity." Fruitful dialogue is always possible when both sides agree that they have not really given sufficient thought to the same question or find it too difficult to resolve.[31]

Unknown to most of the fathers in the Council and noted in my previous chapter, an Ecumenical Conference of Roman Catholics, Orthodox, Anglicans, and Protestants was currently engaged in what would be a fruitful discussion of Tradition and traditions in the life of the church. This was at the Fourth World Conference on Faith and Order at Montreal in July 1963. It sought to reach an understanding of "Tradition" that all Christians, not least those who claimed their tradition was to have no tradition, could recognize, and distinguish this from "traditions" lowercase, meaning church customs.

---

29. Barth, *Ad Limina Apostolorum,* p. 54.

30. Barth, *Ad Limina Apostolorum,* p. 54.

31. Enzo Bianchi, "The Centrality of the Word of God," in Giuseppe Alberigo, Jean-Pierre Jossua, and Joseph A. Komonchak, ET Matthew J. O'Connell, *The Reception of Vatican II* (Tunbridge Wells, UK: Burns & Oates, 1987), pp. 115-36.

It suggested among other formulae: "We exist as Christians *sola traditione,* by tradition alone. Tradition then in this sense includes the preaching of the Word and worship, Christian teaching and theology, missions and also witness to Christ in the lives of members of the Church." The Commission had received comments from Yves Congar who had just completed his own major study on this subject.[32] Later in discussions at the Council, Congar's view was that the gospel cannot be known solely from Scripture or solely from Tradition. But he is pleased that the Council no longer speaks of two sources of revelation.[33]

A question arises as to whether most of *Dei Verbum* had Barth's approval because it shows his influence. Ratzinger thought that the new approach to divine revelation, an approach he welcomed because it was centered on Christ, owed much to the dialectical theology of Karl Barth and to the personalist philosophy of Ebner and Buber. Ratzinger also read Barth's report on the Council and says he agrees with Barth that *Dei Verbum* was a real moving forward from the footsteps of previous Councils, Trent and Vatican I. He was very conscious that the way the original schema was presented made no contribution to ecumenical dialogue and would have destroyed all hope of the coming together again of the separated brethren. Ratzinger was then, like Küng, one of the young theological experts at the Council.[34]

One final word from Barth on a subject that is so obviously central to his whole theology, the Word of God. He once complained, again in the relaxed atmosphere of an informal meeting with students, that in Roman Catholicism, one begins with the existence of the church. Jesus Christ is no longer its free Lord, but is bound up with the existence of the church itself.[35] How delighted he would then be to see how in the Council's new document about the church, we begin with Christ, the Light of the World, *Lumen Gentium.*

---

32. Patrick Rodger and Lukas Vischer, eds., *The Fourth World Conference on Faith and Order, the Report from Montreal 1963,* p. 24. Observers Albert Outler and Kristen Skydsgaard were experts.

33. Congar, *Journal,* 15 and 22 October 1965 — on this theme.

34. Emery de Gaál, *The Theology of Pope Benedict XVI: The Christocentric Shift* (New York: Palgrave Macmillan, 2010), p. 94; Joseph Ratzinger, "Dogmatic Constitution on Divine Revelation, Origin and Background," in *Commentary on the Documents of Vatican II,* vol. 3, ed. Herbert Vorgrimler, pp. 155-69.

35. John D. Godsey, ed., *Karl Barth's Table Talk* (Edinburgh: Oliver & Boyd, 1963), p. 4.

Lumen Gentium

Lumen gentium cum sit Christus. "Since Jesus Christ is the light of the nations, this holy Synod, called together in the Holy Spirit, strongly desires to enlighten all people with his brightness, which gleams over the face of the church. . . ." The opening sentence of the Vatican Council's document is surely all that Barth would hope for. It is centered on Christ and it has a missionary thrust. For Barth the most significant fact about the Council was the rediscovery of the Word of God. The second was the rediscovery of Christ. "In all the documents Jesus Christ has the most important role. We do not have in Vatican II a Church which insists on its own importance. Certainly it does do this. But the real focus is Jesus Christ."[36]

As for mission,[37] Barth was often critical of his own tradition, the Reformers in general, and what he calls the classical doctrine of the church. All suffer from "holy egoism." The church is seen as an end in itself. There is no sense of mission to the world or existing for the world.[38] Was not the Protestant world of the sixteenth and seventeenth centuries characterized by "that pronounced lack of joy in mission and even readiness for it?" And though the Roman Catholic Church performed better in this respect, it also suffered from putting the emphasis on "the world for the Church, than its opposite, the Church for the world." What became, asks Barth of "2 Corinthians 5:19 that it was the world which God reconciled to himself in Jesus Christ, or of the well-known John 3:16 that it was the world which He loved so much that He gave for it His only begotten Son?"[39] The very title, *Lumen Gentium,* certainly makes the point that the church, like Christ, is there for all. Indeed, for all nations. The Christian community has "its wonderful freedom to recruit across the frontiers of nations . . . being one and the same *una catholica* in all, existing within them as a universal people, indeed as *the* universal people."[40] The title was Pope John XXIII's idea. It expressed one of his burning convictions. But was it just a coincidence that about this time

---

36. Karl Barth, conversations with students at Bossey.

37. On Barth and mission, see John G. Flett, *The Witness of God: The Trinity, Missio Dei, Karl Barth and the Nature of Christian Community* (Grand Rapids: Eerdmans, 2010).

38. In recent Faith and Order work on ecclesiology there is a growing emphasis on mission in successive documents: *The Nature and Purpose of the Church* (1998) became *The Nature and Mission of the Church* (2006). *The Church, Towards a Common Vision* (2013) begins with "God's Mission and the Unity of the Church."

39. Barth, *Church Dogmatics* IV/3, pp. 766-67.

40. Barth, *Church Dogmatics* IV/3, p. 741.

the World Council of Churches had its Third Assembly in New Delhi under the banner "Jesus Christ, the Light of the World"? In its opening worship, all shared this prayer:

> We have come together in this place out of many nations because Christ who is the light of the world has shined in our hearts to give the light of the knowledge of the glory of God, and because he has set us as lights in the world and bidden us let our light shine.[41]

Could it be that the same Spirit was moving different Christians in different places to say the same prayer even though in the previous decade, and this is hard to believe, Roman Catholics had been forbidden even to say the Lord's own Prayer together with Protestants?

Vatican Documents about the Church

In this section I will now focus on what *Lumen Gentium* says about "the mystery of the Church" and what Barth has to say about this. In another chapter I deal with polity, how the church is governed according to Vatican II and should be governed according to Barth, though we may find that Barth, on a matter that is so important for the Reformed tradition, is surprisingly undogmatic and adaptable! He is certainly not going to tell Rome to behave like a good Protestant church, partly because he has little experience of such, and perhaps also because his cordial meeting with the pope and others in Rome has mollified his views.

It is important to remember that *Lumen Gentium* is not the only Council document about the church. In one sense you could say all her documents are about the church, for they concern her worship, her teaching, her relationships to peoples of other faiths, to other churches and ecclesial communities as well her own nature and structure. What to deal with and where, was a decision the commissioners of the Council had to decide, and if we are looking for answers to our own questions we may not find them where we expect them to be. Hence Barth, for example, would ask, "Why is the most grievous, the most fundamental schism — the opposition of Church and synagogue [Romans 9–11; Ephesians 2] not dealt with in the Decree on Ecumenism?" because the relationship of the church and the Jews is for

41. W. A. Visser 't Hooft, ed., *The New Delhi Report* (London: SCM, 1962), p. 2.

Barth, as he believes it was for Paul, an ecumenical issue. Likewise we might be surprised that a document that has so much to say about "the People of God" needs a separate document about the "Apostolate of the Laity," who after all constitute some 95 percent of God's people.

People of God and/or Body of Christ

Barth's first "question for clarification" was "in the relationship of chapters I and II" (in *Lumen Gentium*): Is the "Body of Christ" subordinated to the "People of God" or vice versa? We are never told what the pope or others questioned in Rome answered — it was agreed before the visit that such responses were private and confidential — but it is not difficult to see why this question is asked.

In the process of debate, the Council fathers altered the order of the main sections so that "People of God" are mentioned before the Hierarchy. This is one of the major "innovations" that is usually noted. Barth's chapter references appear to be wrong. Chapter 1 does mention "Body of Christ" (1,3) but also explains that the New Testament uses a variety of images to describe the church (1,6). According to a well-known study by Reformed theologian Paul S. Minear in 1960, there are nearly a hundred such images, one of which is "light" as in "Lumen Gentium" and Matthew 5:14, "you are light for all the world." For Roman Catholic theologian Avery Dulles,[42] the reason for this great variety is that no one image can do justice to the "mystery of the Church" but each image can complement another.[43] Minear's study was prompted by the Faith and Order Commission of the World Council of Churches as an ecumenical exercise to discover or rediscover the relationship of the church to Christ as depicted in different images. The book has been reprinted many times, my own copy dated 2004. Rereading it now, one regrets that neither the bishops in Council nor Barth had studied Minear, because he warns against fastening on one image to justify our par-

42. Avery Dulles, *Models of the Church* (1974), new expanded edition (New York: Image Books, 2002).

43. Paul S. Minear, *Images of the Church in the New Testament* (Louisville: Westminster John Knox, 1960). Minear later took part in an Ecumenical and Interfaith Conference at the University of Notre Dame in 1966 attended by a number of Vatican II bishops, experts, and observers including Butler, Congar, Rahner, Raymond Brown, George Lindbeck, and Robert McAfee Brown. He offered a detailed critique of *Dei Verbum*. See John H. Miller, ed., *Vatican II: An Interfaith Appraisal* (Notre Dame: University of Notre Dame Press, 1966), pp. 68-88.

ticular polities. One of the *periti,* Karl Rahner, would make the same point in a critique submitted to the bishops.[44] Minear does, however, single out two images, or rather, groups of images, for special attention: People of God and Body of Christ.[45]

As with *Dei Verbum,* the debate is almost as important as the final decree. Here too basic issues were fiercely contested, so much so that the chapter in Alberigo's *History* has the heading "Beyond an Ecclesiology of Polemics." But some of the polemicists are more ecumenically minded than others and that in itself is a source of hope. They show that there were bishops and their theologian advisors *in* the Council who were pressing for the kind of ecclesiology that people *outside* like Barth had long been pleading for. For Barth, who thinks of the church in a dynamic way as an "event" rather than a rigidly regulated institution, it would be heartening to see that much of the debate could be summed up, as it is by Giuseppe Ruggieri in the chapter I refer to, as "a conflict between a juridical conception of the church as a society, reflected in the unyielding defence of the identification of the Catholic Church and the Mystical Body, and a conception of the church that was more sensitive to its mystery."[46] We also have here a clue to the answer to Barth's question, which image had priority — "Body of Christ" or "People of God"? Because the encyclical *Mystici Corporis* made the Body of Christ image seem so juridical, a move in a different, more dynamic direction would favor something like the "pilgrim people of God." Nine months or so after discussions on the original schema began, it was Cardinal Suenens of Belgium who came up with the radical suggestion that before speaking about the Hierarchy, we should first speak of the People of God whom the hierarchy are called to serve. All agreed that we should first speak about Christ, then about Christ's people. Suenens is forever associated with the saying, "We are all co-responsible now"; lay or clergy, all that happens in the church is our shared concern. We are *all* God's People.

Are we answering Barth's question about People of God and Body of Christ? What was Barth's own answer? How does Barth think of the church? First, he prefers the description "community" or "congregation" to that of "church," because these words imply an active gathering and coming together

44. *History of Vatican II,* vol. 2, p. 312.

45. Paul Minear, *Images of the Church.* "People of God," pp. 66-104, includes holy nation, Israel, Abraham's sons, elect, remnant — enough to make Barth's point about Israel-Church as the elect; "Body of Christ," pp. 173-220, includes body of life, body of the saints, diversities of ministries, spiritual body, plus a discussion of the meaning of "head of the body."

46. *History of Vatican II,* vol. 2, p. 281.

in response to the Word rather than a corporation. In terms of polity, he liked his colleague Erik Wolf's suggestion of the church being a "christocratic brotherhood." The church is "the community of the Lord and those who are elected by him and thus made His brethren."[47] Nearest to the sense of the divine mystery is Barth's own description of the Christian community as the earthly historical form of the existence of Jesus Christ.

Barth's detailed ecclesiology is given in volume IV of *Church Dogmatics,* first published in the original German edition in 1953, but before that he had given the keynote address at the First Assembly of the World Council of Churches on "The Church, the Living Congregation of the Living Lord Jesus Christ" and in 1936 had delivered four lectures on *The Church and the Churches* in preparation for the Second World Conference on Faith and Order that was held in Edinburgh in 1937. In 1936 Barth declares that "[t]he quest for the unity of the Church must in fact be identical with the quest for Jesus Christ as the concrete Head and Lord of the Church." "Jesus Christ as the one Mediator between God and man is the oneness of the Church." We must be on our guard lest the motives that stir us in our search for unity "lead us in a quest which looks past Him." "If we listen to the voice of the Good Shepherd, then the question of the unity of the Church will most surely become for us a burning question." And he has just described the call for unity as "the claim urged by Jesus Christ upon us."[48] So what is clear here is that Barth's thinking about the church, like that of the opening chapter of *Lumen Gentium,* is thoroughly Christological.[49]

Body of Christ, Head of the Body

In the Amsterdam address, Barth is equally adamant that all talk of the church is futile unless centered on Christ. All New Testament images — Body or Bride of Christ, People, Flock, etc. — center on Christ. But next, more than anywhere else in his writings, Barth will repeatedly insist that the church is a dynamic reality: "The Church exists by *happening.* The Church exists as the *event* of this *gathering together.*"[50] This is a different emphasis

47. Barth, *Church Dogmatics* IV/2, p. 680.

48. Karl Barth (1936), *The Church and the Churches,* new edition with foreword by William G. Rusch (Grand Rapids: Eerdmans, 2005), pp. 13-15.

49. See Kimlyn J. Bender, *Karl Barth's Christological Ecclesiology* (Aldershot, UK: Ashgate, 2005).

50. Barth's keynote address can be found in WCC's *The Universal Church in God's Design*

from that in Vatican II. It is more complementary than corrective or contradictory. It has some parallel with the fact that the Vatican Council itself is regarded as an "event," a happening.[51] Alberigo refers to Lutheran observer Skydsgaard's description of the council as "an event in search of the gospel."[52] In the minds of Suenens and Pope John XXIII,[53] the council was more akin to a "New Pentecost" rather than a built-in structure of the church. The tension between "event" and "institution" is explored in a later chapter. Roman Catholic critics insist the church can be both.

In *Church Dogmatics* IV/1 Barth argues that the very word *ecclesia* implies an assembling or congregating and so an event. He then states that "the community is the earthly-historical form of the existence of Jesus Christ Himself."[54] As such it is the Body of Christ. In the Amsterdam address he describes the church as the Body of Christ but makes a very important distinction from what he sees as Roman Catholic ecclesiology:

> With respect to its Head, the Church is divine in nature and manner. As the Body of that Head, it is without doubt and unequivocally human. In and of itself, it is an element of creaturely and therefore threatened reality. Its existence is an existence secured, unthreatened, and incontestable only from above, only from God, not from below, not from the side of its human members. In the event of God's Word and Spirit, it is secured from danger, justified, sanctified, cleansed, and preserved from evil by the fact that it is from above, from God and only by this. In its Lord Jesus Christ [but also, only in Him] is its security.[55]

What Barth is resisting is an identification of Christ and the church, so to speak without remainder, so that the church is Christ, possesses Christ, and there is no appeal to Christ beyond and above the church. The church is a continuation of the incarnation. For Barth, "to speak of a continuation

---

(London: SCM, 1948), pp. 67-76 and reprinted in Karl Barth, *God Here and Now* (London: Routledge, 2003), pp. 75-104.

51. The understanding of Vatican II as "event" is explored at various points by Giuseppe Alberigo in *The History of Vatican II*, which he edited, and in Massimo Fagioli, *Vatican II: The Battle for Meaning* (New York: Paulist Press, 2012).

52. *History of Vatican II*, vol. 5, p. 614.

53. Léon Joseph Suenens (1974), ET Francis Martin, *A New Pentecost* (London: Collins, 1977), p. x.

54. Barth, *Church Dogmatics* IV/1, pp. 651, 661.

55. Karl Barth's Amsterdam Address, in *God Here and Now*, p. 83.

or extension of the incarnation is not only out of place but blasphemous."[56] If this is the thinking in *Mystici Corporis,* Roman Catholic commentators on *Lumen Gentium* are anxious to reassure Barth, or any other such critic, that Vatican II has moved on. Aloys Grillmeier states:

> There is no question of an extension of the hypostatic union to include the Church, as is definitely stressed in the Encyclical *Mystici Corporis* of Pius XII. The analogy "Incarnation-Church" is clearly distinguished from such misleading notions as "a continual incarnation" or "prolongation of the incarnation."

Instead, he insists, a comparison with the incarnation is made by "an excellent analogy."[57] Equally reassuring is Hans Küng's exposition. It is expressed with his usual clarity in *The Church,* his detailed ecclesiology written after Vatican II and first published in 1967:

> It is mistaken and misleading, therefore, to talk of the Church as a "divine-human" being, a "divine-human" reality, phrases which stress the unity but overlook the difference between Christ and the Church, and suggest that Christ is simply a part of the Church rather than its Lord, the head of the Body. Christ is not wholly contained in the Church.

And earlier Küng had made the point that the biblical image of "the Body of Christ" will be misunderstood unless related to "people of God" because the latter reminds the church that it is the people of God "on a journey from Old Testament election through the present toward the future." In this concept temporal categories are supremely important, whereas "Body of Christ" is dominated by the idea of the union of the church with its glorified Lord. The two images are integrated in Paul's theology and need to be integrated in ours.[58] Barth, like Küng, underlines the important biblical distinction, found in *Colossians* and *Ephesians,* between the Head of the Body and the Body of Christ. His first "critical question" on *Lumen Gentium* was: "Wherein lies the difference between Christ, as Lord, King and Judge, and his church?"[59]

This distinction between Head and Body may become less clear, at least

---

56. *Church Dogmatics* IV/3, p. 729.

57. Aloys Grillmeier, "The Mystery of the Church," in *Commentary on the Documents of Vatican II,* vol. 1, ed. Herbert Vorgrimler, pp. 146-48.

58. Hans Küng (1967), *The Church* (London: Search Press, 1968), pp. 237, 224-25.

59. Barth, *Ad Limina Apostolorum,* p. 23.

to Protestant understanding, if the pope as "Vicar of Christ" is thought in any way to take the place of Christ as Head of the church. Barth's son Markus, in his Commentary on Ephesians 1:22, says rather mischievously, "Vicars of this head are not mentioned in Ephesians."[60] According to Paul Minear, "The thought of Jesus Christ as head . . . articulates the perception of a single sovereignty." In *Colossians*, the head is the creative source, the first principle, the preeminent one, the king and lord.[61] Karl Rahner recalls Congar saying: Christ does not need a Vicar. Christ stays with his church.[62]

People of God and Vox Populi

Two further points about "People of God." Barth would be pleased to learn that years after the Council, Roman Catholic and other theologians have come to see the significance of this Old Testament term for ongoing Jewish Christian relations. For example, Cardinal Kasper of the Pontifical Council for Christian Unity has written that if we take *Nostra Aetate* seriously, "then post-Biblical Judaism and the Church are not two covenant peoples; they are one covenant people," that is, People of God.[63] This is very much Barth's view with his insistence that we should hold together Israel and the church as Israel church.[64] But the second post-Conciliar reaction would not please Barth or Roman Catholics like Bradford Hinze, who lament the muffling of so much reforming zeal. "People of God" is accused of promoting a democratic ideology of the church.[65] Critics seem to forget that all the Decrees of Vatican II were subjected to a democratic process requiring a two-thirds majority in favor! The concept "People of God" has promoted grassroots movements, a popular church from below, a church of the poor — in short, so it is stated, a sociological rather than theological view of the church as a sacred

---

60. Markus Barth, *Ephesians*, Anchor Bible (New York: Doubleday, 1974), p. 158.

61. Minear, *Images of the Church*, pp. 207-8.

62. Karl Rahner, *Theological Investigations* XXII (London: Darton, Longman & Todd, 1991), p. 193.

63. Elizabeth T. Groppe, "Revisiting Vatican II's Theology of the People of God after Forty-five Years of Catholic Jewish Dialogue," *Theological Studies* 72, no. 3 (September 2011): 586-619; Kasper, Foreword in Philip A. Cunningham et al., eds., *Christ Jesus and the Jewish People Today* (Grand Rapids: Eerdmans, 2011).

64. Barth, *Church Dogmatics* II/2, pp. 201-5.

65. See James Provost and Knut Walf, *The Tabu of Democracy within the Church* (London: SCM/Concilium, 1992). This book includes essays on "Democracy in Dominican Government" and one by Miroslav Volf on "Democracy and Charisma."

mystery with her sacramental character whose hierarchy and clergy mediate salvation. Such was the reaction of an Extraordinary Synod of Bishops, convened in 1985 to review the reception of the Council.[66] Clearly some were alarmed at what Peter Hebblethwaite had earlier described as *The Runaway Church* because "the Council set in motion a process which, once started, the official Church was powerless to halt."[67] Biblical phrases like People of God had given too many people exalted ideas about their status. But then in better moments we are told that even the pope is only the servant of the servants of God and that all the baptized are equal. Pope, bishops, clergy, and people are all the "People of God."

Subsistit in

This single phrase in *Lumen Gentium* 8, "this church of Christ . . . subsists in the catholic church" and repeated in the Decree on Ecumenism, *Unitatis Redintegratio* 4, sparked off a great controversy among commentators that never seems to die down. There is even an erudite discussion about whether the Council was thinking in classical Latin or scholastic Latin[68] as it could make a difference as to whether the Council was repeating the traditional claim that the church referred to in the Creed as "one, holy, catholic and apostolic" *is* the Roman Catholic Church we now know, or finds its fullest expression and so "subsists" in the Roman Catholic Church, "although outside its structure many elements of sanctification and of truth are to be found."[69] One Roman Catholic *peritus,* Gustave Thils, can see why the debate is inconclusive. The fathers at Vatican II recognized there was a problem. A problem cannot be solved by an expression, not even by *subsistit in!*[70]

The whole controversy seems to have passed Barth by. It is not mentioned in his report of discussions at the Vatican, nor does he appear to have commented on it in subsequent talks and interviews about his assessment of

66. Bradford Hinze, "Ecclesial Impasse: What Can We Learn from Our Laments?" *Theological Studies* 72, no. 3 (September 2011): 470-95.

67. Peter Hebblethwaite, *The Runaway Church* (London: Collins, 1975), Foreword.

68. Francis Sullivan SJ, "The Meaning of *Subsistit in,*" *Theological Studies* 69 (March 2008): 116-24. Barth was aware of the phrase as used by Aquinas. See *Church Dogmatics* II/2, §33.

69. See, for example, Francis A. Sullivan SJ, "The Meaning of *Subsistit in* as Explained by the Congregation for the Doctrine of the Faith," *Theological Studies* 69 (March 2008): 116-24, and earlier articles in the same journal.

70. Gustave Thils, *L'Église et les Églises* (Paris: Desclée de Brouwer, 1967), p. 46.

Vatican II. It would be rash to claim he never mentioned it. Someone, somewhere will quote the contrary! My guess is that Barth would not object to *subsistit in* provided it is not interpreted exclusively, for the same paragraph says "outside its structures many elements of sanctification and of truth are to be found which, as proper gifts to the church of Christ, impel towards catholic unity." This may seem grudging but marks a step forward. As Francis Sullivan explains: "One would look in vain for such positive statements about non-Catholic churches in any Papal document prior to Vatican II."[71] Barth is adamant that each church ought to take herself seriously as the church of Christ. Each church has a special responsibility and a special character that should never be denied "for the sake of internal or external peace, by trying to exist in a kind of nondescript Christianity."[72] What would hurt him and hurts most of us is to be continually told that our churches are not churches.

The document *Dominus Jesus* issued by Cardinal Ratzinger and the Congregation for the Doctrine of the Faith in 2000 appears to take a harder line than Vatican II when it asserts "that the Church of Christ, despite the divisions which exist among Christians, continues to exist fully *only* in the Catholic Church."[73] The Orthodox churches, though not named, are the exception. The "Church of Christ is present and operative in them." But for the rest, our "ecclesial communities . . . are not Churches in the proper sense."[74] Barth, like Calvin before him, is much more generous. For all their criticisms, the Reformers never denied that the "Papal Church" was a church. That is why Barth in that early lecture, "The Concept of the Church" (1927), accepted that when Roman Catholics and Protestants each spoke about the church they were talking about the same thing. Indeed, it is precisely because Roman Catholicism is a church and believes in being the church that it presents this inescapable challenge. The Protestant church is asked by the Roman Catholic Church "whether and how far it is Church."[75] For too many of Barth's Protestant contemporaries the question seemed not to be important.

Such a question becomes a dominant concern in the whole of Barth's

71. Thils, *L'Église et les Églises*, p. 124.

72. Barth, *Church Dogmatics* IV/1, p. 678.

73. See Nicholas Lash's critical comments on *Dominus Jesus* in "In the Spirit of Vatican II," in *Theology for Pilgrims* (London: Darton, Longman & Todd, 2008), pp. 253-84, 269.

74. *Dominus Jesus*, paragraphs 16, 17. The phrase "in the proper sense" is not found in Vatican II.

75. Karl Barth, "Roman Catholicism: A Question to the Protestant Church" (1928), in ET Louise Pettibone Smith, *Theology and Church: Shorter Writings, 1920-1928* (London: SCM, 1962), p. 312.

theology. He is, as Lutheran theologian Reinhard Hütter recognizes, engaged in a "dialectical catholicity," in a sustained dialogue with Rome and confrontation with neo-Protestantism. Where Rome and neo-Protestantism conflict, Barth's sympathies are with Rome, though they would not make him a Roman Catholic tomorrow.[76] Hütter goes on to criticize Barth for not coming up with a more concrete, less abstract ecclesiology of his own. How could he? In my view, Barth did not do this because he could not do this — not without Rome. All our ecclesiologies must in Barth's view be "provisional." If all churches recognized this, that could be an ecumenical breakthrough.[77] Barth is also respecting the Reformers' intentions. They did not wish to form a new church but to reform the one they already belonged to, the Catholic Church known to us as the Church of Rome.

Eucharist Makes the Church?

"Why is it that among the four marks of the church in Acts 2:42 [devotion to the apostles' teaching, fellowship, breaking of bread, and prayers] it is the third [eucharist] that is designated as constitutive for the life of the church?" This is Barth's second "critical question."[78]

It is not clear from the references to Acts 2:42 in *Lumen Gentium* what Barth is objecting to. When the same text appears in the Decree on the Liturgy, *Sacrosanctum Concilium* 7, we read "Christ is always present to his church, especially during the liturgy," but we are also told that Christ is present through the word and when the church is praying or singing hymns. This is surely an advance from any suggestion that Christ *only* becomes present at the moment of consecration of the Bread and the Cup. Barth was once asked by students if he thought communion should be celebrated each Sunday. He

76. Reinhard Hütter, "Karl Barth's 'Dialectical Catholicity': Sic et Non," in *Bound to Be Free: Evangelical Catholic Engagements in Ecclesiology, Ethics, and Ecumenism* (Grand Rapids: Eerdmans, 2004), pp. 78-94.

77. Barth, *Church Dogmatics* IV/2, pp. 621, 719; Christian Duquoc (1985), ET John Bowden *Provisional Churches* (London: SCM, 1986); Anglican Reformed International Commission, *God's Reign and Our Unity* (London: SPCK/Edinburgh: St. Andrew Press, 1984), para. 30: "The Church is thus a provisional embodiment of God's final purpose for all human beings and for all creation."

78. Barth did not live to complete his intended treatment of the Lord's Supper as part of the doctrine of reconciliation, though much can be gleaned from earlier volumes of *Church Dogmatics*. See Paul D. Molnar, *Karl Barth and the Theology of the Lord's Supper* (New York: Peter Lang, 1996).

said, yes it should. "It should be the climax of every service," and he quoted John Calvin in support. But he also emphasized, and at the time (c. 1953), in contrast to Rome, the continued importance of preaching. "When we preach we do the same thing as the Roman Catholic priest does when he is celebrating the transubstantiation. We should not give the people less than the Roman Catholic Church gives.[79] P. T. Forsyth, sometimes seen as Britain's "Barth," spoke of the sacrament of preaching. He made a similar comparison to Barth's: "The Catholic form of worship will always have a vast advantage over ours so long as people come away from its central act with the sense of something done in the spirit world, while they leave ours with the sense only of something said in the present world."[80]

Local Church and/or Universal Church

Which has priority, the local or the universal church? The question on my reading is not clearly answered in *Lumen Gentium,* nor is it asked by Barth. It became a major issue in a strong debate between two high-ranking Cardinals in 1999-2001, Joseph Ratzinger, soon to become Pope Benedict XVI, and Walter Kasper, President of the Pontifical Council for Promoting Christian Unity.[81] Asked which comes first, Ratzinger favors the universal church. Kasper says both! It may all seem a rather abstract debate until you realize how much depends on it in practice. A common complaint among conscientious Roman Catholics is that their church has become more centralized than ever before. In the words of Catholic theologian Bradford Hinze:

> The post–Vatican II period, especially since the beginning of the Papacy of John Paul II in 1978 has become characterised by struggles between proponents of increased centralization in the exercise of church authority,

79. Karl Barth, *Table Talk,* pp. 21-22.

80. P. T. Forsyth, *Positive Preaching and the Modern Mind* (1907; London: Independent Press, 1957), pp. 41, 53.

81. Kilian McDonnell, "The Ratzinger/Kasper Debate: The Universal Church and the Local Churches," *Theological Studies* 63 (2002): 227-50; Paul McPartlan, "The Local Church and the Universal Church: Zizioulas and the Ratzinger-Kasper Debate," *International Journal for the Study of the Christian Church* 4 (2004): 21-31. Earlier in 1987, the Joint Working Group between the Roman Catholic Church and the World Council of Churches embarked on a study of "The Church: Local and Universal," *Faith and Order Paper* 150 (Geneva: WCC, 1990). It raised the question of priority and insisted that local and universal are simultaneously important and belong together, paras. 21-24.

and those cultivating the authority of the local church, as well as national and regional Episcopal conferences.[82]

Hinze sees the struggle "encapsulated" in the Kasper-Ratzinger debate. Which side is Barth on? Unusual for him, I would say both! That is, Kasper's. The church, even if we take her beginning as Pentecost in Jerusalem, is both local and universal. Barth's Amsterdam address has a strong emphasis on the local congregation. "The Church is the 'event of a gathering together,' and in this sense a 'living congregation.'"[83] In a claim that is more akin to Eastern Orthodox ecclesiology than to Rome's, Barth asserts "the one Church exists in its totality in each of the individual communities."[84] But equally strongly, Barth affirms, as he did in the 1936 address: "in Him the Church is once for all, and in spite of every multiplicity of churches, made one, and does not await our desires, capacities or labors of ours for its unification." This faith is also a command laid upon us: "We are claimed for the unity of the Church . . . our action . . . is directed inevitably towards the uniting of the Church."[85] What Barth opposes, and here his views coincide with an early statement by the World Council of Churches, is any suggestion that there is a sort of "super church," set over and above local churches. He recognizes that in the New Testament there were helpful human links between churches. "What we do not find in the New Testament is the existence of what might truly be called a Church government which is superior to the individual communities and the external guarantee of their unity as the community of Jesus Christ." The Jerusalem community "occupied a position of peculiar dignity at any rate up to AD 70. But there can be no question of the others being ruled through it or by it."[86] Barth recognizes that one community may make demands on another and so might a central authority, but such demands should be carefully scrutinized.[87] The basic church law is one of service, not domination. In Timothy Gorringe's phrase, Barth is "against hegemony."[88] A favorite text is Paul's ideal, "not that we have dominion over your faith but are helpers of your joy" (1 Cor. 1:24).[89]

---

82. Hinze, "Ecclesial Impasse," pp. 470-95, 473.

83. Karl Barth, "The Church, the Living Congregation of the Living Lord Jesus Christ," in God Here and Now, p. 83.

84. Barth, Church Dogmatics IV/1, p. 673.

85. Barth, The Church and the Churches, pp. 33-34.

86. Barth, Church Dogmatics IV/1, p. 673.

87. Barth, Church Dogmatics IV/2, p. 691.

88. Timothy J. Gorringe, Karl Barth Against Hegemony (Oxford: Oxford University Press, 1999).

89. Barth, Church Dogmatics IV/1, p. 674.

Authority beyond the Local Church

The "Toronto Statement" of the newly formed World Council of Churches declared in 1950 "the World Council of Churches is not and must never become a super church."[90] This leaves open a still unresolved question of what exactly the World Council of Churches is. Barth may have underestimated the need for wider Councils with some authority to act on behalf of local churches, though he does admit "an institution which demands and maintains the oneness of the locally separated communities is not completely impossible."[91] In thinking about the Vatican Council when it was still in process he felt forced to ask, "But why is it that the voice of Rome made a far greater impression than the voice of Geneva?"[92] Barth of course knows enough about the World Council to know the answer to his own question, but he is not satisfied with the answer. How could he be? The non–Roman Catholic churches are too divided among themselves ever to speak with one voice, and even when they have, as they often have, good things to say together, for example on "human rights, the problems of race, minorities, refugees, and colonialism, the task of the United Nations, atomic and general disarmament," their voice is muted. By contrast, in a Roman

> encyclical the same things were not only talked about but *proclaimed*, that Christianity and the world were not only taught but also *summoned* unreservedly and bindingly with an appeal to the highest authority, and that they received not only advice and admonition but also *directives*.

One can argue with Barth and it is tempting to do so here. He is after all contrasting the attention paid to Pope John XXIII's justly famous encyclical *Pacem in Terris* (1963) with statements made by the World Council. A fairer comparison would be between Vatican II and a World Council Assembly. But Barth is surely right in longing for the day when on some urgent issue the churches speak out boldly and with one voice.

The Barmen Declaration, scripted by Barth for the Confessing Church in Germany, pulls no punches: "Jesus Christ, as he is attested for us in Holy Scripture, is the one Word of God which we have to hear and which we have

---

90. "The Church, the Churches and the World Council of Churches," agreed at Central Committee, Toronto 1950; W. A. Visser 't Hooft, *The Genesis and Formation of the World Council of Churches* (Geneva: WCC, 1982), Appendix V.

91. Barth, *Church Dogmatics* IV/1, pp. 672-73.

92. Barth, *Ad Limina Apostolorum*, p. 76.

to trust and obey in life and in death." No Christian can argue with that, or so we must hope. Barmen then went on to challenge the Führer Principle and the form of leadership and decision making appropriate for the church. On such issues we are not agreed. It is to a consideration of "Popes and Polities" that we now turn.

CHAPTER FOUR

Responding to Vatican II, Part 2

Barth as Questioner

Critics of Barth's ethics often complain that Barth does not tell us what to do, and ecumenical critics of his ecclesiology wish he would tell us what a united church should look like. Barth's response is similar in both cases: we have to listen to what the Living Lord is saying to his Living Church, today.[1] Barth does not offer a blueprint for a united church — this we must discern together. And he will not tell Rome what she ought to do about the pope or curia or future councils. This is a vocation for Roman Catholics. What he can do and does do is offer some questions. He set off for Rome with a whole series of questions, some addressed directly to the pope. Questioning is very important for Barth:

> May God never relieve of this questioning! May he enclose us with questions on every side! May he defend us from any answer which is not itself a question! May he bar every exit and cut us off from all simplifications! May the cavity at the cartwheel's centre, which Lao-Tse perceived long ago, be delimited by a ring of questions! In that central void the answer to our questioning is hidden; but since the void is defined by questions they must never for one moment cease.[2]

---

1. Paul T. Nimmo, *Being in Action: The Theological Shape of Barth's Ethical Vision* (London: T. & T. Clark, 2007), p. 18; David Clough, *Ethics in Crisis: Interpreting Barth's Ethics* (Aldershot, UK: Ashgate, 2005), p. 132; Nigel Biggar, ed., *Reckoning with Barth* (London: Mowbray, 1988), pp. 108-11.

2. Karl Barth, ET Edwyn Hoskyns, *The Epistle to the Romans*, 6th ed. (Oxford: Oxford University Press, 1933), p. 254.

The above quotation is from Barth's Commentary on the Epistle to the Romans and cited by the Anglican theologian Bishop Stephen Sykes in an essay in which he in turn questions Barth about "authority and openness in the Church." There is an implied challenge to Barth in Sykes's immediate response to the quotation: "This openness to the question, What are we to do? can not, of course, be taken as a substitute for action." And he goes on to note Barth's approval of the fact that when Rome decides what should be done, she speaks with authority and gets on with it.[3]

In the following section we hear Barth asking a series of questions. They are questions often shared with Roman Catholics, aware that not all is well with their church. But in the past and still today they cannot always be asked openly for fear of censorship or accusations of disloyalty. Observer Bishop Moorman commends a comment once made by former Anglican, Abbot Christopher Butler, active in the Council: "Let us not be afraid of scholarly and historical truth. Let us not be afraid that our scholars may be lacking in loyalty to the Church and to traditional doctrine."[4] Well said! But questions about some "traditional doctrines" are out of bounds — the ordination of women, for example. And though Vatican II posed questions about bishops and collegiality, it did not question the role of the pope. To his credit, Pope John Paul II raised that question later and addressed it, not just to his fellow Roman Catholics, but to us all in his encyclical *Ut Unum Sint, That All May Be One* (1995). His was not, of course, a completely open question. He had no doubt that Christ willed his church to have a pope. He was asking how a pope might be of greater service. A fair question.

Humanae Vitae and the Challenge to Papal Authority

When Barth was born in 1886 the question of how the Roman Catholic Church should be governed, whether by pope or by bishops or by both, was unresolved. This was mainly because the First Vatican Council, which had been convened to deal with this and other topics, was prevented from completing its work by the outbreak of the Franco-Prussian War in 1870.

---

3. Stephen Sykes, "Authority and Openness in the Church," in *Karl Barth: Centenary Essays*, ed. S. W. Sykes (Cambridge: Cambridge University Press, 1989), pp. 69-86, 72; Karl Barth, *The Epistle to the Romans*, p. 254.

4. Cited by John R. H. Moorman, "Observers and Guests of the Council," in *Vatican II by Those Who Were There*, ed. Alberic Stacpoole (London: Geoffrey Chapman, 1986), p. 166.

The Council was adjourned. It was never officially closed.[5] Its declaration on papal infallibility may be regarded as "unfinished business." Questions of the collegiality of bishops, including the bishop of Rome, of councils and, not least, of the curia proved too hot to handle even at Vatican II. So many issues of church government remained ripe for further consideration by the time Barth died in 1968. Barth was born into this ongoing debate.

Shortly before he died, the response of Roman Catholic laywomen and men and many of their clergy to the papal encyclical *Humanae Vitae,* condemning forms of artificial contraception, provoked a grassroots crisis of papal authority. In an age of simplistic sound bites, with which the Vatican still finds it hard to come to terms, the headline ran, POPE BANS PILL.[6] The encyclical in fact had many more positive things to say. Technically, it was not an infallible document and the pope never said it was, but many conscientious Roman Catholics were very uneasy about disagreeing with the pope even when they believed he was wrong.[7] The encyclical exposed a crisis of authority. In the United States it also provoked a high-level public debate. Moral theologian Charles Curran and some thirty colleagues published in the *New York Times* their "Mayflower Declaration," challenging the pope's arguments.[8] Other learned theologians like Gregory Baum, John Haughey, and Bernard Häring voiced their views on "The Right to Dissent" and the responsibility of theologians to comment on all church teaching. Curran was given the sack. Authority, however, is two-way. It has to be accepted or it is not authoritative. When it comes to deciding what we should do in bed, it was hard for married couples to agree that a celibate pope knows best. A sad aspect of the whole affair was that the previous pope, Pope John XXIII, had established a special commission of "experts" that included a respected North American couple, the Crowleys of Chicago. His successor decided not to listen to their advice.[9]

5. Norman P. Tanner SJ, English editor, *Decrees of the Ecumenical Councils,* vol. 2 (London: Sheed & Ward, 1990), Vatican I; Vatican II, Introduction.

6. Peter Hebblethwaite, *Paul VI: The First Modern Pope* (London: HarperCollins, 1993), pp. 517-21.

7. For a detailed defense of the document as sound Catholic teaching and "infallible," see Janet E. Smith, *Humane Vitae: A Generation Later* (Washington, DC: Catholic University of America Press, 1991).

8. Mark S. Massa SJ, *The American Catholic Revolution: How the Sixties Changed the Church for Ever* (Oxford: Oxford University Press/Scholarship Online, 2010), pp. 49-55; Charles Curran, *Faithful Dissent* (London: Sheed & Ward, 1987); *Loyal Dissent: Memoir of a Catholic Theologian* (Washington, DC: Georgetown University Press, 2006).

9. Peter Hebblethwaite, *Paul VI,* pp. 467-73.

Barth entered into the debate in a general and very genial letter to Pope Paul VI in September 1968.[10] He assured the pope that he constantly thinks of his special "Peter-ministry." He says he is "confident that it will be given to you and given to you again and again, to fulfil this ministry with joy, no matter how great the burden may be." He then mentions *Humanae Vitae*. Barth does not feel competent to comment on the medical aspects. His own Roman Catholic doctor is better qualified to do this. (Was this a not-so-subtle hint? Barth, a theologian who had now been married fifty-five years and had one daughter and four sons, did not feel competent to pontificate on family planning.) What he does note is "the problem of church authority which has become such a burning issue by reason of the encyclical." The question of authority is also a matter "to be discussed and settled" by us in what Barth calls "the Catholic Church" (in the narrower sense). The major point he queries is the constant appeal in the encyclical to natural law. "In this regard, I for one cannot reconcile the encyclical with the fine constitution *Dei Verbum* of the recent council." Barth would not know that Germain Grisez, leading theologian among the "New Natural Lawyers," is both credited and blamed for influencing the pope.[11] But he nonetheless assures the "Holy Father" of "my great respect in spite of this serious difference."

Papacy as a Question for All Christians

A pope's authority had been challenged; the papacy needed help. In 1995, nearly thirty years after *Humanae Vitae* and Barth's death, Pope John Paul II was formally inviting other "Church leaders and their theologians to engage with me in a patient and fraternal dialogue"[12] on the subject of the papacy. The pope was aware, as he had explained to the Ecumenical Patriarch, His Holiness Dimitrios I, that "for a variety of reasons and against the will of all concerned, what should have been a service sometimes manifested itself in a very different light." He felt duty bound as a matter of obedience to Christ to exercise the ministry of being bishop of Rome, but he added, "I insistently

10. Karl Barth, *Letters 1961-1968*, Letter 303, pp. 312-15. A. G. Cardinal Cicognani replied on behalf of the pope and sought to clarify questions of natural law. See Appendix 17, Letter of 11 November 1968, pp. 357-58.

11. Nicholas Bamforth and David A. J. Richards, *Patriarchal Religion, Sexuality and Gender* (Cambridge: Cambridge University Press, 2008), pp. 76-77; Gary Willis, *Papal Sin* (New York: Doubleday, 2000).

12. *Ut Unum Sint*, para. 96.

pray the Holy Spirit to shine his light upon us, enlightening all the Pastors and theologians of our Churches, that we may seek — together, of course — the forms in which this ministry may accomplish a service of love recognised by all concerned."[13] His predecessor Paul VI had been more forthright: "The Pope, as we all know, is the gravest problem in the path of ecumenism." His biographer, Peter Hebblethwaite, calls this "an astonishing remark" and adds, "Paul was the first pope to have taken his critics seriously."[14] Many welcomed John Paul II's initiative in making the problem of the papacy a matter for ecumenical concern. It is still hard to tell if the responses made any difference to the way the papacy operates, and ten years later John Paul II's long reign came to an end and we had a new pope. Cardinal Ratzinger became Pope Benedict XVI in April 2005. His election would have pleased his predecessor. The response of contemporaries in and beyond the Roman Catholic Church was more mixed.[15]

The pope, or rather the papacy as an institution, may be a problem, but it is here to stay. It is a given, from Rome's point of view, not negotiable. What can be negotiated, at least in theory, is how the pope may best serve what Pope John Paul II described as "the full and visible communion of all those Communities in which, by virtue of God's faithfulness, his Spirit dwells." Greater emphasis on collegiality and also on subsidiarity, where local issues are locally decided, could make the exercise of primacy more acceptable to other churches. The pope believed he had

> a particular responsibility in this regard, above all in acknowledging the ecumenical aspirations of the majority of Christian Communities and in heeding the request made of me to find a way of exercising the primacy which, while in no way renouncing what is essential to its mission, is nonetheless open to a new situation.[16]

In line with such "ecumenical aspirations" some non–Roman Catholics are now open to the possibility that there could be "a pope for all Christians." The American Reformed theologian Robert McAfee Brown, who had

13. *Ut Unum Sint*, paras. 95, 96.

14. Hebblethwaite, *Paul VI*, p. 9.

15. William G. Rusch, ed., *The Pontificate of Benedict XVI: Its Premises and Promises* (Grand Rapids: Eerdmans, 2009). For strong criticism see Hans Küng, *Can We Save the Catholic Church?* (London: William Collins, 2013); ET John Bowden, *Memoirs II: Disputed Truth* (London/New York: Continuum, 2008). Küng and Ratzinger were once colleagues in Tübingen and both were *periti* at Vatican II.

16. *Ut Unum Sint*, para. 95.

been an observer at Vatican II, was at first dubious about the exercise and says so in his introduction to a set of essays under the title *A Pope for All Christians*. Like many, he changed his mind about the papacy because of Pope John XXIII. "By his style he persuaded the world that the issues were worth examining."[17] But such admiration for a particular pope presents its own challenges. The Jesuit theologian Norman Tanner describes this as the "Hebblethwaite syndrome."[18] We long for the perfect pope and are almost permanently disappointed when he does not arrive! Even Pope John has his critics for not doing enough in his short reign to reform the curia. For Tanner, this becomes an argument to place more hope in councils because councils are less at the mercy of one voice.[19] A similar point was made by John Calvin in connection with collegiality when he said:

> Men's faults or failings cause it to be safer and more bearable for a number to exercise government, so that they may help one another, teach and admonish one another, and, if one asserts himself unfairly, there may be a number of censors and masters to restrain his wilfulness.[20]

Can Only a Pope Get Things Done and Speak for All Christians?

Pope John XXIII enthralled many of us because he saw the need for an ecumenical council and invited non–Roman Catholics to be participant observers. Robert McAfee Brown was one of them. His own account of the Council, published in his autobiography, *Reflections over the Long Haul: A Memoir*, is worth reading, not least for his witty and perceptive asides. The pope's "advisors opposed the very notion of a council and fought it every inch of the way. They lost. Let a Protestant say it: There are occasional advantages in having papal power. The planning proceeded apace."[21] Barth once told Küng he would like to be pope just for a day "to set many ecumenical matters right."[22]

17. Robert McAfee Brown, Introduction in Peter J. McCord, *A Pope for All Christians* (London: SPCK, 1976), pp. 3-4.

18. Peter Hebblethwaite is the author of biographies of Pope John XXIII and Pope Paul VI.

19. Norman Tanner, *The Church in Council: Conciliar Movements, Religious Practice and the Papacy from Nicaea to Vatican II* (London: Tauris, 2011).

20. Calvin, *Institutes* (1559), IV.20.8.

21. Robert McAfee Brown, *Reflections over the Long Haul: A Memoir* (Louisville: Westminster John Knox, 2005), p. 202.

22. Küng, *Disputed Truth: Memoirs II*, p. 341.

Brown gives an honest account of the anti-Catholic stereotypes with which he grew up and how he became openly committed to dialogue after meeting "Catholics of a sort we had never even seen before — open, gracious, ironic and eager to pursue common concerns despite apparently insurmountable obstacles further down the line." As a result, he was invited to represent the World Alliance of Reformed and Presbyterian Churches, as it was then called, as an observer at Vatican II. He took his preparation for this event very seriously, even to the point of tracking down an old copy of *The Vocabulary of the Mass in Twenty Lessons, for Priests Making a Late Vocation* so that he could join in the Latin responses and know what he was saying.

Even the best of councils need a spokesperson, someone to communicate their views. The World Council of Churches only assembles once every seven years. It has its subgroups like the Central Committee and the Executive, but much of the work of representing the 349 member churches falls to the General Secretary, and most of the media reports concern what the Secretary said in various encounters all round the world. He or she is not a pope, but the office involves a global ministry similar to what became such a feature of John Paul II's long reign. Likewise, the United Nations has a Secretary-General who may or may not adopt a high profile like Dag Hammarskjöld, or be more discreet like the present incumbent, Ban Ki-moon, but either way, the office becomes the person the media turn to when they want to know what the United Nations Organization is thinking or doing. Some form of "papal" leadership is not out of the question. Hammarskjöld once likened his office to being a kind of "secular pope."[23] Why not "a pope for all Christians"?

How Does Barth Contribute to the Debate?
Barth on Pope and Polity

How does Barth contribute to this debate? After meeting with Pope Paul VI, shortly after the Council, Barth assured any old-style Protestant critics: "The Pope is not the Antichrist!"[24] His exclamation is intended to express his humor at the very thought. Barth never said the pope was the Antichrist. (He reserved that charge for the so-called *analogia entis* in what Bishop

---

23. W. H. Auden, Foreword to Dag Hammarskjöld, *Markings*, ET Leif Sjöberg and W. H. Auden (London: Faber & Faber, 1964), p. 20.

24. Karl Barth, *Ad Limina Apostolorum*, p. 17.

Stephen Sykes describes as his "persistent misrepresentation of the 'Catholic view.' ")[25] The sixteenth-century Reformers, Luther and Calvin, did call the pope the Antichrist and so did the Westminster Confession. But unlike Barth, the Reformers never met the pope. Had they done so in the sixteenth century it might not have altered their judgments. By common consent there were no good popes in the Reformation era. By the twentieth century, perhaps as a result of the Reformation and Counter-Reformation, popes were better. From a Protestant perspective, as fallible human beings like the rest of us, they could err and did err, for example in the way in which they handled the rise of totalitarian regimes in Germany and Italy and military dictatorships in Latin America,[26] but they could still be respected for the sincerity of their convictions and holiness of life, and possibly also because they were trying to exercise a much-needed global ministry. None would doubt that Pope John was a man of God, inspired by the Holy Spirit. His successor Paul VI would be widely respected as a good theologian. So was Pope Benedict XVI. Had Calvin met the pope, the two would not have understood one another even though both spoke Latin. Barth's encounter with Pope Paul was with a fellow theologian who had read some of his books and could sense how well informed Barth was about the documents and debates in the Council. Barth, as I noted earlier, was one of the first Protestant theologians to have an in-depth meeting and discussion with the pope. This was his reaction:

> The way in which Paul VI received us and took leave of us was dignified and human in the highest sense. He impressed me as an intelligent and, in his own way, a definitely humble, pious person. During that hour there was no moment when I was forced to think of the title he bears of *Pontifex Maximus*. On our side it should be noted clearly that he did not call himself "Vicar of Christ" in any of the documents of the Council but simply, "Bishop, servant of the servants of God." If I on my part had opportunity to wish him something, it would be a greater measure of "cheerful confidence" in relation to those inner tensions in his church which in part made the Council necessary and in part are the result of the Council. But you would yourself have to be Pope in order to know how hard it must be,

25. Karl Barth, Preface to *Church Dogmatics* I/1, p. xiii: "I regard the *analogia entis* as the invention of the Antichrist"; Sykes, "Authority and Openness," p. 73.

26. Even Pope Francis has been vulnerable to criticisms of what he did or failed to do as priest and bishop during the military dictatorships in his native Argentina. See Paul Vallely, *Pope Francis: Untying the Knots* (London: Bloomsbury, 2013), pp. 63-94.

in the midst of already existing problems and those which have newly developed, to serve the cause of true freedom and that of necessary order, as Paul VI obviously seeks to do. One thing will make his name remembered in the history of the church and the world: his courageous and persistent commitment to peace among the nations, and especially in Vietnam.[27]

Barth would know and be delighted that Paul VI was the first pope to be invited to address the United Nations. He did so in October 1965. His speech met with a standing ovation. What was great about it was its whole tone. Here was a Christian leader seeing his God-given vocation to speak up for all humanity, not least the poor and the millions who had suffered in war. Who but a pope committed to peace among the nations could dare to speak on behalf of the whole Christian church without for one moment asserting such a claim?[28] The Vatican Council, now in its final session, responded to the pope's lead and pledged itself in *Gaudium et Spes* to working with the United Nations and its agencies.[29] According to Peter Hebblethwaite, Rome is the only church or religion to have done that. It would be fair to add that the World Council of Churches has in fact done so, too.

Barth might not have known what a momentous role Pope John XXIII played in averting "World War III" during the Cuban Missile crisis of October 1962, so soon after the Council opened. Congar cries out in his Journal for October 24th: "Nuclear War COULD break out." Gerald Fogarty, writing up this part of the *History of Vatican II*, adds: "Had it been known at the time, this correspondence between the Pope and the Communist leader would probably have surprised a world still engaged in the Cold War. It set in motion a series of events that would not bear fruit for almost thirty years." It was noted that the Communist leader Khrushchev seemed to pay more attention to the pope's entreaties than the Roman Catholic President Kennedy of the United States. Norman Cousins of the United States later had a friendly meeting with Khrushchev in which Khrushchev said how much he had in common with the pope: "We both come from peasant families." He then went on to make this remarkable statement with which Pope John would surely concur:

---

27. *Ad Limina Apostolorum*, p. 16. See also the biography by Peter Hebblethwaite of "a good and holy man who proclaimed the need for a Civilisation of Love," in *Paul VI*, p. 1; "Vicar of Christ"; see *CD* IV/1, p. 723.

28. Hebbelthwaite, *Paul VI*, pp. 436-41.

29. The main references in *Gaudium et Spes* 84, 90 are to "international institutions which already exist."

His goal, as you say, is peace. It is the most important goal in the world. If we don't have peace and the nuclear bombs start to fall, what difference will it make whether we are Communists or Catholics or Capitalists or Chinese or Russians or Americans? Who could tell us apart? [Turning then to the Cuban Missile Crisis, he recalled:] The Pope's appeal was a real ray of light. I was grateful for it. Believe me, that was a dangerous time.[30]

And as noted earlier, Pope John's successor received high praise from Barth for the stance he too had taken for peace in the world, this time over Vietnam.

Barth speaks warmly of the pope and of many other Christians he encountered in Rome "with whom I could not only speak candidly and seriously, but also join in hearty laughter." Any talk of "conversions" from us to Rome or from Rome to us is beside the point. What is significant for all is "a conscientiously necessary 'conversion' — not to another church, but to Jesus Christ, the Lord of the one, holy, catholic and apostolic church."[31] It is a theme that dominates the opening paragraphs of Pope John Paul's encyclical. The pope says:

> The Bishop of Rome himself must fervently make his own Christ's prayer for that conversion which is indispensable for "Peter" to be able to serve his brethren. I earnestly invite the faithful of the Catholic Church and all Christians to share in this prayer. May all join me in praying for this conversion.[32]

Papal Infallibility?

On his visit to the United States in 1962,[33] Barth was often asked about the Vatican Council and about the pope and in particular about "Papal Infallibility." On the first, he said it was still not clear what the main purpose of the Council was. Perhaps even the pope did not know. If he was expected to criticize Rome for her teachings about infallibility, he instead showed

---

30. Gerald P. Fogarty, "The Council Gets Underway," in *History of Vatican II,* vol. 2, pp. 102-3; Norman Cousins, *The Improbable Triumvirate: John F. Kennedy, Pope John, Nikita Khrushchev* (New York: W. W. Norton, 1972).

31. Barth, *Ad Limina Apostolorum,* pp. 17-18.

32. *Ut Unum Sint,* para. 4.

33. Barth's lectures in the USA for part of his *Evangelical Theology: An Introduction* (London: Collins Fontana, 1965).

sympathy with the need of a church to speak with authority. Yes, only God is infallible and Christ is the Head of the church, but claims to infallibility are not unknown even in his own Reformed tradition. If the pope would recognize that there is only one infallible head of the church there would be no more trouble.[34]

Hans Küng's critical study of infallibility was not published in Barth's lifetime. It first appeared in German, *Unfehlbar?* in 1970,[35] but in his meeting with theological students at Tübingen, where Küng was a professor, Barth explained that he had often discussed the question with Küng. There was a need to clarify what exactly was meant by infallibility and also what was involved in the papal claim to be "vicar of Christ."[36] Küng discussed the question at some length in his *Strukturen der Kirche* (1963)[37] and escaped censorship. He even has a Preface by Cardinal Cushing of Boston. A few years later in *Die Kirche* (1967) (*The Church*) he devoted no more than a couple of pages to "Infallibility." It had become clear that it was not a helpful dogma. He asked himself the question: If Vatican I had not pronounced this dogma, would Vatican II have done so? and he suggests that this is most unlikely given the totally different style and approach of Pope John XXIII:

> He revealed a new or rather a very old ideal of Petrine ministry, and instead of seeing the primacy as a more or less dictatorial sovereignty over spiritual subjects, he saw it as a discreet call to serve his brethren inside and outside the Catholic Church, which must be inspired by love and understanding for mankind in the modern world and subject to the true Lord of the Church.[38]

Barth would be aware that though the pope was declared to be infallible in 1870, the claim was asserted for the first and, so far, the only instance in 1950 when Pope Pius XII declared that "the Immaculate Mother of God, the ever-Virgin Mary, having completed the course of her earthly life, was

---

34. Barth at Chicago Press Conference, 19 April 1962, in Barth, *Gespräche 1959-62* (Zürich: Theologischer Verlag, 1995), pp. 448-49.

35. Hans Küng, ET Eric Mosbacher, *Infallible? An Enquiry* (London: Collins Fontana, 1972).

36. Barth, meeting with Students at Tübingen, 2 March 1964, in Barth, *Gespräche 1964-68* (Zürich: Theologischer Verlag, 1997), pp. 105-6.

37. Hans Küng, ET Salvator Attanasio, *Structures of the Church* (London: Burns & Oates, 1965), pp. 305-51.

38. Hans Küng (1967), ET Ray and Rosaleen Ockenden, *The Church* (London: Search Press, 1968), pp. 449-50.

assumed body and soul into heavenly glory." The First Vatican Council had set out, though clearly not in sufficient detail, the conditions in which the pope speaks infallibly:

> We teach and define as a divinely revealed dogma that when the Roman pontiff speaks *ex cathedra*, that is, when in the exercise of his office as shepherd and teacher of all Christians, in virtue of his supreme apostolic authority, he defines a doctrine concerning faith or morals to be held by the whole church, he possesses, by the divine assistance promised to him in blessed Peter, that infallibility which the divine Redeemer willed his church to enjoy in defining doctrine concerning faith or morals. There- fore, such definitions of the Roman pontiff are of themselves, and not by consent of the church, irreformable.
>
> So then, should anyone, which God forbid, have the temerity to reject this definition of ours; let him be anathema.[39]

So understood, teachings about artificial contraception, priestly celibacy, and possibly even the nonordination of women as priests are not infallible.[40] In theory they could be changed. Indeed, some Roman Catholic theologians like Cardinal Avery Dulles are almost prepared to admit that the infallibility dogma is useless because it is so hedged around with numerous qualifica- tions and has rarely been used.[41] Professor Adrian Hastings regarded it as an embarrassment: "Many non–Roman Catholics can envisage and even desire an ecumenical primacy, but absolutely no one finds the claims of Vatican I acceptable. Why do all our ecumenical friends find our case here so wholly unconvincing?"[42] Another historian, Brian Tierney, adds that claims made for infallibility are the opposite of what was originally intended in the Middle Ages. Then the purpose of the dogma was to limit, not to assert, the power of the pope. The Franciscan theologian Petrus Olivi, 1248-1298, was anxious

---

39. Tanner, *Decrees of the Ecumenical Councils*, p. 816.

40. See Avery Dulles, *John Paul II and the Teaching Authority of the Church* (Nash Lecture Campion College, University of Regina, 1997), pp. 9-10. Dulles thinks John Paul II's Apos- tolic Letter, *Ordinatio Sacerdotalis* (1994), which rules out the ordination of women, "points towards infallibility." But on this see Elisabeth Schüssler Fiorenza and Herman Häring, *The Non-Ordination of Women and the Politics of Power* (London: SCM/Maryknoll, NY: Orbis Concilium, 1999), p. vii.

41. See Mark G. Powell, *Papal Infallibility: A Protestant Evaluation of an Ecumenical Problem* (Grand Rapids: Eerdmans, 2009).

42. Adrian Hastings, *The Tablet*, March 1991, quoted in Luis M. Bermejo SJ, *Infallibility on Trial* (Westminster, MD: Christian Classics, 1992).

that the pope's affirmation of the Franciscan Order and its vows of poverty and renunciation of property should not be undone by a later pope with a different opinion. Tierney also argued that contrary to a widely held view, neither Bonaventure nor Thomas Aquinas said anything about the pope being infallible.[43]

Hans Küng's restatement is much more ecumenically acceptable. By the Providence of God the whole church is indefectible. The church is maintained in Truth. Individual church leaders, including popes, may err. Reformers like Calvin and the Anglican authors of the Thirty-Nine Articles of Religion in the *Book of Common Prayer* also accepted that individual church councils could err. But the promise of Christ in Matthew 16:18 remains constant and secure. On this rock, Christ builds his church and the gates of hell will not prevail against her. Christians of different traditions stand by this biblical text but without agreeing that the promise was made to Peter in his own right and not to the church he then represented, or that the pope is the successor of Peter and that the "rock" is Christ.

Is the Pope Successor of Peter?

Prior to the Council and his meeting with Pope Paul VI, Barth has two main comments to make on this whole discussion. The first concerns the question of Peter and his successors; the second, on whether any dogma or confession should be regarded as "irreformable."

On the claim that popes are successors of Peter, Barth in *Church Dogmatics* II/2 dismissed the very suggestion:

> There can be no doubt that the Evangelists gave him [Peter] a prominence over the rest of the apostles as their spokesman, for this is repeatedly evidenced in the text. Exegetically, however, the question does not even arise whether this is also true of his successors on the Roman Episcopal throne in their relation to the bishops of other communities, for there is no passage in the New Testament which even hints at such an interpretation.[44]

What makes the church invincible is Jesus, not Peter; Peter's calling by Jesus, not Peter's faith and confession. "Peter and these twelve — gathered

43. Brian Tierney (1972), *Origins of Papal Infallibility, 1150-1350* (Leiden: E. J. Brill, 1988), pp. 93-130.

44. *Church Dogmatics* II/2, p. 440.

and invited by Jesus to the Lord's Supper to partake of His body and blood — are indeed according to the clear statement of Matthew 16,18, the foundation and invincibility of the Church of Jesus Christ."[45] This is Barth in 1942. In a later volume, Barth cites the work of his Lutheran colleague Oscar Cullmann and his study, *Petrus* (1952),[46] to query whether Peter was ever bishop of Rome and to make the general point that "[i]t certainly cannot be maintained that the existence of a synodal or episcopal organ to guarantee the unity of the communities is essential to the New Testament idea of the church, even if the texts do not record all the actual and perhaps very strong connections which did exist in New Testament days."[47]

In line with this emphasis on Christ rather than Peter, Barth in later interviews recalled the remark of a French Dominican whom he had first met in wartime when this brave man was part of the Resistance to Hitler. Evidently they often spoke and argued about the papacy until one day Father Maydieu said, "Don't let us speak about the Pope, let us speak about Jesus Christ." After this "high point," says Barth, controversy was no longer the main topic of conversation. Then real Christian dialogue could begin and did.[48]

Barth's point about the lack of a biblical basis for the papacy and the wider argument about apostolic succession retain their force. In the various ecumenical symposia and responses to *Ut Unum Sint* it is not hard to find even Roman Catholic scholars who agree with Barth. Brian Daley SJ says: "The New Testament writings, of course, say nothing directly about a continuing function of leadership like Peter's within the later community of disciples, and give no hint of a process for appointing successors to his role as 'rock,' 'shepherd' and source of strength for the others."[49] Another Jesuit, Klaus Schatz, admits that though individual or particular arguments for the papacy may be doubtful and though the papacy has changed in response to different historical circumstances, "a fundamental line can be traced back almost to the beginning." "Almost" sounds like conceding that in the very

---

45. *Church Dogmatics* II/2, p. 441.

46. Oscar Cullmann (1952), ET Floyd V. Filson, *Peter: Disciple, Apostle, Martyr,* 2nd rev. ed. (London: SCM, 1962).

47. *Church Dogmatics* IV/1, p. 674; Cullmann, *Peter: Disciple, Apostle, Martyr,* pp. 34-41.

48. *Gespräche 1964-68,* p. 187 in Interview with Georg Puchinger, 15 April 1965, and later with Henri-Charles Tauxe, 1 and 2 May 1965.

49. Brian E. Daley SJ, "The Ministry of Primacy and the Communion of Churches," in Carl E. Braaten and Robert W. Jenson, eds., *Church Unity and the Papal Office: An Ecumenical Dialogue on John Paul II's Encyclical* Ut Unum Sint (Grand Rapids: Eerdmans, 2001), p. 35.

beginning the papacy was not directly instituted by Christ.[50] It is also a historic fact that original lists of popes do not count Peter as the first pope, or Pope Sextus would then have been called Septimus. But as noted earlier, the value of the papacy can be defended on other grounds, not least as a way of uniting different congregations. One has the impression that after his meeting with the pope, Barth was at least sympathetic to the burdens of office such a universal ministry entails even if he might still have considered that these burdens were self-imposed by poor exegesis and not least because he did not believe that the unity of the church is dependent on the pope. In their conversations, Pope Paul seemed to agree that in the description of non–Roman Catholics as *fratres sejuncti,* the real emphasis is intended to be on the fact that as Christians we are brothers. Might this be a form of ecumenical partnership and collegiality, I wonder?

Irreformable Dogmas?

Barth's second main concern is about papal claims and dogmas that are "irreformable." To repeat what was said at Vatican I: "Therefore, such definitions of the Roman pontiff are of themselves, and not by consent of the church, irreformable." Here Barth affirms what he had first learned from his study and lectures on the Reformed Confessions in 1923. All such confessions were provisional in the sense that they offered the best statements that theologians and churches felt able to offer at the time but were open to further refinement or correction. So the Zurich Council, following Zwingli's own practice, stated:

> Once again, we desire that whoever is able to advise us better or differently by the true divine Scriptures, we shall gladly receive such advice from them with particular gratitude and joy. Hereby we also once again ask each and everyone, that is whoever finds us in some way to have erred against God and his word of the holy gospel, or to be wrong, to point it out in a friendly way out of the true word of God and of the gospel for the sake of the honour of God, of truth, and Christian love. We shall receive and welcome such with the highest gratitude.[51]

50. Klaus Schatz SJ, "Historical Considerations concerning the Problem of the Papacy," in *Petrine Ministry and the Unity of the Church: Toward a Patient and Fraternal Dialogue,* ed. James F. Puglisi (Collegeville, MN: Liturgical Press, 1999), p. 3.

51. Karl Barth (1923), ET Darrell L. Guder and Judith J. Guder, *The Theology of the Reformed Confessions* (Louisville: Westminster John Knox, 2002), p. 24.

And likewise the Bern Consensus of 1532:

If anything were presented to us by our pastors or others which might lead us closer to Christ and in the power of God's Word be more supportive of common friendship and Christian love than the views presented here, we will gladly accept it and not block the course of the Holy Spirit. For it is not directed backwards to the flesh but always forwards towards the image of Christ Jesus our Lord.[52]

In his Gifford Lectures in Aberdeen in 1937 and 1938, Barth expounded the Scots Confession of 1560 and quoted this disclaimer in the original Scottish dialect — one wonders what it might have sounded like with a Swiss-German accent!

That gif onie man will note in this our confessioun onie artickle or sentence repugnant to God's Halie word, that it will pleis him of his gentleness and for Christian charities sake to admonish us of the same in writing; and we upon our honours and fidelities, be God's grace do promise unto him satisfaction fra the mouth of God, that is fra his haly scriptures, or else reformation of that quhilk he sal prove to be amisse.[53]

As for his own theology, Barth never pretended to have said the last word. Who but God can speak the final word? He was not ashamed to admit he had changed his mind[54] and indeed his whole approach. He had revised his groundbreaking Commentary on Paul's Epistle to the Romans, changed from Christian Dogmatics to Church Dogmatics and yet again to Evangelical Theology. But had not Calvin also done the same in successive revisions of his *Institutes of the Christian Religion?* Critics of Barth may feel they are confronted by a man who is sure he is right. Perhaps he is. But there is also a lightness of touch and ability not to take himself too seriously.

The angels laugh at old Karl. They laugh at his trying to capture the truth about God in a book on dogmatics. They laugh because volume follows volume, each thicker than the last, and as they laugh they say to each other: "Look! There he goes with his barrow full of volumes on dogmatics."

---

52. Barth, *Theology of the Reformed Confessions,* p. 24.

53. Karl Barth, ET J. L. M. Haire and Ian Henderson, *The Knowledge of God and the Service of God: The Gifford Lectures 1937 and 1938* (London: Hodder & Stoughton, 1938).

54. Karl Barth, *How I Changed My Mind* (Edinburgh: Saint Andrew Press, 1969).

Barth could have laughed at himself in this way, which is why one of his pupils, Martin Rumscheidt, felt free to publish this sketch as an epilogue in his honor.[55]

The Reformers, especially Calvin, lacked Barth's sense of humor but, at their best and in their confessions, they sought to offer a theology of grace and were themselves gracious enough to admit that they might sometimes be wrong and open to correction. It would be saying too much to claim that Vatican II followed their example. What it did do was to depart from the style and tone of the Counter-Reformation Council of Trent and its stern anathemas. For example, Trent had declared:

> If anyone says that this catholic doctrine concerning justification, set out in this present decree by this holy council, detracts in any way from the glory of God or the merits of Jesus Christ our Lord, and does not rather make clear the truth of our faith, and the glory alike of God and of Jesus Christ: let him be anathema.[56]

Vatican II had no anathemas. Nor did it claim that any of its teachings were irreformable dogmas. Even so, it is very hard for a church that has previously made such statements and regards some of her teachings as infallible ever to admit that she was wrong. It may also be fairer to accept that our forefathers in earlier councils acted in good faith but their decisions are no longer binding. This is the stance taken by Lutherans and Roman Catholics in the *Joint Declaration on the Doctrine of Justification:*

> The doctrinal condemnations of the 16th century, in so far as they relate to the doctrine of justification, appear in a new light. The teaching of the Lutheran churches presented in this Declaration does not fall under the condemnations from the Council of Trent. The condemnations in the Lutheran Confessions do not apply to the teaching of the Roman Catholic Church presented in this Declaration.
>
> Nothing is thereby taken away from the seriousness of the condemnations related to the doctrine of justification. Some were not simply pointless. They remain for us "salutary warnings" to which we must attend in our teaching and practice.[57]

---

55. Karl Barth, *Fragments Grave and Gay,* ed. Martin Rumscheidt (London: Collins Fontana, 1971), pp. 124-25.

56. Council of Trent, Canons concerning Justification 33 in Norman Tanner, *Decrees of the Ecumenical Councils,* p. 681.

57. *Joint Declaration,* paras. 41, 42.

A footnote in the *Joint Declaration* refers to a study by the Roman Catholic scholar Karl Lehmann and the Lutheran theologian Wolfhart Pannenberg, *The Condemnations of the Reformation Era: Do They Still Divide?* (1990). Harding Meyer, the Lutheran ecumenical theologian who helped write the *Joint Declaration,* will surely also have recalled that a similar understanding was reached in the *Leuenberg Agreement between Reformation Churches in Europe* in 1973. Here the parties concerned, mainly Lutheran and Reformed churches, also said that "we take the decisions of the Reformation fathers seriously" but that the condemnations "are no longer an obstacle to church fellowship."[58] All this shows that it is perfectly possible for churches today to respect the decisions they made when separated from each other, learn from each other and from other churches through meetings and formal dialogues, and move on. They may then conclude, in the words of the *Joint Declaration:* "We give thanks to the Lord for this decisive step forward on the way to overcoming the division of the church. We ask the Holy Spirit to lead us further toward that visible unity which is Christ's will."

On this whole question, Barth could quote and did quote the Reformed slogan, *ecclesia reformata sed semper reformanda.* All church decisions are relative and provisional and have need of constant reform. This is also true of church constitutions.[59] Vatican II offers rather cautious support for such a conviction in its Decree on Ecumenism: "In its pilgrimage on earth Christ summons the church to continual reformation, of which it is always in need, in so far as it is an institution of human beings here on earth."[60] But the caveat is that insofar as the church may be viewed as divine and sacramental, it has no need of reform.

What More Did Barth Say about Hierarchy and Apostolic Succession?

Though I have tried hard to argue that Barth's theology has much to offer all Christians of all traditions, when it comes to church polity there is no hiding the fact that his starting point is Reformed. It is not simply biblical and "catholic" in the widest sense. And since Calvin as one of the founding fathers

---

58. *Agreement between Reformation Churches in Europe* (*Leuenberg Agreement*) (Frankfurt am Main: Verlag Otto Lembeck, 1973), vol. 3, pp. 17, 27. Leuenberg documents are published in three languages: German, English, and French.

59. *Church Dogmatics* IV/1, p. 660; IV/2, p. 748.

60. *Unitatis Redintegratio* 6.

of the Reformed tradition was more of a churchman than Luther, one will expect the Reformed to have more decisive views about church government than the Lutherans. If all one knew about Barth was that he was a minister of the Swiss Reformed Church one might presume to know what his attitude to the papacy, to bishops and apostolic succession, church councils, clergy and laity, even the ordination of women might be. We could take it for granted that on all these points he would differ from Rome. But then we would be doing what Barth warns against. We would be dealing in abstractions like "Protestant pastors" or "Catholic priests." Barth abhorred such generalizations. Rome is not monolithic. There are different sorts of Protestants. And precisely because he is a Reformed theologian, we should expect him to give his own account of the hope that is in him rather than blindly echo the dictates of some higher human authority or church tradition.

Barth's engagement with Rome and the Second Vatican Council made many audiences and interviewers curious to know more about his views on church government. For this reason the *Gesamtausgabe* volumes of his speeches in the years 1959-68 are especially valuable. Questioners from different perspectives, including Roman Catholics, had the opportunity of face-to-face dialogue and the freedom to challenge Barth's views or at least to ask for clarifications. Their publication enables us as readers to have some experience of what it must have been like to be a student sharing in a seminar but with the added bonus of seeing someone other than Barth chairing and directing the discussion.

Barth makes a few general observations, which I will then explore in the more detailed treatment on the Christian community that he offers in the final volumes of *Church Dogmatics*. Asked about bishops, he said he had nothing against bishops[61] even though questioners would know that Barth's own church, like most Reformed churches, is not episcopally ordered. The exception is the Reformed Church in Hungary, though even there we are informed that the position of bishop carries administrative rather than hierarchical authority.[62] He was opposed to claims for superior office in the church. A church should be properly ordered, but church constitutions are human creations rather than expressions of divine right. The Presbyterian order did not come down from heaven, "nicht von Himmel gefallen."[63] Seventeenth-

---

61. Barth, *Gespräche 1964-68,* p. 300.

62. Jean-Jacques Bauswein and Lukas Vischer, *The Reformed Family Worldwide: A Survey* (Grand Rapids: Eerdmans, 1999), p. 210.

63. *Gespräche 1964-68,* p. 300.

century Presbyterians said it did and spoke of the "divine right of presbytery." In his more detailed expositions, Barth responds to such questions as these:

Does It Matter to God How the Church Is Ordered?

Yes, indeed! In *Church Dogmatics* IV/2 Barth devotes some fifty pages to a consideration of "The Order of the Community." Because the community witnesses to the "reconciliation of the world with God accomplished in Jesus Christ," which is "the great campaign against chaos and therefore against disorder," the community herself must be an ordered community. "Disorder is wrong." If this sounds obvious, we need to be aware that for Protestants at the time to speak so strongly about church law and church order was a controversial and highly contested subject. Barth draws on a number of studies including that by fellow Swiss Reformed theologian Eduard Schweizer, which in its English translation has the title *Church Order in the New Testament*. He is particularly indebted to his friend Erik Wolf. Schweizer compares the different ecclesiologies of the different Gospels and other New Testament writings and makes the general point that church order in the New Testament is "gospel testimony."[64]

Wolf is quoted by Barth for his description of the church as a "christocratic brotherhood" or "brotherly Christocracy."[65] Barth is highly critical of Rudolf Sohm and Emil Brunner because of the way they describe the community as spiritual and voluntary and "evade the christological question and answer" as to its order. Church order is Christ's rule. Church law is the community's obedient response to Christ.

The key point being made here is that the church is not simply a sociological organization that adapts for its own use patterns of government found in secular society. Barth would be aware, though he does not say so in this section, that the Church of Rome is sometimes accused of adopting the imperial style of the Roman Empire, the Orthodox that of Byzantium, and Reformed churches in Europe and the United States that of Western democracies. Then in recent years, the Orthodox churches accused the World Council of Churches of being too parliamentary. They therefore helped change the whole style of decision making at the WCC so that most matters

---

64. Eduard Schweizer (1959), ET Frank Clarke, *Church Order in the New Testament* (London: SCM, 1961), p. 229.

65. *Church Dogmatics* IV/2, p. 680.

are now agreed by consensus, not by majority votes. To all of which Barth offers this response:

> Because in the direction of Church affairs we are still in the sphere of service, it is better either to avoid terms like monarchy, aristocracy or democracy, with their clear suggestion of the exercise of power, or at any rate to use them in such a way that in the understanding of the rule of the Church on a Christocratic basis, "rule" is always firmly interpreted as outstanding service.[66]

Earlier in the same volume, Barth cites Mark 10:42 about secular rulers who lord it over their subjects "as a procedure which is not to have any place in the community," and in this context the saying of Jesus from the same Gospel passage, "whoever would be great among you should be the servant of all" (Mark 10:44).[67] For this reason Barth would also explain that of all the titles given to the pope, the one that is most appropriate is "servant of the servants of God."[68] George Caird, an observer at Vatican II on behalf of the Congregational churches and a noted New Testament scholar, commented that though we should not overdo the contrast between the magisterium, or magisterial versus ministerial authority, as his own tradition was wont to do, there was a clear shift in Council documents to put the emphasis on ministerial service. A "magister" need not mean a dictator but simply one who teaches and helps others to learn.[69] Hence we should not too easily dismiss the idea of a Catholic magisterium. Whatever the style of a particular polity, whether in church or state, Timothy Gorringe rightly argues that "from his 1911 article on 'Jesus Christ and the Movement for Social Justice' to the last, posthumously published fragments of the *Dogmatics* on the 'lordless powers,' from first to last his [Barth's] work is against hegemony." Hence the title of his study.[70] But Gorringe fails to appreciate just how important it is in Barth's thinking for the church to be structured in this way. The rejection of all patterns of domination in the church can serve as an example as to

66. *Church Dogmatics* IV/2, p. 693.

67. *Church Dogmatics* IV/2, pp. 175, 691.

68. *Gespräche 1964-68*, p. 359. The title was used by Gregory the Great and is quoted by Pope John Paul II in *Ut Unum Sint* 88 as a "beautiful expression."

69. George B. Caird, *Our Dialogue with Rome: The Second Vatican Council and After* (Oxford: Oxford University Press, 1967), pp. 62-63.

70. Timothy J. Gorringe, *Karl Barth Against Hegemony* (Oxford: Oxford University Press, 1999), p. 1.

how we can live together in society as a whole. Church law in Barth's view should be exemplary.[71]

Barth recognizes that "there are demands which the community has to address to its members" and demands that one community has to make on another or a central authority on all, but all such demanding has to be closely scrutinized "to be sure that it is not the abstract demanding of dominion, or the abstract assertion of privileges and claims and dignities, but only the demanding of service." Nor can any leader or any church or council ignore the fact that all stand under a demand. In effect Barth is saying no one is above the law of service.[72]

What about the Hierarchy?

Reformed churches like to think of themselves as nonhierarchical. In his *Institutes* Calvin had said that though some called the government of the church a "hierarchy," this is, he said "an improper term (it seems to me), certainly one unused in Scripture. For the Holy Spirit willed men to beware of dreaming of principality or lordship as far as the government of the church is concerned."[73] The point here is that "hierarchy" like all forms of "arche" or "ocracy" is associated with rule, not simply with order. For Presbyterians, a common emphasis is on the parity of ministers. All ministers are of equal status even though they may have different functions. In my own United Reformed tradition a moderator of assembly or a moderator of a synod is not a superior grade of minister, and in the former case the office is only temporary. One is elected to serve for two years. All ministers are paid the same stipend because all are equally valued.

In his first major treatment of the topic in his *Göttingen Dogmatics*, lectures given in 1925-26, Barth accepts Calvin's fourfold structure of ministry of pastors, doctors, elders, and deacons but insists there are no gradations of rank but all are equally forms of service.[74] All depend on the inward call from Christ and the outward call from the community. There is no hierarchy. Thirty years later in *Church Dogmatics* IV/3 (1959), Barth's view of hierarchy

71. *Church Dogmatics* IV/2, pp. 719-26.
72. *Church Dogmatics* IV/2, pp. 691-92.
73. Calvin, *Institutes of the Christian Religion* (1559), IV.4.4.
74. Karl Barth, *Unterricht in der Christlichen Religion* III (Zürich: Theologischer Verlag, 2003), pp. 375-76; Kimlyn J. Bender, *Karl Barth's Christological Ecclesiology* (Aldershot, UK: Ashgate, 2005), pp. 74-75.

could be regarded as more nuanced and more ecumenical. It is found in the subsection dealing with "the upbuilding of the community." "Building," he notes, is a good biblical metaphor, drawn from the construction industry and applied to the Christian community in 2 Corinthians 5 and Ephesians 4. In 1 Peter 2, Christians are "living stones" and Christ "the corner stone." Like all metaphors, comparisons must not be pushed beyond their limitations. Humanly speaking, the work of building the Christian community is never finished and the finished or final edifice is "the new Jerusalem which comes down from God out of heaven" (Rev. 21:2). It is not of our making. Such texts give added support for Barth's emphasis on the provisional nature of the church.

Workers on a building site have to be organized, but Barth insists that the pattern of organization must be different for the up-building of the Christian community:

> The only thing is that, as distinct from ordinary construction, there are no superior and inferior functions and tasks, nor can there be a rigid hierarchy of those taking part but only a very flexible hierarchy corresponding to the directness with which each receives orders from the Lord Himself. In this building new dispositions may be made at any time by which (without any question of degradation on the one side or decoration on the other) the last become first and the first last: a leading worker or overseer again dropping back into the ranks and having an important contribution to make as a labourer; and a labourer or apprentice, without any long training or experience, having the opportunity to work at a higher or even the very highest job.[75]

If such seems idealistic and even impractical it could be pointed out, for example, that abbots in many monastic communities often return to the ranks after a period of high office in their communities. Likewise it is not unknown for bishops, and even archbishops, in the Church of England to return to parish ministry or some other sphere of service. What is unknown, save for rare exceptions, is for popes to do likewise! Barth's real objection to rigid hierarchies is that they establish distinctions of superiors and inferiors that condone practices of domination and subjection, but he may also be making the point that even in the church no one is indispensable. Popes should be allowed to retire, as Pope Benedict did in 2013. They should also be allowed to die if they are old and ill. Too many of us kept praying that

---

75. *Church Dogmatics* IV/2, p. 631.

John Paul II should live on. The Holy Spirit has and will help us discern new leaders when the time comes. Practicing what he preached, Barth himself contemplated a time when the next funeral would be his and afterward he might be forgotten. It did not seem to trouble him. The church of Christ would survive without him![76] And to date, so has his theology!

What about the Laity?

For Barth, laypeople also have a place in a flexible hierarchy. This, as we shall see, is a great understatement. Laypeople certainly have a place and it is not at the bottom, as in the traditional pyramid image of church structure. In Roman Catholic thinking, the hierarchy is often contrasted with the laity. Not for Barth. Barth does not like the terms "layman, laywoman"; neither did some of his predecessors in the Reformed tradition. In the *Göttingen Dogmatics* he quotes the Reformed theologian Turretini: *"discrimen inter clericos et laicos figmentum papale est."*[77] Later he would say we are all members of the people of God, the λάος Θεού. On this there was a growing ecumenical consensus. Vatican II rediscovered the laity.[78] So did the World Council of Churches.[79] Congar dealt with the subject in depth in 1956, *Jalons sur une théologie du laicat,* and the Reformed theologian Hendrik Kraemer made this the subject of his Hulsean Lectures at Cambridge in 1958. At a more popular level, English readers had Gibbs and Morton's *God's Frozen People* (1964). In Germany, the founding father of the Protestant Kirchentag, Reinhold von Thadden-Trieglaff, was a layman and saw the Kirchentag as the occasion when laypeople from all over Germany and beyond would gather to think about their faith and responsible citizenship. This lay movement has gone on growing in popularity and now brings together 100,000 or more people every two years in a major German city. The first was held in 1949

---

76. *Church Dogmatics* III/4, p. 589.

77. *Unterricht in der Christlichen Religionen* III, p. 373.

78. In addition to the emphasis on "People of God" in *Lumen Gentium,* the Council also issued a Decree on the Apostolate of the Laity, *Decretum de apostolatu laicorum,* which Barth discusses in his *Ad Limina Apostolorum,* pp. 31-32.

79. The World Council of Churches from its formation in 1948 had a Department of the Laity. This was led first by Hendrik Kramer and later by Hans Ruedi Weber. When the emphasis was more general on the Renewal of Congregational Life © 1971, "the word 'laity' tended to disappear from ecumenical discussion." See Nicholas Lossky et al., *Dictionary of the Ecumenical Movement* (Geneva: WCC, 2002).

in Hanover.[80] So Christians of many different traditions were rediscovering the laity in the final decades of Barth's life.

They were not agreed about the implications of their discoveries for the church. Congar, for example, spent most of his opening chapters criticizing a Protestant and Barthian emphasis on the church as a community to the exclusion of its God-given institutional structure of sacraments and hierarchy.[81] The Protestant emphasis was one-sided and heretical. But he had also to admit that there was a tendency to identify the church with the clergy. He quoted the English historian F. M. Powicke in support of a common assumption among Anglicans that to go "into the church" means to become a clergyman. This expression is still common. There is, in other words, one-sidedness on both sides, but for Congar this is only heretical when the emphasis is only on the community, for in his view the hierarchy has never been mentioned to the exclusion of the community.[82]

His argument is not convincing. Hopefully this approach is better: just as there is a high-level argument among respected Roman Catholic theologians as to which comes first, the church universal or the local church, so a case can be made for starting with the Christian community rather than with the hierarchy. Vatican II did this in *Lumen Gentium* but did not follow it through. Barth begins with the Christian community and goes on to speak of the "ministry of the community." Or rather, as with *Lumen Gentium* with Christ, then with Christ's calling of the community. Then follows the detailed description of the ministry and mission of the community and the Spirit's gifts to the community so that it can fulfill its ministry of witness in its many different aspects. Barth's emphasis throughout is communal and involves all the "people of God."

Before outlining twelve different tasks for the ministry of the community, Barth dismisses an alternative approach of outlining what he calls "forms of the Church's ministry." In his view there is no biblical basis for doing this. The lists of ministries in Romans 12, 1 Corinthians 12, and Ephesians 4 do not tally. They are different because they are adapted for different circumstances and communities. They can serve as examples and give us direction, but "the only sensible course is to ask concerning the basic forms of the Church's ministry already revealed in them, not to treat and expound

80. Werner Hühne, *A Man to Be Reckoned With: The Story of Reinhold von Thadden-Trieglaff* (London: SCM, 1962).

81. Yves Congar (1956, 1964), ET Donald Attwater, *Lay People in the Church*, rev. ed. (London: Geoffrey Chapman, 1965), p. 31.

82. *Lay People*, pp. 47, 48.

them as norms of the differentiation of ministry which are valid once and for all."[83]

We may even say that there is now an ecumenical consensus about ministry in the New Testament. The Faith and Order document *Baptism, Eucharist and Ministry* drawn up by theologians from the Roman Catholic, Orthodox, Anglican, and Protestant churches, and more widely studied and commented on than any previous Faith and Order document, accepts that "the New Testament does not describe a single pattern of ministry." But having said this it goes on to commend that "the threefold ministry of bishop, presbyter and deacon may serve today as an expression of the unity we seek."[84]

The Ministry of the Community: Is Barth's Radically Different Approach to Questions of Ministry Ecumenically Helpful?

The Roman Catholic Church was delighted with the conclusion in *Baptism, Eucharist and Ministry* about the threefold ministry. Other churches, including, my own, were not so sure.[85] Barth might not wish to argue about this, for his whole approach is radically different. *Baptism, Eucharist and Ministry,* like *Lumen Gentium,* like Barth, starts with "The Calling of the Whole People of God," but after the first six paragraphs on this theme it devotes the remaining fifty to the "Ordained Ministry." Barth by contrast is more consistent. Having reached the conclusion that ministry is the task of the whole Christian community, he follows this through to show how *all* the people of God may participate. If we are mainly interested in the threefold ministry of bishops, presbyters, and deacons we may not get much help from Barth. But in contrast to *BEM* and the documents of Vatican II, those who are not ordained will no longer feel they have been so quickly forgotten.

Already we have a hint of a radically different approach when Barth states in the opening paragraphs:

The ministry of the community is given this concrete definiteness as a ministry to God and man by its institution and ordination as such in the

83. *Church Dogmatics* IV/3, p. 860.

84. World Council of Churches Faith and Order Document 111, *Baptism, Eucharist and Ministry* (Geneva: WCC, 1982), M19, M22. In addition to this report there are now six volumes of *Churches' Responses to BEM* plus two volumes of concluding summaries and assessments.

85. Max Thurian, ed., *Churches Respond to BEM,* vol. 6 (Geneva: WCC, 1988), p. 31; *Churches Respond to BEM,* vol. 1 (Geneva: WCC, 1986), p. 108.

discipleship of Jesus Christ. He and the Gospel which He proclaims and which proclaims Him, is the content of the witness which is alone at issue in its ministry.[86]

It is the ministry of the community that is "instituted" and "ordained," not just the ministers. Then when Barth lists the various tasks it is easy to see, even from their description, that none is exclusively the ministry of the ordained. These are the tasks:[87]

1. It is our office to praise God.
2. The explicit proclamation of the gospel in the assembly of the community
3. The instruction that is to be given in the community
4. The speech and action of the community which are for the most part directed outwards to the world, and are therefore characteristically apostolic . . . excellently summed up in the word "evangelization"
5. Mission "in which the community has to speak apostolically in the narrower sense"
6. In relation to the speaking community, "the ministry of theology"
7. The community prays as it works.
8. The cure of souls — "the activity of the community as a sign and witness to individuals both within itself and in the nearer or more distant world around"
9. Personal examples of Christian life and action
10. Diaconate — the rendering of service
11. Prophetic action — the action of the community in the ministry of its witness
12. Establishing fellowship — the Christian community acts in the fact that it establishes fellowship, first and supremely by attesting "the supreme fellowship," namely that of the Father with the Son and the Son with the Father in the Holy Spirit.

The last point includes baptism and the Lord's Supper, about which Barth admits "there is more to be said" than that such actions "establish fellowship" and about which he might indeed have said much more had he lived not only to complete his fragment on baptism but also his exposition of Communion in a fifth volume of *Church Dogmatics*.[88]

86. *Church Dogmatics* IV/3, p. 831.
87. *Church Dogmatics* IV/3, pp. 865ff.
88. *Church Dogmatics* IV/3, p. 901; Paul D. Molnar, *Karl Barth and the Theology of the*

None of the above twelve tasks of ministry is exclusively clerical, which is not to say that the clergy are excluded or that the community has no need of experts and leadership. For example, in connection with 8, the cure of souls, Barth states: "Within the community it may indeed, like all other functions, be the concern of those specially called and gifted in this regard. Yet no Christian can escape responsibility for it." And all also share in this ministry through common prayer.[89] Barth is particularly scathing about people who pride themselves on being "no theologian":

> All indolent talk of non-theological laymen will thus be quietly refuted. For if theology understands itself as an integrating element in the ministry of the community, the conclusion is natural enough that every Christian is responsible for it and indeed has to think of himself as a theologian.[90]

He elaborated the same point in his lecture in the United States in 1962, reprinted in *Evangelical Theology*:

> Every Christian as such is called to be a theologian. . . . It is always a suspicious phenomenon when leading churchmen (whether or not they are adorned with a bishop's silver cross), along with certain fiery evangelists, preachers, or well-meaning warriors for this or that practical Christian cause, are heard to affirm, cheerfully and no doubt also a bit disdainfully, that theology is after all not their business. "I am not a theologian; I am an administrator!" a high-ranking English churchman once said to me. And just as bad is the fact that not a few preachers after they have exchanged their student years for the routine of practical service, seem to think that they are allowed to leave theology behind them, as the butterfly does with its caterpillar existence, as if it were an exertion over and done with for them.[91]

Later, in interviews, Barth is asked by a young Roman Catholic theologian: "What is theology?" His reply is that theology is "ein Lebensakt," which could be translated as "theology is our life," for as Christians we do

---

Lord's Supper: A Systematic Investigation (New York: Peter Lang, 1996). Molnar argues: "Although Barth never lived to complete his intended treatment of the Lord's Supper as part of the doctrine of reconciliation, there is enough material in the rest of the *Church Dogmatics* from which to grasp his position on the subject" (p. 3).

89. *Church Dogmatics* IV/3, p. 885.
90. *Church Dogmatics* IV/3, p. 882.
91. *Evangelical Theology*, p. 42

not say "cogito ergo sum" but "credo ergo sum," I believe and therefore I am.[92] What is particularly impressive in this regard is the way in which Barth, then in his eighties, so obviously enjoyed and valued theological discussions with parishioners in various churches, Roman Catholic and Protestant, in his home city of Basel, and he clearly respected all the people he was speaking with.[93] One can also sense that when Barth was preaching in Basel prison, the prisoners themselves were fellow theologians not least because they made "deliverance to the captives" a matter of their own, and his, life and death.[94] Barth would also enjoy the prison chaplain's joke that in order to hear him preach "one had to break the law and be put in jail"![95]

Responding to Vatican II's Unfinished Agenda: Laity, Community of Women and Men?

In several of his last speeches and discussions and in his report on his visit to Rome, Barth responds to various points made about ministry in the documents of Vatican II, in *Lumen Gentium,* in the *Decree on the Apostolate of the Laity,* and the *Decree on the Missionary Activity of the Church.* Rather mischievously he notes that "[i]f Mary is the 'perfect example' of the apostolate of the laity, and as such 'Queen of the Apostles,' does this make the apostolate of the laity superior to all other forms of apostolate?"[96] "Does the desire that the laity be active include also the women mentioned in paragraph 9" of this document on the laity?[97] He wonders, too, why the lay apostolate is not more closely linked to People of God rather than seen as a response to the needs of the times.[98] And why are the laity given the task of testimony when this could be the task of the whole church? He raised the same query in relation to *Lumen Gentium.*[99] All of which could

---

92. "Gespräch mit Seigi Yoshinaga," from Tokyo in *Gespräche 1964-68,* pp. 456-58.

93. Karl Barth, *Gespräche 1964-1968* (Zürich: Theologischer Verlag, 1997).

94. Karl Barth (1959), ET Marguerite Wieser, *Deliverance to the Captives* (London: SCM, 1961); also ET A. T. Mackay, *Call for God: New Sermons from Basel Prison* (London: SCM, 1967).

95. "Remarks by the Preacher and the Prison Chaplain," in *Deliverance to the Captives,* p. 11.

96. Barth, *Ad Limina Apostolorum,* p. 32.

97. *Ad Limina Apostolorum,* p. 31.

98. *Ad Limina Apostolorum,* p. 31.

99. *Ad Limina Apostolorum,* pp. 32, 21.

be a polite way of asking why there is a separate document on the laity? Might this not suggest that Rome, despite the fact that "people of God" was placed before "hierarchy" in *Lumen Gentium,* still tended to identify the church with the hierarchy? To which, Barth asks, "[A]re the laity part of the hierarchy? Are lay people also with the pope, bishops, priests and deacons 'partakers of the function of Christ'?" Finally, in relation to *Gaudium et Spes,* Barth asks, "Where is the prophetic function of the Council in the face of the real problems of the middle of our century?" Prophecy, as we have seen, is in Barth's analysis one of the functions of the ministry of the community.

One would expect a theologian from the Reformed tradition to look critically at Roman Catholic ecclesiology. Some of his criticisms echo the Reformers before him. But Barth is also aware and in fact delighted that Rome at Vatican II was in the process of a genuine renewal and rethink. And so often in the process, as anyone can see from reading or, best of all, attending the Council debates, there is an attempt to balance conflicting emphases. Can one speak of the pope without denigrating a council? Can one emphasize that we are all members of the people of God and give proper attention to the importance of a hierarchy, even a flexible hierarchy, and the need for more priests? In short, and looked at positively, the Council opened up a discussion that needs to continue. In this, though Barth is no longer with us, or not visibly so, his comments and criticisms can still be helpful and should still be heard.

And just as Barth noted in that early essay how Rome poses a question to the Protestant — and indeed to other churches — so the arguments in the debates at Vatican II engage us all. Most churches underestimate the vocation of those who are not ordained. After an outburst of enthusiasm in the 1960s, "the laity" ceased to be of special interest. The Roman Catholic theologian Paul Lakeland could therefore say in his *Liberation of the Laity* (2003) that very little had been written on the subject since Yves Congar.[100] As already noted, even the World Council of Churches ceased to have a Department of the Laity. Most churches too are involved, or should be involved, in debates about the service and ministry of women. In many local Roman Catholic congregations there is more lay participation than in many Protestant congregations. And even in Protestant and in ecumenical assemblies male and clerical speakers predominate and often dominate. The nonrecognition of each other's ordained ministers

---

100. Paul Lakeland, *Liberation of the Laity* (New York: Continuum, 2003), p. 1.

still remains a major cause of division. Perhaps Barth himself grew tired of endless debates about apostolic succession, episcopacy, and so forth and opted for a more inclusive framework of the "ministry of the community." His approach has much to commend it — and to all churches, not just Rome.

Collegiality?

Readers may notice that despite my opening paragraphs, I have said little about Barth and collegiality. This is because Barth appears to have little to add. Collegiality remained after the Council another unresolved issue.[101] Bishops returned from some of the early synods frustrated at their lack of influence. They might be consulted but they were not allowed to decide. The Dominican theologian Edward Schillebeeckx, one of the expert theologians at Vatican II, detects in the Council a tension between "charisma and institution." Without institutional support, ideas like co-responsibility and collegiality are doomed to disappear: "One cannot in fact honestly speak of the equality of all in the church (Galatians 3:28) if one does not specify, or provide institutional safeguards for, the forms which follow from this equality."[102] This, after the Council, Rome failed to do.

Surely Barth as a theologian from a church with a strong conciliar tradition would have more to say. The bishops of the Church of England in their response to *Ut Unum Sint* had specified collegiality as their first concern when assessing Rome's Magisterium and linked this with the *sensus fidelium* and the relationship of the pope to the curia.[103]

Barth may not have commented directly on arguments about collegiality, but the whole tone of the comments we have noted is collegial. He is, as Gorringe explains, "against hegemony." With the Confessing Church and the Barmen Declaration he helped to write, he is opposed to "the Führer Principle" in church or state and so with the state appointment of a Reich Bishop to rule over the church in Germany. Thesis Four cites Matthew 20:25 and parallels about "rulers in the world" and declares:

101. Mary McAleese, *Quo Vadis? Collegiality in the Code of Canon Law* (Dublin: Columba, 2012).

102. Edward Schillebeeckx, ET John Bowden, *The Church: The Human Story of God* (London: SCM, 1990), p. 209.

103. House of Bishops Occasional Paper, *May They All Be One: A Response of the House of Bishops of the Church of England to Ut Unum Sint* (London: Church House, 1997), para. 19.

The various offices in the church do not establish a dominion of some over others; on the contrary, they are the exercise of the ministry entrusted to and enjoined upon the whole congregation.

We reject the false doctrine, as though the church, apart from this ministry, could and were permitted to give to itself, or allow to be given to it, special leaders vested with ruling powers.[104]

Eberhard Busch in his recent commentary on the Declaration explains that "the various offices" may refer to the pattern of ministry outlined by Calvin of Christ as Prophet, Priest, and King and which some Lutheran congregations also accepted. But he makes the general observation: "At the very least it is clear that the task of leadership in the church is distributed onto various shoulders."[105] In other words, leadership is shared. It should be collegial.

Collegial Theology

There are those who argue more strongly than Barth that theology should be a collegial exercise, not the work of single authors operating in relative isolation. Barth was clearly indebted to a diverse company of earlier theologians, not always so good at working in partnership with contemporaries. As we saw, the World Council of Churches once experimented with a group of twenty-five distinguished theologians of whom Barth was one, and often, according to Newbigin, "at his most polemical." Barth, Baillie, Brunner, and Niebuhr were each strong-minded theologians who lacked the ecumenical diplomacy of a bishop like Newbigin.[106] Theirs could never be an easy, docile collegiality, but one could claim that they were aware, and Barth was certainly conscious of the fact, that they had constantly to defend their convictions before such contemporary critics. They were mutually accountable, and that surely is part of collegiality.

More sympathetic critics have come to see Barth as a great conversation partner. This is the theme of a set of essays in John McDowell and Mike Higton's *Conversing with Barth*. They set out to refute James Barr's complaint

104. Eberhard Busch (2004), ET *The Barmen Theses Then and Now* (Grand Rapids: Eerdmans, 2010), p. 61.

105. Busch, *The Barmen Theses*, p. 64.

106. Lesslie Newbigin, *Unfinished Agenda: An Autobiography* (London: SPCK, 1985), p. 131.

that Barth "paid little attention to other people's opinions," and they share Paul van Burren's appeal to other theologians to enter into conversation with Barth's theology and "never to dismiss this man as a relic of an antique world or as a conservative or reactionary who will not move with the times."[107] Or, as Robert McAfee Brown said in his Foreword to Barth's *Credo:* "The reader has the privilege of disagreeing with Barth. He no longer has the privilege of ignoring him."[108]

Barth's close interaction with Rome was made possible because he regarded Roman Catholic theologians like Erich Przywara, Hans Urs von Balthasar, and Hans Küng as colleagues. Collegiality is about treating such contemporaries and even our predecessors like Congar and Barth as colleagues and relating to them.

107. John C. McDowell and Mike Higton, eds., *Conversing with Barth* (Aldershot, UK: Ashgate, 2004), Introduction.

108. Robert McAfee Brown, "Foreword" in Barth (1935), ET J. Strathearn McNab, *Credo: A Presentation of the Chief Problems of Dogmatics with Reference to the Apostles' Creed* (London: Hodder & Stoughton, 1964), p. ix.

CHAPTER FIVE

Reforming or Converting Karl Barth: Roman Catholic Critics

Dialogue Is Two-Way

Dialogue is two-way. Ecumenical dialogues can have a double effect on those who take part in them. We become more self-conscious, even more thankful and proud of our own tradition. But we might also become more understanding of and sympathetic toward our partners and see the need for our own reform. Barth in Lutheran Göttingen and Roman Catholic Münster rediscovered his own Reformed roots even to the point where a witty Methodist-Episcopalian commentator, Stanley Hauerwas, would joke about "his obscure references throughout his *Church Dogmatics* to Protestant scholastics unknown to anyone else."[1] Although he had resisted the title of lecturer in "Reformed Dogmatics," he needed to think more deeply about his own Reformed tradition than he had done as a Reformed pastor in Geneva and Safenwil. He did this through lectures on Zwingli and Calvin and the Reformed Confessions. Then growing contact with Roman Catholic theologians from his time at Münster to Vatican II and its aftermath made him more sympathetic toward Rome without making him a Roman Catholic.

Dialogue could lead to conversion. In a famous footnote to his address on "Church and Theology" delivered at Göttingen in 1925, Barth admitted that if he had to choose between the way the Reformation was interpreted by Schleiermacher-Ritschl-Troeltsch and Roman Catholic understanding of the church, "if I were forced to make a choice between the two evils, I should

---

1. Stanley Hauerwas, *With the Grain of the Universe* (London: SCM, 2002), p. 159.

in fact, prefer the Catholic."[2] And at the time he was sometimes accused of being too pro-Catholic. Forty years later, Barth rejoiced at the way he was received by the pope and cardinals in Rome. He had earlier noted how he was often better understood by Roman Catholics than by people in his own tradition, but he saw no need to become a Roman Catholic. On the contrary, he rejects the very idea of such conversions:

> "Conversions" from us to the Roman Catholic Church or from there to one of our churches have as such no significance (*peccatur intra muros et extra!*). They can have significance only if they are in the form of a necessary "conversion" — not to another church, but to Jesus Christ, the Lord of the one, holy, catholic and apostolic church. Basically both here and there it can only be a matter of each one heeding in his place in his own church the call to faith in the one Lord, and to his service.[3]

Understood in this way, Christians in other traditions can aid the process of our conversion to a deeper relationship to Christ and to what the Groupe des Dombes, Roman Catholic–Reformed and Lutheran dialogue partners, call *For the Conversion of the Churches*.[4] In this chapter I try hard to take seriously some Roman Catholic critics of Karl Barth in the conviction that at his best he was open to such criticisms and, if need be, to such correction. He was certainly painfully aware that much in his own tradition was in desperate need of what we might describe as "catholic reform." We will look at some key Roman Catholic criticisms of Barth's theology such as a recent study, *Ecclesial Mediation in Karl Barth*.[5] I shall concentrate on the questions they raise rather than on those who raise them. Catholic critics will be listened to as those who make serious challenges to a brother Christian theologian to review his own thinking about our human cooperation in the work of reconciliation and about the church as a mediator of salvation, the nature of sacraments, and other common concerns. In a later chapter, we shall see that some of the so-called church-dividing issues like justification may have been resolved. And earlier, we have seen that we *may* have reached greater mutual understanding about Mary, Scripture and Tradition, about "a

---

2. Karl Barth, "Church and Theology," in ET Louise Pettibone Smith, *Theology and Church: Shorter Writings, 1920-1928* (New York: Harper & Row, 1962), p. 314.

3. Karl Barth, *Ad Limina Apostolorum*, pp. 17-18.

4. Groupe des Dombes (1991), ET James Greig, *For the Conversion of the Churches* (Geneva: WCC, 1993).

5. John Yocum, *Ecclesial Mediation in Karl Barth* (Aldershot, UK: Ashgate, 2004).

pope for all Christians," and the importance of councils. I say "may" because there are always those who sincerely believe that agreements have not gone far enough, gone too far, or that we must simply beg to differ.

One further point should be made before we listen to Barth's Roman Catholic critics. Let us agree that only those who are Roman Catholics can reform Rome. It would surely be presumptuous to suggest otherwise. But Pope John XXIII did ask non–Roman Catholic communions to, so to speak, "cross over to Macedonia and help us," just as centuries ago, the same Holy Spirit had said this to Paul (Acts 16:9). And John Paul II in *Ut Unum Sint* explicitly asked all Christians to help him be a better pope. His appeal is worth quoting in full. He refers to his vocation as pope:

> This is an immense task, which we cannot refuse and which I cannot carry out by myself. Could not the real but imperfect communion existing between us persuade church leaders and their theologians to engage with me in a patient and fraternal dialogue on this subject, a dialogue in which, leaving useless controversies behind, we could listen to one another, keeping before us only the will of Christ for his church and allowing ourselves to be deeply moved by his plea "that they may all be one . . . so that the world may believe that you have sent me."[6]

Many bishops at Vatican II did aid the process of reform by listening to Barth. They did so because they recognized Barth as a brother in Christ who is in some sense in "a real but imperfect communion" with the Church of Rome, for as the Decree on Ecumenism so clearly states: "Those who believe in Christ and have been truly baptised are in some kind of communion with the catholic church." Again, the much-discussed phrase in *Lumen Gentium*, "*subsistit in*," suggests that the whole church catholic is larger and more comprehensive than the actual Roman Catholic Church herself. It is big enough to embrace a "Protestant" theologian like Barth. And despite Rome's earlier suspicions of the ecumenical movement, even in 1925, while still at Göttingen, Barth joked with his friend Eduard Thurneysen about the remarkable approval they were receiving from papists. One whom he nicknames Athanasius said that Catholic theologians would not ignore Barth's "admonitions without loss: Eduard, we shall get to the Council yet!"[7] Indeed they might! Barth was invited to the Council in 1962, though by then too

---

6. *Ut Unum Sint* para. 96.

7. Karl Barth, ET James D. Smart, *Revolutionary Theology in the Making: Barth-Thurneysen Correspondence, 1914-1925* (London: Epworth Press, 1964), p. 205.

old and too ill to attend its sessions but fit enough later, in 1966, to engage in lively discussions in Rome with Pope Paul VI and others, including Karl Rahner and Joseph Ratzinger, later Pope Benedict. Such was Rome's long-standing respect for Karl Barth.

Converted Critics

Contrary to Barth, mutual understanding between members of the Church of Rome and other Christians may sometimes be helped by Christians who have converted to Rome and yet remained ecumenically sensitive to and appreciative of the churches and traditions they came from. Barth too easily dismissed such conversions from one church to another. It is true they do not solve the unity problem, but it can mean we have, so to speak, "friends at court." Louis Bouyer was a Lutheran pastor who converted to Roman Catholicism but remained sympathetic to the spirit of Protestantism though not to its form, as one can see in his well-known book, *The Spirit and Forms of Protestantism*.[8] Others who have at some stage converted are among today's leading Roman Catholic theologians or were Barth's contemporaries. Avery Dulles, one of Rome's best-known ecclesiologists, was once a Presbyterian, the son of John Foster Dulles, best known as Secretary of State to Eisenhower but before that one of the United States' pioneers in both the United Nations and the World Council of Churches. The ecumenically minded Roman Catholic Archbishop, Basil Hume, had a Scottish Presbyterian father. Abbot Christopher Butler had previously been Anglican and was a great ecumenical advocate at Vatican II.[9] The Dominican Fergus Kerr was once a Scottish Episcopalian. He demonstrates a critical appreciation of Barth, who was more closely followed in Scotland than in England. Janet Martin Soskice, eminent Roman Catholic and feminist theologian, grew up as a rather lukewarm Canadian Anglican but when she came to take the faith more seriously carefully weighed up the strengths and weaknesses of Rome and found that the former outweighed the latter. Rome seemed to her to have a better claim to be the church than any other. And though

8. Louis Bouyer (1954), ET A. V. Littledale, *The Spirit and Forms of Protestantism* (London: Collins Fontana, 1963). Boyer was strongly influenced by Roman Catholic ecumenist Dom Lambert Beauduin. See his *Veilleur avant l'Aurore: Colloque Lambert Beauduin* (Paris: Éditions de Chevetogne, 1978).

9. Christopher Butler, *The Theology of Vatican II* (London: Darton, Longman & Todd, 1967); *A Time to Speak* (Southend, UK: Mayhew McCrimon, 1972).

Yves Congar was always a Roman Catholic, he attributes his Jewish and Protestant sympathies to his early upbringing. Barth early on had experienced both the benefits and weaknesses of personal conversions from one tradition to another. His colleague at Göttingen, Erik Peterson, was a Lutheran who converted to Roman Catholicism but who in the process had, with Erich Przywara SJ, helped Barth think more deeply about the incarnation. Barth would also be aware that interconfessional conversions were not always so fruitful. He was not impressed by Friedrich Heiler, who changed from being Roman Catholic to Lutheran because he came to value the Protestant's "evangelical freedom." Barth was very critical of his Protestant version of the Mass and felt that Heiler had a "dreamy pious" concept of the church.[10] Converts may help us see that there is truth on the other side but not if they offer easy compromises or concoct what is sometimes called an "ecumenical mishmash" for the liturgy.

Is Barth Sufficiently "Catholic"?

At a much more profound level Barth is asking himself the question that troubled the sixteenth-century Reformers: What is so wrong in the Church of Rome that it justifies our separation from Rome? And Barth and the heirs of the Reformation ask themselves: What differences still continue to be church-dividing? In response Roman Catholics may ask, indeed must ask: Is Barth's theology and in particular his ecclesiology "sufficiently catholic"? What, from a Roman Catholic point of view, prevents Barth's being accepted as a catholic theologian?

The question is not easily answered. Readers of Hans Urs von Balthasar's pioneering exercise in dialogue, *The Theology of Karl Barth*, originally published in German in 1951, may quickly form the impression that the difficulties in what Balthasar calls "Prospects for Rapprochement" are all on Barth's side. As a Roman Catholic theologian there is nothing in Barth's theology that von Balthasar feels he must reject, that is, once he has dismissed the whole argument about the *analogia entis* in Barth's account as "extremely simplistic" and "in fact downright fraudulent." Earlier he had said "the greatest doubts surround what Barth means by Church," but at the time, 1951, those sections of *Church Dogmatics* dealing with ecclesiology had still

10. Amy Marga, *Karl Barth's Dialogue with Roman Catholicism* (Tübingen: Mohr Siebeck, 2010), pp. 84-86, 63-65.

to be published.[11] There is also the vexed question even among Roman Catholics as to who in the end decides what Roman Catholic theology is truly "Catholic." As noted earlier, many of Rome's best-known theologians in the twentieth century were at some stage or other regarded as suspect. They include Yves Congar, Henri de Lubac, John Courtney Murray, Karl Rahner, Dom Lambert Beauduin, Hans Küng, Charles Curran, Leonardo Boff, and Edward Schillebeeckx. The first four were later reinstated and even acknowledged as a major influence in the thinking of Vatican II. At the same time, there would be many Roman Catholic theologians who would have serious questions about Balthasar himself. Fergus Kerr observes that "throughout the 1950s Balthasar was a lonely figure." He was not invited to Vatican II as one of the *periti* though later honored in 1969 by Pope Paul VI. Today the secondary literature about him is "overwhelmingly positive in tenure."[12] This is, says Kerr, "perhaps surprising — unless critics do not know where to start" because, like Barth, he wrote so much! Such Catholic candor! In short, Barth was no more suspect as a "catholic theologian" than Balthasar, who is now "widely regarded as the greatest Catholic theologian of the century," and who publicly acknowledged just how much he owed to Barth, his colleague in the University at Basel.[13] Hans Küng remains suspect, but not because of his affection and respect for Barth. And let us remember Barth's greatest accolade in the eyes of Rome, that he was, according to Pius XII, the greatest theologian since Thomas Aquinas. High praise indeed!

No Roman Catholic in Barth's lifetime would doubt Aquinas's Catholic credentials, though they would differ widely in their understanding of "the "Angelic Doctor.""[14] What are the most fundamental reservations Roman Catholics have about Barth?

By "fundamental" I mean issues that remain after other disagreements have been talked through. Balthasar in his pioneering dialogue with Barth could not find "remaining differences . . . that justify a split in the Church," but added:

---

11. Hans Urs von Balthasar, ET Edward T. Oakes SJ (San Francisco: Ignatius Press, 1992), pp. 379-83. Barth deals with ecclesiology in volume IV. The first part appeared in German in 1953, part 2 in 1955, and part 3 in 1959.

12. But see also Karen Kirby, *Balthasar: A (Very) Critical Introduction* (Grand Rapids: Eerdmans, 2012).

13. Fergus Kerr, *Twentieth Century Catholic Theologians* (Oxford: Blackwell, 2007), pp. 121-44.

14. Kerr, *Twentieth Century Catholic Theologians*, p. 1.

Of course, we are not claiming that our investigations have set aside all reasons for a split between Protestants and Catholics in general, or between Barthian and Catholic theology in particular. As we said earlier, there could well be important reasons in ecclesiology for still justifying in Barth's eyes and that of his followers this division: for example, an infallible Magisterium, the number and praxis of the sacraments, the veneration of the saints and especially of the Mother of the Lord. Certainly profound differences of opinion still exist here. But these differences can no longer be justified on the basis of positions developed in treating creation and covenant.[15]

This is von Balthasar in 1951. In later years he was more inclined to stress the importance of all the differences that he listed here and be less enthusiastic about Barth and about Vatican II.[16] In *The Office of Peter and the Structure of the Church,* he is very much on the defensive, anxious to counteract "a deep seated anti-Roman attitude within the Catholic Church."[17]

Six Fundamental Roman Catholic Criticisms of Barth

I explore six "fundamental" Roman Catholic concerns about Barth's ecclesiology:

- Ecclesial mediation
- Sacraments
- Human cooperation in salvation
- The church as institution as well as event
- The work of the Holy Spirit in the church
- The church universal
- The question of woman

On each of these topics Roman Catholics are not Barth's only critics. Barth's theology may reflect a "weakness" that is common in his own Re-

---

15. Hans Urs von Balthasar (1951), ET Edward T. Oakes SJ, *The Theology of Karl Barth* (San Francisco: Communion Books, 1992), p. 386.

16. Benjamin Dahlke, *Karl Barth, Catholic Renewal and Vatican II* (London: T. & T. Clark, 2012), p. 154.

17. Hans Urs von Balthasar (1974), ET Andrée Emery, *The Office of Peter and the Structure of the Church* (San Francisco: Ignatius Press, 1986), p. 9.

formed tradition or Protestantism in general. Such points are important to note if we are in search of a more comprehensive catholicity than can be expressed by one theologian's identity with Rome. For example, Eugene Rogers, author of a well-known study of Thomas Aquinas and Karl Barth, in a more recent essay has criticized Barth for allowing "the Son to eclipse the Spirit." He is repeating a criticism made by Robert Jenson (Lutheran) and Rowan Williams (Anglican) but resisted by fellow Roman Catholic theologian Philip Rosato in 1981[18] and more recently by a number of Pentecostal theologians who one might expect to be most likely to accuse Barth of neglecting the Holy Spirit.[19]

The "Question of Woman,"[20] to repeat a question raised by Barth's faithful assistant, Charlotte von Kirschbaum, might seem out of place in such a list. Yet insofar as Rome's own feminist theologians are not only critical of their own church but also of Barth for his own ambivalence on an urgent issue for all churches, their criticisms ought to be heeded. A catholicity that seems to undervalue half the human race is surely not catholic enough.

Misunderstandings or Valid Criticisms?

I shall resist the temptation to defend Barth except where a criticism loses its force because based on a misunderstanding of what Barth is trying to do. For example, Colm O'Grady in the first major Roman Catholic study of *The Church in Catholic Theology: Dialogue with Karl Barth*, accuses Barth of neglecting the universal church.[21] Reformed theologian Lukas Vischer concedes this is a weakness in Reformed ecclesiology in general: "Reformed

18. Philip Rosato, *The Spirit as Lord: The Pneumatology of Karl Barth* (Edinburgh: T. & T. Clark, 1981).

19. Eugene F. Rogers Jr., "The Eclipse of the Spirit in Karl Barth," in *Conversing with Barth*, ed. John C. McDowell and Mike Higton (Aldershot, UK: Ashgate 2004), pp. 173-90; Robert Jenson "You Wonder Where the Spirit Went," *Pro Ecclesia* (1993): 296-304; Pentecostal theologian Frank Macchia was impressed by Barth's emphasis on "Baptism with the Holy Spirit," and Veli-Matti Kärkkäinen accepts that Barth might later have begun again with "a more fully pneumatological approach"; see "Karl Barth and the Theology of Religions," in *Karl Barth and Evangelical Theology*, ed. Sung Wook Chung (Grand Rapids: Baker Academic, 2006), pp. 236-57, 240.

20. Eleanor Jackson, ed., *The Question of Woman: The Collected Writings of Charlotte von Kirschbaum* (Grand Rapids: Eerdmans, 1996).

21. Colm O'Grady MSC, *The Church in Catholic Theology: Dialogue with Karl Barth* (London: Geoffrey Chapman, 1970), pp. 255, 305.

churches are so deeply divided that they are unable to form a universal communion capable of transcending effectively the boundaries of nations."[22] Both critics fail to appreciate a vital aspect of Barth's and Reformed ecclesiologies. They are provisional. They emerge from a genuine attempt to honor the Reformers' intention to reform the universal Church of Rome, not to provide an alternative or replacement. The nearest equivalent to Rome's geographical universality would be the World Council of Churches with its 560 million members in over 110 countries, but even its strongest defenders, who at one time included Lukas Vischer as Director of the Faith and Order Commission, know that it makes no claim to be either a "Church" or "a genuinely Ecumenical Council" after the manner of Nicea or Constantinople. Barth is convinced that the church must be one and catholic in the double sense of wholeness and being universal. He cannot accept Rome's claims to be its one and only true expression.

Provisional Ecclesiology

Barth made the point that ecclesiology must be provisional.[23] So did the ecumenical dialogue between the Anglican Consultative Council and the World Alliance of Reformed Churches, *God's Reign and Our Unity:*

> The Church is . . . a provisional embodiment of God's final purpose for all human beings and for all creation. It is provisional in a double sense: only part of the human family has been brought into its life, and those who have been so brought are only partly conformed to God's purpose.

The church is provisional because it awaits the coming kingdom of God. The church is "a provisional embodiment of God's purpose of reconciliation."[24] Vatican II preferred to state: "the Church is in Christ . . . a sacrament or instrumental sign of intimate union with God and of the unity of all humanity."[25] This gives the church its "universal mission." In Rome's

---

22. Lukas Vischer, "The Ministry of Unity and the Common Witness of the Churches Today," in *Petrine Ministry and the Unity of the Church,* ed. James F. Puglisi (Collegeville, MN: Liturgical Press, 1999), pp. 137-52, 149.

23. *Church Dogmatics* IV/1, p. 660; IV/2, pp. 620-21.

24. *Report of the Anglican-Reformed International Commission 1984: God's Reign and Our Unity* (Edinburgh/London: Saint Andrew Press/SPCK, 1984), paras. 30, 35.

25. *Lumen Gentium* 1.

view, Christ himself has given the universal church its permanent structure through Peter, the apostles, and their successors to carry out his commission to "go . . . to all nations and make them my disciples" (Matt. 28:19). Barth accepts the commission but is not convinced that the structures of his own or any other church can claim to be more than provisional. In this he disagrees with the official Roman view but not with Roman Catholic theologians like Christian Duquoc, author of *Provisional Churches*.[26]

Criticisms of Barth: Ecclesial Mediation

Lumen Gentium 8 declares: "Christ, the one mediator, set up his holy church here on earth as a visible structure, a community of faith, hope and love . . . and through it he pours out grace and truth on everyone." And in the previous paragraph we read: "In this (mystical) body the life of Christ is communicated to believers, who by means of the sacraments in a mysterious way are united to Christ." Roman Catholic critics of Barth think he understates the church's share in mediation.

Like many Roman Catholic commentators, John Yocum is extremely fair and generous in his judgments. He regards Barth as a polemical theologian who sometimes overstated his case in arguments with his opponents. Barth in *Church Dogmatics* II/2, first published in 1942, was much more positive about ecclesial mediation than he was in later subsections of *Church Dogmatics* IV (1953-67), especially the unfinished fragment, volume IV/4 on baptism, where he rejects the whole notion of sacraments. In *CD* II/2, p. 197, Barth states:

> [A]ll the election that has taken place and takes place in Jesus Christ is <u>mediated</u> [my underlining], conditioned and bounded by the election of the community. It mirrors in its <u>mediate</u> and <u>mediating character</u> the existence of the one Mediator, Jesus Christ, Himself.[27]

Yocum checks this against the German original, which uses the word *vermittelt,* which in this context means mediate and in others could be translated as arrange or adjust.

---

26. Christian Duquoc, ET John Bowden, *Provisional Churches* (London: SCM, 1986). The book would be more helpful ecumenically if Duquoc showed more knowledge of and interest in other churches.

27. John Yocum, *Ecclesial Mediation in Karl Barth* (Aldershot, UK: Ashgate, 2004), p. 58.

Yocum appreciates Barth's concern in response to 1 Timothy 2:5 to affirm that Christ Jesus is the "one Mediator between God and man." He accepts that Barth "wishes to rule out . . . any view of creaturely mediation in which human action threatens the unique effectiveness of the work of Jesus Christ for salvation. But in the whole of *Church Dogmatics* IV on "The Doctrine of Reconciliation":

> [T]he polemical interest pushes Barth's thought in this volume in directions which have deleterious consequences for his theology as a whole, especially for the coherence of his account of the life and mission of the Church with some important tracts of biblical data.[28]

In Yocum's view, human action and divine action do not need to be sealed off from each other, though this is increasingly the tendency in Barth's theology.[29]

The Jesuit theologian Philip Rosato, commenting on Barth's *Ad Limina Apostolorum,* says that for Barth the Council seemed to prefer "sacramental mediation of Christ rather than evangelical testimony to him" and Barth's pointed question, "Is it the Church which saves and renews the world?" Rosato thinks Barth's criticisms of Council documents are "one sided interpretations."[30]

Baptism and Sacraments

In the first document agreed by the Council, Vatican II declares:

> The purpose of sacraments is to make people holy, to build up the body of Christ, and finally to express a relationship of worship to God. They not only presuppose faith; they also nourish it, strengthen and express it, both through words and through objects. This is why they are called sacraments of faith. It is true that they confer grace.[31]

28. Yocum, *Ecclesial Mediation in Karl Barth,* pp. 92-98. Note that the Reformed–Roman Catholic Dialogue, *Towards a Common Understanding of the Church* (1991), states in para. 86 that it does not wish to say "that the Church exercises a mediation complementary to that of Christ."

29. Yocum, *Ecclesial Mediation in Karl Barth,* p. 96.

30. Philip J. Rosato SJ, *"Ad Limina Apostolorum in Retrospect,"* in *Karl Barth, Centenary Essays,* ed. Stephen Sykes (Cambridge: Cambridge University Press, 1989), pp. 87-114, 99-101, 104.

31. *Sacrosanctum Concilium* para. 59.

Barth could accept much that is said in this paragraph, but in his last writings he has difficulties with the whole notion of sacraments and with the claim that they "confer grace." Rome cannot accept Barth's denials. But judging by her response to the ecumenical convergence text *Baptism, Eucharist and Ministry* (1982), Barth's reservations about sacraments expose, in Rome's view, a weakness that is more widely shared.

All churches were invited to respond to *Baptism, Eucharist and Ministry*. The Roman Catholic Secretariat for Promoting Christian Unity did so in 1987. It congratulated Faith and Order for its fifty years of work on this subject and appreciated the fact that it was only in the last twenty years or so that Roman Catholic theologians had shared in the discussions. But there is more work to be done:

> On the notion of sacrament, *BEM* shows that there are many aspects that Christians can affirm together. But, because of the importance of seeking agreement on baptism, eucharist and ministry as a step towards Christian unity, we believe that the on-going work of Faith and Order must include a further and deeper ecumenical exploration of the notion of sacrament and sacramentality. . . . There is an absence of a clear concept of sacrament [and sacramentality] in *BEM*. Further work is needed on this.[32]

Barth, of course, is not to be blamed for this. The fault may also lie with the New Testament! That is why Barth's son Markus, as a distinguished New Testament scholar, raised the question back in 1951, whether in the New Testament, baptism is a sacrament — *Die Taufe ein Sakrament?*[33] He admits that his own answer though radical was less radical than his father's. He also tells us that his father might have been uneasy about his own (Karl Barth's) conclusions because he requested that his unfinished Fragment on the subject should not be published until after his death though the lectures had been prepared in 1962. In the Preface, dated Easter 1967, Karl Barth acknowledges his debt: "In face of the exegetical conclusions of my son's book, I have had to abandon the 'sacramental' understanding of baptism."[34] Any detailed concordance will show us that "sacrament" is not a New Testament word. Its nearest equivalent in the Greek is *mysterion*. Markus Barth

---

32. Roman Catholic Response in Max Thurian, ed., *Churches Respond to BEM*, vol. 6 (Geneva: WCC, 1988), pp. 6-7.

33. Markus Barth, *Die Taufe, Ein Sakrament?* (Zürich: Evangelischer Verlag, 1951). This is a detailed exegetical study of some 550 pages of all references to baptism in the New Testament.

34. *Church Dogmatics* IV/4, p. x.

discusses the interpretation of this term both in his book on baptism and his later Commentary on Ephesians[35] in relations to Ephesians 5:32.

Markus Barth explains that *mysterion* in this text is interpreted as sacrament by the Catholic Church ever since the Fourth Lateran Council in 1215. In the immediate context the discussion in Ephesians is about marriage, and on the basis of this text, marriage is called a sacrament. Calvin disputed this translation and hence the whole argument about marriage being a sacrament.[36] The Reformers did not, however, doubt that baptism and the Lord's Supper were sacraments. Karl Barth himself underlined this in his comments on the Scottish Confession of 1560 in his Gifford Lectures, *The Knowledge of God and the Service of God* delivered at Aberdeen, Scotland in 1937 and 1938. His affirmation is worth quoting because, as our Roman Catholic critic John Yocum notes, it contradicts his later stance:

> It is noteworthy that from beginning to end the right conception of [church] service is expounded from the aspect of the sacraments. Our sixteenth-century forefathers were far from valuing the sacraments lightly. In opposition to Roman Catholicism they made inquiry about the *true* sacraments. . . . One might be astonished that in a document so strictly reformed as this, at this point the prayers and confession of faith of the congregation are not mentioned at all and preaching only incidentally. What is spoken of here is simply Baptism and the Lord's Supper, and in the main only the Lord's Supper. How the Reformed church has been misunderstood — by herself as well as by others — when later the impression prevailed that she was a church without sacraments, even a church hostile to the sacraments.[37]

Barth at this stage has no difficulty in accepting a definition of sacraments which he thinks all, including the Scottish Confession and the ancient church accept, namely that "a sacrament is an action in which God acts and man serves, his service taking the form of the execution of a divine precept." Likewise in his *Epistle to the Romans* Barth states: "Baptism is a sacrament of truth and holiness; and it is a sacrament because it is the sign which directs us to God's revelation of eternal life and declares . . . the

35. Markus Barth, *Ephesians* (New York: Doubleday, 1974).

36. Calvin, *Institutes* IV.19.36.

37. Karl Barth, ET J. L. M. Haire and Ian Henderson, *The Knowledge of God and the Service of God: Recalling the Scottish Confession of 1560* (London: Hodder & Stoughton, 1938), pp. 190-91; Yocum, *Ecclesial Mediation*, pp. 135-37.

Word of God."[38] And in *The Teaching of the Church Regarding Baptism*, based on a lecture first given in 1943, Barth raises no objection to the fact that baptism and the Lord's Supper "are distinguished from other activities of the Church" by being called a "sacrament," though he makes the additional intriguing comment that "it is even more important to realise that all the activities of the Church are in their way sacramental," which might suggest that at this stage Barth might not have strong objections to Rome's description of confirmation, penance, marriage, and ordination etc. as "sacraments."[39]

Yet even at this earlier stage, if we compare what Barth says about the sacrament of baptism with what is stated in the baptismal formulae of the Roman Catholic Church, what seems to be missing is an appreciation of how God may use physical things like water to convey, communicate, and mediate his gracious presence. In the Baptismal Rite (1969), authorized after Vatican II, the priest tells the congregation: "My dear brothers and sisters, God uses the sacrament of water to give his divine life to those who believe in him. Let us turn to him and ask him to pour his gift of life from this font onto this child he has chosen."[40] This is not Barth's language. Barth would put the emphasis on God's election of the candidate for baptism, not on the actual rite and the water of baptism. Indeed Barth is adamant in making this qualification:

> In view of the points established regarding the nature and potency of baptism, manifestly one cannot properly maintain what would be here asserted by Roman and Lutheran and Anglican baptismal teaching: namely, that water-baptism conferred by the Church is *as such* a causative or generative means by which there are imparted to man the forgiveness of sins, the Holy Spirit and even faith — a means by which grace is poured out upon him, so that he is saved and made blessed — a means by which his

38. Karl Barth, ET Edwyn Hoskins, *The Epistle to the Romans*, 6th ed. (Oxford: Oxford University Press, 1933), p. 192, comment on Romans 6:3.

39. Karl Barth (1943), ET Ernest Payne, *The Teaching of the Church Regarding Baptism* (London: SCM, 1948), pp. 5, 16; *Epistle to the Romans*, p. 192.

40. Max Thurian and Geoffrey Wainwright, eds., *Baptism and Eucharist: Ecumenical Convergence in Celebration* (Geneva: WCC, 1983), p. 22. The book enables us to compare different rites. See also Thomas F. Best, ed., *Baptism Today: Faith and Order Paper 207* (Collegeville, MN: WCC/Liturgical Press, 2008), which summarizes the thinking about baptism in different church traditions. So does Dagmar Heller, *Baptized into Christ: A Guide to the Ecumenical Discussion of Baptism* (Geneva: WCC, 2012).

rebirth is effected, by which he is taken into the covenant of the grace of God and incorporated in the Church.[41]

In his later work, baptism with water is our human response to the prior action of God in baptizing us with the Holy Spirit. The two are treated separately though Barth insists they belong together: "Baptism with the Holy Spirit does not exclude baptism with water. It does not render it superfluous. Indeed, it makes it possible and demands it." Even so, one cannot say that baptism is absolutely necessary for salvation. Barth can find no support for this view in the New Testament in frequently cited texts like Mark 16:16 and John 3:5: "Obviously it was neither possible nor desirable to tie the work of God, of Jesus Christ, of the Holy Spirit, in any obvious way to baptism as a *medium salutis*."[42]

I said at the beginning of this chapter that I would let Barth's critics state their case and I would not jump to Barth's defense. But here, where we are dealing not so much with outright criticism as with contrasting emphases, a brief comment and summary is in order. Three quick points: First, we can agree with Yocum[43] and other commentators that in his rejection of the whole notion of sacraments, Barth is not being consistent with his own theology. The point is also made by his Reformed advocate Thomas Torrance,[44] by his Reformed interpreter George Hunsinger,[45] by Lutheran student Eberhard Jüngel,[46] and more gently by John Webster,[47] Anglican. Paul Molnar tries hard to defend Barth but admits to "ambiguity" in Barth's treatment of sacraments.[48] Second, according to Webster, Barth as a polemical theologian (Yocum) is engaged in an argument against "over inflation of ecclesial activity"[49] and what

---

41. *Teaching of the Church Regarding Baptism*, p. 26.

42. *Church Dogmatics* IV/4, pp. 41, 155.

43. Yocum, *Ecclesial Mediation*, p. 45.

44. Thomas F. Torrance, *Theology in Reconciliation* (London: Catholic Book Club, 1975), p. 99.

45. George Hunsinger, *Disruptive Grace: Studies in the Theology of Karl Barth* (Grand Rapids: Eerdmans, 2000), pp. 275-76.

46. Eberhard Jüngel, "Karl Barth's Lehre von der Taufe," in *Barth-Studien* (Gütersloh: Mohn, 1982).

47. John Webster, "Baptism with Water," in *Barth's Ethics of Reconciliation* (Cambridge: Cambridge University Press, 1995), pp. 148-73, 172.

48. Paul D. Molnar, *Karl Barth and the Theology of the Lord's Supper* (New York: Peter Lang, 1996), pp. 233-38.

49. John Webster, *Ethics of Reconciliation* (Cambridge: Cambridge University Press, 1995), p. 172.

seem to him to be overstated claims for what the performance of the rite of baptism accomplishes. Barth is offering a corrective. Third, the same can be said about Barth's reservations about infant baptism. Baptism is a serious act of obedience. Its model is Jesus' own baptism. It should not be entered into lightly. Infant baptism may give the impression that we can become followers of Christ in our sleep:

> But the baptism which inaugurates the life of the Christian was once, and is properly, the very expressive exponent of the very concrete turning in the life of man which in its singularity is expressly related to the singularity of the person and act of Jesus Christ, i.e., to His baptism. . . . It is the perverted ecclesiastical practice of administering a baptism in which the baptised supposedly becomes a Christian unwittingly and unwillingly that has obscured the consciousness of the once-for-allness of this beginning, replacing it by the comfortable notion that there is not needed any such beginning of Christian existence, but rather than we can become Christians and be Christians in our sleep.[50]

But here let two distinguished Roman Catholic theologians, one a Dominican and the other a Jesuit, offer their reassurance to Barth's concerns first about infant baptism and then about sacraments. In a recent book, *Take the Plunge: Living Baptism and Confirmation,* Timothy Radcliffe, one-time Master of the Dominicans, tells us with great enthusiasm that "Christianity will flourish in the twenty-first century if we grasp that the Church is above all the community of the baptized. Baptism is the great mystery of faith." (Note his word "mystery," not "sacrament"!) To be baptized is the greatest honor that can happen to any Christian. A greater honor than being made a cardinal, or dare he say it, becoming pope! And he cites the present pope, Benedict. As a younger priest he had felt that candidates for baptism or their parents must show strong evidence of personal faith. Then he came to appreciate even more that Christ is the Lord of mercy, ever welcoming. Says Radcliffe, "We must offer Christ's open hospitality to those who hang around on the edge," those who offer "just the smallest hints of faith."[51] Despite his conviction that infant baptism was "one of the many disorders from which the church suffers," Barth rejected the suggestion that he should now be baptized on confession of his personal faith. He said: "I regarded

---

50. *Church Dogmatics* IV/3, p. 517.

51. Timothy Radcliffe OP, *Take the Plunge: Living Baptism and Confirmation* (London: Bloomsbury, 2012), pp. 1, 13.

and still regard it as more correct and important to take my one baptism very seriously."[52]

On his visit to Rome, Barth had conversations with Karl Rahner and other theologians who had been experts at the Council. He asked Rahner, Ratzinger, and Semmelroth "to let me hear their somewhat divergent views on Mariology."[53] Had time permitted, they could usefully have discussed the whole question of sacraments. Rahner would explain that the whole notion of sacraments was a fairly late development in the history of the church. Using the same word to describe very different things such as penance, marriage, ordination, and communion was bound to cause confusion. As one alternative, Rahner describes sacraments as "events." This is very much Barth's language. They are events in which the church in Christ "actualises herself." A sacrament as an event is "an objective symbol, a physical embodiment." In a later essay, Rahner likens sacraments to gestures. He says that to understand sacraments,

> we must first keep in mind that everywhere in human life, and not only in the religious domain, there are gestures that express something; signify something, but in addition also *bring about* that which they signify. Where the Church addresses such a gesture to a person in a solemn and official way, we have to do in this gesture of the Church with what we call a sacrament.
>
> When the Church admits a baby into the community; when she lets a person share the Lord's Supper . . . in such gestures decisive situations are marked with holy signs, and such gestures effect what they signify.[54]

And he adds: "In a long history of reflection on her faith, the Church has become aware that she has seven such fundamental gestures." Would Barth find such an argument persuasive? I hope so, if not for seven sacraments at least for two. Rahner is quite clear that all along, the initiative lies with God. They proceed from God's desire to save people and to call for their response. That too is Barth's concern. He suspects that Rome is sometimes inclined to usurp the Lordship of Christ. Rahner also concedes that without such a response, sacraments remain an empty manifestation of God's love.

52. Letter of Karl Barth to a Mrs. Gowalezyk, member of a community that teaches believer's baptism, 7 April 1965, *Letters 1961-1968*, p. 189.

53. Barth, *Ad Limina Apostolorum*, p. 14.

54. Karl Rahner, "Questions on the Theology of Sacraments," in *Theological Investigations XXIII* (London: Darton, Longman & Todd, 1992), pp. 189-90, and "Marriage as a Sacrament," in *Theological Investigations X*, pp. 199-202.

Human Cooperation in Salvation

The Dominican theologian Fergus Kerr treats Barth with great respect and often with great admiration as for his "brilliant, even 'inspired' thesis . . . to ground a whole vision of what it is to be human precisely on the history on one particular human individual — on Jesus Christ raised from the dead."[55] But he is also aware as a former Protestant or Scottish Episcopalian, of a Protestant tendency to see all forms of human cooperation in salvation as competition with God. He notes the point made by John Webster in his Introduction to Eberhard Jüngel's response to the Roman Catholic Lutheran Agreement on Justification, *The Joint Declaration*, in *Justification: The Heart of the Christian Faith*. For him the emphasis on *solus Christus*, by Christ alone, is undermined by secondary centers of salvation such as Mary and the church. Jüngel, says Webster, may appear to be "driven by a competitive understanding of divine and human action, in which acts have to be assigned *either* to God *or* to creatures — an understanding shared of course by Barth."[56] Kerr comments, "Whether co-operation is necessarily competition is an interesting question." It is a Protestant dilemma not found in Aquinas, who often quoted as a favorite text, Isaiah 26:12: "Lord, you will bestow prosperity on us; for in truth all our works are your doing." This text for Thomas excludes all competitiveness between divine and human agency.[57]

To illustrate Kerr's point one can quote Barth's famous comment on the fatal "and" as the single word that divides Roman Catholics and Protestants. Asked in an interview in 1962,[58] "What is the greatest obstacle for rapprochement between Reformed and Roman Catholic?," Barth said it is the word "and." When we say Jesus, Roman Catholics says Jesus **and** Mary; when we say obey Christ, Roman Catholics say **and** his Vicar on earth. When we claim that the sole source of revelation is Scripture, Roman Catholics say **and** Tradition. This is Barth before Vatican II had begun to debate such issues. At the time, he had a real fear that the Council might create a

---

55. Fergus Kerr, *Immortal Longings: Versions of Transcending Humanity* (London: SPCK, 1997), p. 45.

56. John Webster, Introduction to Eberhard Jüngel, ET Jeffrey F. Cayzer, *Justification, the Heart of the Christian Faith: A Theological Study with an Ecumenical Purpose* (Edinburgh: T. & T. Clark, 2001), pp. x-xi.

57. Fergus Kerr, *After Aquinas: Versions of Thomism* (Oxford: Blackwell, 2002), p. 143, and with reference to Aquinas *ST* 1.105.5.

58. Karl Barth, *Gespräche 1959-62*, pp. 530-31, interview with Tanneguy de Quénétain about Barth and the ecumenical movement.

new dogma and call Mary "Co-Redeemer." We know from the *History of Vatican II* and the strongly argued debates in Mariology that it records, that his fear was well grounded. Many did want to call Mary Co-Redeemer. And though the outcome of this debate was to set all thinking about Mary within the document about the church of which Mary is a preeminent member, *Lumen Gentium* accepts that "in the church the blessed Virgin is invoked by the titles of advocate, benefactress, helper and mediatrix," but insists: "This, however must be understood in such a way that it takes nothing from the dignity and power of Christ, the one mediator and adds nothing on to this." The document cites 1 Timothy 2:5-6: "There is one God, and there is one mediator between God and human beings, the man Christ Jesus who gave himself as a ransom for them all."[59] What Barth regards as the fatal "and" is still in evidence here and readily explained by the fact that all Vatican II documents aimed at a consensus and required a two-thirds majority even when, as on Mariology, the bishops were at times almost equally divided.

In his comments on the documents of Vatican II and particularly that on Divine Revelation, *Dei Verbum,* the bogey word is "both." "What are we to think when we read in section 9 that **both** [tradition and Scripture] flow 'from the same divine wellspring'?"[60] Barth is not a "both/and man." Should he be? Are we human beings only recipients of what God has done for us in Christ or do we also cooperate in salvation? It is a fair question, for certainly some forms of Protestant preaching can give the impression that there is nothing more the congregation can do.

In the predominantly Roman Catholic city of Münster, Barth in 1927 had lectured on Paul's Letter to the Philippians.[61] He observed that the text, "with fear and trembling, work out your salvation" (Phil. 2:12) had "become a crux of Protestant dogmatics and a repeatedly quoted *dictum probans* of the Catholics." But he feels "the old dispute is now softened" once we perceive that nothing was further from Paul's mind than to command us to attend to our own salvation. Barth interprets the whole text as meaning "live as a Christian . . . show and prove oneself what one is as a Christian." Is he perhaps sidestepping a debate that still needs to be held, or has he answered this by describing the Philippians as "co-partners in grace" (Phil. 1:5)?

Roman Catholics tend to find in their church's theology a better synthesis of divine and human activity than they find in Barth. Yves Congar in

---

59. *Lumen Gentium* paras. 62, 60.
60. Barth, *Ad Limina Apostolorum,* p. 50.
61. Karl Barth (1927), ET James Leitch, *The Epistle to the Philippians* (London: SCM, 1962).

Dialogue between Christians regards Barth as a human genius, but! Barth's emphasis on the sovereign causality of God and lack of emphasis on our own co-causality with God has "reinforced an element of heresy which has been disastrous in its effects." He does not explain what these effects were.[62] In *Tradition and Traditions* Congar both accepts Barth's criticism that Rome has tended to make the church, and so therefore the pope, the sole judge and so deprived Scripture of its sovereignty, but at the same time he thinks that Barth and Protestant thought in general separate "Christ in too radical manner from his Body, the Church."[63] Colm O'Grady is convinced that Barth "speaks of the divine and human Church as two distinct realities, and attributes salvific mediation only to the divine Church, that is, to the Holy Spirit." He restates the Catholic position: "The Holy Spirit indwells his Church and uses it as his instrument so that the human Church lives the life of the Spirit and cooperates with him in the achievement of its unity, sanctity, catholicity and apostolicity."[64] Hans Küng makes a criticism of Barth's criticism: "Barth misunderstood the 'cooperari' of the Council of Trent. The justification of all through redemption in Christ by God's verdict is exclusively God's work. This is Catholic teaching." He goes on to explain that on what he calls the "subjective" side of the saving event, Trent sees the human being as cooperating in what God is doing. He talks of involvement rather than collaboration: "*Cooperari* means getting oneself involved in what God alone has put into execution." The God who elects us into his covenant "wants a true partner, not a robot or a puppet, but a man responding to him with a personal, responsible, active and heartfelt Yes."[65]

The Jesuit theologian John Macken offers a detailed study of *The Autonomy Theme in the Church Dogmatics: Karl Barth and His Critics*. He comments on Protestant theologian Trutz Rendtorff. Rendtorff criticized Barth for not giving any substantial reality to the church. The church for Barth has no more than a shadowy existence and in the end is not that important. But Macken thinks that Rendtorff misunderstands Barth's rather enigmatic statements, for example: "The world would be lost without Christ; the world

62. Yves Congar, ET Philip Loretz, *Dialogue between Christians: Catholic Contributions to Ecumenism* (London: Geoffrey Chapman, 1966), p. 12.

63. Yves Congar, ET Michael Naseby and Thomas Rainborough, *Tradition and Traditions: An Historical and Theological Essay* (London: Burns & Oates, 1966), pp. 466, 409.

64. Colm O'Grady, *The Church in Catholic Theology: Dialogue with Karl Barth* (London: Geoffrey Chapman, 1970), pp. 127, 279.

65. Hans Küng, *Justification: The Doctrine of Karl Barth and a Catholic Reflection* (London: Burns & Oates, 1964; new edition 1981), pp. 264-65.

would not necessarily be lost if there were no church; the Church would be lost if there were no counterpart in the world." "Jesus Christ can go his own autonomous way without reference to the church," says Rendtorff.[66] He can, but he chooses not to. In an "act of free grace" Christ claims the service of the church. But Macken in defending human autonomy in Barth also recognizes that Barth can be his own strongest critic. He cites an extract from the *Humanity of God* but one that can only be understood in its context.

Barth is reviewing his earlier theology: "It must now quite frankly be granted that we were at that time only partially in the right." The whole talk was of the "wholly other," the "infinite qualitative distinction" between God and humanity. The suggestion was that all the Bible was interested in was God. "Redemption was viewed as the abolition of the creatureliness of the creature." And, "Did not the whole thing frequently seem more like the report of an enormous execution than the message of Resurrection which was its real aim?" Then comes the passage cited by Macken:

> Was the impression of many contemporaries wholly unfounded, who felt that the final result might be to stand Schleiermacher on his head, that is to make God great for a change at the cost of man? Were they wrong in thinking that actually not too much had been won and that perhaps in the final analysis it was only a new Titanism at work?[67]

Church as Event and Institution

Continuity in the church through a line that can be traced back to Peter and the first Apostles appointed by Christ is very important in Roman Catholic theology. Not so for Barth. He appears to be less concerned with the church's foundation and existence than with what happens now: "The Church exists as the event of this gathering together." The church is "a dynamic reality. . . . The Church exists by happening."[68] By contrast the *Catechism of the Catholic*

---

66. John Macken SJ, *The Autonomy Theme in the Church Dogmatics: Karl Barth and His Critics* (Cambridge: Cambridge University Press, 1990), pp. 124-27; *Church Dogmatics* IV/3, p. 826.

67. Macken, *The Autonomy Theme*, p. 159; Karl Barth, ET John Newton Thomas and Thomas Wieser, *The Humanity of God* (London: Collins, 1961), pp. 42-43.

68. "The Church: The Living Congregation of the Living Lord Jesus Christ" (1948), in ET Paul M. van Buren, *God Here and Now* (London/New York: Routledge, 1964, 2003), pp. 75-104.

Church declares: "The Lord Jesus endowed his community with a structure which will remain until the Kingdom is fully achieved. Before all else there is the choice of the Twelve with Peter as their head. Representing the twelve tribes of Israel they are the foundation stones of the new Jerusalem."[69] Because such a structure is a permanent feature of the church we are often told, for example, that the church cannot ordain women as priests because Christ chose only men to be apostles. Nor could one contemplate a church without bishops for they are the successors of the apostles. This understanding is not of course peculiar to the Church of Rome. Nor is the criticism of viewing the church as primarily an "event" rather than an institution something only voiced by Roman Catholics. But first let's hear the Roman Catholic response to Barth as voiced by his "dialogue partner," Colm O'Grady.

Colm O'Grady says that Roman Catholics assert the uniqueness of revelation to the apostles but this is continued — "the uniqueness does not exclude a continuation, in the sense that the unique revelation has to be transmitted by the Holy Spirit in and through, and therefore also by, human historical means so that it can reach the end of the world."[70] He will then devote a whole chapter in which he argues that "The Church is Event and Institution" and he will ask Barth: "[I]s the Church never continuously the Church?" In reply to his own question, O'Grady states: "The Church is also a constant reality, and the source of the repeated event of its gathering." He quotes Karl Rahner in support:

> [The Church] is a visible society; as really visible it must continually realize its historical, spatio-temporal tangibility through the actions of men. It must become "event" over and over again. It is not as if these "events" in their separated individuality in space and time founded the Church anew. An actualism of this sort, which would basically deny the social constitution of the Church, tradition, apostolic succession and any real Church law of divine right, is foreign to Catholic ecclesiology.[71]

If Barth is the target for such a critique but also the spur to a more balanced judgment, Rahner does not say so; but Lesslie Newbigin does. As a fellow Reformed theologian and leader in the newly formed World Council

---

69. *Catechism of the Catholic Church* (London: Geoffrey Chapman, 1994), para. 765.

70. O'Grady, *The Church in Catholic Theology.*

71. O'Grady, *The Church in Catholic Theology,* pp. 252-53; Karl Rahner, in Karl Rahner and Joseph Ratzinger, *The Episcopate and the Primacy* (New York/Edinburgh: T. & T. Clark, 1962), p. 24.

of Churches, he heard Barth's keynote address at Amsterdam and felt that Barth carried the emphasis on what he calls "this dynamic doctrine of the Church," which can be found in the Reformers, to "almost this extreme point." The church becomes a "series of totally disconnected events." There is no place in Barth's picture "for a continuing historical institution, nor for any organic relation between different congregations in different places and times."[72] Again, I will not jump to Barth's defense. Newbigin is reacting to the repeated emphasis on "event" (*Ereignis*) in Barth's Amsterdam address. He is also, unlike Barth, trying to be diplomatic in his zeal for church unity. He is more like Melanchthon where Barth is more like Calvin. Newbigin was a pioneer in the formation of the United Church of South India (1947) and one of her first bishops.

Barth's emphasis on the church as event has its Roman Catholic defenders. The so-called Bologna school in *The History of Vatican II* interprets the Council as an "event," as Giuseppe Alberigo, the editor, says in the first volume in 1995: "At thirty years' distance, Vatican II appears as an event that, independently of and despite its limitations and lacunae, made the hope and relevance of the gospel relevant once again." The Council is not just a collection of several hundreds of pages of texts but is better understood as "a stimulus to the community of believers to accept the disquieting confrontation with the word of God and with the mystery of human history."[73] Edmund Schlink, Lutheran observer from Germany, says: "Without doubt the conciliar decisions are correctly interpreted only if they are interpreted against the background of the whole conciliar <u>event</u>."[74]

Congar in his *My Journal of the Council,* in recording the comments of various observers on the Document on the Church, notes that Greek Orthodox theologian Nissiotis said that the eucharist was the basis for the structure of the local church and that "real participation in the Body of Christ unceasingly recreates the Church."[75] There are echoes here of Barth's event ecclesiology. Congar does not note that Nissiotis was at one time a

---

72. Lesslie Newbigin, *The Household of God* (London: SCM, 1953), p. 50.

73. Giuseppe Alberigo and Joseph A. Komonchak, *History of Vatican II*, vol. 1 (Maryknoll, NY: Orbis/Leuven: Peeters, 1995), p. xi. See also Massimo Faggioli, *Vatican II: The Battle for Meaning* (New York: Paulist Press, 2012), p. 15, where "event" is seen as one of the main "hermeneutical principles" used by Alberigo and his colleagues.

74. Edmund Schlink, ET Herbert J. A. Bouman, *After the Council* (Philadelphia: Fortress Press, 1968), pp. 46-47, quoted in Faggioli, *Vatican II: The Battle for Meaning,* p. 43.

75. Yves Congar, ET Mary John Ronayne OP and Mary Cecily Boulding OP, *My Journal of the Council* (Collegeville, MN: Liturgical Press, 2012), p. 330.

student of Barth's. He does not criticize the observers' comments but simply says how impressed he is. "The quality of this meeting was exceptional." The observers are very well informed.

Much earlier (1958) and even before the Council was announced, the Roman Catholic theologian Heinrich Fries published a study that is both critical of and sympathetic to Barth: *Kirche als Ereignis*.[76] He deals first with Vatican I where he sees the question about the church as one of its chief themes, then also with the encyclical of Pope Pius XII, *Mystici Corporis*. But for us the most interesting section of the book is the final chapter, "The Church as Event according to Karl Barth's Doctrine of the Church." Fries sees Barth's emphasis on the event character of the church as entirely consistent with Barth's emphasis on the sovereign freedom of God, the One who in Jesus loves in freedom. Reconciliation is itself an event, the free act of the true God and the fulfillment of the covenant between God and humanity. He explores the way the theme is developed in Barth from his Commentary on the Epistle to the Romans to the volume IV/2 of the *Kirchliche Dogmatik*, first published in German in 1955. Volume IV/3 would appear in 1959. He is also very conscious of an anti–Roman Catholic tendency in Barth, despite his friendship with Roman Catholic theologians like Küng and von Balthasar, a tendency that was very evident in his "attack" at Amsterdam in 1948, sparked as it was then by Rome's absence from the ecumenical movement. We need to hold together here and now and forever the church as both a substantial reality (*Wirklichkeit*) and an event (*Ereignis*). He sees Barth as opening up a search that engages our whole existence and so needs to continue.

Fries with Karl Rahner would later advocate what both regarded as a realistic program for church unity, *Einigung der Kirchen — reale Möglichkeit* (1983).[77] Later still he would lament how little had changed after the Council in his sad little book, *Leiden an der Kirche* (1989), in English, *Suffering from the Church: Renewal or Restoration* (1995).[78]

Other studies of the church as "event" that should be mentioned include those by Barth's former student, the Belgian Dominican Jérôme Hamer[79]

---

76. Heinrich Fries, *Kirche als Ereignis* (Düsseldorf: Patmos-Verlag, 1958).

77. Heinrich Fries and Karl Rahner, ET Ruth C. L. Gritsch and Eric W. Gritsch, *Unity of the Churches: An Actual Possibility* (Philadelphia: Fortress Press, 1985).

78. Heinrich Fries, ET Arlene Swidler and Leonard Swidler, *Suffering from the Church: Renewal or Restoration* (Collegeville, MN: Liturgical Press, 1995). The book includes important essays on post-Vatican II Roman Catholicism by Leonard Swidler and Peter Neuner.

79. Jérôme Hamer, *L'Occassionalisme Théologique de Karl Barth* (Paris: Desclée de Brouwer, 1949).

and Reformed theologian Jean-Louis Leuba.[80] Rather surprisingly there are no references to Barth in this particular work by Leuba. Medal Kehl offers a detailed study of the Church as Institution in recent German and Roman Catholic ecclesiology. He refers to Barth, and also to Brunner, Bonhoeffer, and Moltmann but clearly sees no need to regard Barth's thinking about the Church as Event as a rival alternative to the Church as Institution. Hans Küng would appear to have Barth's thinking in mind when he holds together the actual existence of the church and the event of its being constantly created: "There is no Church which is not created and must constantly be created; and none is created without the operation of the Spirit."[81] In this section of *The Church,* he refers to section §62, "The Holy Spirit and the Gathering of the Christian Community" in *Church Dogmatics* IV/1, where Barth writes of the freedom of the Holy Spirit and how the church exists only as "it is gathered and lets itself be gathered and gathers itself by the living Jesus Christ through the Holy Spirit." Barth explains that all the usual distinctions between "being and act, status and dynamic" have to be abandoned. The church *is* and the church *exists* when certain actions take place. Though Küng relates the Holy Spirit more closely to the church than is perhaps evident in Barth, he makes the point that though the Spirit is domiciled in the church, the Spirit is not domesticated by the church nor under the control of the church. It is this shared conviction about the Spirit's freedom that leads to that dynamic view of the church which Küng also shares. Though he says the Holy Spirit is promised to those who hold office in the church, the Spirit is not the Spirit of office but the Spirit of God and is free to act in other ways and by other means and even outside and beyond the church,[82] meaning, surely, the church as "institution."

One final comment on "event ecclesiology." Barth in his Amsterdam address speculated that "the congregational form of Church may yet have a future also among us." He was quoting Friedrich Loofs back in 1901![83] The same might also now be said of "event ecclesiology." The Anglican Methodist Report on *Fresh Expressions in the Mission of the Church* (2012) refers to the analogy of being church as a performance and then adds a caution, which, as we have seen, has become the standard criticism of Barth:

---

80. Jean-Louis Leuba, *L'institution et l'événement* (Neuchâtel: Delachaux, 1950).

81. Hans Küng (1967), ET *The Church* (London: Search Press, 1968), p. 176.

82. Küng, *The Church,* pp. 176-77.

83. Karl Barth, "The Church: The Living Congregation of the Living Lord Jesus Christ," in *God Here and Now,* p. 104.

The performance analogy allows the Church to be understood as an "event," though such language needs to be used with caution lest the impression is given that it lacks historical visibility and continuity. The Archbishop of Canterbury [Rowan Williams] helpfully points out . . . "church" is "what happens when people encounter the Risen Christ Jesus and commit themselves to sustaining and deepening that encounter in their encounter with each other."[84]

Archbishop Williams adds the proviso that what is needed then are "ways of identifying the same living Christ at the heart of every expression of Christian life in common."

The Work of the Holy Spirit in the Church

Critical questions here follow on from the debates about the Church as Institution or Event. Is the Holy Spirit continuously at work in the Institution of the Church? Has Barth done justice to this question as far as Roman Catholics are concerned? After all, the Council of Trent claimed that it was "lawfully assembled in the Holy Spirit."[85] And Vatican I claims that "the holy Spirit was promised to the successors of Peter . . . that, by his assistance, they might religiously guard and faithfully expound the revelation or deposit of faith transmitted by the apostles."[86] Vatican II in *Lumen Gentium*, the document on the church, begins with a Trinitarian basis and so proceeds to say of the Holy Spirit that it was sent to "sanctify the church continually and so that believers would have through Christ access to the Father in one Spirit (see Ephesians 2,18)." It adds that "the Spirit dwells in the church and in the hearts of the faithful as in a temple (see 1 Corinthians 3,16; 6,19). He leads the church into all truth (see John 16,13)."[87] It also claims that "this holy synod" is "called together in the Holy Spirit."[88]

84. Anglican Methodist Working Party, *Fresh Expressions in the Mission of the Church* (London: Church House Publishing, 2012), para. 1.8.10. "Fresh Expressions" is an example of a mission strategy that explores new ways of "being church" in a society where most people have only a minimal contact with existing church structures of any tradition.

85. Trent, Session 2, 7 January 1546. Norman Tanner, *Decrees of the Ecumenical Councils* (London: Sheed & Ward, 1990), p. 660.

86. Vatican I, chapter 4 on Infallible Teaching; see Tanner, *Decrees of the Ecumenical Councils*, p. 816.

87. *Lumen Gentium* 4.

88. *Lumen Gentium* 1.

Reinhard Hütter, Lutheran, criticizes Barth for his "abstract ecclesiology." He applauds Barth for early on seeing the importance of real engagement with Rome but is critical of Barth's "dialectical catholicity," which he says is inherently linked to his "disembodied pneumatology." He contrasts Barth with Luther:

> While for Luther the Holy Spirit becomes "embodied" in particular practices (and therefore, for him, a beginning with the concrete practices is also possible in his ecclesiology), for Barth the church's practices remain, as witnessing responses, radically distinguished from the Holy Spirit's activity. . . .
>
> One major challenge for us is to understand the Spirit and the church in a way that avoids transcendental moves by giving due account of the Spirit's embodiment in distinct practices. . . . Only a return to concrete ecclesial traditions, doctrines, and liturgical, communal, and moral practices will allow us to address each other concretely and face the concrete, pressing nature of the brokenness of Christ's body in the world.[89]

When he wrote this, Hütter was a Lutheran professor at Duke Divinity School. Later he became convinced by his own argument, as outlined above, that concrete practices that embodied the Spirit's activity are best found in Roman Catholicism. He therefore became a Roman Catholic. The gist of his criticism is that Barth leaves the Holy Spirit floating in the air. Hütter wants to point to specific church practices, institutions like the papacy and magisterium, and say, here is the Holy Spirit, this is what the Spirit is, and is doing in the church. Does Barth fail to satisfy this request? Evidently, yes.

A related criticism is that the Spirit in Barth's theology is disembodied and potentially redundant. Eugene Rogers, author of a well-known study of Thomas Aquinas and Karl Barth, writes of "The Eclipse of the Spirit in Barth."[90] Even in the first volume of *Church Dogmatics,* the Holy Spirit seems to be redundant since all that the Spirit does is really done by Christ. It is Christ who sets us free for freedom despite the earlier reference to the Spirit.

---

89. Reinhard Hütter, "Karl Barth's 'Dialectical Catholicity,'" in *Bound to Be Free: Evangelical Catholic Engagements in Ecclesiology, Ethics, and Ecumenism* (Grand Rapids: Eerdmans, 2004), pp. 78-94, 92-93.

90. Eugene F. Rogers Jr. "The Eclipse of the Spirit in Karl Barth," in McDowell and Higton, *Conversing with Barth,* pp. 173-90; Philip J. Rosato SJ, *The Spirit as Lord: The Pneumatology of Karl Barth* (Edinburgh: T. & T. Clark, 1981).

Barth may mention the Spirit often but he does not, according to Rogers, give the Spirit a distinct role. He cites the well-known article by the Lutheran theologian and former student of Barth's, Robert Jenson, "You Wonder Where the Spirit Went."[91] Throughout the *Church Dogmatics*, "Christological statements render pneumatological ones superfluous." Or, almost superfluous. Rogers finds more emphasis on the Spirit in the first and then in the final volume of *Church Dogmatics*. He comments: "Appropriately, it is in his belated treatment of the sacraments, at the end of his career, that Barth's doctrine of the Spirit becomes lively again." Through the distinct but related actions of "Baptism with the Spirit" and "Baptism with Water," the Holy Spirit applies the work of Christ to individual human beings. He finds a parallel in what another scholar has said of Gregory Nazianzen's understanding of the Spirit: "What Christ has accomplished universally, the Spirit perfects particularly."[92]

Orthodox theologians criticized Barth because of his support for the "Filioque" clause in the Nicene-Constantinopolitan Creed. Yves Congar agrees with them. In *I Believe in the Holy Spirit*, volume 3, he notes how his own attitude has changed. The point at issue for him is not a dogmatic argument about the Trinity but a canonical argument about authority. The Roman and Western church altered *the* Ecumenical Creed, without consulting the Eastern churches. They may have a theological reason for stating that the Holy Spirit proceeds from the Father *and the Son,* but they had no right to alter the decision of an Ecumenical Council. That they did so was one reason for the divisions between East and West in 1054.[93]

The Church Universal

Colm O'Grady applauds Barth's statement that "the Church is catholic or it is not Church" but feels there is no place in his ecclesiology for the church universal:

91. Robert Jenson, "You Wonder Where the Spirit Went," *Pro Ecclesia* 2 (1993): 296-304.

92. Rogers, "The Eclipse of the Spirit in Karl Barth," p. 187.

93. Yves Congar (1980), ET *I Believe in the Holy Spirit*, vol. 3 (New York: Seabury Press/ London: Geoffrey Chapman, 1983), pp. 204-6. See also Lukas Vischer, ed., *Spirit of God, Spirit of Christ: Ecumenical Reflections on the Filioque Controversy,* Faith and Order Paper 103 (Geneva: WCC/London: SPCK, 1981). Jean-Miguel Garrigues offers a Roman Catholic comment, pp. 149-63; also Alasdair Heron on "The Filioque in Recent Reformed Theology," including Barth, pp. 110-20. See also David Guretzki, *Karl Barth on the Filioque* (Aldershot, UK: Ashgate, 2009).

For Barth there is no universal power of extension of the one Church, nor actual universal extension of one Church. There is a universal plurality of forms of the one Church in self-sameness . . . [but] there is no place in his ecclesiology for a universal Church, nor consequently for the unity of a universal Church.[94]

And earlier he had stated: "I do not think that Barth does justice to the universal and institutional church. Basically his position is that of Congregationalism." And again, "In Barth's ecclesiology there is no place for universality." This is, in O'Grady's judgment, the price Barth has to pay for "the denial of the pope as the successor of him to whom Christ said: "I have prayed for you that your faith may not fail; . . . strengthen your brethren. Feed my lambs. . . . Tend my sheep." This is, of course, a price the Orthodox are also prepared to pay and yet find ways of affirming the church universal in each local community. Barth is vulnerable in O'Grady's eyes because he pays no attention to bishops or indeed any precise form of ordained ministry or hierarchical order.[95]

I mentioned earlier[96] the high-level debate within the Church of Rome between Cardinal Ratzinger as he then was and Cardinal Kasper about which has the priority, the universal or the local? Ratzinger says the universal; Kasper says both have equal priority. Despite the strong emphasis in Barth on the local congregation, he would probably agree with Kasper and with the Orthodox, for Barth sees the local congregation as an expression of the church catholic and universal.

The Question of Woman, a Question Addressed to Barth *and* Rome

Vatican II and Women

Barth has more to say about the partnership of women and men in Church and Society than Vatican II but not enough to help Roman Catholic feminist critics of their own church. Ann Loades (Anglican),[97] the editor of an anthology of feminist theology, Roman Catholic and Protestant, comments that the document on the laity is one of the few places where the contribu-

94. O'Grady, *The Church in Catholic Theology*, p. 305.
95. O'Grady, *The Church in Catholic Theology*, pp. 255, 286.
96. See pages 98-99 and footnote 75.
97. Ann Loades, *Feminist Theology: A Reader* (London: SPCK, 1990), p. 184.

tion of women is even mentioned: "Since women are increasingly taking an active part in the whole life of society, it is important that their participation in the various fields of the church's apostolate should also increase." It sees as an example "those men and women who assisted Paul in the preaching of the gospel" according to Acts 18:18 and Romans 16:3.[98] *Gaudium et Spes* also refers to changes in society, or what the document earlier calls "signs of the times" that the church should respond to: "Women are now at work in almost every sphere of life, and it is fitting that they should play their full part according to their disposition. Everyone should recognise and encourage the sharing in cultural life which is suitable and necessary for women."[99] (It is notable that some women observers helped the Commission prepare this document in which women now get a mention!) There is very little serious theological reflection in such comments. Barth might be pleased and even feel he is being quoted when *Gaudium et Spes* asserts: "God, however, did not create the human person a solitary; from the very beginning 'male and female God created them' (Genesis 1,27), and their coming together brings about the first form of the communion of persons. For by natural constitution the human person is a social being who cannot live or develop without relations with others."[100] It goes on to assert that there is a basic equality between women and men.[101] There is little here that a feminist would call "radical," but we have moved on from times when "catholic theology" assumed that only men were made in the image of God and women had this distinction only by association with men.

What was radical at the time was the invitation to women to attend as auditors at the Council. Never before had women been invited to an ecumenical council and possibly in earlier times, even for Vatican I in 1869-70, few if any had questioned their absence. By 1962 as the Council itself was noting, attitudes had changed. The media and married Protestant observers were among the first to notice. A headline in a Belgian paper said, "The Church is not racist but it does not admit women to its Council." United States Congregationalist observer Douglas Horton wondered what was so unreal about a congregation of 3,000 people and then realized it was the ab-

---

98. *Apostolicam Actuositatem* paras. 9 and 10.

99. *Gaudium et Spes* 60.

100. *Gaudium et Spes* 12; Barth, *Church Dogmatics* III/4, p. 116 — §54 "Freedom in Fellowship," where Barth expounds the theme of "fellow humanity" corresponding to the fact that God himself exists "in relationship and not in isolation."

101. *Gaudium et Spes* 29.

sence of any women.[102] His colleagues Ralph Calder and Viscountess Stansgate contemplated nominating a woman observer.[103] Should the observers set an example they hoped the Council would follow? Horton thought not. Observers were Rome's guests. Even so, a hint to Cardinal Willebrands had been dropped and a moderate response did follow. Karl Rahner, one of the Roman Catholic *periti*, commented: "When the doors of the Second Vatican Council were opened to laymen as well as to clerics it was taken for granted that this applied initially to men only. But in reality the correctness of this assumption is far from self-evident."[104] An expert on world poverty, Lady Jackson (Barbara Ward) was not allowed to address the assembly because she was a woman[105] and attempts were made to bar women journalists from attending Mass at the Council.[106] When at last laypeople were admitted as auditors, they were all men; but a year later, 1964, twenty-three women joined them.[107] And even then they had to be eased in. First they were welcomed in their absence! The pope did not notice that no women had as yet responded to his invitation to attend. The invitations had not been sent! Then they sat at the back. Little by little they were allowed nearer the front. One or two even shared in the Mixed Commission that prepared *Gaudium et Spes* and its cautious recognition of the changing place of women in society.

Barth of course was not there to observe all this, but would he, did he mind? I think he would, though my comment might surprise some of Barth's Roman Catholic feminist critics. In his comments on the *Decree on the Apostolate of the Laity,* Barth asks: "Does the desire that the laity be active include also the women mentioned in this paragraph?" He notes as part of this question

102. Carmel McEnroy, *Guests in Their Own House: The Women of Vatican II* (New York: Crossroads, 1996), p. 13.

103. Ralph Calder to Douglas Horton, 7 April 1964, in Theodore Louis Trost, *Douglas Horton and the Ecumenical Impulse in American Religion* (Cambridge, MA: Harvard University Press, 2002), p. 224. Viscountess Stansgate became best known in England as the mother of the famous Labour politician Tony Benn. She offered to help fund a woman observer if the idea was acceptable. They consulted Cardinal Willebrands.

104. Karl Rahner, "The Position of Woman in the New Situation in Which the Church Finds Herself," ET David Bourke, *Theological Investigations VIII*, pp. 75-93, 82.

105. *History of Vatican II*, vol. 4, pp. 25, 27. Later she did take "an outstanding part" in the 1971 Synod of Bishops. See Joan Morris, *Against Nature and God* (Oxford: Mowbray, 1974), p. 173.

106. Anne E. Carr, *Transforming Grace: Christian Tradition and Women's Experience* (San Francisco: Harper & Row), p. 30.

107. Their names are given in McEnroy, *Guests in Their Own House,* p. 297. Women could attend the third and fourth sessions, 1964 and 1965.

that this lay activity is to be exercised "both in the Church and in the world, in both the spiritual and temporal orders." He also questions why the lay apostolate of men and women is seen as a response to "the needs of the times" rather than an implication of seeing the church as "People [*laos*] of God."[108]

Women Arguing with Barth

On the eve of Vatican II one of Karl Rahner's Jesuit students, Haye Van der Meer, submitted a doctoral thesis, *Women Priests in the Catholic Church?*[109] Its author had clearly read Karl Barth and his assistant, Charlotte von Kirschbaum, and was well informed about debates in other churches, especially in the Lutheran churches of Scandinavia and in the Church of England. Even at this relatively early stage, the work shows how Roman Catholics found it impossible to ignore what other churches were saying about the role of women in the church even when they were convinced that other churches were wrong. But Van der Meer's thesis is tantalizing! He keeps his own personal convictions pretty much to himself. He says he has no wish to say whether the policy of the Roman Catholic Church is right or even whether it could be altered. So why do all this research for nothing? One might well ask! And he is also cautious in his criticisms of Barth. He tells us he cannot go along with Barth where Barth rejects the idea of spelling out male and female characteristics, but this is because it might raise too many other issues. Yet this is actually quite important. Some of the arguments against the ordination of women are based on male assumptions about the nature of women. It is important for feminists that Barth tries to avoid such stereotyping. Van der Meer appears to take a stronger line when he disagrees with Barth about the exegesis of 1 Corinthians 14:34ff., about women being silent in the congregation. Van der Meer says that even this passage is not at all clear "in forbidding women to speak in the congregation completely for all time." Barth says the injunctions have to be taken seriously but that "it is certainly foolish to try to make an inflexible rule of the particular interpretation of Paul in this instance."[110] Agreed! Alas, in this instance, Barth does

108. Karl Barth, *Ad Limina Apostolorum*, p. 31.

109. Haye Van der Meer (1962), ET Arlene and Leonard Swidler, *Women Priests in the Catholic Church: A Theological and Historical Investigation* (Philadelphia: Temple University Press, 1973).

110. Van der Meer, *Women Priests in the Catholic Church*, p. 23; Barth, *Church Dogmatics* III/4, p. 156.

succumb to stereotyping when he insists that "[t]he essential point is that woman must always and in all circumstances be woman; that she must feel and conduct herself as such and not as a man."[111] He would need to reread de Beauvoir more carefully. She is famous for asserting that "one is not born a woman, rather one becomes a woman." Being male or female is not simply biological but a social construct.

Roman Catholic feminists tend to dismiss Barth. Foremost among them is Mary Daly. Daly in *Beyond God the Father* (1973) links together Tertullian, Clement, Jerome, Augustine, Aquinas, Luther, Calvin, Knox, Barth, Bonhoeffer, and Teilhard de Chardin and refers to "the blatant misogynism of these men," a view that is quoted and supported by another feminist writer, Anne E. Carr.[112] Daly became so critical of her own church that she ceased being a Roman Catholic but not before commenting: "Meanwhile in other Christian churches things have not really been that different. Theologian Karl Barth proclaimed that woman is ontologically subordinate to man as her 'head.'"[113] Mary Daly became the first woman to preach at Harvard in its 336-year history. This was in 1971. She said she was tired of being told that "in Christ there is neither male or female" (Gal. 3:28) for "everywhere else there damn well is!"[114] In a later book, *Pure Lust* (1984), Barth is dismissed for his "sadomasochistic theology." Such comments do not really help. What is lacking in Daly and others is an attempt to understand why Barth thinks as he does and then carefully expose the weaknesses in his arguments. Any careful reader can discern that Barth is not at his best even when being prompted by his theological assistant, Charlotte von Kirschbaum. He is struggling to assert that women and men are equal and that subordination does not mean inferiority; that it is equally good for men to lead and equally good for women to follow. Similar expositions, particularly of Paul, can be found in Barth's Swiss and Reformed contemporary, Jean-Jacques von Allmen's *Maris et Femmes d'après Saint Paul* (1951).[115] The argument is not convincing. But

---

111. *Church Dogmatics* III/4, p. 156.

112. Mary Daly, *Beyond God the Father* (Boston: Beacon Press, 1973, 1977), p. 22; Carr, *Transforming Grace*, p. 98.

113. Daly, *Beyond God the Father*, p. 3.

114. Loades, *Feminist Theology: A Reader*, p. 186.

115. Jean-Jacques von Allmen, *Maris et Femmes d'après Saint Paul* (Paris: Delachaux et Niestlé, 1951), p. 36. Von Allmen argues that the best aid to the emancipation of women is the evangelization of men away from attitudes of domination and tyranny to being a loving husband. The hierarchical relationship of husbands to wives reflects that of Christ to the church as in Ephesians 5.

given the fact that in Barth's lifetime women in Switzerland still did not have the vote, feminists might ask whether for all his expositions of Scripture, Barth is here more influenced by the patriarchal attitudes of Swiss men than by open-minded listening for the Word of God. Some Reformed churches in Switzerland had ordained women in the 1920s and 1930s; most did not do so until 1966, that is, only shortly before Barth's death in 1968. Though not a feminist, Barth was ahead of most of his Swiss contemporaries both in his support for the extension of the franchise and the ordination of women. In an essay that first appeared in 1946, "The Christian Community and the Civil Community," he stated:

> If, in accordance with a specifically Christian insight, it lies in the very na-
> ture of the State that this equality must not be restricted by any difference
> of religious belief or unbelief, it is all the more important for the Church
> to urge that the restriction of political freedom and responsibility not
> only of certain classes and races but, supremely, of that of women is an
> arbitrary convention which does not deserve to be preserved any longer.
> If Christians are to be consistent there can be only one possible decision
> in this matter.[116]

In his lectures on *Evangelical Theology*, delivered in Chicago in 1962, Barth scolds his countrymen's "narrow-minded rejection of voting rights for women."[117] He did not live to see those rights being granted. Women were also excluded from voting in some Reformed church councils and to this, too, Barth strongly objected: "The exclusion of women from parochial and synodical synods is undoubtedly an arbitrary convention — an anom-aly which in our church, as in others, deserves only to be abolished." He welcomed the fact that Zurich had decided in favor of women voting in the church in a resolution dated July 1963.[118] Barth also supported the ordina-tion of women. He entered into heated newspaper discussion on this issue in 1932.[119]

---

116. Karl Barth, "The Christian Community and the Civil Community" (1946), in *Com-munity, State and Church* (Gloucester, MA: Peter Smith, 1968), p. 175.

117. Karl Barth, ET Grover Foley, *Evangelical Theology: An Introduction* (London: Collins Fontana, 1965), p. 77.

118. Karl Barth, *Letters 1961-1968*, p. 175.

119. See Letter of Eduard Thurneysen to Barth, 21 July 1932 and notes, *Karl Barth-Eduard Thurneysen Briefwechsel*, Band 3 (Zürich: Theologischer Verlag, 2000), pp. 244-45; Renate Köbler, *In the Shadow of Karl Barth: Charlotte von Kirschbaum* (Louisville: Westminster John Knox, 1989), p. 108.

Unlike the Vatican Council before its final sessions, Barth did have female counselors. They included Henrietta Visser 't Hooft, wife of the first General Secretary of the World Council of Churches, Sarah Chakko, first woman President in the WCC, and of course his longtime secretary and theological assistant, Charlotte von Kirschbaum, author of *The Question of Woman.* Critics like Mary Grey think von Kirschbaum deserves more than a passing reference or occasional footnote.

Be that as it may, all three were capable of arguing with Barth and did so from early on in his professorial career. But he also conceded that "the question of what woman is or should be is a matter for woman herself to decide." Rahner admitted that his own essay "The Position of Woman" did not say much.[120] As a married man with a family of sons and daughters, Barth was better placed than a celibate priest and professor like Rahner to listen to women. Critics will tell us he did not always hear what they were saying.

Henrietta Visser 't Hooft engaged in an argument with Barth as early as March 1934. Her question is prompted by Barth's Commentary on Paul's First Letter to the Corinthians, *The Resurrection of the Dead,* and his acceptance of Paul's argument that "man was not created for woman's sake, but woman for the sake of man." In response, Barth wrote a friendly letter the following month but with a detailed defense of Paul. She wrote again in May, stating that she thought Barth had not really understood her question. The letter remained unanswered though to be fair to Barth, he was now embroiled in the church conflict with Hitler and about to be expelled from Germany and his teaching post in Bonn. Undeterred, she takes up the correspondence with Barth in 1941, this time asking for his reaction to an article she had written in 1934, *Eva, wo bist du?,* but again receives no reply. This is a pity, for she expounds a critical point that both Barth and Paul overlook, that Jesus himself, in Mark 10, gave priority to Genesis 1:27 where man and woman are together made in the image of God and there is no suggestion there, in contrast to Genesis 2, that man was created first and so has priority. Soon after the Amsterdam Assembly of 1948, she voices her despair: "Why is Professor Barth so destructive on the question of women's work in the Church and for the Church?" She had, however, helped to persuade her husband, as General Secretary of the World Council of Churches, that the relationship of women and men, their co-humanity in God's covenant, was "one of the deepest, unsolved problems of humanity." Willem Visser 't Hooft therefore

---

120. Karl Rahner, "The Position of Woman in the New Situation in Which the Church Finds Herself," *Theological Investigations* VIII, pp. 75-93.

supported his wife in establishing in the WCC a department for the Cooperation of Men and Women in Church and Society.

Visser 't Hooft's original mistake was to give Barth a leading role at Amsterdam in the establishing of such a department. The women involved soon got the impression that Barth was not taking them seriously, even when they quoted Paul in Galatians on the overcoming of all discrimination between master and slave, man and woman in Christ. Barth described his own experience in the group as absolutely shattering. He had never been so terrified. Eberhard Busch gives this more restrained account of the encounter. Barth "did not succeed in convincing the 'Christian women'" that "besides writing Galatians 3.28 (which was about the one thing that they joyfully affirmed), Paul also said several other things on the relation between men and women which were important and right."[121] Among his critics was Sarah Chakko, an Orthodox Syrian woman from India, first Chairperson of the Commission on the Life and Work of Women in the Church and shortly to become the first woman President in the WCC. She proved herself more than a match for Barth.

Sarah Chakko, Madeleine Barot, famous for her Bible studies at Bossey, and Cornelia van Asch van Wyck asked for a meeting with Barth to discuss his exposition of Genesis 2 and texts in Paul. Visser 't Hooft describes their confrontation.

> Barth was especially scared of Sarah Chakko. Maybe it was because there was something so dignified about Sarah. She had something a little royal about her. And she really challenged him. She contended with the others that, having affirmed the woman and given such a beautiful exegesis of her place in the Genesis account of Creation, he somehow "pulled the rug out from underneath" when he turned to the Pauline teachings on the place of women. He then undid whatever good might have been done by his Genesis commentary.[122]

It is only fair to point out that in the setting of the WCC a woman like Sarah Chakko and her colleagues were free to argue with Barth. Her Roman

---

121. Eberhard Busch, ET John Bowden, *Karl Barth: His Life from Letters and Autobiographical Texts* (London: SCM, 1976), p. 358. Paul in Galatians 3:27-28 states: "Baptized into union with him, you have all put on Christ like a garment. There is no such thing as Jew and Greek, slave and freeman, male and female; for you are all one person in Christ Jesus."

122. M. Kurian, *Sarah Chakko: A Voice of Women in the Ecumenical Movement* (Thiruvalla, India: Christhava, 1998), p. 99.

Catholic sisters could not argue with the pope or even with the fathers at the Council, for some subjects were off limits. "Women" among them! The ordination of women to the priesthood is not open for discussion even though eminent Roman Catholic theologians like Nicholas Lash and Lavinia Byrne wish to discuss it. We are simply told, this time by the Sacred Congregation for the Doctrine of the Faith (1976), that "the Church in fidelity to the example of the Lord does not consider herself authorised to admit women to priestly ordination." In May 1994, Pope John Paul II published an open letter stating that the question of women's ordination was definitely closed. The following year, Carmel McEnroy lost her job because of her "public dissent" with Magisterial teaching because she persisted in discussing the issue. Two thousand people signed a letter of support, urging the pope to let the debate continue.[123] The Vatican response is that the issue is closed. There is nothing to discuss. The first disciples were all men. End of argument! Or, are the implications of Jesus' choice a subject for debate? According to at least one Roman Catholic expert, such teaching cannot be regarded as "infallible" even when repeated by a pope.[124] And George Tavard asks and answers his own question: "Who can authorise the Church to do what it has never done before if not the Church itself as it is guided by the Holy Spirit to act upon new discernments of the signs of the times?"[125]

Vatican II in fact opened up a discussion that no pope is able to suppress. I soon discovered a wealth of literature on the subject, much of it challenging, sometimes openly provocative. One is introduced to Deborah Halter, Executive Director of the Women's Ordinations Conference in the United States and author of *The Papal "No": A Comprehensive Guide to the Vatican's Rejection of Women's Ordination*[126] and a set of essays edited by James Coriden, *Sexism and Church Law*.[127] Canon Law can be quoted in support of an open debate, for according to Canon 212:3, quoted by Halter: it can indeed be the duty of "the Christian faithful" to voice their opinions on matters that concern the good of the church, the common good, and the dignity of persons. And those like Halter who take this advice to heart wish

123. McEnroy, *Guests in Their Own House*, p. 273.

124. Kelley A. Raab, *When Women Become Priests: The Catholic Women's Ordination Debate* (New York: Columbia University Press, 2000), p. 32.

125. George Tavard, *Vatican II and the Ecumenical Way* (Milwaukee: Marquette University Press, 2007), p. 35.

126. Deborah Halter, *The Papal "No": A Comprehensive Guide to the Vatican's Rejection of Women's Ordination* (New York: Crossroad, 2004).

127. James Coriden, *Sexism and Church Law*, cited by Deborah Halter.

to assure us that they are asking questions about the male-only priesthood "not as an act of thoughtless rebellion" but rather as "an act of loyal reflection that leads to and nurtures a mature faith." When we are children we may have to accept "no" for an answer, but as mature adults we need to know the reasons why. In theory, this was recognized by the Congregation for the Doctrine of the Faith. The Commission's President, Archbishop Enrico Bartoletti, said that the purpose of *Inter Insigniores,* The Declaration on the Admission of Women to the Ministerial Priesthood (1976), was to help the faithful understand why ordination was "not being granted to women." He had told Pope Paul VI that it was "urgent to give a fully justified answer" to women's exclusion rather than issue a disciplinary "niet!"[128] But it is fair to add that though women are excluded in theory, in practice they are in demand for their pastoral ministrations. In Quebec, for example, 70 percent of the church's pastoral work is carried out by women.[129]

Women like Henrietta Visser 't Hooft and Sarah Chakko did not find Barth's reasoning convincing, let alone that of the Doctrine of the Faith, but they were allowed to argue with Barth. Sarah Chakko was not primarily interested in questions of ordination in her own Orthodox tradition or in other churches. She is a spokesperson for women at a time when the laity, women and men, were being rediscovered. See the pioneering studies by Yves Congar OP and Hendrik Kraemer (Reformed).[130] In response to questions at the Amsterdam Assembly on a report on the "Life and Work of Women in the Churches," she said that "the question of the ordination of women was only a minor part of the whole problem. There were many other matters relating to the service of women which it would be good to discuss, and it surely could not be so very dangerous to discuss the ordination of women."[131] Here she was not simply voicing her own opinion but reporting on the answers to a questionnaire sent out by the World Council to its member churches. This had evoked what Visser 't Hooft, the General Secretary, described as "an extraordinarily wide and keen response and had made it clear that this ['Life and Work of Women in the Churches'] had become a vital issue in many

128. Halter, *The Papal "No,"* p. 42.

129. Mary Ellen Sheehan, "Vatican II and the Ministry of Women in the Church," in *Vatican II and Its Legacy,* ed. Mathijs Lamberigts (Leuven: Leuven University Press, 2002), pp. 469-86, 479.

130. Yves Congar (1957), ET Donald Attwater *Lay People in the Church,* rev. ed. (London: Geoffrey Chapman, 1965); Hendrik Kraemer, *A Theology of the Laity* (London: Lutterworth, 1958). The WCC also established a Department of the Laity and a journal *Laity,* 1955-1968.

131. Kurian, *Sarah Chakko,* p. 98.

countries." And the amount of material collected was so considerable that the report Sarah Chakko referred to could only be regarded as a very short and provisional summary. A fuller report was needed and was indeed produced some four years later, edited by another distinguished ecumenical pioneer, Kathleen Bliss. It also showed that "Women and the Ordained Ministry" was not the only issue of concern to women and their churches and ended with this interesting observation from a woman in Berlin:

> The questions you have asked are certainly very interesting but please do not be angry if I say that the most important question has not been asked at all. The life of the church is no longer carried on chiefly through its organisations, but in the houses and families, the factories and offices where Christians meet with others. So the first question should be: What does the Church mean in the lives of women? What chance does the Church give to women to be its representatives at home and in their work?[132]

Ecumenical bodies can claim to have pioneered the way. The WCC inquiry into the "Service and Status of Women in the Churches" preceded by twenty years a similar investigation by the Roman Catholic Church among its own members. Roman Catholic women like Lavinia Byrne tell us that though she had raised questions about women's ordination back in 1988, the issue ceased to be so abstract and academic once she started working with a national ecumenical body, what was then the Council of Churches for Britain and Ireland, now Churches Together in Britain and Ireland. She then came into contact with ordained women ministers in different churches and could see for herself how genuine and effective was their vocation to serve God in this way. How can something that is right in one church be regarded as so wrong in another? And other women like Elisabeth Wendel-Moltmann, who experienced the loneliness of pioneering a trail for women theologians and women ministers, tell us that "the question of women" can only be answered by women and men, from different churches, working together. She pays tribute to the help she received from Iwand, Wolf, Weber and, not least, her husband Jürgen Moltmann, and to other ecumenically minded theologians like Hans Küng and Philip Potter, one-time General Secretary of the World Council of Churches and currently married to one of Germany's women bishops. Sadly, she has this comment to add: "Barth and Bonhoeffer, whom I had previously regarded as important social thinkers,

---

132. Kathleen Bliss, *The Service and Status of Women in the Churches* (London: SCM, 1952), pp. 9, 201.

were no good on the women's question." But she also admits that one of the few books available for women like herself, who were only just beginning to question the fact that the church was "Man's Church," was the book by Barth's assistant, Charlotte von Kirschbaum's *Die Wirkliche Frau,* first published in 1944. Reading Kirschbaum today may only make us conscious of its date. But then we need to appreciate that she and Barth were pioneers. Indeed, Barth scholar Clifford Green comments that Barth deserves credit "for being perhaps the only European male theologian addressing these issues in the 1940's and 1950's." In doing so, Barth acknowledged his debt to *Die Wirkliche Frau* and to Charlotte von Kirschbaum. In the Preface to *Church Dogmatics* III/3, written in 1950, he says how much he and his readers owe

> to the twenty years of work quietly accomplished at my side by Charlotte von Kirschbaum. She has devoted no less of her life and powers to the growth of this work than I have myself. Without her co-operation it would not have advanced from day to day, and I should hardly dare contemplate the future which may yet remain to me. I know what it really means to have a helper *(Gegenuber).*[133]

The reference is to God's word to Adam that "it is not good for man to be alone." God provides a partner or helpmeet.

"Helpmeet," from the Authorized Version of Genesis 2:20's description of Eve, is easily misunderstood as suggesting woman's subordination to man. It is good to be reminded that when the expression is used in the Old Testament, in fifteen out of twenty-one instances it refers to God as the helper of humanity, hardly a subordinate role! Barth's personal relationship with von Kirschbaum, his secretary, was and may always be a matter of some controversy; so too the question of the actual contribution she made to his work and how far the *Church Dogmatics* was their joint project. Her own illness and death was one of the reasons why the work was never finished. Gentler judgments by scholars like Green may help us regard the Barth-Kirschbaum professional relationship as an illustration or paradigm of the man-woman relationship described in *Church Dogmatics* III/4/§54, "Freedom in Fellowship." The man-woman relationship experienced by von Kirschbaum and described in this section and in her own book would not suit today's feminists. It comes too close to what Halter calls "anthropological subordinationalism" as found in Aristotle, Augustine, and Aquinas. Barth tries hard to make the

133. *Church Dogmatics* III/3, p. xiii.

point that men and women are equal but different. The difference is that the man leads, the woman follows, but this does not mean that woman is inferior to man. The same point had been made by von Kirschbaum. The argument is based on some readings of Scripture. And therein lies a problem that Barth's critics, Henrietta Visser 't Hooft and Sarah Chakko, had once pointed out and that Clifford Green explains. Barth was overanxious to hold together different parts of Scripture and not face the conflict that has to be recognized between Galatians 3:28 and texts that call on women to be obedient to their husbands and keep silent in church.[134]

Moving on from Barth: Post–Vatican II Partnership of Barth Scholars and Feminists

If Protestant feminists like Elisabeth Wendel-Moltmann found little support from Barth, and if Roman Catholic feminists rarely troubled to look for help in his direction, this need not be the last word. We can have a shared concern for the good of the church as a whole and the Roman Catholic Church in particular. By her attitude to women, the Roman Catholic Church continues to alienate many of her most faithful women supporters. Pope John XXIII may have opened a window in the Vatican so that the Holy Spirit could blow in, but as far as women like Deborah Halter are concerned, it is a case of "Vatican II: A Window Unopened."[135] Sister Joan Chittister writes of "one step forward, two steps back." Women cannot feel completely at home in a man's church.[136] Open discussion is still strongly discouraged, sometimes censored, as in Deborah Halter's own case. Barth scholars who are free to debate and are prepared to argue with Barth, and who are sympathetic to "the question of woman" can liberate us all from the sort of theological reasoning that has only served to keep women out of positions of leadership in any church, especially the Church of Rome. Help is available from the ecumenical community of women and men and their theological *periti*. Help is also available from Barth himself and from scholars who acknowledge how

---

134. Clifford Green, "Karl Barth's Treatment of the Man-Woman Relationship: Issues for Theological Method," in *Reflections on Bonhoeffer*, ed. Geoffrey B. Kelly (Chicago: Covenant Publications, 1999), pp. 228-40.

135. Halter, *The Papal "No,"* ch. 3.

136. Joan Chittister OSB, "Wanted, the Other Half of the Church," in Austen Ivereigh, ed., *Unfinished Journey: The Church Forty Years after Vatican II* (London/New York: Continuum, 2003), pp. 95-96.

much they have learned from him. Here I list a number of points made by Barth and Barth scholars, finding where possible, Roman Catholic comment on the same themes.

But first a word of encouragement from Charlotte von Kirschbaum herself. She said in 1949 that she was searching for a (Protestant) Doctrine of Woman: "May others, who can do it better, take up this concern of ours and continue the quest."[137] Even her search was in its own way ecumenical, for she was engaged in discussion with a popular Roman Catholic writer, Gertrud Le Fort, author of *Die Ewige Frau* (1934), Edith Stein, a convert from Judaism, and Simone de Beauvoir, the author of *Le Deuxieme Sexe* (1949) who was influenced by the existentialism of Jean-Paul Sartre.[138] She also quotes an Anglican clergyman, R. W. Howard, and a series of lecture-sermons he gave in Oxford on the theme *Should Women Be Priests?*[139]

Barth was not interested in "political correctness" or keeping up to date with the "signs of the times." He was critical of *Gaudium et Spes,* one of the few Council documents that has much to say about women — women helped to write it! — for its lack of a theological base. Pope John Paul II's encyclical *Mulieris Dignitatem: On the Dignity and Vocation of Women* (1988) does have a stronger theology. It takes as a key text, Galatians 4:4, "God sent forth his Son, born of a woman." Barth's starting point is different and from the point of view of partnership, better. We, women and men, are partners, in a covenant relationship with God and with one another. The fundamental relationship is that between two people who are different but equal, between man and woman. Our "ordination to be in covenant relation with God" has as its counterpart that our humanity has by its very nature the character of co-humanity.[140]

Barth is more concerned with the service of the community rather than with "office" and hence with the vocation of *all* Christian women and men. The Roman Catholic theologian Elisabeth Schüssler Fiorenza can sympathize with this. She explains in *The Discipleship of Equals* (1993) that from

---

137. From the Foreword to *Die Wirkliche Frau* (1949); *The Question of Woman*, p. 53.

138. *Church Dogmatics* III/4, pp. 161, 172; Helena M. Tomko, *Sacramental Realism: Gertrud Le Fort and German Catholic Literature in the Weimar Republic and Third Reich, 1924-1946* (London: Maney Publishing, 2007).

139. Charlotte von Kirschbaum, *The Question of Woman*, p. 202; R. W. Howard, *Should Women Be Priests?* (Oxford: Basil Blackwell, 1949). The Synod of the Church of England answered Howard's question in 1992. In 2014 it decided that women could also become bishops.

140. Karl Barth, "Freedom in Fellowship: Man and Woman," *Church Dogmatics* III/4, pp. 116-240.

her first book on "the ministries of women in the Church," *Der vergessene Partner* (1964), she was not primarily concerned with arguing for women's ordination "because this might only enhance the clericalisation of the church." "Only such a positive theological understanding of lay ministry can provide the basis for the professional ministry of women."[141]

Barth scholar, translator, and at one time possible successor to Barth in Basel, Thomas Torrance, makes a number of points in his argument for the ordination of women that directly or indirectly have Barth's support.[142]

- First, as in Barth, the virgin birth of Jesus means the setting aside of the male in the conception of Jesus and so rules out any claims to male superiority.
- Torrance goes on to make the point that is clear in the Greek text of the Creed but obscured by what were then the current English translations. These state that "Jesus Christ . . . for us *men* and our salvation . . . was incarnate of the Holy Spirit and the Virgin Mary and became man." Modern translations now say "for us" and that Christ became "truly human." The Greek word, *anthropos,* embraces men and women where "man" no longer does. Likewise, we are to understand "The Word became flesh" in John 1, as affirming the humanity rather than the masculinity of Christ. Hence it is wrong to argue from the incarnation to the essential maleness of priests if they are to represent Christ. Christ, as divine and human, transcends categories of gender.
- Further, it is, in Torrance's view and that of Archbishop George Carey, whom he cites, "a serious theological error" to see the male priest as essential if the priest is to be an eikon of Christ. This is to misunderstand the whole biblical notion of eikon or image. It is an expression of our human relationship to God. Torrance, even more than Barth, has made a study of the church "fathers" and asserts that to the best of his knowledge no council of the universal church ever claimed that only a male human being could image or represent Christ. "This strange pseudo-theological idea is a modern innovation evidently put forward by some rather reactionary churchmen in the 19th century." Torrance's argument against the misuse of the idea of representation of Christ has more recently been supported by Methodist theologian Frances Young

141. Elisabeth Schüssler Fiorenza, *The Discipleship of Equals: A Critical Feminist Ekklesia-logy of Liberation* (London: SCM, 1993), pp. 13, 15, 17.

142. T. F. Torrance, *The Ministry of Women* (Edinburgh: Handsel Press, 1992).

and studies by a Jesuit, John D. Laurence, *"Priest" as a Type of Christ.* In theory, any baptized Christian, man, woman, or child, can represent Christ and is called to do so.[143]

- It is only fair to concede that Torrance does not deal with claims that because the church is the Bride of Christ, the priest as representative of Christ needs to be male. For Torrance, it is Christ who presides at the eucharist. Human beings do not take his place.

Barth scholars Clifford Green,[144] Paul Fiddes,[145] and Timothy Gorringe[146] support the criticisms made earlier by Henrietta Visser 't Hooft and Sarah Chakko of Barth's uncritical use of New Testament texts that are assumed to support woman's subordinate role. Trevor Hart, another Barth scholar, dismissed the way such texts are used by those opposed to women's ordination as though their meaning was "crystal clear." Describing himself as an "evangelical" theologian, he quotes and rejects the sort of statement made in this case by a fellow evangelical theologian, Roger Beckwith of Oxford:

> One cannot fail to see that, according to Biblical teaching, men and women can no more cease to be in a relationship of authority and subordination than they can cease to be the creatures of God. [Hence] the exclusion of the subordinate partner in the human race from the principal offices in the Christian ministry . . . is as inevitable today as it was in the first century.[147]

Contrary to Roger Beckwith, one can study the New Testament and fail to see what he sees. Rome set up a Biblical Commission to do just that and reached the conclusion that the Scriptures themselves did not rule out the ordination of women to the priesthood. John Wijngaards made a study of

143. Frances Young, *Presbyteral Ministry in the Catholic Tradition* (London: Methodist Sacramental Fellowship, 1994); John D. Laurence SJ, *"Priest" as a Type of Christ* (New York: Peter Lang, 1984).

144. Green, "Karl Barth's Treatment of the Man-Woman Relationship."

145. Paul Fiddes, "The Status of Women in the Thought of Karl Barth," in *After Eve,* ed. Janet Martin Soskice (London: Collins, 1990), pp. 138-55. Paul Fiddes is Baptist; Janet Martin Soskice is Roman Catholic.

146. Timothy Gorringe, *Karl Barth: Against Hegemony* (Oxford: Oxford University Press, 1999), pp. 207, 209, 229. Gorringe says, "We can accept his [Barth's] fundamental theological principles without his unacceptable conclusions."

147. Cited in Trevor Hart, *Evangelicals and the Ordination of Women to the Priesthood* (Edinburgh: Movement for Whole Ministry, Occasional Publication 7, 1994), pp. 4-5.

nine biblical texts cited in arguments against the ordination of women. None stood up to closer scrutiny. He was shocked to see how the papal declaration *Inter Insigniores* simply ignored the advice of the Biblical Commission.[148] A very balanced account of Paul's teaching on women and post-Pauline traditions is given by Roman Catholic scholar Elisabeth Schüssler Fiorenza in her well-known study, *In Memory of Her: A Feminist Theological Reconstruction of Christian Origins*. Paul did affirm Christian equality and freedom as in Galatians 3:28, but the way he applied this understanding to the needs of the Corinthian congregation could set a precedent for Christian teaching about the subordination of women that was developed in the post-Pauline tradition.[149]

This "post-Pauline" tradition of woman's subordination may also be evident in the Lutheran concept of "Orders of Creation," which Dietrich Bonhoeffer accepted but Barth himself sought to reject. Renate Bethge, wife of Bonhoeffer's biographer, endured the consequences when they asked Bonhoeffer to give the address at their wedding. He told the couple: "You Eberhard have all the responsibility . . . and you, Renate, will help your husband and find your happiness in that."[150] Alas, Karl Barth, often Bonhoeffer's mentor, might have said the same! And suffered the same rebuke from such a woman! Though did Renate Bethge think that way in 1943 or only much later?

In Memory of Her by Elisabeth Schüssler Fiorenza exposed the fact that though Jesus said the woman who anointed him would forever be remembered, the men who wrote the Gospels forgot her name. The woman who first discovered that Jesus was alive is also sometimes forgotten or otherwise maligned. Marga Bührig, a President of the WCC, criticizes Barth for making no mention of Mary Magdalene in his Commentary on the resurrection witnesses in 1 Corinthians 15.[151] But Charlotte von Kirschbaum dismisses Mary Magdalene's claim to be called "apostle to the apostles."[152] Since then,

---

148. John Wijngaards, *The Ordination of Women in the Catholic Church* (London: Darton, Longman & Todd, 2001), pp. 4-6; McEnroy, *Guests in Their Own House*, p. 270.

149. Elisabeth Schüssler Fiorenza, *In Memory of Her* (London: SCM, 1983), p. 236. See also footnote 150.

150. Renate Bethge, "Bonhoeffer's Picture of Women," in Guy Carter et al., *Bonhoeffer's Ethics* (Kampen: Kok Pharos, 1991), pp. 194-99; Dietrich Bonhoeffer, "A Wedding Sermon from a Prison Cell," May 1943, in *Letters and Papers from Prison*, enlarged ed. (London: SCM, 1971), pp. 41-47.

151. Marga Bührig, *Woman Invisible: A Personal Odyssey in Christian Feminism* with Postscript by Lavinia Byrne (London: Burns & Oates, 1993), p. 21.

152. Charlotte von Kirschbaum, *The Question of Woman*, pp. 78-79.

New Testament scholarship has taken more notice of these "invisible women."[153] All credit to Barth that in his Commentary on Romans 16 he defends the fact that Romans was addressed to real women and men, laypeople, who might have understood Paul better than the theologians! He also notes that "[i]n the middle of the first century a community-sister took the letter from Corinth to Rome."[154] Where would we be without Phoebe, or Junia?![155] A later commentator, James Dunn, points out that a third of those giving leadership in the house churches in Rome were women.[156] Carmel McEnroy, speaking up for the women at Vatican II, ends with this plea:

> Women of the Church everywhere claim your power. As successors of Mary Magdalene — not the sinful woman, but the apostle to the apostles, fulfil the command of Jesus to go and tell Peter and the other disciples what you see and hear: Jesus is risen and continues to rise in women and all who are put down in church and society.[157]

Can Barth, with the Help of His Critics, Women and Men, Help Reform Rome?

Hans Küng was probably not the first to tell Barth that he would never understand the Roman Catholic Church simply by reading Denzinger. He quoted Rahner's reference to "the vicious circle of Denzinger theology."[158] Constitutions and legal documents can't give you the feel for a living church. This is why Alberigo and his colleagues in the *History of Vatican II* argue very convincingly that it is not enough to read the Council documents. You need also to enter into the debates. Barth, as we know, was not able to do this until after the Council. Had he done so earlier, he would have relished the sort of encounters between bishops, experts, and observers that are now so powerfully described in Yves Congar's recently translated *My Journal of the Council*.

---

153. See for example Ann Graham Brock (Lutheran), *Mary Magdalene: The First Apostle, the Struggle for Authority* (Cambridge, MA: Harvard University Press, 2003).

154. Karl Barth, *The Epistle to the Romans* on Romans 16:1-16.

155. On Junia, see Eldon Jay Epp, *Junia: The First Woman Apostle* (Minneapolis: Fortress Press, 2005).

156. James D. G. Dunn, *Romans 9–16*, Word Biblical Commentary (Dallas: Word, 1988).

157. McEnroy, *Guests in Their Own House*, p. 272.

158. Küng, *Justification*, p. 109.

Congar gave strict instructions that his *Journal* was not to be published until after his death. We can see why! He offers quite sharp comments about many of his contemporaries and is not afraid to criticize the pope, Paul VI, for making ecumenical gestures but not having the depth of theology to carry them through. Such comments and the honest accounts of weak moments in the Council that one finds both in Congar and *The History* portray a church that is not afraid to admit its failings but is bent on searching for a better way. Barth at his best wanted to be part of that process. That is why the Catholic critics of Barth tend to be very sympathetic in their criticisms of him and why we non–Roman Catholics should accept that Barth's own theology is in need of further reformation, not least by faithful women as well as men.

But Congar, too, has his women critics. The Dominican sister Cecily Boulding has lovingly helped translate a *Journal* of nearly a thousand pages but can't resist this comment before ending with respectful admiration for one of the last century's greatest Christian ecumenists: "Congar was an inveterate grumbler; the *Journal* is laced throughout with a stream of criticisms and complaints." But much more attractive is Congar's account of his personal debt to his own mother, Tere, who died during the Council, and the fact that when, at some major ceremony, little Catholic boys were given a leading role, Congar asked, "But why were there no little girls?"[159] If there had been then (1965), they would be mature Christian women now who still desperately need our support and a church in which they feel "at home."[160]

---

159. Mary Cecily Boulding OP, "Congar at the Second Vatican Council," in Yves Congar, *My Journal of the Council,* pp. xxxvii-xlvi, xlvi.

160. Many women would also not feel at home in the Church of England after its vote in the House of Laity, 20 November 2012, not to accept women bishops. Synod in February 2014 later agreed that women could be bishops and could be consecrated later that year. Earlier, opponents tended to revive two old arguments: first, that it is not "catholic teaching"; second, that it is not biblical. Both arguments can be challenged, and a careful reading of Barth and the Bible will help, especially if all can agree that for Barth and the Bible the question of women's place in church and society was still in process of debate, that there are unresolved contradictions. Even so, Barth supported the ordination of women as ministers, and if he had Reformed doubts about bishops these had nothing to do with whether bishops were male or female but more to do with hegemony and prelatical domination of the kind the citizens in Calvin's Geneva had once endured when a bishop and his army laid siege to the city.

CHAPTER SIX

Differences That Still Divide?

After Vatican II, Are There Still Differences That Divide?

Vatican II opened up a path for dialogue that Rome had previously barred. The dialogues continue and have achieved some notable agreements such as the Joint Declaration on Justification by Faith. The question is, are there still some church-dividing differences? My hunch is that the only church-dividing difference is the church itself. This is also what Barth and Küng thought.[1] We can reach agreement on faith, can live together despite different emphases in ethics but remain divided in our understandings of what the church is and is called to become.[2] But first a recap on the progress we can all observe just by attending Mass and which Barth himself welcomed in his final years, shortly after the ending of the Council and his own visit to Rome in 1966.

Anyone attending Mass in a Roman Catholic Church one Sunday and Communion in a Protestant or Anglican church the next Sunday may wonder if we are still divided in faith, even in our understanding of the eucharist. Many of us now follow a common lectionary of Bible readings, based on the three-year cycle in the Missal, and are not far from having a common liturgy. Nothing is said in the actual text of the Mass about transubstantiation, and

---

1. Karl Barth, Letter to Dr. B. A. Willems OP of Nijmegen, 6 March 1963, in ET Geoffrey W. Bromiley, *Karl Barth Letters, 1961-1968* (Edinburgh: T. & T. Clark/Grand Rapids: Eerdmans, 1981), pp. 93-94.

2. Faith and Order Commission, World Council of Churches, *The Church, Towards a Common Vision*, Faith and Order Paper 214 (Geneva: WCC, 2013), shows both large measures of agreement or convergence but also disputed questions like the church as sacrament or the limits to diversity.

for many non–Roman Catholics the only two references that seem unfamiliar are the request to "blessed Mary, ever virgin" to pray for us, and talk of the "sacrifice of the Mass." In both instances further exposition may make such differences acceptable. It becomes harder and harder to explain why we cannot share communion together. Barth had a similar experience when, as I have already noted, in his more infirm old age he spent Sundays listening to two sermons on Swiss radio, one Catholic and the other Protestant. The preaching, he said, is on the whole better than it was, and what is more, it had become more ecumenical:

> What I have heard has been ecumenical preaching, even when the term has not been used. I mean that there has not been any confessional debate, obviously not because of some tacit or express radio agreement, but because neither side has seemed to feel any need for it. In spite of Chapter VIII of the Church Constitution of Vatican II, I have heard on the Roman Catholic side no extolling of the Mother of God, only muted references to the authority of the Petrine office and no direct stress on the meritoriousness of good works. And on the Reformed side no allusions to the power and craft of the devil resident in Rome and no insistence on "Here I stand; I can do no other." Obviously some things have been said on both sides out of respect for the fathers, but not in active attack or defense. Again, not all Roman Catholics like the Reformed style of preaching, nor do all the Reformed like the Roman Catholic style. But in what is said on either side, the element of dissent is, for those who have ears to hear, much less significant than the material consensus, that is, an increasing concentration on the gospel.[3]

If confessional differences have indeed been put to one side so that worshipers and preachers can concentrate on the gospel, we may thank the ecumenical movement and Vatican II and those who contributed to them, not least Reformed theologians like Barth himself and his Roman Catholic colleagues and contemporaries like Congar, Rahner, von Balthasar, and Küng. They probed and challenged the differences that once divided us and did so, so successfully in some instances, that those differences have almost disappeared. I offer three examples:

---

3. Karl Barth, "Radio Sermons Catholic and Evangelical," in *Final Testimonies*, ed. Eberhard Busch, trans. Geoffrey Bromiley (Grand Rapids: Eerdmans, 1977), pp. 44-45.

Justification by Faith

I begin with "justification by faith." Disagreement about justification by faith is one of the reasons, some say *the* main reason, why Protestants and Roman Catholics are divided. Need they be? Not any more. Roman Catholics and Lutherans can now confess together: "sinners are justified by faith in the saving action of God in Christ." Roman Catholics and Lutherans can agree that "[b]y grace alone, in faith in Christ's saving work and not because of any merit on our part, we are accepted by God and receive the Holy Spirit, who renews our hearts while equipping and calling us to good works." All we need to do is "accept that we are accepted," as Lutheran theologian Paul Tillich once said, and then act on this great news. This is the agreement officially endorsed by both churches at Augsburg on Reformation Day, 31 October 1999, in a Reformation city, and known as the *Joint Declaration on the Doctrine of Justification.*[4] We are justified through grace by faith and no longer justified in using "Justification" as the main reason for dividing the church, for separating as Protestants from the Church of Rome. Justification need not be a church-dividing issue any more.

This historic agreement had many antecedents, including the debates that took place in colloquies between Roman Catholics and Protestants in the decade before the Council of Trent was convened in 1545. Barth mentions in particular the Colloquy at Ratisbon in 1541.[5] He commends the efforts of the Romanist theologian Cardinal Caspar Contarini who wrote a treatise on Justification in which he outlines both Luther's arguments and the Romanist response. Barth implies that the whole issue might have been resolved had the church been prepared to listen to Contarini. It might have been resolved if Reginald Pole, the Englishman much admired by Ratzinger and who was known to be sympathetic to Luther's views, had become pope in 1549. He missed election by one vote. At the Council of Trent, opening in 1545 and after various sessions ending in 1563, the argument about justification by faith as against justification by good works might again have been resolved had the Lutherans accepted the invitation to attend. This is one of the arguments submitted by Hans Küng. Then for the next four hundred years we enter a dark period in which Catholics and Protestants sometimes fought

---

4. *Joint Declaration on the Doctrine of Justification: Official Common Statement by the Lutheran World Federation and the Catholic Church* (Geneva: Lutheran World Federation, 1999).

5. Karl Barth, *Church Dogmatics* IV/1, p. 624; Peter Matheson, *Cardinal Contarini of Regensburg* (Oxford: Clarendon Press, 1972).

but rarely spoke to each other, let alone discussed their faith. Differences became polarized. But after Trent we did not need to wait until 1999 to realize that agreement on this divisive issue was possible. A bright young Roman Catholic student, Hans Küng, discovered such a consensus forty years earlier in 1957 in his thesis on Karl Barth and Justification. The official report, *The Joint Declaration on the Doctrine of Justification,* makes no reference to Küng or Barth, probably because these two theologians were, so to speak, unofficial, and partly because, by 1999, Küng's reforming zeal had cast doubt on his Catholic credentials. However, Cardinal Kasper in one of the early seminars about this groundbreaking agreement was much more generous.

In 2001 Kasper succeeded Edward Cassidy as President of the Pontifical Council for Promoting Christian Unity. In an address at Yale University, he described his experience as a German living through the Hitler era. He recalled how life-saving ecumenical understanding could be when Christians of different traditions were herded together in the same camps. Even informal conversations among fellow prisoners may pave the way for closer unity. He continued:

> These doctrines have divided Lutherans and Roman Catholics for more than four hundred years, bringing great suffering to individuals and to many of the peoples of Europe. Nevertheless, in their common resistance to the inhumane unchristian system of the Nazis, in the concentration camps and trenches of the Second World War, many Catholics and evangelical Christians discovered that they were not as far apart as they seemed. . . . Ecumenical theology after 1945 was able to make use of these experiences. We could mention a whole host of theologians from both sides who prepared the way for what has now been achieved, particularly Karl Barth and Karl Rahner. We are like dwarfs on the shoulders of these giants. I could also mention Hans Küng, Harding Meyer, George Lindbeck, Wolfhart Pannenberg, and many others.[6]

It is sad, even ungracious, that more is not said about the pioneering work of Hans Küng and his friendship and partnership with Karl Barth, for here we have a splendid example of real Christian dialogue. And, what is more, here is real evidence that so-called Protestant outsiders and insiders who are not official spokespeople can change their church's thinking, even

6. Walter Kasper, "The Joint Declaration on the Doctrine of Justification: A Roman Catholic Perspective," in *The Joint Declaration on the Doctrine of Justification,* ed. William G. Rusch (Collegeville, MN: Liturgical Press, 2003), p. 15.

Rome's, even the Lutherans'. Their agreement roused a lot of excitement at the time, more I think than the official agreement forty years later.

Barth enjoyed reading Küng's book[7] even though in places Küng is highly critical of Barth. And Barth in turn raised questions about whether there was after all agreement between official Roman Catholic theology and his own, or only with a Catholic theologian who had been reading Trent after reading Karl Barth! Karl Rahner in some thoughtful comments on this exchange highlighted two key principles that made their dialogue so real. Barth as author of what he had written should be accepted as his own best interpreter. Barth is best qualified to say what Barth thinks and to say whether or not Küng has correctly interpreted him. And yes, as a Roman Catholic theologian, Rahner can vouch for the fact that Küng's theology is Roman Catholic theology. Rahner is a better judge of this than Barth. In dialogue we let the other speak for himself. We do not presume to know better.

Küng's book is in two parts. Part one is entirely devoted to an outline of Barth's theology. Its value is greatly enhanced by being publicly endorsed by Barth in his friendly "Letter to the Author," printed in the first and subsequent editions:

> I here gladly, gratefully and publicly testify not only that you have adequately covered all significant aspects of justification treated in the ten volumes of my *Church Dogmatics* published so far, and that you have fully and accurately reproduced my views as I myself understand them; but also that you have brought all this beautifully into focus through your brief yet precise presentation of details and your frequent references to the larger historical context.[8]

In the second half, Küng offers what he modestly calls "An Attempt at a Catholic Response." Such a modest claim might be expected from an unknown student, not yet thirty, writing about one who was then the best-known Protestant theologian in the world, but not all brilliant students are noted for their humility! So it helps Küng's exposition of Catholic doctrine to have the backing of Karl Rahner: "Küng's presentation is Catholic."[9] At this stage, 1957, Rahner was already well established as one of Rome's

---

7. Hans Küng, *Rechtfertigung: Die Lehre Karl Barths und eine katholische Besinnung* (1957), ET Thomas Nelson and Sons, *Justification*, 4th ed. (London: Burns & Oates, 1981).

8. Küng, *Justification*, p. xxxix.

9. Karl Rahner SJ, "Barth's Agreement with the Catholic Doctrine of Justification," in ET Kevin Smith, *Theological Investigations IV* (London: Darton, Longman & Todd, 1966).

leading theologians, a Jesuit and, at the time, professor at Innsbruck. Later he would prove to be something of an ecumenical pioneer when he put forward with Hans Frei a serious proposal for church unity, *Unity of the Churches: An Actual Possibility* (1983).[10] Earlier he had been one of the *periti* at Vatican II.

As well as encouragement from Rahner, Küng also had support from Hans Urs von Balthasar. He had just published in 1951 what Barth also agreed was one of the best books about Barth. It was also largely thanks to Balthasar and the publishing house he had founded that Küng's thesis was so quickly in print. So we are now talking about three Roman Catholic scholars, not just one, who were and would become among Rome's best-known theologians in the last half of the twentieth century, and their conversation with one whom Küng's Roman Catholic biographer, Herman Häring, describes as the Protestant theologian with the greatest authority.[11] It may be unofficial, but in other respects here is a dialogue carried out at the highest level. Hans Küng's book is still worth reading, is still in print, and, like all his later writings, is beautifully readable. Here is just a brief summary of questions asked and answers given.

Barth's theology of justification poses the question: "Does Catholic theology really take justification seriously as the free sovereign act of God?" And on the other side, Roman Catholics challenge Barth with this question: "Does God's grace really affect man?" The questions arise because of a Protestant suspicion that Catholic theology and the Council of Trent in particular put too much emphasis on humanity's share in our own salvation and conversely, that Protestants like Barth so emphasize God's initiative and action as to leave us human beings with nothing more to do than accept that they are accepted. Questions are still being asked and massive tomes written about whether there is much space for human action in Barth's theology.[12] As part of his Catholic response, Küng argues that had Barth been more sympathetic he would have seen that Rome does put the emphasis on God's action. The confrontational style of Reformation debates led each side

10. Heinrich Fries, Karl Rahner (1983), *Unity of the Churches: An Actual Possibility* (Philadelphia: Fortress Press, 1985).

11. Hermann Häring, ET John Bowden, *Hans Küng: Breaking Through* (London: SCM, 1998), p. 34.

12. John Macken SJ, *The Autonomy Theme in the Church Dogmatics: Karl Barth and His Critics* (Cambridge: Cambridge University Press, 1990); Holly Taylor Coolman, "Divine and Human Action in Thomas Aquinas," in Bruce L. McCormack and Thomas Joseph White OP, eds., *Thomas Aquinas and Karl Barth* (Grand Rapids: Eerdmans, 2013), pp. 262-79.

into an unbalanced, one-sided emphasis.[13] So because the Protestants were concentrating on what God had done, Roman Catholics, in response, were almost bound to sound more anthropological than theological, in putting more emphasis on our human response. But it is also a mistake to isolate Trent. One needs to look at Catholic theology as a whole. Yet Küng has to admit that "it is not always easy to perceive the living Catholic teaching in its fullness." He would also voice a comment he later attributed to Barth himself that it is not always possible to hear the voice of the Good Shepherd from the throne of Peter.[14] And on the question posed to Barth: "Does Karl Barth take Justification seriously as the Justification of man?," Küng's answer is a simple "Yes."

Küng can be criticized for appearing to suggest that the differences between Catholics and Protestants were largely verbal. Thus at one point he explains: "Protestants speak of declaring just which includes making just and Catholics of making just which presupposes declaring just. Is it not time to stop arguing about imaginary differences?"[15] Trevor Hart of Aberdeen thinks that Küng implies that to reach agreement "all that needs to be done is a little clarification and tweaking of terms and concepts." He is convinced that "there remain significant points of difference which ought not to be glossed over in an enthusiasm for ecumenical progress." But he also admits that one of the difficulties is the way in which Catholics and Protestants like Barth use "justification" and "sanctification."[16] For Barth, justification looks back to what God has done for us in Christ. Sanctification is an ongoing process. It is about what God is doing with us. So stated, it is worth asking Barth if he would agree to this distinction. Alas, the question posed in 1999 comes too late for Barth who died in 1968, though not too late for Küng who is still alive and well and publishing.

I should add that Eberhard Jüngel, in the third edition of his detailed defense of the Lutheran understanding of *Justification: The Heart of the Christian Faith*, is not convinced by Küng's arguments. He offers, according

---

13. John O'Malley, *Trent: What Happened at the Council* (Cambridge, MA: Belknap, Harvard University Press, 2013), p. 116, poses a different contrast: "Trent's decree was the intellectual's emotionally cool response to Luther's spiritual anguish."

14. Hans Küng, *My Struggle for Freedom* (London: Continuum, 2003), pp. 130-31.

15. Küng, *Justification*, p. 221.

16. Trevor Hart, *Regarding Karl Barth* (Carlisle, UK: Paternoster Press, 1999), pp. 69, 72-73; George Hunsinger, "A Tale of Two Simultaneities: Justification and Sanctification in Calvin and Barth," in *Conversing with Barth*, ed. John C. McDowell and Mike Higton (Aldershot, UK: Ashgate, 2004), pp. 68-89.

to John Webster, "the most substantial contribution" to the debate about the *Joint Declaration* "from the *non placet* Lutheran side."[17] *Non placet* was the standard expression of dissent at Vatican II.

In the ongoing debate, the attempt is made to involve more traditions. The original 1999 agreement is between Lutherans and Roman Catholics. Methodists, Anglicans, Reformed, and observers from the World Council of Churches' Faith and Order Commission have since been drawn into the discussion. The World Methodist Council confirmed its support at its meeting in Seoul in 2006. Anglicans had already formulated their comments and agreements on justification in the Second Anglican–Roman Catholic International Commission as part of a wider consideration of "Salvation and the Church" in 1987. The difficulty for other churches is the assumption that justification by grace through faith is the heart of the gospel. Even a renowned Lutheran ecumenist, Harding Meyer of the Strasbourg Ecumenical Institute, in an article titled "One in Christ" (1981), warned against imposing "a specifically Lutheran perspective on the Catholic partner." Harding Meyer helped to draft the *Joint Declaration*. His one-time colleague at Strasbourg and fellow Lutheran, André Birmelé, reports that the Lutherans in this dialogue wanted to assert that Justification is "*the* indispensable criterion which constantly serves to orient all the teaching and practice of our churches to Christ," but the Catholics would not agree to such an emphatic "the."[18] Here the Catholics are agreeing with Barth but without saying so!

Karl Barth in his rather mischievous manner doubted whether Martin Luther himself would wish to sum up the whole gospel in terms of justification. After all, as Barth noted, this is not a major theme in the Gospels themselves nor in much of the rest of the New Testament outside Romans and Galatians. One is on surer ground in asserting that the center of the gospel is Jesus Christ. The Lutheran scholar, Eberhard Jüngel, famous for earlier studies on Barth, and, as we saw earlier, now one of the key protagonists in this debate with Rome, does not dispute this but argues that it is precisely the doctrine of justification that makes "the confession of Christ

---

17. Eberhard Jüngel (3rd ed., 1999), ET Jeffrey F. Cayzer, *Justification: The Heart of the Christian Faith* (Edinburgh: T. & T. Clark, 2001), pp. 177, 184, 187, 223.

18. André Birmelé, "Joint Declaration on the Doctrine of Justification — A Decisive Step Forward," in *Justification and Sanctification in the Traditions of the Reformation,* ed. Milan Opočensky and Páraic Réamonn (Geneva: World Alliance of Reformed Churches, 1999), p. 141; Michael Weinrich and John Burgess, eds., *What Is Justification About? Reformed Contributions to an Ecumenical Theme* (Grand Rapids: Eerdmans, 2009). Project sponsored by World Alliance of Reformed Churches.

the centre of the church." He challenges the following passage in the *Church Dogmatics*.[19] Barth enters into a detailed consideration of Luther's view in *Church Dogmatics* IV/1 and comes to this conclusion:

> The *articulus stantis et cadentis ecclesiae* is not the doctrine of justification as such, but its basis and culmination; the confession of Jesus Christ, in whom are hid all the treasures of wisdom and knowledge (Colossians 2,3); the knowledge of His being and activity for us and to us and with us. It could probably be shown that this was also the opinion of Luther. If here, as everywhere, we allow Christ to be the centre, the starting point and the finishing point, we have no reason to fear that there will be any lack of unity and cohesion, and therefore of systematics in the best sense of the word.
>
> The problem of justification does not need artificially to be absolutised and given a monopoly. It has its own dignity and necessity to which we do more and not less justice if we do not ascribe to it a totalitarian claim which is not proper to it, or allow all other questions to culminate or merge into it.[20]

In more recent essays that form part of the Reformed response to *The Joint Declaration*, Katherine Sonderegger argues that our thinking about justification by faith is distorted unless we think also of those who are justified, about those who are called and elected in Christ, those who are predestined. "Predestination forms the necessary context to justification as shadows to light; without it justification itself loses definition." One can see why this subject is almost overlooked in the *Joint Declaration*. Trent was arguing with Luther not with Calvin. Predestination and election were not matters of controversy. But prior to the Reformation, and what she calls "modern theological culture," earlier theologians saw the connections. It was those whom God calls that he also justified. They did not ignore, as is the modern habit, belief in divine decrees.[21]

Justification as a dogma can too easily be isolated from life. That is one reason why Barth commends Bonhoeffer's comment on justification in his famous critique of "cheap grace" in *The Cost of Discipleship*, "easily the best

---

19. Jüngel, *Justification*, Introduction by John Webster, p. viii.

20. *Church Dogmatics* IV/1, pp. 527-28; Jüngel, "Theological Reservations: An Analysis of Karl Barth," in *Justification*, pp. 18-31.

21. Katherine Sonderegger, "Called to Salvation in Christ: Justification and Predestination," in *What Is Justification About?* Weinrich and Burgess, eds., pp. 122-38.

that has been written on this subject," says Barth.[22] First published in 1937, an abridged version had appeared in English in 1948. Here is a summary, slightly rearranged, of "cheap grace":

> Cheap grace means the justification of sin without the justification of the sinner. Grace alone does everything, they say, and so everything can remain as it was before.
>
> Cheap grace means grace as a doctrine, a principle, a system. It means forgiveness of sins proclaimed as a general truth. . . . An intellectual assent to that idea is held to be of itself sufficient to secure remission of sins. . . . Instead of following Christ, let the Christian enjoy the consolations of his grace.
>
> Cheap grace is grace without discipleship, grace without the cross, grace without Jesus Christ, living and incarnate.[23]

The phrases have become so memorable that it is easy to ignore the context. The contemporary context for Bonhoeffer was of course the conflict with Hitler. The cost of discipleship cost Bonhoeffer his life. He was executed for his opposition to Hitler in April 1945. He has become one of the twentieth century's best-known martyrs. But in the book, the context is the Reformation and its sequel. Rome distorted Christian discipleship by erecting a double standard, one for monks and another for the rest of us. But Bonhoeffer also rails against enthusiasts and Anabaptists and later fellow Lutherans who treat grace in the way he has described it, so that justification by grace through faith makes no difference to how Christians live.

It is also possible, and this is something neither Barth nor Bonhoeffer appear to have noticed, to read the Council of Trent's "Decree on Justification" as a protest against cheap grace! Trent, as Küng persuaded Barth, was not wholly bad. And if it was a one-sided reaction to Luther, Luther was also one-sided when he rejected the Letter of James and its emphasis on active obedience, as an "epistle of straw." So, as if to put the record straight, the Decree of Trent cites James: "Hence it is very truly said that faith without works is dead," and also Galatians about faith working through love.[24] Trent affirms that "no one, however much justified, ought to think that he is

---

22. *Church Dogmatics* IV/2, p. 505.

23. Dietrich Bonhoeffer, *The Cost of Discipleship*, ET R. H. Fuller and Irmgard Booth, 6th ed. (London: SCM, 1959), pp. 35, 41.

24. Norman P. Tanner SJ, ed., *Decrees of the Ecumenical Councils* (London: Sheed & Ward, 1990), pp. 673-74.

exempt from the observance of the commandments."[25] Cheap grace is grace without discipleship, said Bonhoeffer, and he quotes Luther and the way he could be misunderstood, perhaps, we might now admit, in ways that Trent anticipated. Luther had taught "grace alone can save; his followers took up the doctrine and repeated it word for word. But they left out its invariable corollary, the obligation of discipleship."

Barth accepted that justification by faith is very important, but the doctrine ought not to be treated in isolation. In redirecting our gaze to Christ rather than a doctrinal controversy, Barth may also be nearer to the lived faith of ordinary Christian men and women. Official church agreements among theologians are one thing; lived faith of the people in the pews another. This is a point made by Karl Rahner in one of his later essays and echoed in some recent comment on the *Joint Declaration*. How many ordinary members of Lutheran or other Protestant congregations pay much attention to justification by grace through faith? How many Roman Catholics know much about the teaching of the Council of Trent? Surely for most people, Catholic or Protestant, faith is expressed in different ways but is nonetheless genuine. The faithful, and we should call them such, believe in God, entrust their lives to the living God of grace and forgiveness; they say their prayers, are baptized, and celebrate the Lord's Supper. They recognize Jesus Christ crucified and risen as Lord. This is their faith. What is more, it is a faith that is neither exclusively Protestant nor Catholic. Most of us Christians no longer see ourselves as divided in faith. This was Rahner's view, the view of one of Rome's top theologians.[26]

Related to this observation is a fact noted by Lutheran professor David Yeago of South Carolina. He is personally deeply supportive of the *Joint Declaration* but adds, "I cannot help admitting that its approval by my own denomination was made easier by the fact that, beyond a few slogans, very few Lutherans any longer employ the language of justification and grace to talk about anything central to their lives."[27] He is not happy about this and even less about the fact that a protest by some Lutherans against the *Declaration* was ignored by the Lutheran authorities — a clear sign, he thinks, of the

25. Council of Trent, "Decree on Justification," chs. 7 and 11, in *Decrees of the Ecumenical Councils,* ed. Norman P. Tanner, pp. 673-75.

26. Karl Rahner, "Realistic Possibility of Unification in Faith," in *Theological Investigations* XXII, ET Joseph Donceel SJ (London: Darton, Longman & Todd, 1991), pp. 67-79.

27. David Yeago, "The Ecclesial Context of Ecumenical Reception," in *The Ecumenical Future: Background Papers for "In One Body through the Cross,"* ed. Carl E. Braaten and Robert W. Jenson (Grand Rapids: Eerdmans, 2004), p. 31.

real status of the doctrine. But this could also support Rahner's contention that at the grassroots level of local congregations, Roman Catholics and Protestants are not divided in faith.

But Rahner also conceded that the papacy and papal infallibility still divide us. Are there other issues?

In his friendly "Letter to the Author" that is now part of Küng's *Justification,* Barth commends the young author for taking "a rather sizeable step" but urges him not to stop now he has begun. "Do not content yourself with the fine beginnings you have made in this important search." He then lists some of the items for a future ecumenical agenda:

> It will certainly take quite an effort, once (as we hope) the central area has been cleared to make somewhat plausible to us matters like Transubstantiation, the Sacrifice of the Mass, Mary, and the infallible papacy and the other things with which we are confronted . . . in the Tridentine profession of faith.[28]

Küng had in fact urged Barth to see Trent in the context both of Reformation controversies and what Newman called the "Development of Doctrine" and so not to find the whole of Catholic doctrine in one set of conciliar decrees. He then adds some items of his own that Barth needs to reexamine so as to overcome what he describes as "the intransigence of Barth's opposition to Catholic teaching, especially in the area of Church and Sacrament (ecclesiastical tradition, the primacy of the Pope, Mariology and, beyond that, in regard to 'natural' knowledge of God)." Finally, a comment that is so topical it could have been written yesterday, not back in 1957. Please take a look at our Catholic life, says Küng, at our practice, not just our doctrines. Protestants, he suggests, are too discreet and diplomatic to be helpful. It would help if they were prepared to "charge the Catholic Church with 'abuses' which might occur anywhere."[29] The invitation is general and the so-called "abuses" not specified, but anyone reading Küng in the twenty-first century will immediately think of the scandal of sexual abuse carried out by priests and too often covered up or ignored by the hierarchy. It could indeed happen anywhere but is a special embarrassment to a church that makes great claims for her own holiness, catholicity, and divine origins in the will of Christ.

---

28. Karl Barth, in Küng's *Justification,* p. xlii.
29. Küng, *Justification,* pp. 278, 282.

Natural Knowledge of God and the *Analogia Entis*

Anyone familiar with religious controversies of the Reformation era will know that it was quite common to label your opponent the Antichrist.[30] The biblical term is found in the Letters of John and only there but is sometimes linked with a reference in 2 Thessalonians 2 to the adversary or wicked one "who enthrones himself in God's temple." Even before the sixteenth-century Reformation, the term was often applied to the pope. The British historian Christopher Hill finds references in Joachim of Fiore (1135-1202), the Waldensians, Wyclif and the Lollards, Jan Huss and the Hussites, all in the centuries before Luther. Continuing this polemic against the papacy, the Westminster Confession of 1647 declares:

> There is no other head of the Church but the Lord Jesus Christ; nor can the Pope of Rome, in any sense be head thereof; but is that Antichrist, that man of sin and son of perdition, that exalteth himself in the Church against Christ, and all that is called God.[31]

But with the dawning of what is sometimes called polite ecumenism, where, even when we disagree, we refrain from insulting, the use of such strong language becomes an embarrassment. Hence the shock that is still felt when we find "Antichrist" in Barth and find it, as in the Reformers and their ancestors, in Barth's dispute with Rome. Taking the term literally, the concern is with anyone who is against or is usurping the place of Christ. Barth does not apply this term to the pope. He applies it to a particular way of doing theology. Any theology that does not begin and end with the revelation of God in Christ could be this "Antichrist." And if we are to be in dispute with the church of Christ, the church that according to the Creed is one, holy, catholic, and apostolic, we must have a good and serious reason for our separation. Nothing could be more serious than the suspicion that something is "Antichrist" and so must be rejected.

In one of his early lectures, Barth sees the Roman Catholic Church as posing a challenge to the Protestant Church: "Roman Catholicism: A Question to the Protestant Church." The question was posed personally, notably in his encounter and friendship with the Jesuit scholar Erich Przywara, as well as in dogmatic statements. Barth was living and working in the Roman Catholic city and university of Münster. This is the start of what

---

30. Christopher Hill, *Antichrist in Seventeenth Century England* (London: Verso, 1989).
31. The Westminster Confession 1647, chapter 25, "Of the Church," para. 6.

his biographer, Eberhard Busch, describes as his "Encounter with Catholicism."[32] The lecture was delivered in various places in 1928. It is "the substance of the Church to be the house of God." The challenge of Catholicism, and it is a very positive challenge, is that "it has kept at least the claim to the knowledge of this substance and has guarded it," whereas those whom Barth calls the new Protestants have lost it so that it might be "meaningless to call ourselves any longer by the name of the Protestant Church,"[33] the emphasis there being on the claim to be church. This is the "Church" context for Barth's strident criticism of Rome in the first volume of his *Church Dogmatics*. Barth feels bound to exclude the search for any other foundation for theology than the Word of God, any way of appealing to so-called natural knowledge of God. Roman Catholics may regard the *analogia entis*, basically the analogy of God's being and existence and humanity's being, as legitimate. Barth cannot. "I regard the *analogia entis* as the invention of the Antichrist, and I believe that because of it, it is impossible ever to become a Roman Catholic, all other reasons for not doing so being to my mind shortsighted and trivial."[34]

Eighty years after this Preface was written, the outburst still provokes detailed scrutiny among Protestant and Roman Catholic scholars. Two major studies appeared in 2010-11. The disputed points are highly technical. Thankfully, I think it hardly necessary to go into too much detail, as even if Barth did believe that this was *the* church-dividing issue in 1932, he would not do so now. But in support of this conclusion we need to understand why Barth felt so strongly about the *analogia entis* and whether my contemporary commentators, Protestant and Roman Catholic, consider the issue a major point of difference or a misunderstanding that an ecumenical seminar might resolve.

Why was the issue so important for Barth? According to Eberhard Busch, his one-time assistant and later biographer, Barth saw the dividing line "in the Catholic attempt to claim control over God's grace instead of allowing it the controlling power." This was "the one fundamental error of Catholicism." Barth had invited his Jesuit friend Erich Przywara to his sem-

---

32. Eberhard Busch, *Karl Barth: His Life from His Letters*, ET John Bowden (London: SCM, 1976), pp. 177-89; Amy Marga, *Karl Barth's Dialogue with Catholicism in Göttingen and Münster* (Tübingen: Mohr Siebeck, 2010).

33. "Roman Catholicism: A Question to the Protestant Church," in ET Louise Pettibone Smith, *Karl Barth, Theology and Church: Shorter Writings, 1920-1928* (New York: Harper & Row, 1962), pp. 313-14.

34. *Church Dogmatics* 1/1, Preface, p. xiii.

inar in Münster in 1931 on "the problems of natural theology." It was the title and subject of Przywara's forthcoming book, *Analogia entis,* that "enabled Barth to pin-point the reason for his dissent from Roman Catholicism." In conversations that Busch reports, Barth interpreted the phrase as meaning "there is a Being superior to God and creation in respect of which a comparison would be possible between Creator and creature. Over against that I would say; that is not the case."[35]

Bruce McCormack takes us back to an earlier encounter with Przywara and to an article he wrote for *Stimmen der Zeit* in 1923, and which was quite complimentary to Barth and his colleagues. In this article about "God in Us or God above Us," he contrasted Barth's wholly other God with Augustine's *analogia entis.* McCormack adds the comment: "a momentous phrase destined to play a large role in Barth's future debate with Catholicism." For further detail, McCormack refers to Barth's lecture on "Fate and Idea in Theology."[36] In this lecture given at Dortmund in 1929 Barth explains the term in this way: "Everything that is exists in mere dissimilarity to the Creator, yet by having being it exists in greatest similarity to the Creator. That is what is meant by *analogia entis.*" And in reference to Aquinas, Barth interprets him as saying "*Analogia entis* means that every existing being and we as human beings participate in the *similitude Dei.* The experience of God becomes an inherent human possibility and necessity." Protestants need to reject this, even though Barth admits that Aquinas developed the idea in "an extraordinarily penetrating and consistent manner." For what is at stake is this. God's Word as God's Word is new, not something we have already heard and know already; "the Word says something new — not something more strongly and clearly that human beings knew anyway and that they could also experience in some other way."[37]

Whether or not Barth understood Aquinas, the general consensus at the ecumenical conference on the *analogia entis* in Washington, D.C., in 2008 was that he misunderstood Przywara.[38] Przywara himself said he was misunderstood, describing Barth's view as "a grotesque distortion" and claiming

35. Busch, *Karl Barth: His Life,* pp. 177-78, 215, 284.

36. Bruce McCormack, *Karl Barth's Critically Realistic Dialectical Theology: Its Genesis and Development, 1909-1936* (Oxford: Clarendon Press, 1995), pp. 320-21, 383-91.

37. "Fate and Idea in Theology," in H. Martin Rumscheidt, *The Way of Theology in Karl Barth: Essays and Comments* (Alison Park, PA: Pickwick Publications, 1986), pp. 33, 38.

38. Archbishop J. Augustine Di Noia OP, Foreword in Thomas Joseph White OP, *The Analogy of Being: Invention of the Antichrist or the Wisdom of God?* (Grand Rapids: Eerdmans, 2011), p. xi.

that the *analogia entis* was only what the Fourth Lateran Council of 1215 had once taught — at a time, before the Reformation, when "Christianity was still unified."[39] The Council declared that "between creator and creature there can be noted no similarity so great that a greater dissimilarity cannot be seen between them." That Council was in turn defending the theology of Peter Lombard against charges made against him by Joachim of Fiore. In the course of the argument, the Council talks of God's perfection and makes this point I have noted: "For between creator and creature there can be noted no similarity so great that a greater dissimilarity cannot be seen between them."[40] If Barth really thought that the analogy of being meant that humanity could presume to have too much in common with God, this sentence should have put him right.

The Washington Conference was itself a fine demonstration of one of Barth's great convictions that as theologians we should go on asking questions: "May God never relieve us of this questioning. May he enclose us with questions on every side! May he defend us from any answer which is not itself a question! May he bar every exit and cut us off from all simplifications."[41] In a conference intended to honor both theologians, one Roman Catholic, the other Reformed, Przywara and Barth, "two earthen vessels, two witnesses to Christ," a distinguished gathering of Roman Catholic, Protestant, and Orthodox theologians set themselves the question, "Is the Analogy of Being the Antichrist or the Wisdom of God?" They came to the conclusion that it is neither. Only Christ may be called "the wisdom of God." What they affirmed was the value of the questioning that each theologian put to the other. What they illustrated is that such questioning need not be church-dividing. Sadly, in such an ecumenical conference they would not have been permitted to break bread together, but the cause of their separation was not the *analogia entis* that Barth once stated was the key issue separating him from Rome. They could also recall that despite their disagreements, Barth and Przywara remained good friends. Indeed, Bruce McCormack, one of our foremost Barth scholars, noted at the conference that Barth's early de-

39. John R. Betz, "After Barth: A New Introduction to Erich Przywara's *Analogia Entis*," in *The Analogy of Being*, ed. White, p. 75; Lateran IV, Constitutions 2.

40. Tanner, ed., *Decrees of the Ecumenical Councils*, p. 232, "On the Error of Abbot Joachim."

41. Karl Barth, *The Epistle to the Romans*, ET Edwyn C. Hoskyns, 6th ed. (London: Oxford University Press, 1933), p. 254, in relation to Romans 7:12-13; Stephen Sykes, "Authority and Openness in the Church," in *Karl Barth: Centenary Essays*, ed. Stephen Sykes (Cambridge: Cambridge University Press, 1989), p. 72.

bates with Przywara were carried out in a friendly manner, "without the pyrotechnics of the Preface to *Church Dogmatics* 1,1." What had changed a few years later was Hitler's coming to power. This put Barth on high alert as he saw in the views of the German Christians and their acceptance of Hitler the consequences of natural theology.[42]

The friendly atmosphere earlier was because both were open to learning from the other. Openness is another of Barth's big themes. Both theologians were open to being corrected. Prompted by Przywara, Barth thought more deeply than he had done about the incarnation. Przywara thought more deeply than he had done about sin.

Disciples or rather students of Przywara would modify the sharpness of the original debate so that the argument could become much more constructive and reconciliation possible. Gottlieb Söhngen put much more emphasis on the priority of God making himself known through his activity, and made the analogy of being subordinate to the analogy of faith. This was much more acceptable to Barth, so much so that in the second volume of *Church Dogmatics* (*CD* II/1, pp. 81-82) he declared, "If this is the Roman Catholic doctrine of *analogia entis* then I must withdraw my earlier statement that I regard the *analogia entis* as the 'invention of anti-Christ.'" But at the time Barth was not convinced that Söhngen's views were accepted as official Roman Catholic thinking. Barth died long before one of Söhngen's pupils, Joseph Ratzinger, became pope. As a learned theologian whose doctoral dissertation was supervised by Söhngen, Ratzinger, as he then was, would be familiar with the Barth-Przywara debate. He made Natural Theology part of his Inaugural Lecture at Bonn in 1959, arguing against Pascal and others that the God of the philosophers was the same as the God of Abraham, Isaac, and Jacob. But he also admitted that theologians needed to take care before using the philosophers' terms.[43]

Sixty years before the Washington conference, Hans Urs von Balthasar drew on the later thinking of Przywara and of Söhngen to demonstrate that there was no good reason to regard Barth's preferred term, the analogy of faith, as incompatible with the analogy of being. Barth, he believed, would surely agree with Przywara that the real heart of the faith was "God in Christ in the Church." As for the *analogia entis*, "This is an issue that hardly merits

---

42. Bruce L. McCormack, "Karl Barth's Version of an 'Analogy of Being': A Dialectical No and Yes to Roman Catholicism," in *The Analogy of Being*, ed. White, p. 104.

43. Emery de Gaál, *The Theology of Pope Benedict XVI: The Christocentric Shift* (New York: Palgrave Macmillan, 2010), pp. 74-75. See also Kenneth Oakes, *Karl Barth on Theology and Philosophy* (Oxford: Oxford University Press, 2012).

Barth getting so excited about it, and it is certainly not worth splitting the Church because of it."[44]

There I might cheerfully leave the subject, confident that on this issue Roman Catholics and Protestants can be reconciled, but for the fact that one of the most recent commentators remains unconvinced. Keith Johnson thinks that Barth rejected Przywara's views not because he did not understand them but because he did. Barth never changed his mind, but he did change his criticism because he felt Roman Catholics had come to agree with the criticism he made. Johnson remains convinced that people like Przywara have a totally different idea of the church from Barth: "Roman Catholics like Przywara believe that the Catholic Church exists as the concrete visible form of God's self-revelation in the world, and they hold that this revelation serves as a pattern for how God relates to creation as a whole." He is not convinced by Balthasar's understanding of Barth: "Clearly, von Balthasar's account of Barth's theology stands in contradiction to my own." He suspects that dialogues too readily gloss over the issues that still divide. I am not sure this is fair. But to his credit, Johnson cites Barth's own conclusion, voiced to students in Hans Küng's city of Tübingen in 1964, in the era of the Second Vatican Council: "We want to understand one another; we do not want to fight about words. Therefore I have now discontinued the battle against the idol of the *analogia entis*. I no longer fire along the front. In the end this entire discourse about analogy became boring for me."[45] As far as we know, in conversations with Pope Paul VI about the Council, Barth never mentioned the subject. They had plenty of other issues to discuss.

Mary and Joseph, Immaculate Conception, and the Assumption of the Blessed Virgin

In his discussions with Karl Rahner, Joseph Ratzinger, the future Pope Benedict, and with Pope Paul VI, Barth noted:

> We did not pass over the difficult point of Mariology. The Pope had heard that I preferred Joseph, the foster father of Jesus, as the prototype of the nature and function of the church to the "handmaid of the Lord" who was

44. Hans Urs von Balthasar, *The Theology of Karl Barth* (1951), ET Edward T. Oakes (San Francisco: Ignatius Press, 1992), p. 257.

45. Keith Johnson, *Karl Barth and the Analogia Entis* (London: T. & T. Clark, 2010), pp. 84, 163, 192, 234.

subsequently elevated to the position of Queen of heaven. He assured me he would pray for me, that in my advanced age I would be given deeper insight into this problem.[46]

Earlier I suggested that Protestant views on Mary may have had a decisive influence on the way in which the Second Vatican Council came to articulate the church's faith about her. At the time of the Reformation, Mariology was not a source of division. The Reformers did not question that Jesus was, as the Creed states, "born of the Virgin Mary," and they believed this, not because it was in the Creed but because this is what the New Testament, in the Gospels of Matthew and Luke, proclaims. The three leading Reformers, Luther, Zwingli, and Calvin, differ in their emphases. Oxford church historian Diarmaid MacCulloch writes of "Luther's warmth towards Mary" and of a "more chilly overall attitude to Mary in Calvin's Geneva."[47] Luther and Zwingli accepted the title given to Mary by the Council of Ephesus in 431 that Mary is the "mother of God" because the Word, though eternal, "united to himself hypostatically the human and underwent a birth according to the flesh of her womb." Calvin was not happy with the title "Mother of God" and preferred to say that she is the "mother of the Son of God." Barth notes Calvin's reservations about *theotikos* but adds his own judgment that "the description of Mary as 'mother of God' was and is sensible, permissible and necessary as an auxiliary Christological proposition."[48] All three Reformers agree that Mary is significant for faith because she is the mother of Jesus, not in her own right. They are aware of tendencies in medieval Catholicism where believers might wish to move beyond the veneration of Mary to the worship of Mary. Mary for Calvin is a good human model of listening, understanding, and witnessing. The church, which is our real mother, not Mary, should follow her example. The community must be urged to imitate Mary, not to adore her. Calvin appeals to an early Council, that of Carthage in 397, against what he calls the wicked custom of praying to the saints and of asking the Virgin Mary to bid her Son do what we request. Again, following Mary's example rather than offering her special honor, we should not be afraid when confronted with the mysteries of our faith to ask how can this be, as Mary did when told by the angel that she was to be the mother of Jesus.[49]

46. Barth, *Ad Limina Apostolorum,* pp. 14-15.
47. Diarmaid MacCulloch, "Mary in Sixteenth Century Protestantism," in *The Church and Mary,* ed. R. N. Swanson (Woodbridge, UK: Boydell Press, 2004), pp. 201, 203.
48. *CD* I/2, pp. 138-39.
49. John Calvin, *Institutes of the Christian Religion* III.20.22; IV.17.25.

One can find all these points elaborated in a little more detail in the courageous study by that unofficial but rightly respected dialogue partnership of Roman Catholics and Protestants in France and French-speaking Switzerland, the Groupe des Dombes: *Mary in the Plan of God and in the Communion of Saints*. It was originally published in French and in two parts in 1997 and 1998. As they state in the Introduction, "After over fifty years of patient ecumenical work in the area of doctrine . . . the Dombe Group believe that a further bold step is now possible: to tackle the subject of the Virgin Mary."[50] In their view, there was full agreement in the first millennium about the place of Mary. Disagreement began to surface at the time of the Reformation and hardened in the post-Reformation era. They describe the attitude of the Reformers to Mary as "ambivalent." For example, Zwingli kept the Feast of the Assumption while he was minister in Zurich, not so much out of theological conviction but through pastoral sympathy for the popularity of devotion to Mary.

Such arguments as there were, could be described as debates within the medieval Catholic Church about devotion to Mary and her part in the plan of salvation. After the Reformation and the Counter-Reformation of the Council of Trent, debates were polarized as Protestant versus Roman Catholic. The two sides grew apart as did their thinking about Mary independently of each other, though not without some sensitivity about how the other side might react. Rome promulgated two dogmas, the Immaculate Conception in 1854 and the Assumption of the Virgin Mary in 1950, the first and only dogma that is officially regarded as "infallible" following the dogma of Papal Infallibility pronounced at Vatican I in 1870. Some Protestants, but not Barth, raised questions about the Virgin Birth, a subject the Reformers themselves never questioned. The so-called "Higher Criticism" exposed the fact that compared with the resurrection the manner of Jesus' birth was not a major article of faith. It might even for many be an unnecessary obstacle to belief.

Barth's convictions were on this point more Catholic than Protestant, though for un–Roman Catholic reasons. One reason why he wanted to say more about Joseph was because Joseph's nonparticipation in the actual conception of Jesus is a perfect illustration of Barth's point that in no way are we human beings equal partners in our own salvation. There is no possibility of

---

50. Alain Blancy and Maurice Jourjon and the Dombes Group, ET Matthew J. O'Connell, *Mary in the Plan of God and in the Communion of Saints: Toward a Common Christian Understanding* (Mahwah, NJ: Paulist Press, 1999), paras. 15, 30-35; Catherine E. Clifford, *The Groupe des Dombes: A Dialogue of Conversion* (New York: Peter Lang, 2005), pp. 222-33.

ever hailing Joseph as our co-redeemer. He might also have noted that Calvin had said more about Joseph as the guardian of Jesus and observed that Jesus' genealogy is traced through Joseph as well as Mary (Matt. 1:16; Luke 3:23).

Barth first observes that the birth of Jesus by the Virgin Mary is "a dogma which Catholics and Protestants have on the whole believed and taught unanimously and as a matter of course."[51] We believe it, however, not just because it is accepted by the church but because we see the need for such a dogma as a correct interpretation of revelation. Birth through Mary or as in Galatians 4:4, being "born of a woman," affirms Christ's humanity, but the miracle and mystery of Christmas is proclaimed in this way: "The virginity of Mary in the birth of the Lord is the denial, not of man in the presence of God, but of any power, attribute or capacity in him for God."[52] Though not mentioned at this point, Barth may again have in the back of his mind objections to Przywara's ideas about human openness to God and our natural human capacity because of the *analogia entis*. Barth continues: "[W]e must take care to avoid traces of Roman Catholic Mariology and must not regard the human creatureliness represented by the *virgo* as in principle an openness for the work of God which still belongs to man in spite of the Fall." Or again, "It is not, then, as if at this point a door is opened which can lead to Mariology and thus to a doctrine of the goodness of the creature and its capacity for God, to a doctrine of the independent holiness of the Church."[53] And on the clause that tells us that Jesus was conceived by the Holy Spirit, Barth has this to add: "Through the Holy Spirit and only through the Holy Spirit can man be there for God, be free for God's work on him, believe, be a recipient of His revelation, the object of the divine reconciliation."[54]

I have left out of this account most of Barth's small-print exposition of biblical texts and the arguments of Protestant theologians like Schleiermacher and Emil Brunner and earlier Protestant writers like Polanus and F. Turretini. Barth's sympathies are with the earlier dogmaticians. They, unlike so many moderns, appreciated the need for "a spiritual understanding of the spiritual." What we might describe as Barth's "Catholic," but not just Roman Catholic, sympathies are shown in the way in which he agrees with the Orthodox[55] theologian Nicolas Berdyaev's reaction to Brunner's book:

---

51. *CD* I/2, p. 174; Dustin Resch, *Barth's Interpretation of the Virgin Birth: A Sign of Mystery* (Farnham, UK: Ashgate, 2012).

52. *CD* I/2, p. 188.

53. *CD* I/2, pp. 195, 196.

54. *CD* I/2, p. 198.

55. For an Orthodox comment see Andrew Louth, *Mary and the Mystery of the Incarna-*

The sigh of N. Berdyaev is mine too: "I read Brunner's book with tremendous interest, because I felt in him tenseness and acuity of thought, religious sensibility. But when I reached the passage in which Brunner confesses that he does not believe in Jesus Christ's birth of the Virgin, or at least confronts it with indifference, my mood became sad and the matter grew tedious. For it seemed to be as though everything had now been cancelled, as though everything else was now pointless."[56]

What has Barth to say about the two Marian dogmas on the Immaculate Conception and the Assumption, the second being promulgated in his lifetime in 1950 and the first in 1854 during the papacy of Pius IX, shortly to become the first infallible pope? Even before reading Barth one could predict that any Protestant theologian would reject both dogmas because neither has any firm biblical basis. Roman Catholic theologians like the recent Pope Benedict XVI readily concede this. Joseph Ratzinger, as he then was, notes in his commentary on the document on Divine Revelation, *Dei Verbum* of Vatican II, that this was one reason why the Roman Catholic Church needed to rethink the authority of Scripture and Tradition: "The controversy concerning the dogma of 1854 was a further milestone, for which — in default of Biblical proof — tradition was made responsible, which could now, however, no longer be understood as the simple passing on of something that had been handed down once and for all." And he adds that the dogma of 1950, the bodily assumption of the Virgin Mary into heaven, "placed the idea of the Church's knowledge through faith in the forefront of the idea of tradition."[57]

The "controversy" Ratzinger refers to was not only an internal debate in the Roman Catholic Church but fully ecumenical, a fact that is the more remarkable given that in the century that spans the two dogmas and that of Papal Infallibility, Rome was not interested in what other Christians might think. At least this was the official stance. There were, however, many sensitive Roman Catholics who feared that such declarations of what Christians ought to believe would only make it more difficult for Protestants to "return" to Rome.

---

tion: *An Essay on the Mother of God in the Theology of Karl Barth* (Oxford: SLG Press, 1977, 2002).

56. CD I/2, p. 184. The reference to Berdyaev is to *Orient und Occident*, Heft 1 (1929), p. 19. Brunner's book is the *Mediator*. Barth was even less impressed with his more recent publication, *Man in Revolt*. It "is so bad my only possible attitude to it is silence."

57. Joseph Ratzinger, "Dogmatic Constitution on Divine Revelation," in *Commentary on the Documents of Vatican II*, vol. 4, ed. Herbert Vorgrimler (New York: Herder & Herder/London: Burns & Oates, 1968), pp. 155, 156.

Barth's reaction is blunt: "Mariology is an excrescence, i.e. a diseased construct of theological thought. Excrescences must be excised."[58] Barth accepts the *theotikos* because in his view, and that of Reformers like Luther and Zwingli, it is a statement about Christ. He will object to the two Marian dogmas precisely because they are primarily, if not exclusively, about Mary. He opposes what he calls "an independent Mariology (as it is called)" as "one of those characteristically Roman Catholic enterprises against which there has to be an Evangelical protest not only for their arbitrariness in form but also for the precariousness of their content." And his reason:

> The content of the biblical attestation of revelation does not give us any cause to acknowledge that the person of Mary in the event of revelation possesses relatively even such an independent and emphatic position as to render it necessary or justifiable to make it the object of theological doctrine that goes beyond the one statement made, or even of a mario-logical dogma.[59]

Barth is aware that both the dogma of the Immaculate Conception and that of the Assumption had a long history. The First Lateran Council of 649 made the perpetual virginity of Mary a dogma in 649, but he is clearly pleased to note that Anselm, Bernard of Clairvaux, Thomas Aquinas, and Bonaventura, theologians he greatly respected, had reservations about such a dogma though Duns Scotus did not. His *Kirchliche Dogmatik* I/2 from which the above quotations are taken was published in 1938, twelve years before Pope Pius XII declared the Assumption of the Blessed Mary a binding article of faith, but he would not be surprised when this happened. He notes that the ascension of Mary into heaven was celebrated even in the seventh century, and he adds that "its final definition as a dogma was almost inevitable."[60] He may not have known that Elizabeth of Schönau's vision, sometime in the twelfth century (c. 1156), in which she saw Mary enthroned in heaven, aided belief in Mary's bodily assumption and that this vision is portrayed in a painting in the York Psalter of 1170, but the thought that dogma might be based on a dream and not on revelation in Scripture would have appalled him.[61] *Church Dogmatics* III/2 was also published before the official dogma,

---

58. *CD* I/2, p. 139.
59. *CD* I/2, p. 139.
60. *CD* I/2, p. 141.
61. Henry Mayr-Harting, "The Idea of the Assumption of Mary in the West, 800-1200," in *The Church and Mary*, ed. R. N. Swanson (Woodbridge, UK: Boydell Press, 2004), pp. 104-5.

namely in 1948, so Barth in effect is offering his criticism in advance. This is what he had to say:

> The Roman Catholic definition of the assumption of Mary as a dogma of the faith, quite apart from anything else, is an additional proof of its profound lack of understanding of the basic difference between the situation and order of the New Testament and that of the Old. In the New Testament order the exaltation of the one man Jesus Christ, in which the exaltation of His own is already latently accomplished, is followed by only one assumption of which nothing can be said because it has not yet happened, namely, the assumption of the community to meet its Lord when He comes again at the final revelation in which the exaltation which has already occurred in Jesus Christ will be made manifest.[62]

Barth's judgments are much more severe than the conclusions reached in recent dialogues with Rome. The Groupe des Dombes (1998) concedes that under Pius XII the Marian movement reached its high point and that the declaration of 1950 "placed a new major difficulty in the way of ecumenical dialogue," but the Groupe now feels able "to move beyond controversies inherited from the past and better understand our respective positions on each of the two Marian claims." They do so in part by constantly emphasizing that Mary, like every human being, is dependent on Christ for her holiness. So "filled with grace" in Luke 1:28, which as Barth noted when translated as in the Vulgate as *gratia plena* "has given rise to so many mariological speculations, against which it ought to have constituted a serious warning," is interpreted by the Groupe des Dombes in the light of Ephesians 1:6: "[I]f Mary was filled with grace in a unique way, it was in order to bear witness to the fact that we in turn are touched by the superabundant gift of grace that God has bestowed on us in his beloved Son." And though they admit that the doctrine of the Immaculate Conception is "not formally attested in the Scriptures, it is to be understood in the light of God's plan in the history of salvation." In the end, there is an agreement to differ but without needing to divide. Roman Catholics can interpret the dogmas within a hierarchy of truths and relate them to the center of the Christian faith. Protestants simply say they do not find such dogma helpful.[63]

The Anglican–Roman Catholic International Commission report, *Mary, Grace and Hope in Christ* (2005), builds on previous agreements when the

62. CD III/2, p. 638.
63. *Mary in the Plan of God*, paras. 98, 274, 275; Barth, CD I/2, pp. 139-40.

main subject was "Authority in the Church." Its conclusions include as "Advances in Agreement" this statement:

> That the teaching about Mary in the two definitions of the Assumption and the Immaculate Conception, understood within the biblical pattern of the economy of hope and grace, can be said to be consonant with the teaching of the Scriptures and the ancient common traditions.[64]

The tone is very different from Barth's. Have Barth's strong protests against nineteenth- and twentieth-century developments in Mariology been ignored in the interests of ecumenical consensus? Not at all. On the contrary, one can argue, and I have argued, that strong warnings by non–Roman Catholics like Barth against excessive Mariologies influenced the debates at Vatican II, restrained those anxious to hail Mary as Co-Redeemer, and thus made it possible for both Protestants and Roman Catholics to be faithful to the position both held before Trent when Mary was not a church-dividing subject. Or, as another Oxford church historian, Judith Maltby, says, "Mary was not a 'target' of the Reformers."[65] Let all sing Magnificat, Mary's song!

The observers at Vatican II were delighted that after some painful discussions, the bishops agreed not to have a separate document on Mariology but to incorporate what they wished to say about Mary in their document about the church. My own university tutor, Professor George Caird, who was an observer at Vatican II, was delighted at this:

> We Protestants cannot be too grateful for the courage and generosity with which the Council Fathers have grasped this particular nettle. They have recognised what a serious obstacle their Mariology has been to Protestants, and they could hardly have done more without seriously imperilling the simple faith of millions of loyal Roman Catholics. Whatever residual doubts we may have, we can have real sympathy with a portrayal of Mary which puts all the emphasis on her role as a member of the Church who

---

64. Anglican Roman Catholic International Commission, *Mary, Grace and Hope in Christ* (Harrisburg, PA/London: Morehouse, 2005), para. 78.

65. Judith Maltby, "Anglicans, the Reformation and the Anglican Roman Catholic International Commission's Agreed Statement: *Mary, Grace and Hope in Christ*," *Theology* 110, no. 855 (May-June 2007): 171-79. Maltby is critical of the way her Anglican colleagues misuse history in support of Protestant devotion to Mary and thinks the views of the International Commission on Mary might be distorted by the fact that all but two of the twenty-one commissioners were men.

shares with other members the need of redemption, and as a symbol of the Church's present faith and future glory.[66]

So much for the Immaculate Conception! Caird was a Reformed theologian and biblical scholar, at the time a member of the Congregational Church in England and Wales and later of the United Reformed Church. He would claim that his understanding of Mary is shaped entirely by accounts of Mary in the New Testament. Some Roman Catholics might be alarmed by his interpretation. They would say, and did say, that proper respect was not being shown to the Mother of our Lord if she was included as a sort of appendix to a document about the church. The pope, Paul VI, was aware of some of these objections[67] and so felt the need to make quite clear his own views on Mary, whatever the Council might decide. Before the final vote on *Lumen Gentium,* the pope gave his judgment: "We declare/*declaramus*" Mary is "Mother of the Church."[68]

Barth had clearly studied *Lumen Gentium* in detail when he met the pope. He was aware that even some of Rome's greatest theologians held different views about Mary. He simply asked: Are the predicates of Mary, Advocate, Auxiatrix, Adjutrix, and Mediatrix in paragraph 62, to be understood only in the context of pious invocation? — a view he thought Ratzinger held. And if so, should the Immaculate Conception and the Assumption also be seen as pious invocation? Differently expressed, the contrast is sometimes made between devotion and dogma, aids to prayer or theological propositions. We are not told what the pope said in reply except that when Barth admitted a preference for Joseph, the pope said he would pray that he might be given deeper insight. On a different document, the Decree on the Apostolate of the Laity, Barth rather mischievously asked, "If Mary is the perfect example of the apostolate of the laity and as such Queen of the Apostles and therefore of Peter and his colleagues and successors, is it then necessary to speak of the superiority of the apostolate of the laity to all other forms of the apostolate of the Church?" Again we do not know what the pope's response or that of his fellow bishops was to such a radical suggestion.[69]

Strengthened by the whole approach of Vatican II, Barth must have felt on solid grounds when he persuaded an unknown Roman Catholic theo-

---

66. George B. Caird, *Our Dialogue with Rome* (Oxford: Oxford University Press, 1967), pp. 45-46.

67. *History of Vatican II,* vol. 3, p. 368.

68. *History of Vatican II,* vol. 4, pp. 446-48.

69. *Ad Limina Apostolorum* 23.1.5; 32.

logian not to deliver a lecture on Mariology. Barth commends the care the writer has taken in the lecture he sent to Barth for comment, but he raised the question, "Could Mariology as such be a legitimate theme for theology?" Barth thinks not. So did Vatican II, hence the subject of Mary became part of a wider consideration of the church, not a separate topic.[70] In *Lumen Gentium*, Mary is the subject of chapter 8: "The blessed Virgin Mary, Mother of God, in the mystery of Christ and the Church."

Two final comments on the Vatican document about Mary. As Reformed observer George Caird noted, this was a very sensitive subject for Roman Catholics to handle. Opinions among the bishops in Council were deeply divided. Luis Tagle in the *History of Vatican II* describes the period when a number of highly controversial decisions came before the Council as "the Black Week of Vatican II," 14-21 November 1964. On November 18th, the pope declared that he would bestow on Mary the title "Mother of the Church." The author notes that "the text on the Blessed Virgin had split the assembly almost exactly in half, making it possible to have at least a thousand fathers in favor of the title. Numbers here are important, whatever the Roman Catholic Church may sometimes say about 'democracy' because Council documents required a two-thirds majority. The pope was aware that the title was 'requested by fathers from various parts of the world.'"[71] The title also reflected his own convictions. But opinion would also be divided as to the wisdom of a pope at such a universal Council choosing to act unilaterally. Peter Hebblethwaite, Paul VI's biographer, says the pope "made what seemed like a mistake." Tagle notes that "[e]ven the mild Semmelroth considered the proclamation the worst part of a very bad day." Peter Hebblethwaite asks himself the question, "Why did Paul do it?" and concludes: "Sometimes the simplest answers are best." Paul used the title, "Mary, Mother of the Church," because he believed in it. So did the otherwise radical "conciliarist," Cardinal Suenens. But if the pope's decision was a "mistake" it was, so Hebblethwaite explains, because he was disagreeing with the Theological

70. *Ad Limina Apostolorum* 59-62; "A Letter about Mariology" dated Basel, 21 October 1966, *Letters*.

71. Alberic Stacpole OSB, "Mary's Place in *Lumen Gentium*," in *Mary and the Churches: Papers of the Chichester Congress 1986 of the Ecumenical Society of the Blessed Virgin Mary* (Dublin: Columba, 1987), pp. 85-94. Stacpole thinks Paul VI was perfectly in order. Methodists in *Mary, Mother of the Lord* (Peterborough, UK: Methodist Publishing House, 1995), p. 38, raise no objection: "Mary can be seen as mother of all Christians and of the Church," but remains also a fellow disciple. See also for other ecumenical studies, Robert W. Jenson and Carl E. Braaten, eds., *Mary, Mother of God* (Grand Rapids: Eerdmans, 2004).

Commission, which repeatedly and unanimously had rejected the title because it appeared to place Mary *outside* the church whereas the whole thrust
of conciliar Mariology was to include her *within* the church, as the first or
leading disciple, and the "type" of the church, in St. Ambrose's expression.
"[Pope] Paul was in opposition with expert theological opinion."[72]

If the pope, for various reasons, rejected the consensus of the Council, as of course Roman popes are entitled to do, the Council as such paid
great respect to the separated brethren and the observers who acted as their
spokesmen. This is clear in paragraphs 62, 67, and 69 of *Lumen Gentium*
VIII as noted above. This is a welcome advance. Some Roman Catholics had
previously objected in 1854, 1870, and 1950 to Vatican dogma about the Immaculate Conception, Infallibility, and the Assumption of the Blessed Virgin
on the grounds that it would make relations with Protestants and also with
the Orthodox more difficult, but their objections went unheeded. Inspired by
Pope John XXIII, Vatican II was determined to listen to non–Roman Catholic
theologians and this time tried hard to respond to what they were saying.
Above all, they heard and accepted the criticism that whatever was said about
Mary must not detract from the shared belief that we are saved by grace
through faith in Jesus Christ, Savior of the World and Son of God. After list-
ing titles by which Mary is invoked, *Lumen Gentium* states: "This [invocation
of Mary] must be understood in such a way that it takes nothing from the
dignity and power of Christ the one mediator, and adds nothing on to this."[73]

Hierarchy of Truths

Some differences are more important than others, and not all differences
need be church-dividing issues. The Vatican Council's teaching on a "hierarchy of truths" may offer the potential for agreement even where differences
remain.

Barth asks: "What is the meaning of 'an order or hierarchy of truths'
in Catholic teaching which 'vary in their relation to the foundation of the
Christian faith'? What are the 'essentials' of the faith?"[74] Barth cites *Unitatis
Redintegratio* 11:

72. Luis Antonio G. Tagle, "The Black Week of Vatican II, November 14-21 1964," in
History of Vatican II, vol. 4, pp. 446-47; Peter Hebblethwaite, *Paul VI, the First Modern Pope*
(London: HarperCollins, 1993), pp. 368-69.

73. *Lumen Gentium* 62.

74. Barth, *Ad Limina Apostolorum*, p. 28.

In ecumenical dialogue, when catholic theologians join with other Christians in common study of the divine mysteries. . . . When comparing doctrines with one another, they should remember that in catholic doctrine there exists an order or "hierarchy" of truths, since they vary in their connection with the foundation of the Christian faith.

And 4:

All in the church must preserve unity in essentials. But let all, according to the gifts they have received, maintain a proper freedom in their various forms of spiritual life and discipline, in their different liturgical rites, and even in their theological elaborations of revealed truth. In all things let charity prevail. If they are true to this course of action, they will be giving ever better expression to the authentic catholicity and apostolicity of the church.

Twenty years later Barth's questions were still being asked in ecumenical circles. I am not sure they were being answered! George Carey, later Archbishop of Canterbury, welcomed the notion. Answering his own question, "Can Protestants and Catholics get together?" he replied: "The Second Vatican Council, in fact, opened new possibilities through a statement in the *Decree on Ecumenism*. The *Decree* suggested that closer agreement among Christians is possible if we think in terms of an hierarchy of truths."[75] He wrote this in 1985. Earlier in 1970 George Lindbeck, who had been a Lutheran observer at Vatican II, used the hierarchy of truths to suggest that the Marian dogmas need not be imposed on Christians who had not originally agreed to them provided they were accepted as "legitimate optional theological opinions." He quoted in support the Roman Catholic ecumenical theologian Thomas Stransky, who had set out some clear examples of how the teaching that some doctrines are more central than others might be applied: "Grace has more importance than sin; the Holy Spirit more than our Lady; the resurrection of Christ more than his childhood; baptism more than penance; the eucharist more than the anointing of the sick."[76]

75. George Carey, *A Tale of Two Churches: Can Protestants and Catholics Get Together?* (Downers Grove, IL: InterVarsity, 1985), p. 160, cited in Mark A. Noll and Carolyn Nystrom, *Is the Reformation Over?* (Grand Rapids: Baker Academic, 2005), p. 33.

76. George A. Lindbeck, *The Future of Roman Catholic Theology* (London: SPCK, 1970), p. 107; Thomas Stransky, "The Separated Churches and Ecclesial Communities," in *Vatican II on Ecumenism*, ed. Michael Adams (Dublin: Columba, 1967), p. 55. Stransky is a joint editor of the *Dictionary of the Ecumenical Movement*, 2nd ed. (Geneva: WCC, 2002), and wrote the article on the Joint Working Group.

The Joint Working Group between the Roman Catholic Church and the World Council of Churches embarked on a study of "The Notion of 'Hierarchy of Truths'" in 1985 and issued its report in 1990.[77] They begin by noting that "[t]he concept has aroused ecumenical hopes, but the expression still needs clarification of its use in the Decree and of its implications for ecumenical dialogue." Earlier, in 1987, Professor William Henn OFM, one of the Roman Catholic participants in this study, in a separate account had listed a number of theologians who agreed that the notion was a "very promising step for ecumenism." They included Schlink, Dumont, Thils, Kuppers, and Valeske, while Cullmann and Lortz said it was probably the most revolutionary statement of Vatican II. Henn says that Congar was probably one of the originators of the expression.[78] The Joint Working Group Report makes no mention of Congar but tells us that the idea was first introduced to the Council by Archbishop Pangrazio (Italy) in November 1963 and later in October 1964 by Cardinal König from Vienna.

The Group finds some sort of consensus in regarding some truths and teachings as more central than others, though it avoids being too specific. There is, or so they suggest, a consensus — for example that the first seven ecumenical councils are more important than others, that baptism and the eucharist have priority over other sacramental acts, and that some biblical passages "bear witness more fully to the fulfilment of God's promise and revelation in Jesus Christ through the Holy Spirit in the church."[79] Such examples are fine but very general. What some of us might hope to hear is that because some truths are more central than others, Roman Catholics could for example accept that most of us share the same apostolic faith as outlined in the Nicene-Constantinopolitan Creed of 381 and need not be required to accept, for example, the two Marian dogmas, the point made by George Lindbeck. The report warns that "[t]here is no picking and choosing of what God has revealed."[80] But what if there is genuine doubt as to whether God has revealed such truths that have no direct support in Scripture? To my mind, the Joint Working Group skates around such issues. In answer to Barth's question, we still do not know what is meant by an order or hierarchy of truths.

77. Joint Working Group (JWG) between the Roman Catholic Church and the World Council of Churches, Faith and Order Paper 150, *The Notion of "Hierarchy of Truths": An Ecumenical Interpretation* (Geneva: WCC, 1990).

78. William Henn, *The Hierarchy of Truths according to Yves Congar* (Rome: Editrice Pontificia Università Gregoriana, 1987), p. 1.

79. *JWG* para. 11.

80. *JWG* para. 25.

The *Malta Report* (1972) on conversations between Lutherans and Roman Catholics refers to the "hierarchy of truths" in a couple of paragraphs but does not clarify what the phrase means.[81] Nor do we learn much more from the Methodist–Roman Catholic Dialogue "Speaking the Truth in Love" (2001). Roman Catholics speak of a "hierarchy of truths." John Wesley spoke of an "analogy of faith" — which sounds rather like Barth — but whether either term helps us know what is most central and what is not is left unclear.[82] In their earlier dialogue (1995), they find agreement on "essential doctrines" like the Trinity and then state:

> But within the ecumenical dialogue also "the hierarchy of truths" of Catholic doctrine should always be respected; these truths all demand due assent of faith, yet are not all equally central to the mystery revealed in Jesus Christ, since they vary in their connection with the foundation of the Christian faith. This may be helpful when we discuss those doctrines which are important for the teaching and spirituality of the Catholic Church, but which will not be easily accepted by Methodists, e.g. the teaching about Mary in relation to Christ and the church.[83]

Part of the difficulty in reaching agreement is that different traditions have long operated with something like a hierarchy of truths, so the idea seems more familiar and workable than it really is. In my own Reformed tradition, one of our journals cited Richard Baxter's motto: "In necessary things unity; in doubtful things liberty; in all things charity"; but even in Baxter's day (1615-1691) Christians found it impossible to agree on what was essential for unity, and Baxter spent the last thirty years of his life in virtual exile as a Nonconformist when with a little more agreement, or liberty, he could have become a bishop of the Established Church. Twentieth-century ecumenical thinkers like Oscar Cullmann say there can be no unity without some concessions, while Karl Rahner pleads for tolerance on matters that he

81. Joint Lutheran Roman Catholic Study Commission, *The Gospel and the Church Malta Report 1972*, in Harding Meyer and Lukas Vischer, *Growth in Agreement I* (Geneva: WCC, 1984), paras. 24, 25.

82. Joint Commission between the Roman Catholic Church and the World Methodist Church Council, *Brighton Report: Speaking the Truth in Love* (2001), reprinted in Jeffrey Gros, Thomas F. Best, and Lorelei Fuchs, *Growth in Agreement III: International Dialogue Texts and Agreed Statements, 1998-2005* (Geneva: WCC, 2007), para. 23.

83. *The Word of Life: A Statement on Revelation and Faith* (1995), reprinted in Jeffrey Gros, Harding Meyer, William G. Rusch, *Growth in Agreement II: Reports and Agreed Statements of Ecumenical Conversations on a World Level, 1982-1998* (Geneva: WCC, 2000), para. 116.

and his colleague Heinrich Fries regard as less essential. In the proposals they offer that could make the unity of the churches an actual possibility, they say: "[N]ot every member is required to agree . . . to every single proposition which the Church itself considers part of its binding confession."[84]

Barth was also asking: "What are the essentials" that "all in the church" must preserve if there is to be unity? Of course we know what Barth himself would say: "Jesus Christ!" Unlike the Lutherans he would not necessarily expound this as "justification by grace through faith." The Joint Working Group Report speaks of "the mystery of Christ" but admits that this in itself has not been enough to make our communion in the Holy Spirit fully visible, and this is due in part to disagreement about "the ordering of truths around the central mystery."[85] So we are back to the tantalizing difficulty of a phrase that too easily raises false hopes because we think we know what it means.

In the next and final chapter I consider how we may rediscover our unity by responding to Pope John's vision of a more attractive Roman Catholic Church, the actual experience of the Council, and Barth's concept of "event."

84. Heinrich Fries and Karl Rahner (1983), ET Ruth Gritsch, Eric Grosch, *Unity of the Churches: An Actual Possibility* (Philadelphia: Fortress Press, 1985).

85. *JWG* paras. 29, 31.

CHAPTER SEVEN

The Rediscovery of Unity

Roman Catholics are understandably critical of any suggestion that a united church is something that has now to be created, as it were from scratch, by pooling together the best insights of the different traditions. Traditionally she has claimed the church is already one and her unity clearly visible. Come and see! Return to Rome! Rome is Home! The appeal should not be dismissed too quickly. Michael Ramsey, Archbishop of Canterbury at the time of Vatican II, once declared: "The ultimate goal of the ecumenical movement was reunion with Rome, but, indeed, not with the Roman Church in its present form."[1] It was a way of saying there can be no reunion without reform.

Some of the bishops at Vatican II, including England's Cardinal Heenan, were still appealing to the rest of us to "return to Rome." Congar is blunt in his dismissal: "Heenan: he spoke at length to say little. HE SPOKE IN TERMS OF RETURN."[2] Hans Küng, writing before the start of the Council, was confident that Pope John XXIII had better hopes in mind than "all the wholly theoretical and ineffectual appeals to 'return' which have run out so often."[3] His comment about "theoretical appeals" prompts me to look beyond the theory to the practice of unity, and this is what I propose to do. But first a comment about the Council's main document on church unity.

---

1. Archbishop Michael Ramsey, *Le Monde*, 15 September 1963 and cited in *History of Vatican II*, vol. 2, ed. Giuseppe Alberigo and Joseph A. Komonchak (Maryknoll, NY: Orbis/Leuven: Peeters, 1995-2006), p. 540.

2. Yves Congar, *My Journal of the Council*, 30 November 1962.

3. Hans Küng (1961), ET Cecily Hastings, *The Council and Reunion* (London: Sheed & Ward, 1961), p. 4.

Unity in Theory and Practice: Vatican II as an Example of Unity

Unitatis Redintegratio is often heralded as *the* document that marks the Roman Catholic Church's entry into the modern ecumenical movement and serious dialogue with other ecclesial communities. I propose something different. The Council, and not any particular Council document, is a much better expression of real progress in "the restoration of unity among all Christians." The Council in its sometimes painful and courageous pilgrimage from the sort of views once expressed by Heenan and Ottaviani — Rome is right, the rest of you are wrong — became a much better example of the church seeking to answer Jesus' prayer that all may be one, than the Decree on Ecumenism or any such statement.

I say this for three particular reasons. All such documents too easily sound just like nice ideas. Even the World Council of Churches' New Delhi Statement, agreed in November 1961, after the announcement of Vatican II but before the start of the Council, can only point to a theory and a belief, not to a practice:

> We believe that unity which is both God's will and his gift to his Church is being made visible as all in each place who are baptised into Jesus Christ and confess him as Lord and Saviour are brought by the Holy Spirit into one fully committed fellowship, holding the one apostolic faith, preaching the one Gospel, breaking the one bread, joining in common prayer and having a corporate life reaching out in witness and service to all and who at the same time are united with the whole Christian fellowship in all places and all ages in such wise that ministry and members are accepted by all, and that can act and speak together as occasion requires for the tasks for which God calls his people.[4]

The statement, largely the work of Reformed theologian Lesslie Newbigin, Bishop of the recently formed United Church of South India, remains, despite its incredibly long sentence, and despite more recent variations,[5] one of the best expressions of the unity we seek — but it remains just that, an expression of a hope. Second, and by contrast, what actually *happened*

---

4. *The New Delhi Report: The Third Assembly of the World Council of Churches 1961* (London: SCM, 1962), p. 116; Lesslie Newbigin, *Unfinished Agenda: An Autobiography* (London: SPCK, 1985), pp. 171-72.

5. *The Busan Report: The Tenth Assembly of the World Council of Churches 2013*. The Assembly adopted a Unity Statement intended to offer a more holistic vision of the unity we seek.

at Vatican II can serve as a real-life example of what happens as unity is restored. The Council did not fulfill the vision of New Delhi. All non–Roman Catholics, and even at one point Roman Catholic women journalists, were excluded from communion, but it does at best show us a real company of men, and later a few women, drawn from every continent and many different Christian traditions, searching and praying for unity and sometimes discovering it. The belief expressed in *Unitatis Redintegratio* 3, that "those who believe in Christ and have been truly baptised are in some kind of communion with the catholic church, even though this communion is imperfect," was *actually* embodied in the meetings during the Council and in the encounter Barth experienced when he met and talked and prayed with Pope Paul VI and other bishops and theologians. Unity has to be embodied so that we can be seen to be one. Jesus Christ is not just a nice idea. He is a human being whom we — our ancestors — heard with their own ears, saw with their own eyes, touched with their own hands, "the Word that gives life. This life was made visible" (1 John 1:1-2). Likewise, his Body, the Body of Christ, is not just a concept but a community gathered in Christ and by Christ. Unity is something we can experience as well as discuss. Vatican II, says Alberigo, editor of its *History* and expert on earlier Councils like Florence, was not just decrees but a community of believers, confronted by the Word of God.[6] Bea relished the whole experience of the Council: "Ever since the end of the Council's first period I have repeatedly stated that the fruits of the Council were to be sought, to a large extent, less in the actual documents than in the whole experience of the Council, represented by those who took part in it."[7] The "experience of being together, going together slowly toward a common purpose" gives us, says George Tavard, a consultant who worked with Bea in the Unity Secretariat at Vatican II, "the spiritual experience of binding the Body of Christ, structuring the Church as the gathering of the People of God."[8]

Third, and this is great news, the experience of unity is much better than the theory! This is the reverse of what is sometimes said: "Roman Catholic

6. Giuseppe Alberigo, "Vatican II et sa Héritage," in *Vatican II and Its Legacy*, ed. Mathijs Lamberigts and Leo Kenis (Leuven: Leuven University Press, 2002), p. 1; Giuseppe Alberigo, ed., *Christian Unity: The Council of Ferrara-Florence 1438/9-1989* (Leuven: Leuven University Press, 1991).

7. Stjepan Schmidt SJ, *Augustin Bea: Cardinal of Unity* (New York: New City Press, 1992), p. 453.

8. George Tavard, *The Church Tomorrow* (London: Darton, Longman & Todd, 1965), p. 118.

theology has beautiful language about the church yet there is often a gap between the rhetoric and practical realities."[9] Having met a few people who were at Vatican II and read the reports and debates of many more, I have fallen in love with the Council. I am not so drawn to *Unitatis Redintegratio.* It marks a step forward, but the Council went further. Pope John XXIII's vision of the Council and the pope himself attracts our response in a way that a document that is so hedged around with claims and qualifications can never do.

Jewish Comment: The Joy of Acceptance

I discovered recently a superb example of how the experience of friendship and acceptance is so much more powerful than any document about unity. Some Jewish men from the United States went to Rome to hear at firsthand Rome's renunciation of centuries of anti-Semitism and blaming Jews for the death of Christ. As they met and talked with some of their bishops from the United States they experienced amazing friendship and fraternal love that their ancestors had probably never known.[10] They were deeply moved. The experience was better than the document *Nostra Aetate.* One of Barth's distinguished Jewish admirers, Michael Wyschogrod, can also explain why: "The non-Christian religions are spoken *about,* not spoken to." Jews, especially, would feel they are not being spoken to when all issues about the churches' complicity in the holocaust are glossed over, a point Barth strongly criticized in *Nostra Aetate.* He expected "an explicit confession of guilt here." It did not come.[11]

---

9. Patrick Connolly, "Receptive Ecumenical Learning and Episcopal Accountability within Contemporary Roman Catholicism — Canonical Considerations," in *Receptive Ecumenism and the Call to Catholic Learning,* ed. Paul D. Murray (Oxford: Oxford University Press, 2008), pp. 241-52, 241.

10. Rabbi Marc H. Tanenbaum, "A Jewish Viewpoint," in *Vatican II: An Interfaith Appraisal,* ed. John H. Miller (Notre Dame: University of Notre Dame Press, 1966), pp. 349-57, 357.

11. Michael Wyschogrod, *Abraham's Promise: Judaism and Jewish Christian Relations* (Grand Rapids: Eerdmans, 2004/London: SCM, 2006), p. 180. For his comments on Barth see also "A Jewish Perspective on Karl Barth," in Donald K. McKim, *How Karl Barth Changed My Mind* (Grand Rapids: Eerdmans, 1986), pp. 156-61; *Ad Limina Apostolorum,* p. 36.

Pope John XXIII's Vision

The pope surprised the world by his announcement of a Council. His vision caught the imagination not only of ecumenically minded Christians in other churches but of the world's media. As World Council of Churches' observer Lukas Vischer noted: "Hundreds of journalists and television teams streamed into Rome" and the Council "became an abiding subject of interest in the secular press."[12] It became a public event in the way that no council or church assembly had ever been before.

Moments of inspiration are hard to describe, and in the early months after the surprise announcement in January 1959 the pope often fumbled in his explanations of what he had in mind, or should we say, what Christ himself was summoning his church to become. This pope was a man of prayer, unlike most of the popes the Reformers had to endure in the sixteenth century. He felt inspired by God to call a Council. But one of his most attractive explanations is reported by one of Barth's young Roman Catholic admirers, Hans Küng, in his popular little paperback, *The Council and Reunion* (1961):

> The Ecumenical Council will be a demonstration, uniquely far-reaching in its significance, of truly world-wide catholicity. What is happening is proof that the Lord is assisting this salutary plan with his holy grace. The idea of the Council did not come as the slowly ripening fruit of long deliberation but was like the sudden flowering of an unexpected spring. . . . By God's grace, then, we shall hold this Council; we shall prepare for it by working hard at whatever on the Catholic side most needs to be healed and strengthened according to the teaching of our Lord. When we have carried out this strenuous task, eliminated everything which could at the human level hinder our rapid progress, then we shall point to the Church in all her splendour, *sina macula et ruga,* and say to all those who are separated from us, Orthodox, Protestants, and the rest: Look, brothers, this is the Church of Christ. We have striven to be true to her, to ask the Lord for grace that she may remain for ever what he willed. Come; here the way lies open for meeting and for homecoming; come; take, or resume, that place which is yours, which for many of you was your fathers' place. O what joy, what a flowering even in civil and social life, may be looked for by the

12. Lukas Vischer, "The Council as an Event in the Ecumenical Movement," in *History of Vatican II*, vol. 5, pp. 485-539, 489-91. See below how Pope Francis was in 2013 the most talked-about name on the Internet.

whole world if once we have religious peace and the re-establishment of the family of Christendom.[13]

The quotation, taken from an address to diocesan presidents of Italian Catholic Action, says it all. The pope wanted to make the Church of Rome more attractive. He succeeded. He holds before us the prospect of "truly world-wide catholicity" to which our representatives, the observers, would be able to contribute. They would demonstrate by their presence a more comprehensive catholicity than that already "subsisting" in the Church of Rome.

What then was so special about this Council? With the help of theological advisors Karl Barth and Yves Congar and some of their colleagues, Reformed and Roman Catholic, I offer the following answers as to why I see the Council itself as a model of the unity we seek.

The Council Was an "Event"

This understanding of Vatican II is picked up by Alberigo and his colleagues in the *History of Vatican II*. It chimes in beautifully with Barth's ecclesiology. It expresses what the pope has said: "The idea of the Council did not come as the slowly ripening fruit of long deliberation but was like the sudden flowering of an unexpected spring." It was not something instituted by a constitution that might require such a Council to be held at regular intervals as had once been envisaged at Constance (1415) in *Haec Sancta* and the related decree *Frequens* with the requirement that Councils be held at regular intervals.[14] Such a requirement is part of the constitution of the World Council of Churches. Assemblies must be held every seven years or so. Nor was it like Nicea, summoned by the emperor to keep the peace and agree on a creed. It was not specifically a reunion council like Florence. On that point, too, Barth was right. The prime aim of Vatican II was not Christian reunion, though it might aid the process. Vatican II did not have to happen. It did. Why? Because, according to the pope, the good Lord said it must! And what is more, the Lord was already offering his help. The Council was

13. Pope John XXIII, address to diocesan presidents of Italian Catholic Action, cited in Hans Küng, *The Council and Reunion* (London: Sheed & Ward, 1961), p. 6. The biblical reference is to Ephesians 5:27.

14. Norman P. Tanner SJ and Giuseppe Alberigo, eds., *Decrees of the Ecumenical Councils*, vol. 1 (London: Sheed & Ward, 1990), pp. 438-39; Francis Oakley *Council over Pope? Towards a Provisional Ecclesiology* (New York: Herder & Herder, 1969), pp. 74-77.

part of his "salutary plan" and was being aided by "his holy grace," which in Barth's theology is another name for Christ. The Council was an "event."

Such an explanation gains credibility even in skeptical minds by the fact that the pope's decision took everyone by surprise. Pope John was an old man. You don't expect an old man to come up with young ideas, but he did. John Wilkins, the editor of *The Tablet*, "could barely believe his eyes when Pope John XXIII summoned the world's bishops to Rome." And when it happened, he exclaimed: "the bravery of it, the confidence of it!"[15] It took one's breath away. The pope himself later reported that the cardinals received the announcement of the Council in "impressive, devout silence." Alberigo adds: "The disturbance felt by these churchmen is easily understood."[16] After all the traumas of Pius XII, "Hitler's Pope?" and all that, anything for a quiet life! Elect an old man who will hold the reins and die quietly. It was not to be. Thank God!

Could it be that church unity will only be "restored" when we allow such comings together "to happen"? British Christians have a superb example of this in what happened at a British Council of Churches' Conference at Swanwick in 1987. Cardinal Basil Hume had come with a carefully prepared speech. No one knew what he was about to say because he decided not to say it. He tore up his prepared script and committed his fellow Roman Catholics, there and then, to join in the new Ecumenical Partnerships of Churches Together.[17] An older ecumenist, Nathaniel Micklem, one of the people to whom this book is dedicated, once remarked: "We must have rules but we must not expect the Holy Spirit to keep *our* rules."

In too many union negotiations we are imprisoned by our own rules. Daniel Hardy in one of his last essays identified as a major problem in reunion the way each church "insists on its own ways as normative." It is a problem that readily afflicts the Church of Rome with its ecclesiology, which is, in Hardy's view, "an impressively dense, closely articulated whole."[18] *Uni-*

15. Austen Ivereigh, ed., Introduction in *Unfinished Journey: The Church Forty Years after Vatican II* (London/New York: Continuum, 2003), p. 2.

16. Giuseppe Alberigo, "The Announcement of the Council," in *History of Vatican II*, vol. 1, pp. 1-54, 2.

17. Martin Reardon, the First General Secretary of Churches Together in England, gives a less dramatic but more accurate account of the Swanwick "event." See Martin Reardon, "Christian Unity," in *Basil Hume by His Friends*, ed. Carolyn Butler (London: Fount/HarperCollins, 1999), pp. 101-12, 110-11.

18. Daniel W. Hardy, "Receptive Ecumenism — Learning by Engagement," in *Receptive Ecumenism and the Call to Catholic Learning*, ed. Murray, pp. 428-41, 430.

tatis Redintegratio tends to measure all other ecclesial bodies by what Rome thinks the church ought to be and is. Perhaps we all do this. But not all make this claim: "[I]t is only through Christ's catholic church, which is the all-embracing means of salvation, that the fullness of the means of salvation can be attained" (*UR* 3), unless by "catholic" we mean something different and more inclusive than the Church of Rome as she now is.

The Restoration of Unity, an Event Not of Our Making

This is, I think, where Barth's event ecclesiology can make a positive contribution to ecumenism. Instead of trying to impose on the other a pre-arranged or even preordained package, we allow unity to happen, expect the Holy Spirit to act. To adapt a section of *Church Dogmatics:* the church becomes one when it is gathered and lets itself be gathered together "by the living Jesus Christ through the Holy Spirit." We can't explain how this happens but it does happen. The event is not ours to control. Barth really does believe that Christ is alive and active![19] He adds a comment: "[T]he saying about the wind which blows and is heard, but we do not know whence it comes or whither it goes (John 3:8) seems to repel any question as to the explanation of the fact that it does blow and is heard."[20] The church is when people "can make a common response with their existence to the work of Jesus Christ received by them as Word." As "Word" addressed to them; not spoken about them as though they were not there! And for all the criticisms that are leveled at Barth — and also at Vatican II — for saying too little about the Holy Spirit, Barth's whole discussion of the church in the last volumes of his *Church Dogmatics* begins with "The Holy Spirit and the Gathering of the Christian Community."[21] But Barth will make it abundantly clear in a later section that he cannot agree with those who dismiss all thought of law and order in the church with the cry echoed by Emil Brunner, "What we need is the Holy Ghost." The Christian community must not order its life like any other human society but on the contrary constantly recognize that Christ himself is the One who orders, commands, and controls and to whom they owe obedience.[22] Christ is the Head of the church. But though this is stated

19. Paul T. Nimmo, *Being in Action* (London: T. & T. Clark, 2007), p. 18, writes of Barth's "profound confidence" that God does speak to us and we are able to hear him.

20. *Church Dogmatics* IV/1, p. 649.

21. *Church Dogmatics* IV/1, pp. 643-50.

22. *Church Dogmatics* IV/2, pp. 681-82.

in the Letters of Paul, the New Testament does not give us a blueprint for all, for all times:

> To discuss the problem of the Church in terms of this criterion [is] a romantic undertaking which makes no serious attempt at theological deliberation. . . . The New Testament does not attest a model of Christian fellowship, but "the life of the Lord in the community," and therefore the basic law which is valid and normative for the community in every age.[23]

Critics of Barth will say that it is not enough to say that Christ is the Head of the church. We need to say more about authority and how decisions are made. This is to misunderstand Barth. Barth recalls how a Roman Catholic colleague told him, "Let's not argue about the Pope, let's talk about Christ."[24] And at that point, says Barth, real dialogue began. Barth is setting priorities. Let us first agree that "the purpose of Church government is to see that Christ and He alone rules in His Church." Or, as was affirmed at the Confessing Synod at Barmen in 1934 in a declaration drafted by Barth: "Jesus Christ, as he is attested for us in Holy Scripture, is the one Word of God which we are to hear and which we have to trust and obey in life and in death."[25] Agreed on that, we then go on to explore together how best the church may discern Christ's will. Barth, on the basis of his known views, might then say that the church needs to be more democratic and its leadership more collegial. But in a serious deliberation with Roman Catholics and others he might be led by God to say something different. So might we.

Saying Yes, "placet," to God's Will

Unity for Barth is God's will. In *Reshaping Ecumenical Theology* (2010), the Anglican ecumenist and widely read expert on the subject, Paul Avis, reminds us: "No one was more insistent on the imperative of Church unity and the scandal of separation than Barth."[26] And he quotes what Barth said

---

23. *Church Dogmatics* IV/2, p. 686, where Barth cites his Reformed colleague Eduard Schweizer.

24. Karl Barth, *Gespräche 1959-1962*, p. 204.

25. Eberhard Busch, ET Darrell and Judith Guder, *The Barmen Theses, Then and Now* (Grand Rapids: Eerdmans, 2010), p. 19.

26. Paul Avis, *Reshaping Ecumenical Theology* (London: T. & T. Clark, 2010), p. 108.

in his 1936 lecture for the Faith and Order Conference in Edinburgh in 1937 and repeated in *Church Dogmatics* IV/1 in 1953:

> There is no justification theological, spiritual or biblical for the existence of a plurality of churches genuinely separated in this way and mutually excluding one another internally and therefore externally. There may be good grounds for the rise of these divisions. There may be serious obstacles to their removal. There may be many things which can be said by way of interpretation and mitigation. But this does not alter the fact that every division as such is a deep riddle, a scandal. . . . For the *una ecclesia* cannot exist if there is a second or third side by side or opposed to it.[27]

Unitatis Redintegratio agrees with Barth! There can only be one church. Neither wishes to be too dogmatic about where or where not she may be found.

Unlike Congar, Barth never gave up in his hopes for reunion. It was God's will. Congar sometimes asked himself, "Do we really want unity?"[28] That was never Barth's question. Unity is God's will even if not our wish.

Praying Together

Barth was not able to attend the Council and join with the fathers in their daily prayer. His Reformed colleague and one-time translator,[29] Douglas Horton, was.

Horton, as retired Dean of Harvard, was the only observer who attended all the Plenary Sessions in the four years of the Council. He was also present at every Mass. Of course — why "of course"? — he was not permitted to receive communion, but this did not color his judgment: "The most important

---

27. Karl Barth, *Church Dogmatics* IV/1, pp. 675-76, cited in part in Avis, *Reshaping Ecumenical Theology*, p. 108; Barth, *The Church and the Churches* (1936), new edition with Foreword by William G. Rusch (Grand Rapids: Eerdmans, 2005), pp. 19-30, "The Multiplicity of the Churches."

28. Bernard Lauret, ET John Bowden, *Fifty Years of Catholic Theology: Conversations with Yves Congar* (London: SCM, 1988), p. 80.

29. Douglas Horton introduced English-speaking readers to Barth with his translation of *The Word of God and the Word of Man* (London: Hodder & Stoughton, 1928), reissued in 1957. He added his own glowing tribute: "People in general have heard Professor Barth gladly because he seems to understand their needs." A more recent translation is now that of Amy Marga, *The Word of God and Theology* (London/New York: Continuum, 2011).

moment at the Vatican Council was the moment of the Mass."[30] And where the celebrants and the liturgies came from different cultures and continents, he appreciated more and more the rich diversity evident in one church.

Barth has his own distinctive take on ecumenical prayer. Prayer is asking for God's help. We are commanded by Christ to pray and so need never doubt that our prayers are heard. Asking God's help is part of the covenant relationship God has established in Christ with all his people. Even when we pray on our own we pray with Christ and with all his people, for all his people, and indeed for all people: "We have seen that one cannot plead one's own cause before God without first and foremost pleading His, which is also the cause of the whole community, of the ecumenical Church and indeed of all creation."[31]

Horton, on the basis of his experience of worshiping together at Vatican II, adds that the best prayer may sometimes be silent: "that moment of silence when all were aware of the presence of Christ in the midst of the company."[32] I find this a most moving observation. It challenges any suggestion that we can only experience Christ's Presence when we receive the consecrated bread and wine from authorized hands. It is also supported by Roman Catholic theologian Nicholas Lash's comments on worship. Under the subheading "A School of Prayer," Lash pleads for more silence. "Ours is a culture of relentless, restless noise. And yet, without some sense of stillness, of sustained attentiveness, we are rendered deaf to ourselves, to each other, and to the mystery of God." Let there be "pools of silence" during the celebration of the liturgy, pauses between petitions of prayer. He is surely suggesting that in the silence, we stop speaking so we can hear God answering.[33]

One of God's answers is to bring us together through prayer. Basil Hume, commenting on his experience of the Swanwick Conference I mentioned earlier, has this to say: "In 1987 and 1990, we were very polite to one another; now we are friends. In 1987 and 1990 we came to watch each other pray; now we pray together." He told the Conference that unity was a gift of God that he felt had been given in abundance during the Conference.[34]

---

30. Address 24 June 1966, cited in Theodore Louis Trost, *Douglas Horton and the Ecumenical Impulse in American Religion* (Cambridge, MA: Harvard University Press, 2002), p. 222.

31. *Church Dogmatics* III/4, pp. 87-115, 110. See also Don E. Saliers, ed., *Prayer, Karl Barth*, 50th anniv. ed. (Louisville: Westminster John Knox, 2002).

32. Trost, *Douglas Horton*, p. 222.

33. Nicholas Lash, "The Church — A School of Wisdom," in *Receptive Ecumenism and the Call to Catholic Learning*, ed. Murray, pp. 63-77, 74.

34. Speech by Basil Hume at Swanwick Conference Centre, Derbyshire, 3 September 1987, in *Basil Hume by His Friends*, ed. Butler, pp. 110-11.

Horton and the other observers prayed together with the bishops and *periti* at Vatican II. We can be sure Barth prayed with them and for them, though from his home in Basel.

Praying together became so important at the Council that in its final months Congar could write in his *Journal:* "Cullmann told me that the Pope would have liked to have a service of prayer with the Observers. But several people had raised difficulties, and the idea has had to be abandoned. There will only be a reception at the end of the Session."[35] No doubt the "several people" remembered that only a few years earlier Catholics and Protestants were not allowed even to say the Lord's Prayer together.

If, as Barth insists, true prayer is asking, it is also expecting something to happen, some "event" not of our making. Our life together is invocation, calling on God.[36]

Responding to the Word

From an ecumenical point of view the Council's decrees, *Dei Verbum, Sacrosanctum Concilium,* and *Lumen Gentium* and several others, are just as important as *Unitatis Redintegratio* on the Restoration of Unity and the guidance later offered in the *Directory for the Application of Principles and Norms on Ecumenism,*[37] issued in 1993.

Most significant of all was the liturgical act of "enthroning" the Bible before the whole assembly of bishops, theological experts, and observers. This, as we have seen, was the action that most impressed Barth when he read about it and challenged Congar as he prepared for it to happen: "I know that in a few moments a Bible will be placed on a throne in order to preside over the Council. BUT WILL IT SPEAK? Will it be listened to? Will there be a moment for the Word of God?"[38] Barth seemed confident that the placing of "the old book of the Gospels" in "the direct line of vision of the bishops" (and observers!) was "more than just a necessary piece of liturgical and ornamental scenery" but on the contrary was a sign

35. Congar, *Journal,* 26 November 1965.

36. Invocation is the theme that runs through the last and unfinished volume of *Church Dogmatics* IV/4, ET Geoffrey W. Bromiley, *The Christian Life* (Grand Rapids: Eerdmans/Edinburgh: T. & T. Clark, 1981).

37. Pontifical Council for Christian Unity, *Directory for the Application of Principles and Norms on Ecumenism* (London: Catholic Truth Society, 1993).

38. Congar, *Journal,* 11 October 1962.

of "the dynamics of the beginning of a reorganization — precisely around the Gospel" for which years of closer Bible study by Roman Catholics had served as preparation.[39]

Fifty years before the Council, the young Karl Barth, pastor at Safenwil, actually proposed that the act of worship at the start of a Synod should be abolished! It had become, in his view, a mere formality. It bore no relation to, and made no difference to, the proceedings that followed. Joining in worship means that the members commit themselves to take "directions from the norms of the world of the gospel, the desire to be at least a community of faith and hope and so the governing body" of such a church.[40] Horton was confident that the reading of Scripture and the celebration of the Mass did make a difference to the way the Council fathers debated and what they decided. It is for those of us who now read the documents to say if we agree. Did the fathers hear the Word?

The first document agreed by the Council was that on the Liturgy. It is full of biblical references. Even when citing fathers of the church like Augustine, the reference is to one of his commentaries. It includes this rationale for a lectionary:

> In order that believers can be provided with a richer diet of God's word, the rich heritage of the Bible is to be opened more widely, in such a way that a fuller and more nourishing selection of the scriptures gets read to the people within a fixed period of year.

As was noted earlier, the Council's decision has, in Barth's view, resulted in much better and more biblical preaching. It also bore fruit ecumenically in the widespread adoption of a Common Lectionary based on the three-year cycle of readings in the Missal. Likewise the *Decree on Ecumenism* does not only quote John 17, that all may be one, but makes frequent references to other parts of the New Testament, though none at all to the Old Testament, despite the desire expressed elsewhere to affirm God's continuing covenant with Israel as his original people. Barth himself would ask the pope and others in Rome why the Decree made no reference to "Abraham's stock" and to "the most grievous, the fundamental schism — the opposition of church

39. Karl Barth, "Thoughts on the Second Vatican Council," *Ad Limina Apostolorum*, pp. 68-69.

40. Karl Barth, ET James D. Smart, *Revolutionary Theology in the Making: Barth-Thurneysen Correspondence, 1914-1925* (London: Epworth, 1964), p. 34, Letter to Thurneysen, 5 October 1915.

and synagogue"?[41] A later Reformed theologian, Walter Brueggemann, then too young to be involved with Vatican II, offers helpful insights from the Old Testament in one of his many "commentaries" in "Rethinking Church Models through Scripture."[42]

Unitatis Redintegratio applauds the "love and reverence, almost a cult, for holy scripture" found among the separated brothers and sisters but highlights a major difference on the question of the authoritative and authentic interpretation of Scripture: "For, according to catholic belief, the authentic teaching office has a special place in the interpretation of the written word of God."

By "authentic teaching office," Rome tends to mean the pope and the Magisterium. Why not the theologians? The query was raised by that great ecumenical leader, Reformed churchman Willem Visser 't Hooft, first General Secretary of the WCC. Like many a church leader or bishop he was too involved in administration to have time to be, in his own judgment, a "theologian," though Barth would hate to hear anyone make that disclaimer. All God's people should be theologians! But he can offer from his own experience this comment: "A bishop may be a good theologian, though this is by no means always the case; but however gifted he is in this direction, his other duties will prevent him giving the necessary time to theological studies." After decades in which there had been "no real dialogue between Catholic theologians and the authorities of their church, it seemed almost a miracle . . . that the Council became the meeting place of the *magistri* and the *magisterium*. Theologians were at last given the opportunity to fulfill their calling. But sadly it did not last. After a few years, the old problem of relationship appeared in a new form." Visser 't Hooft was writing in the 1980s.[43]

The Council, however, saw a positive point arising from this difference: "The sacred utterances provide for the work of dialogue an instrument of the highest value in the mighty hand of God for the attainment of that unity which the Saviour holds out to all."[44] But here, as so often, Council docu-

41. Barth, *Ad Limina Apostolorum*, p. 30.

42. Walter Brueggemann, *Cadences of Home: Preaching among Exiles* (Louisville: Westminster John Knox, 1997), pp. 99-109.

43. W. A. Visser 't Hooft, *Teachers and the Teaching Authorities* (Geneva: WCC, 2000), pp. 66, 77. The unfinished manuscript was not published until twenty years after it was written. For supporting comment from a Roman Catholic theologian, see Charles E. Curran, *Loyal Dissent: Memoir of a Catholic Theologian* (Washington, DC: Georgetown University Press, 2006).

44. *Unitatis Redintegratio*, para. 21.

ments are both generous and grudging. It is unkind in an ecumenical document to describe someone's love of the Bible as "a cult." The same paragraph includes the alteration demanded by the pope or others in authority that we non–Roman Catholics cannot be said to *find* God in the Scriptures even though we are commended for seeking God there.[45] In real dialogue the parties should be able to speak for themselves. We non–Roman Catholics *do* find God speaking to us as we listen for his Word in the Bible, and when, as Calvin would insist, we are guided by the Holy Spirit in our understanding. In my own Reformed tradition the question addressed to ministers and elders is: "Do you believe that the Word of God in the Old and New Testaments, discerned under the guidance of the Holy Spirit, is the supreme authority for the faith and conduct of all God's people?"[46] I do.

But even such an emphasis on a "supreme authority" can be inhibiting unless we also appreciate Barth's convictions about Scripture. Scripture speaks a liberating Word. In a section with the subheading "Freedom under the Word," Barth states:

> When Scripture exercises authority over the church, all the things which under the rule of autonomous faith are either declared essential and indispensable with legalistic zeal, or avoided and rejected with a similar legalistic concern, can at different times have a place or not a place, not merely by permission but by command, not merely because they are harmless, but for salvation: popes and councils, bishops and pastors, the dignity of synods and congregations, leaders and inspired teachers, the ministry of theologians and others in the congregation, the ministry of men and the ministry of women. But why this or that? And not this or that? It is only if the freedom of God's Word is suppressed, or on the presupposition of an "enthusiastic" supplanting of Scripture, that we can wish legalistically to command or forbid.[47]

Receptive Ecumenism

Vatican II and even the *Decree on Ecumenism* can be commended for its openness and readiness to receive from Christians of other traditions and

---

45. See the account of the so-called "Black Week" at Vatican II in *History of Vatican II*, vol. 4, pp. 388-452, 409.

46. *Manual of the United Reformed Church in the United Kingdom*, Schedule B.

47. Barth, *Church Dogmatics* 1/2, p. 694.

their communities. Again, the Council itself and not any particular document is the best expression of this. Nearly 200 theologians from the major
world communions were invited not just to come and watch but to actively
participate and contribute their insights. They were appointed, in many
cases, because they were ecumenically committed. Douglas Horton had
been active in unity negotiations in the United States. Max Thurian came
from the Taizé community. Originally a Reformed monastic community, it
was becoming increasingly ecumenical and remains so today, with brothers
drawn from different communions including the Roman Catholic Church.
Lukas Vischer was Director of the Faith and Order Commission of the World
Council of Churches. Traditionally they could have been dismissed as heretics. Now the popes and council fathers and their expert advisors wanted to
hear and possibly "receive" what they had to offer. In some cases, including
"ecumenism," quite a lot.

"Receptive Ecumenism" seeks to develop that conciliar experience. As
expounded by its leading theologian, and a great personal friend, the lay
Roman Catholic Paul Murray:

> Receptive Ecumenism is concerned to place at the forefront of the Chris-
> tian ecumenical agenda the self-critical question, "What, in any given
> situation, can one's own tradition appropriately learn with integrity from
> other traditions?" And, moreover, to ask this question without insisting,
> although certainly hoping, that these other traditions are also asking
> themselves the same question.[48]

As already indicated, for Roman Catholics, one answer about what can
be learned and received is "love and reverence for holy scripture," but without turning this into a cult! Somewhat glossed over, is some fifty years of
ecumenical experience in conferring with Christians in other traditions in
major conferences like Edinburgh 1910, Stockholm 1925, Lausanne 1927, Oxford and Edinburgh 1937, and by the start of the Council, three Assemblies of
the World Council of Churches: Amsterdam 1948, Evanston 1954, and New
Delhi 1961. There was also the formation of united churches in Canada 1925
and South India 1947. Barth was rather annoyed that "this initiative of the
non-Catholic churches is not explicitly recognised."[49] He might have added
that the theological convictions underpinning "the ecumenical movement"

48. Paul D. Murray, "Receptive Ecumenism and Catholic Learning — Establishing the
Agenda," in *Receptive Ecumenism and the Call to Catholic Learning*, ed. Murray, pp. 5-25, 12.
49. Barth, *Ad Limina Apostolorum*, p. 30.

are also undervalued if ecumenism is only seen as a call to "the catholic faithful to recognise the signs of the times and take an intelligent part in the work of ecumenism."[50] Often taken for granted is the way we all cheerfully sing hymns from other traditions while continuing to reject their authors if, in our view, they were not properly ordained. Reception, like dialogue, is two-way. For Barth and many of his Protestant contemporaries what they (we) needed to receive from Rome was her high view of the place of the church in God's plan of salvation. Barth was saying this in his days at Münster in that famous lecture, "Roman Catholicism: A Question to the Protestant Church" (1928). After Vatican II there was much to be learned and received from Rome in the matter of reform and renewal. He feared "we might be left far behind by a papal church that is making a dynamic recovery."[51]

The Ecumenical Gift Exchange

Closely associated with "Receptive Ecumenism" is the "Ecumenical Gift Exchange." The idea has been developed by Margaret O'Gara and others. Her background is that of a Roman Catholic theological student in a predominantly Protestant faculty, quickly realizing how little she knew about Protestantism and Protestants knew about her own Catholicism.[52] Each side has gifts to offer of which the other is unaware. She quotes *Lumen Gentium*:

> By virtue of this catholicity, the individual parts bring their own gifts to the other parts and to the whole church, in such a way that the whole and individual parts grow greater through their mutual communication of all and their united efforts towards fullness in unity.[53]

The Decree on Ecumenism urges Roman Catholics to acknowledge and esteem the "truly Christian endowments" found among the separated brothers and sisters, to recognize (in them) "the riches of Christ"(4). Roman Catholics are to recognize that "the churches of the East have a treasury from which the Western church has drawn extensively — in liturgical practice, spiritual tradition and canon law"(14). But at other times, the same Decree

---

50. *Unitatis Redintegratio*, para. 4.
51. Barth, *Ad Limina Apostolorum*, pp. 76-77.
52. Margaret O'Gara, *The Ecumenical Gift Exchange* (Collegeville, MN: Liturgical Press, 1998), pp. 29-30.
53. O'Gara, *The Ecumenical Gift Exchange*, p. vii; *Lumen Gentium* 13.

gives the impression that the Roman Catholic Church has everything she needs and the rest of us therefore have little to offer. We may have some of her gifts (3); she has all of them. "Our Lord entrusted *all* the blessings of the new covenant to the one apostolic college of which Peter is the head, in order to establish the one body of Christ on earth into which all should be fully incorporated who belong in any way to the people of God" (3). But here Ladislas Orsy SJ, a participant in the first Durham Conference on Receptive Ecumenism, and canon law expert at Vatican II, comes to our aid. His own tradition, he admits, needs humility and this does not come easily:

> The Catholic community may feel that such a humble attitude is contrary to their fundamental belief since "the Church of Christ . . . *subsists* in the Catholic Church" (*LG8, UR4*). What more can they learn and receive? They can learn and receive a lot: God is rich enough to give them more. The faithful can always progress in their intelligence of faith and their deeds of love. The Church of Christ within the Catholic Church (and for that matter wherever it is present) is a dynamic reality[54] always prompting the community to progress towards its eschatological perfection.[55]

Help from us all is needed to fulfill one particular part of our common calling, namely in realizing the fullness of catholicity and in the restoration of unity, and this is clearly stated in the Decree:

> The divisions among Christians prevent the church from realizing in practice the fullness of catholicity proper to her, in those of her sons and daughters who, though attached to her by baptism, are yet separated from full communion with her. (4)
>
> The restoration of unity is the concern of the whole church, faithful and clergy alike. (5)

Such help will, one hopes, be gladly received. Congar had predicted in his *Journal:* "There can be no doubt that the Council will have the effect of forcing Rome to discover catholicity."[56] Catholicity, that is, in breadth as well as depth. As Ladislas Orsy states, "the Council leaves room for enrichment," and he reminds us that the Decree keeps the best things until last when it

54. Barth would be delighted to hear a Roman Catholic describe the church as "a dynamic reality."

55. Ladislas Orsy SJ, "Authentic Learning and Receiving — A Search for Criteria," in *Receptive Ecumenism and the Call to Catholic Learning*, ed. Murray, pp. 39-51, 45.

56. Congar, *Journal*, 21 November 1962.

recognizes that the task before us, "the reconciling of all Christians," is beyond all our "human powers and capacities."[57]

Catholic Learning

With many of the world's best theologians of all traditions, Vatican II offered an amazing opportunity for "catholic learning" in the fullest sense of the term. It extended this to all the participants in Rome and readers everywhere who followed the debates and read and still read the documents. Rome became one great open university. This was great. Visser 't Hooft described it as "almost a miracle."[58] You could go to lectures by Rahner or Congar, talk about human rights with Robert McAfee Brown and John Courtney Murray from the United States, New Testament theology with Oscar Cullmann or George Caird, what it might mean to be "the Church of the poor" from Professor Míguez Bonino from Argentina. Some would learn for the first time about an "ecumenical movement" or about serious objections to calling Mary "Mediatrix." And such "catholic learning" was vital if one was to have an informed debate about the church or the Restoration of Unity. Nor did it matter if some of these teachers were Methodist or Lutheran, Reformed or Roman Catholic, for in catholic learning, as the Decree on Ecumenism wisely states: "Whatever is truly Christian is never contrary to what genuinely belongs to the faith; indeed, it can always bring a deeper realization of the mystery of Christ and the Church."[59] Congar, we may recall, had said that "the whole truth is grasped only in communion with the whole Church."[60] It got him into trouble once, but now that he was being honored as an expert at the Council it was no sin to listen to him! Dan Hardy, also a participant at the first two Receptive Ecumenism Conferences, raised the question "whether any church can discover the truth of the Church by itself."[61] And Barth, who pleaded that there is no past in the church, urged us all not to dismiss too quickly those whose views challenge our own. "All heretics are relatively heretical, so even those who have been branded heretics at one time or another and condemned for their avowed folly and wickedness must be allowed

57. Ladislas Orsy, "Authentic Learning and Receiving," p. 40; *Unitatis Redintegratio* 24.

58. Visser 't Hooft, *Teachers and Teaching Authorities*.

59. *Unitatis Redintegratio* 4.

60. Yves Congar, *True and False Reform in the Church*, originally published in 1950.

61. Daniel W. Hardy, "Receptive Ecumenism — Learning by Engagement," in *Receptive Ecumenism and the Call to Catholic Learning*, ed. Murray, pp. 428-41, 430.

their say in theology."[62] Barth's theology would reinstate the once-banned Congar and plead that we go on listening to his (Barth's) friend, Hans Küng, whose post-Vatican II theology remains suspect in Rome. Nor should we ever dismiss Schleiermacher. Barth never could.

Universal Catholicity

"Catholic" can also mean "universal" and as such, Vatican II was the most universal Council that has ever been held. Its 2,500 bishops came from every continent and from almost every country. The church, meaning the Roman Catholic Church, was in the view of Karl Rahner beginning to discover herself as "a world Church" even if "manifested only more or less rudimentarily."[63] Rahner, Jesuit theologian from Innsbruck and later Munich, was very conscious that the Council was still dominated by European theologians — like himself and Congar and those Belgians! — and their ways of thinking. Even when there were cultural variations in the celebration of Mass, there were still no African dancers. He should have come to the World Council of Churches Assembly in Harare, Zimbabwe in 1998, but alas he died too soon, 1984. The Council had, however, opened up serious consideration of other world religions and this too was a positive first. The church was involved in a transition that was as dramatic as the change from being a church of the Jews to a church of the Gentiles. Barth would wish he had said of Jews and Gentiles.

A different slant on the same issue is provided by a journalist at Vatican II, Michael Novak, in his popular account, *The Open Church*. He takes up a question posed by Fr. George Tavard.[64] Can the church move away from its old legalistic habits? Will it be Catholic or simply Latin?[65] As a Member of the Secretariat for Christian Unity, Tavard would appreciate that in order to be more "Catholic" the "Latin" church needed more ecumenical help.

62. Karl Barth (1946), ET Brian Cozens and John Bowden, *Protestant Theology in the Nineteenth Century*, new edition (London: SCM, 2001), p. 3.

63. Karl Rahner, "Basic Theological Interpretation of the Second Vatican Council," ET Edward Quinn, *Theological Investigations* XX (London: Darton, Longman & Todd, 1987), pp. 77-89.

64. For an excellent account of Tavard, expert on and at Vatican II and on Calvin and Tillich, see Marc R. Alexander, *Church and Ministry in the Works of G. H. Tavard* (Leuven: Leuven University Press, 1994).

65. Michael Novak, *The Open Church* (London: Darton, Longman & Todd, 1964), pp. 117-18.

The Joint Working Group between the Roman Catholic Church and the World Council of Churches, inaugurated just before the conclusion of Vatican II, took up this challenge. It embarked on a study of "Catholicity and Apostolicity." The Fourth Assembly of the World Council of Churches, meeting at Uppsala in 1968, considered a Faith and Order Report on "The Holy Spirit and the Catholicity of the Church." Both these initiatives illustrate how Vatican II opened up a wider discussion about "The Nature of Catholicity" and how Roman Catholic theologians, including Barth student Jérôme Hamer, were contributing to the debate. At the Faith and Order meeting held in the Jesuit College in Louvain, the attempt was made to broaden the discussion beyond the level of ecclesial disputes and focus more on the call to all the churches to renewal and mission. The Louvain account includes what has long been a controversial statement, that of Ignatius: that "[w]here Jesus Christ is, there is the Catholic Church."[66] This is not quite what Vatican II said!

Pastoral Council

"From a very early date, it was understood that the pope wished the Second Vatican Council to be primarily 'pastoral' in nature." So says Joseph Komonchak in the opening volume of the *History of Vatican II*. But then he has to admit that there was no agreement as to what was meant by "pastoral."[67] A later volume describes the Council as "Doctrinal and Pastoral."[68] This is a more appropriate and helpful description.

Council documents in cold print cannot possibly convey the fact that the Council was pastoral in the best sense of being warm, welcoming, and caring, not least to the observers. Few, perhaps only four, who were there are still alive to tell us. A few more left detailed accounts of their days in Rome. I have drawn heavily on Congar's *Journal* and the five-volume *History of Vatican II*, both of which pay a lot of attention to the observers and what they had to say. If all one knew about Vatican II was what is written in the sixteen major documents, you would never know they were there or what a

66. World Council of Churches, Faith and Order Paper 59, *Faith and Order Louvain 1971* (Geneva: WCC, 1971), pp. 133-40; Ignatius, *Smyrna* 8.2, sometimes contrasted with "where the bishop is there is the Church." See also Carl E. Braaten and Robert Jenson, eds., *The Catholicity of the Reformation* (Grand Rapids: Eerdmans, 1996).

67. *History of Vatican II*, vol. 1, p. 179.

68. *History of Vatican II*, vol. 4, ch. 3, "Doctrinal and Pastoral," pp. 195-231.

difference their presence made to its debates and decrees. But what we can all discover is that the whole tone of this Council was pastoral and caring, and this is one of its lasting legacies. Our theologies and our churches are still being criticized, not least in the reluctance to call churches like my own United Reformed or the Church of England "churches," but there are no anathemas. We are being listened to with love and respect, not simply condemned and dismissed. This is an enormous gain and it has transformed ecumenical relationships ever since. The Council became a model of good practice that is far more eloquent than all that *Unitatis Redintegratio* or any other document has to say. Though not formally part of the World Council of Churches, Rome is a full member of the Faith and Order Commission[69] and of many regional and national councils, and active in experimenting with "revisioning Christian unity" through the Global Christian Forum. All this is the legacy of Vatican II.[70]

The greatest ecumenical compliment to the pope and fathers at Vatican II is to assert that if the sixteenth-century Reformers had been invited to such a Council, the church in the West might still be one. There can be reformation without division. More modestly, we can say that Vatican II vindicates conciliarism, which had too long been suspect in Rome. It also dropped heavy hints in favor of greater collegiality among pope and bishops but failed to carry through the necessary reforms. But it could be that the sheer practicalities of being a world church will make collegiality an obvious necessity. This is the view of Nicholas Lash and others: only the collegiality of the worldwide episcopate, with and under the pope, can sustain the *koinonia* of such a world church. Congar made a similar point.[71] But this claim is not yet recognized, and what Lash laments and criticizes is the way that decades after the Council, the church is "far more rigorously and monolithically controlled by pope and curia than at any time in its history." Synods in their present form are little more than "instruments of papal power."[72] But he continues to hope: "The centralised control from which we suffer,

69. For many years, Rome was strongly represented by Jean-Marie R. Tillard (1927-2000) as a Vice-Moderator of the Faith and Order Plenary Commission.

70. Huibert van Beek, ed., *Revisioning Christian Unity: The Global Christian Forum* (Oxford: Regnum Books International, 2009). The first Forum was held in Limuru, Kenya in 2007.

71. Congar, *Journal*, 15 October 1962.

72. Nicholas Lash, "Vatican II, O Happy Memory and Hope," in *Unfinished Journey: The Church Forty Years After Vatican II*, ed. Austen Ivereigh (London/New York: Continuum, 2003), pp. 13-31, reprinted in Nicholas Lash, *Theology for Pilgrims* (London: Darton, Longman & Todd, 2008), pp. 227-39.

and which has contributed so greatly to the present crisis of authority, was built up in less than a hundred years. It could be put into reverse in less than ten." Since then, another ten years have passed with no sign of progress. In a later essay, Lash cites the Vatican II historian Joseph Komonchak, that the decision was made at the Council "not to resolve a disputed issue." The relation between papal primacy and episcopal collegiality was one of them.[73] It remains unresolved to be resolved.

Subsidiarity

It is ironic that it is papal teaching about subsidiarity that could answer Lash's complaints about excessive centralized control from Rome. The teaching was expounded in Pius XI's encyclical *Quadragesimo anno* (1931). Today, it is more often cited in political discussions, for example about the relative power of the European Community versus national governments, or by neo-conservatives in support of private enterprise, but Pius XII emphasized that it also applied to the church. So did Pope John XXIII. If, as some suggest, it is implicit in some of the documents of Vatican II, the references are not that obvious. The Extraordinary Synod of Bishops in 1985 recommended further study of the issue.[74]

Its fundamental teaching is that decisions should be made as near to the grassroots as possible by those most affected by them. One aim is to encourage a sense of responsibility. On this principle, a congregation should have a major say in the appointment of its priest, a diocese in that of its bishop. In both cases, appointments are not only of concern to local people but also the wider church, so the decision-making process needs to be shared. Subsidiarity can then be linked with what Cardinal Suenens called "co-responsibility." The Jesuit ecumenist Edward Yarnold once commented: "Other Christians need to see this principle of subsidiarity in practice before they accept the Papacy."[75]

---

73. Nicholas Lash, "In the Spirit of Vatican II," in *Theology for Pilgrims*, p. 267.

74. Ad Leys, *Ecclesiological Impacts of the Principle of Subsidiarity* (Kampen: Uitgeverij, 1995).

75. Edward Yarnold SJ, *In Search of Unity: Ecumenical Principles and Prospects* (Slough, UK: St. Paul Publications, 1989), p. 112.

Conciliar Consensus and Discerning Truth through Debate

As for conciliarism, it is a remarkable "achievement," or should we say, sign of the working of the Holy Spirit, that 2,500 bishops from very different cultures and continents could reach consensus and near unanimous agreement on so many contentious issues. *Lumen Gentium* deals with the place of Mary in the church, a subject on which at one stage the Council was almost evenly divided. Yet in the end it was agreed to: 2,151 to five. *Dei Verbum* deals with Scripture and Tradition, also contentious, but had the support of 2,350 bishops and only six against. The *History of Vatican II* and other accounts of the debates expose sharp differences before such agreements were reached. This may or may not demonstrate the truth of the English Puritan John Milton's famous claim:

> Though all the winds of doctrine were let loose to play upon the earth, so Truth be in the field, we do injuriously by licensing and prohibiting to misdoubt her strength. Let her and Falsehood grapple, whoever knew Truth put to the worse, in a free and open encounter.[76]

Vatican II can revive our confidence in the discovery of Truth through debate. I say this despite reading Congar's comment that there were too many set speeches and too little debate in the actual assembly.[77] The real debates took place in the commissions and in the coffee bars, or as individual bishops weighed up and prayed over opposing arguments. In some cases decisions were delayed for a year or more rather than rushed through in a hurry. The Council provided space for "polemical" theologians like Barth as well as rehabilitating theologians like Congar who had been told to keep quiet and stop writing.

Does Barth Have Anything to Add to Discussions about Bishops?

Barth is more interested in the documents of Vatican II than in the process of debate through which they were fashioned, but this is partly because he could read the documents but was not present at the debates. We can, however, glean from earlier comments what he might wish to add.

Barth supported Hans Küng in a campaign in Basel in 1967 to retain the

76. John Milton, *Areopagitica*.
77. Yves Congar, *Journal*, 22 October 1963.

right of the local cathedral chapter to elect their own bishop,[78] something that Nicholas Lash would surely approve. Küng is delighted that Barth is "interested in these questions of church politics" where that other famous professor in Basel, Hans Urs von Balthasar, is not. Thirty years later this practice of subsidiarity seems to be forgotten. Rome makes sure that the bishop is loyal to Rome. Kurt Koch, once radical, now defends every Roman position. His consecration takes place in Rome, not in the local cathedral. By 2006, after ten years as bishop, "a deep gulf has emerged between bishop and people." Hans Küng, of course, has his critics but so do his critics. Unlike Nicholas Lash, he can sound bitter in his disappointment: "I see the freedom of the election of bishops endangered not by the free liberal state, but by an authoritarian Curia which, not unlike the Kremlin, is in process of taking over the episcopate all over the world."[79] He no longer has his friend Karl Barth to turn to. Küng missed him deeply. Hans Küng led the farewell tributes to Barth at the cathedral service in Basel. In a recent study, Küng returns to the attack in his heartfelt plea, *Can We Save the Catholic Church?* and notes that even in the seventh century the people of Rome had the right to elect the pope as Bishop of Rome. Great bishops like Ambrose of Milan and Augustine of Hippo were chosen by the people. Why not the Bishop of Basel?[80] Should Barth have had a vote?

In an early volume of *Church Dogmatics*,[81] Barth makes some sharp observations about Vatican I. Called by an authoritarian pope, without the consent of the cardinals, it inevitably declared the pope infallible. The pope set the agenda, and the possibility of "fraternal discussion and a general decision" had been ruled out in advance because Rome had rejected the idea of government by synods. Barth is aware of a vocal minority of opposition, "mainly German, but also French and Oriental bishops." (How he might relish a conversation with Margaret O'Gara, expert on this very point![82]) They foresaw that a declaration of papal infallibility would weaken the authority of bishops, make relations with the Eastern Orthodox even more difficult, and do nothing to persuade Protestants to return to Rome. What they lacked, says Barth, was a strong theology, a totally different concept of authority in the church.

---

78. Hans Küng, ET *Disputed Truth: Memoirs II* (London: Continuum, 2008), pp. 24-28.

79. Küng, *Disputed Truth*, p. 25.

80. Hans Küng, *Can We Save the Catholic Church?* (London: William Collins, 2013), pp. 85, 307-8.

81. *Church Dogmatics* I/2, pp. 564-72.

82. Margaret O'Gara, *Triumph in Defeat: Infallibility, Vatican I and the French Minority Bishops* (Washington, DC: Catholic University of America Press, 1988).

But as so often in Barth, he is just as, or even more, critical of his own church. The Protestant church at the time was too theologically weak and too divided to offer strong support to the opposition to the Vaticanum. Things might have been different had Vatican I happened in the days of Schleiermacher! Strange praise indeed, coming from one of Schleiermacher's lifelong critics — though always a very respectful critic. The Protestant churches have also succumbed to "Parliamentarianism" in their practice of church government. This last comment is prophetic. Barth, writing in 1938, anticipates by sixty years the strong criticisms voiced by the Orthodox and other churches against the parliamentary style of decision making in the Protestant-led World Council of Churches. As a result of a Special Commission with the Orthodox churches, the World Council members agreed to make all major decisions by consensus.[83] The old style of voting by majorities always leads, as in the British Parliament, to confrontation, a "fight" between Government and Opposition. In consensus decision making, everyone is involved in seeking agreement, not in winning an argument. Minority viewpoints are listened to, not simply brushed aside because their votes don't count. Vatican II, as we have seen, operated a two-thirds majority principle, but its ideal and often its practice were more like consensus, with near unanimity on certain key issues. But, as we can see in this next section, consensus can involve compromises on controversial issues. Barth learned this at Barmen and so did many at Vatican II.

Mission, Ecumenism, or an Interfaith Issue? The Jewish Question

Barth and Vatican II differed about what to say about the Jews and where to say it. The Council saw Judaism as an interfaith issue. Barth, who began his academic career with a study of Paul's Letter to the Romans, saw the continued separate existence of the Synagogue as *the* ecumenical issue, as in Romans 9-11: "Why is the most grievous, the fundamental schism — the opposition of church and synagogue (Romans 9–11; Ephesians 2) — not dealt with here, but only spoken of the relation of the church to 'Abraham's stock' in the Relation-

---

83. Jill Tabart, *Coming to Consensus* (Geneva: WCC, 2003). Dr. Tabart comes from the Uniting Church of Australia, which has practiced consensus decision making for the past twenty years or so. The Society of Friends (Quakers) has an even longer history of such decision making. Both churches have offered expert advice to the WCC Assemblies and Central Committee meetings.

ship of the Church to Non-Christian Religions?"[84] And earlier, and before the Council, in what became the last major volume of *Church Dogmatics,* Barth had written: "Even the modern ecumenical movement suffers more seriously from the absence of Israel than of Rome or Moscow." He said this in 1959, before the Russian Orthodox Church became part of the World Council of Churches at the New Delhi Assembly in 1961, and before the Second Vatican Council committed Rome to the ecumenical movement in *Unitatis Redintegratio* in 1964. Barth also asked why *Nostra Aetate* on interfaith relations had little to say about mission: "Why is the critical and missionary task of the Church in reference to the religions only marginal to the Declaration and not central to it?"[85] And though he would surely welcome what the Council had to say about freedom of religion, he was less happy about its weak theological basis. Hence his description of *Dignitatis Humanae* as a "monstrosity," which his Roman Catholic friend Hans Küng, as a *peritus* to the bishops, ought to have tried to correct. "I find the declaration on religious freedom absolutely terrible," he told Küng in a letter from Basel, shortly before his visit to Rome to discuss *Nostra Aetate, Dignitatis Humanae,* and other documents he had studied carefully as soon as they were published.[86]

But Barth and all those active at the Council, whether as non–Roman Catholic observers, or as bishops and their *periti,* could all agree with Yves Congar: "Twenty years after Auschwitz it is impossible that the Church should say nothing."[87] All those present at the Council were at least twenty when Hitler's horrendous persecution of the Jews was taking place. All those in Europe had seen it happening. In Berlin, a Roman Catholic priest had been arrested by the Gestapo just because he prayed for the Jews and those in concentration camps.[88] What did bishops from Germany now wish to say? The priest, Monsignor Bernhard Lichtenberg, was only doing what the Vatican said priests do: "The Catholic Church has always prayed for the Jewish people. . . . It especially condemns hatred against the people elected by God." This decree was issued in April 1928. Once Hitler came to power

84. Barth, "Decree on Ecumenism," in *Ad Limina Apostolorum,* p. 30. But see also *Lumen Gentium* 16.

85. Barth, "Declaration on the Relationship of the Church to Non-Christian Religions," in *Ad Limina Apostolorum,* p. 36.

86. Karl Barth, Letter to Hans Küng, 16 September 1966, in *Karl Barth Letters, 1961-1968,* p. 220.

87. Yves Congar, *Journal,* 3 May 1964.

88. Kevin Spicer, *Resisting the Third Reich: The Catholic Clergy in Hitler's Berlin* (Urbana: Illinois University Press, 2004), p. 3.

in 1933 and a Concordat with Hitler had been signed, it was safer to ignore it. And what about the Vatican and the Jews? Susan Zuccotti makes her accusations against Pope Pius XII and bishops in Rome in the stinging title of her study: *Under His Very Windows: The Vatican and the Holocaust in Italy:* "Pius XII did not speak out publicly against the destruction of the Jews. The fact is rarely contested nor can it be."[89] But by 1962, the War was long since over — though not the Cold War. Hitler and Mussolini were dead. What did the bishops at the Vatican Council now wish to say? What resistance to such tyranny and what help to the victims had the church offered?

There were some good stories to tell and many of them ecumenical. The Roman Catholic theologian Henri de Lubac, expert at the Council, and the Reformed Church leader, Marc Boegner, an observer, had cooperated in rescue work for Jews in France.[90] What gestures of reconciliation and repentance ought the church, meaning all churches, to make now?

Barth was very conscious that he had not done enough. If he was being too hard on himself, his biographer, one-time assistant and great advocate, Eberhard Busch, set out to put the record straight in his detailed account, *Unter dem Bogen des einen Bundes, Karl Barth und die Juden 1933-1945*, first published in 1996.[91] When Barth read the biography of Dietrich Bonhoeffer, that the author Eberhard Bethge had sent him, he learned many new facts about his younger colleague. "Especially new to me was the fact that in 1933 and the years following, Bonhoeffer was the first and almost the only one to face and tackle the Jewish question so centrally and energetically." And he went on to make his own confession:

> I have long since regarded it as a fault on my part that I did not make this question a decisive issue, at least publicly in the church conflict (e.g., in

89. Susan Zuccotti, *Under His Very Windows: The Vatican and the Holocaust in Italy* (New Haven: Yale University Press, 2002). What can be, and is, argued over is why, if this is true, the Pope felt he had to keep silent.

90. Marc Boegner, ET René Hague, *The Long Road to Unity* (London: Collins, 1970), pp. 295, 305; Henri de Lubac, *Résistance Chrétienne à l'Antisémitisme, Souvenirs* (Paris: Fayard, 1988).

91. Eberhard Busch, *Unter dem Bogen des einen Bundes* (Neukirchen-Vluyn: Neukirchener Verlag, 1996), 537 pages. Busch presents a short account in George Hunsinger, ed., *For the Sake of the World: Karl Barth and the Future of Ecclesial Theology* (Grand Rapids: Eerdmans, 2004), pp. 53-79: "Indissoluble Unity: Barth's Position on the Jews during the Hitler Era," with a response from Katherine Sonderegger, pp. 80-94. See also Katherine Sonderegger, *That Jesus Christ Was Born a Jew: Karl Barth's "Doctrine of Israel"* (University Park: Pennsylvania State University Press, 1992).

the two Barmen Declarations I drafted in 1934). A text in which I might have done so would not, of course, have been acceptable to the mind set of even the "confessors" of that time, whether in the reformed or the general synod. But this does not excuse the fact that since my interests were elsewhere I did not at least formally put up a fight on the matter.[92]

Such strong self-criticism can be more healing than the reproach of others, even of a Jewish writer like Pinchas Lapide. Lapide wrote critically of "no balm in Barmen" *(Barmen ohne Erbarmen)*.[93] As Barth is given much of the credit for Barmen, it is fair for him to also take much of the blame. But also in fairness, it should be added that at the Synod in 1934, Bonhoeffer was not present to add his support but was still serving as a pastor in London, and that it was Barth who urged Bonhoeffer to return to Germany because that is where he was needed in the struggle against Hitler. It should also be recognized that even though Barth failed to encourage his allies in the Confessing Church to embrace a political struggle against a regime that he soon recognized as demonic, Barth himself, as Angela Hancock's recent study *Barth's Emergency Homiletics, 1932-1933*[94] makes so clear, was engaged in active resistance and defiance and for this reason was under constant threat and surveillance to the point that he was expelled from Germany in May 1935. Had he not been Swiss, his fate might have been the same as Bonhoeffer's. Preaching can be a form of resistance. Barth insisted on giving lectures on Homiletics to counteract the fashion for turning sermons into eulogies for the man sent by God to save the German people from their enemies, including the Jews — notions that no amount of clever exegesis of Scripture could honestly support.

Given his own confession of guilt in not doing enough for the Jews, Barth was justified in a criticism he made of *Nostra Aetate:* "Would it not be more appropriate, in view of the anti-Semitism of the ancient, the medieval, and to a large degree the modern church, to set forth an explicit confession of guilt here?"[95] Rome offered no such confession, a point many Jews were

---

92. Karl Barth, Letter to Rector Eberhard Bethge, 22 May 1967, in *Karl Barth Letters, 1961-1968*, p. 250. English edition of Bethge's biography, translated by Eric Mosbacher et al., *Dietrich Bonhoeffer: Theologian, Christian, Contemporary* (London: Collins, 1970).

93. Pinchas Lapide, *Jeder Kommt zum Vater, Barmen und die Folgen* (Neukirchen-Vluyn: Neukirchener Verlag, 1984), p. 31.

94. Angela Dienart Hancock, *Karl Barth's Emergency Homiletics, 1932-1933: A Summons to Prophetic Witness at the Dawn of the Third Reich* (Grand Rapids: Eerdmans, 2013).

95. Karl Barth, *Ad Limina Apostolorum*, p. 36, "Critical Questions," 7.

quick to notice. Instead, the Council offers a very generalized statement that may not ring true in the ears of all who read it:

> Moreover, the church, which condemns all persecutions against any people, mindful of its common inheritance with the Jews and motivated not by political considerations but by the religious charity of the gospel, deplores feelings of hatred, persecutions and demonstrations of anti-Semitism directed against the Jews at whatever time and by whomsoever.[96]

Jewish critics and many Christians could also note that the Council only "deplores" anti-Semitism, it did not "condemn it." All Vatican documents are a compromise in search of consensus. As we can see from the debates as described in *The History of Vatican II*,[97] many of the bishops wished to say more but needed to say something that almost all could agree to say. Despite all this, the great strength of the document is its bold declaration that *all* Jews are not to be blamed for the death of Christ: "Although the Jewish authorities with their followers pressed for the death of Christ, still those things which were perpetrated during his passion cannot be ascribed indiscriminately to all Jews living at the time nor to the Jews of today."[98]

Open-minded readers of the New Testament could have reached that conclusion earlier. Crucifixion was a Roman punishment. All the first disciples of Jesus were Jews. But even a Bible scholar like Martin Luther had no love for Jews and could be quoted in support of the burning of synagogues. Jews were also barred from Geneva before Calvin's arrival and not welcomed back until much later. Calvin was once asked what he thought about Luther's treatise, *On the Jews and Their Lies* (1543). Unfortunately his answer is not known.[99] Bernard Cottret, for one, is convinced that Calvin opposed anti-Semitism.[100] What we do know about later members of Lutheran and Reformed congregations is that many were guilty of anti-Semitism, and their attitudes made it possible for six million Jews to disappear from the streets of Europe before their very eyes. All churches, not just Rome, have such a terrible crime against humanity to acknowledge. It happened on their watch.

---

96. *Nostra Aetate* 4.

97. *History of Vatican II*, vol. 4, pp. 135-66; vol. 5, pp. 211-21.

98. *Nostra Aetate* 4.

99. J. Marius and Lange van Ravenswaay, "Calvin and the Jews," in *Calvin Handbook*, ed. Herman J. Selderhuis (Grand Rapids: Eerdmans, 2009), pp. 143-46, 144.

100. Bernard Cottret, ET M. Wallace McDonald, *Calvin: A Biography* (Grand Rapids: Eerdmans, 2000), pp. 313-19.

When representatives of the Protestant churches in Germany came together in Stuttgart in October 1945 with representatives of the provisional World Council of Churches, they did what Barth, with the support of Niemöller and others urged them to do: say "frankly and clearly, without any qualifications or modification: We Germans have erred, hence the chaos of today — and we Christians in Germany are also Germans!" What they agreed to say still sounds more heart-rending than routine confessions of sin many of us make, Sunday by Sunday:

> Through us endless suffering has been brought to many peoples and countries. True, we struggled for many years in the name of Jesus Christ against a spirit which found its terrible expression in the National Socialist regime of violence, but we accuse ourselves for not witnessing more courageously, for not praying more faithfully, for not believing more joyously, and for not loving more ardently.[101]

Fine words, in contrast to which *Nostra Aetate*'s denunciation of persecutions sounds remote and aloof. But, at least, the Council's document mentioned the Jews and anti-Semitism. Stuttgart did not. And before the Council even met, Pope John XXIII had removed the reference to "perfidious Jews" in the church's liturgy for Good Friday, a term that could make contempt for Jews look like official teaching. This great pope was known and loved for his compassion for Jews. The same could not be said of his predecessors, Pius XII or Pius XI.

A question of what the Roman Catholic Church should say about the Jews had, as I have noted, already been raised in 1928, but the details have only come to light more recently as some of the Vatican archives were opened to researchers.[102] A Catholic movement, the Amici Israel, committed to Jewish-Christian reconciliation, at one time had support from nineteen cardinals and at least 3,000 priests. In 1928 they petitioned the Holy Office at the Vatican for the removal of this invidious phrase: *"oremus et pro perfidis Judaeis."* They encountered strong opposition. What right had an unofficial body to demand changes in the holy liturgy that had been celebrated since 1570? It was soon made clear that they had no such rights and the organi-

---

101. See James Bentley, *Martin Niemöller* (Oxford: Oxford University Press, 1984), pp. 175-77.

102. Hubert Wolf, "The Good Friday Supplication for the Jews and the Roman Curia, 1928-1975: A Case Example for Research Prospects for the Twentieth Century," in *The Roman Inquisition, the Index and the Jews,* ed. Stephen Wendehorst (Leiden: Brill, 2004), pp. 235-58.

zation was ordered to disband. It was even argued, on the basis of Matthew 27:25, that Jews accepted responsibility for the death of Christ: "His blood be upon us and upon our children." Such texts and such interpretations would be fiercely argued in debates at Vatican II about the traditional charge of "deicide." What Pius XI did do in 1928 was to issue a much-needed decree against anti-Semitism. In retrospect, and in the light of whether the Jewish question is an ecumenical or an interfaith issue, it is relevant to note that in the same year, 1928, that Rome rejected moves for better Christian-Jewish relationships, she also, in *Mortalium Animos,* rejected Roman Catholic participation in the growing ecumenical movement. Jews, Anglicans, and Protestants were outside the fold. The remedy was in their hands. Convert! Return to Rome!

Jews should be credited for much of the initiative in putting their concerns on the agenda of Vatican II. Without their urging, it might never have happened. In a survey of Catholic regions in Germany in 1961, only three out of 81 mentioned Jewish-Christian relations as a topic for the Council.[103] Even in 1928, much of the inspiration for the formation of the Amici Israel came from a Jewish convert to Roman Catholicism, Sophie Franziska. Much of the impetus for *Nostra Aetate* belongs to a Jewish professor, Jules Isaac,[104] who asked for, and was granted, a meeting with Pope John. A Jewish convert, John Oesterreicher, and author of the detailed commentary on *Nostra Aetate* in Vorgrimler's commentaries on the *Documents of Vatican II,* says: "That Jules Isaac's visit had a lasting effect on the Pope cannot in my opinion be doubted. Yet it is doubtful if his was the decisive influence."[105] Credit should also be given to Pope John and his close ally, Cardinal Bea. Deputations of Jews came and thanked the pope for all he had done before and during the

---

103. John Connolly, *From Enemy to Brother: Revolution in Catholic Teaching on the Jews, 1933-1965* (Cambridge, MA: Harvard University Press, 2012), p. 240.

104. Jules Isaac (1877-1963) lost most of his relatives in the Holocaust. He escaped with his life only because he was out when the Gestapo called. In the war years he began a major study, *Jésus et Israël* (1947). By the time he met the pope, he had been researching the Christian roots of anti-Semitism for the past sixteen years and taken part in a Jewish-Christian dialogue on the subject at Seelisberg, Switzerland (1947), for which he presented eighteen points as a basis for discussion. See his lecture in Paris 1959, ET *The Christian Roots of Anti-Semitism* (London: Council of Christians and Jews, 1960) and Pierre Pierrard, *Juifs et Catholiques Français* (Paris: Cerf, 1997). Sadly, Isaac died in 1963, two years before the Council was able to agree on what to say about the Jews and where to say it. *Nostra Aetate,* 28 October 1965, was one of the last documents to be agreed.

105. John M. Oesterreicher, "Declaration on the Relationship of the Church to Non-Christian Religions," in *Commentary on the Documents of Vatican II,* vol. 3, ed. Herbert Vorgrimler (New York: Herder & Herder/London: Burns & Oates, 1968), pp. 1-136, 4.

War in saving Jewish people from Auschwitz and the camps. Bea had written a key article, "Are the Jews a Deicide People?," which was considered to be far too controversial for some journals to publish but which Bea later distributed to the Council fathers. He was also quoted by the *Jewish Chronicle* for commending the way in which the World Council of Churches at its Assembly in New Delhi in 1961 had denounced anti-Semitism as a great evil and for saying that the Catholic Church would not lag behind in that regard.[106] Shortly after the Council, he published a study of *The Church and the Jewish People*.[107] When Jules Isaac handed Pope John a detailed dossier of Jewish hopes for the Council, the obvious person to handle the matter was Bea. Bea was at that time the first President of the Secretariat for Promoting Christian Unity. So for mainly practical and administrative reasons, "the Jews" were first regarded as an ecumenical issue at Vatican II. Barth, if he realized this, would be pleased with the fact but not with the explanations.

Not all were convinced that relations with Jews were an ecumenical issue. Even Willebrands had doubts.[108] To cut a long story short, and it was a long story, given the tortuous history of Christian relationships from New Testament times to the Council's closure in 1965, and all the hours of debate since Jules Isaac presented proposals to the pope in June 1960, it was again partly for pragmatic reasons that the Jewish question came to be treated in a different document and not in *Unitatis Redintegratio*. The same happened to "Freedom of Religion and Human Rights." That subject too had been assigned to the Ecumenical Commission but in the end acquired a document of its own, *Dignitatis Humanae*.

The "Restoration of Unity" was sufficiently complicated without adding Human Rights and the Synagogue to the mix. And the "Jewish Question" was then and now so easily confused with political attitudes to the State of Israel and relations with Christians and Muslims in the Middle East. As earlier noted, Barth himself had experienced such controversies when he and others tried to persuade the Second Assembly of the World Council of Churches at Evanston in 1954 to accept a theological statement on "The Hope of Israel."

106. Stjepan Schmidt SJ, *Augustin Bea: Cardinal of Unity* (New York: New City Press, 1992), pp. 501-2.

107. Augustin Cardinal Bea SJ, ET Philip Loretz, *The Church and the Jewish People* (London: Geoffrey Chapman, 1966).

108. Mauro Velati, "Willebrands at the Council," in Peter de Mey et al., *The Ecumenical Legacy of Johannes Cardinal Willebrands, 1909-2006* (Leuven: Peeters, 2012), p. 100. He worked on the subgroup, De Judaeis, but had a clear conviction that the Jews posed a different question than that of "separated brethren."

Barth posed the question of whether we see the Jews as objects of mission or sisters and brothers in the People of God. He believed with Paul (the Jew and Christian?) that God's covenant with Israel was never revoked (Rom. 11:29). What the church should do is witness to God's saving love in Christ in such a way as to make Israel jealous (Rom. 10:19). Vatican II tried hard, but not hard enough, to make the church more attractive to Jews. Its good intentions are summed up in the book by John Connolly, *From Enemy to Brother: The Evolution in Catholic Teaching on the Jews, 1933-1965.*[109]

Concluding Comment

Vatican II was so totally different in style and outcome from Vatican I that it had Barth's enthusiastic support to his dying day. He had no illusions that the Council's hopes for "the restoration of unity" were about to be fulfilled. He told students and staff in conversations at the Ecumenical Institute at Bossey in 1967 that unity would come but it might take a hundred years, which means fifty years from now, or much longer.[110] Difficulties remain, but there are no "irreconcilable differences."[111] In earlier conversations he surprised some of his Protestant listeners when he said he prayed for the pope. Asked a question about "intercommunion," Barth said, just get on with it: "Do it and don't ask questions"![112]

Ecumenical diplomats would be horrified. They can explain why. But why not? Newbigin might say this is Barth at his most polemical. Meanwhile, the nearby Ecumenical Community at Taizé follows Barth's advice. They have long since abandoned separate tables at communion, and Rome knows what they do.[113] Students and staff at Bossey are more cautious. Fifty years after Barth's conversations with an earlier generation, students at this

---

109. John Connolly, *From Enemy to Brother: The Evolution of Catholic Teaching on the Jews, 1933-1965* (Cambridge, MA: Harvard University Press, 2012).

110. Karl Barth, Conversations with Students at WCC Bossey, 23 January 1967, *Gespräche 1964-68*, pp. 582-83.

111. Conversations with Students at Bossey, p. 588.

112. Conversations with Students at Bossey, some of whom were and are Roman Catholic, p. 588.

113. The discreet little notices suggesting that Catholics and Protestants should gather at separate tables for communion have long since disappeared and the fact is recognized in Rome, for even when Brother Roget (Reformed) was the prior, the celebrant was a Roman Catholic priest.

Ecumenical Institute — Anglicans, Baptists, Lutherans, Methodist, Orthodox, Pentecostal, Reformed, and other traditions — often make their way every Sunday to "their own" churches in Geneva.[114] But who can blame them? Their own churches will not permit them to break bread together at Bossey. Calvin's city is big enough to cater for all tastes. Was this what Jesus had in mind when he prayed passionately that all may be one? Was this what Vatican II was all about? What would Barth say? Surely what he said in 1936:

> We have no right to explain the multiplicity of the churches at all. We have to deal with it as we deal with sin, our own and others'.

The "restoration" or "rediscovery" of unity in Christ is a gift and event that must never be taken for granted. It is also for all Christians our common calling. The legacy of the great pioneers, Barth and Congar and many more, and the experience of Vatican II come to us as a gift from God that can still inspire and encourage all who work and pray for unity. People of my generation never knew Barth or shared directly in that great Council, but we know people who did. Ours is the task to try and communicate what we learned from them.

Postscript: Joy and Peace and a New Pope

As I attempt to conclude, a new pope has appeared on the scene. Barth's old friend, Hans Küng, is cautiously hopeful. A new pope could make all the difference to the church that has become too dependent on its popes.[115] But what grabs my attention is an unexpected article in an often-skeptical newspaper: "Why even atheists should be praying for Pope Francis."[116] It is written by a well-known journalist who is also a Jew. What Jonathan Freedland admires about Pope Francis is that through his own simple lifestyle "[h]e is in the business of scraping away the trappings, the edifice of Vatican wealth accreted over centuries, and returning the church to its core purpose, one Jesus himself might have recognised." He adds that given the guile of those in control, the pope will need all the support he can get. A skeptic on

114. Students at Bossey come from every continent and church tradition. The current Director is Ioan Sauca, priest of the Romanian Orthodox Church. My wife and I worked there 2007-2008.

115. Küng, *Can We Save the Catholic Church?*

116. *The Guardian*, 15 November 2013.

the radio responds that all this is just gesture politics and even a pope has no power to change an institution that has existed for 2,000 years. To this, Freedland responds in words that, for me, reflect Barth's belief in the power of the Word: "The pope may have no army, no battalions or divisions, but he has a pulpit — and right now he is using it to be the world's loudest and clearest voice against the status quo. You don't have to be a believer to believe that." To which I wish only to add: You don't have to be a Catholic to support all such efforts in the reform of Rome, while not neglecting your own congregation whose need for a radical *aggiornamento* may be even greater and so painfully obvious to God. And all this, not for our own, church-centered preoccupations, but for the sake of the world God really cares about. Like Vatican II and its outward-looking document *Gaudium et Spes,* and like Barth himself, a new pope can help all of us rediscover joy and hope in God.

Bibliography

Books by Karl Barth

The sequence follows the chronology of Barth's life, starting with his birth in 1886 and dates in which lectures and addresses, books and articles were first given or written. Chronology is important for tracing possible developments in Barth's thought as well as his responses to contemporary events.

Many of Barth's writings can now be accessed online via the Karl Barth Digital Library. I am grateful to the Bodleian Library, Oxford, for this facility.

Karl Barth (Eberhard Busch). *Karl Barth: His Life from Letters and Autobiographical Texts.* ET John Bowden. London: SCM, 1976.

(1914-1925). Barth-Thurneysen Correspondence. ET James D. Smart, *Revolutionary Theology in the Making: Barth-Thurneysen Correspondence 1914-1925.* London: Epworth Press, 1964.

(1921). *The Epistle to the Romans* (2nd edition). ET Edwyn C. Hoskyns. London: Oxford: University Press, 1933.

(1922). *Die Theologie Calvins.* ET Geoffrey W. Bromiley, *The Theology of John Calvin.* Grand Rapids: Eerdmans, 1995.

(1923-1924). *Lectures at Göttingen.* ET Geoffrey W. Bromiley, *The Theology of Schleiermacher.* Edinburgh: T. & T. Clark, 1982.

(1923). *The Theology of the Reformed Confessions.* ET Darrell L. Guder and Judith J. Guder. Louisville: Westminster John Knox, 2002.

(1924-1925). *Lectures at Göttingen: 1924-1925.* ET Geoffrey W. Bromiley, *The Göttingen Dogmatics,* vol. 1. Grand Rapids: Eerdmans, 1991.

(1925). *Witness to the Word: A Commentary on John 1,* Lectures at Münster 1925 and Bonn 1933. ET Geoffrey W. Bromiley. Grand Rapids: Eerdmans, 1986.

(1927). *The Epistle to the Philippians.* ET James W. Leitch. London: SCM, 1962.

(1927). "The Concept of the Church," "Roman Catholicism: A Question to the

Protestant Church" (1928), and other essays in ET Louise Pettibone Smith, *Theology and Church: Shorter Writings 1920-1928*. New York: Harper & Row, 1962.

(1928). ET Douglas Horton, *The Word of God and the Word of Man*. London: Hodder & Stoughton, 1928; new ET Amy Marga, *The Word of God and Theology*. London: T. & T. Clark, 2011.

(1928). *Ethik*. ET Geoffrey W. Bromiley, *Ethics*. Edinburgh: T. & T. Clark, 1981.

(1929). ET R. Birch Hoyle, *The Holy Ghost and the Christian Life*. London: Frederick Muller, 1938.

(1930). *Der Götze Wackelt, Zeitkritische Afsätze, Reden und Briefe von 1930-1960*. Berlin: Käthe Vogt Verlag, 1961.

(1931). *Anselm: Fides Quaerens Intellectum*. ET Ian W. Robertson. London: SCM, 1960.

(1932-). *Die Kirchliche Dogmatik*, 13 part-volumes. Zürich: Evangelischer Verlag, 1932-1967.

(1936-). *Church Dogmatics*, 13 part-volumes. Geoffrey W. Bromiley and Thomas F. Torrance, eds. Edinburgh: T. & T. Clark, 1936-1969. Vol. I/1 revised translation 1975, *Church Dogmatics IV/4, Lecture Fragments: The Christian Life*. Grand Rapids: Eerdmans/ Edinburgh T. & T. Clark, 1981.

(1934, Barth et al.). "The Barmen Declaration" of the Confessing Church in Germany. In Eberhard Busch, *The Barmen Theses Then and Now*. Grand Rapids: Eerdmans, 2010.

"Gospel and Law" (1935). "Church and State" (1938) and "The Christian Community and the Civil Community" (1946). In Karl Barth, *Community, State and Church*. Gloucester, MA: Peter Smith, 1968.

(1936). *The Church and the Churches*, new edition with Foreword by William G. Rusch. Grand Rapids: Eerdmans, 2005.

(1936). *Credo*. ET J. Strathearn McNab, new edition with Foreword by Robert McAfee Brown. London: Hodder & Stoughton, 1964.

(1937-1938). *The Knowledge of God and the Service of God*, Gifford Lectures 1937-1938. ET J. L. M. Haire and Ian Henderson. London: Hodder & Stoughton, 1938.

(1938-). *Eine Schweizer Stimme 1938-1945* (Letters and addresses in wartime Europe). Zürich: Theologischer Verlag, 1945.

(1938). *Trouble and Promise in the Struggle of the Church in Germany, Lecture Margaret Hall, Oxford, 1938*. Oxford: Clarendon, 1938.

(1940-1943). Lectures and Seminars on Calvin's Catechism. ET Gabriel Vahanian, edited by Jean-Louis Leuba, *The Faith of the Church: A Commentary on the Apostles' Creed According to Calvin's Catechism*. London: Collins Fontana, 1958.

(1943). ET Ernest A. Payne, *The Teaching of the Church Regarding Baptism*. London: SCM, 1948.

(1946). *Against the Stream: Shorter Post-War Writing, 1946-52.* London: SCM, 1954.

(1947). ET Brian Cozens and John Bowden, *Protestant Theology in the Nineteenth Century,* new edition with Introduction by Colin Gunton. London: SCM, 2001.

(1947). ET Shirley C. Guthrie, *Learning Jesus Christ through the Heidelberg Catechism.* Grand Rapids: Eerdmans, 1964.

(1948). "The Church: The Living Congregation of the Living Lord Jesus Christ," Address at the First Assembly of the World Council of Churches, Amsterdam 1948. Reprinted in Paul van Buren et al., *God Here and Now.* London: Routledge Classics, 2003.

(1953-1957). ET John Newton Thomas and Thomas Wieser, *The Humanity of God.* London: Collins, 1961.

(1953-1956). ET John D. Godsey, *Table Talk.* Edinburgh: Oliver & Boyd, 1963.

(1954-1959). ET Marguerite Wieser, Preface by John Marsh, *Deliverance to the Captives.* London: SCM, 1961.

(1956). ET *The German Church Conflict.* London: Lutterworth Press, 1965.

(1958). Based on earlier essays in the *Christian Century,* 1938-1958. In *Karl Barth 1886-1968: How I Changed My Mind,* edited by John D. Godsey. Edinburgh: St. Andrew Press, 1966.

(1959-1964). ET A. T. Mackay, *Call for God: New Sermons from Basel Prison.* London: SCM, 1967.

(1959-1962). *Gespräche 1959-1962.* Zürich: Theologischer Verlag, 1995.

(1960-). ET Eric Mosbacher, edited by Martin Rumscheidt, *Fragments Grave and Gay.* London: Collins Fontana, 1971.

(1961). ET Geoffrey W. Bromiley, *Karl Barth Letters 1961-1968.* Edinburgh: T. & T. Clark, 1981.

(1962). ET Grover Foley, *Evangelical Theology: An Introduction.* London: Collins Fontana, 1965.

(1963). *Gespräche 1963.* Edited by Eberhard Busch. Zürich: Theologischer Verlag, 2005.

(1964-1968). *Gespräche 1964-1968.* Edited by Eberhard Busch. Zürich: Theologischer Verlag, 1997.

(1967). ET Keith R. Crim, *Ad Limina Apostolorum: An Appraisal of Vatican II.* Richmond, VA: John Knox Press, 1968.

(1968). "Concluding Unscientific Postscript on Schleiermacher," ET George Hunsinger in *The Theology of Schleiermacher.* Edinburgh: T. & T. Clark, 1982.

(1968). ET Geoffrey W. Bromiley, edited by Eberhard Busch, *Final Testimonies.* Grand Rapids: Eerdmans, 1977.

Books by Yves Congar

Divided Christendom. London: Geoffrey Bles, 1939.
Vraie et Fausse Réform dans L'Église (1950; 2nd edition 1967), new translation, Paul Philibert OP, *True and False Reform in the Church*. Collegeville, MN: Liturgical Press, 2011.
"Amica Contestatio." In World Council of Churches Faith and Order Study, Intercommunion, edited by Donald Baillie and John Marsh. London: SCM, 1952.
The Wide World My Parish. London: Darton, Longman & Todd, 1961.
Lay People in the Church. 1957, 1964; London: Geoffrey Chapman, 1965.
"Ecumenical Experience and Conversion: A Personal Testimony." In *The Sufficiency of God: Essays on the Ecumenical Hope in Honour of W. A. Visser 't Hooft, First General Secretary of the World Council of Churches*, edited by Robert C. Mackie and Charles C. West. London: SCM, 1963.
Report from Rome: The Second Session of the Vatican Council. London: Geoffrey Chapman, 1964.
Dialogue between Christians: Catholic Contributions to Ecumenism. London: Geoffrey Chapman, 1966.
Tradition and Traditions. London: Burns & Oates, 1966.
Diversity and Communion. London: SCM, 1984.
Le Concile de Vatican II: Son Eglise, Peuple de Dieu et Corps du Christ. Paris: Beauchesne, 1984.
The Word and the Spirit. 1984; London: Geoffrey Chapman, 1986.
Fifty Years of Catholic Theology: Conversations with Yves Congar. Edited by Bernard Lauret. London: SCM, 1988.
My Journal of the Council (2002). ET Mary John Ronayne OP and Mary Cecily Boulding OP. Collegeville, MN: Liturgical Press, 2012.

Books about Vatican II

Abbott, Walter M., SJ, ed. *Documents of Vatican II, with Notes and Comments by Catholic, Protestant and Orthodox Authorities*. New York: Guild Press, 1966.
Alberigo, Giuseppe, and James Provost. *Synod 1985: An Evaluation*. Edinburgh: Concilium and T. & T. Clark, 1986.
Alberigo, Giuseppe, Jean-Pierre Jossua, and Joseph A. Komonchak, eds. *The Reception of Vatican II*. London: Burns & Oates, 1987.
Alberigo, Giuseppe, ed. *Christian Unity: The Council of Florence 1438/9-1989*. Leuven: Peeters, 1991.
Alberigo, Giuseppe, and Joseph A. Komonchak, eds. *History of Vatican II*, vols. 1-5. Maryknoll, NY: Orbis/Leuven: Peeters, 1995-2006.

Berkouwer, G. C. *The Second Vatican Council and the New Catholicism*. Grand Rapids: Eerdmans, 1965.

Brown, Robert McAfee. *Observer in Rome*. London: Methuen, 1964.

———. *Reflections over the Long Haul: A Memoir*. Louisville: Westminster John Knox, 2005.

Butler, Christopher. *The Theology of Vatican II*. London: Darton, Longman & Todd, 1967.

———. *A Time to Speak*. Southend, UK: Mayhew-McCrimon, 1972.

Caird, George B. *Our Dialogue with Rome: The Second Vatican Council and After*. Oxford: Oxford University Press, 1967.

Chittister, Joan. *The Way We Were*. Maryknoll, NY: Orbis, 2005.

Ciorra, Anthony, and Michael W. Higgins, eds. *Vatican II: A Universal Call to Holiness*. New York: Paulist Press, 2012.

Connelly, John. *From Enemy to Brother: Revolution in Catholic Teaching on the Jews 1933-1965*. Cambridge, MA: Harvard University Press, 2012.

Cullmann, Oscar. *Entre Deux Sessions du Concile: Expériences et espérances d'un Observateur protestant*. (Originally published in *Foi at Vie* 1.)

D'Costa, Gavin, and Emma Jane Harris. *The Second Vatican Council: Celebrating Its Achievements and the Future*. London: Bloomsbury, 2013.

Donnelly, D., Josef Faméré, et al., eds. *The Belgian Contribution to the Second Vatican Council*. Leuven: Peeters, 2008.

Faggioli, Massimo. *True Reform: Liturgy and Ecclesiology in Sacrosanctum Concilium*. Collegeville, MN: Liturgical Press, 2012.

———. *Vatican II: The Battle for Meaning*. New York: Paulist Press, 2012.

Ganoczy, Alexandre. *Calvin und Vaticanum II, Das Problem der Kollegialität*. Wiesbaden: F. Steiner, 1965.

Grant, Frederick C. *Rome and Reunio*. New York/Oxford: Oxford University Press, 1965.

Greeley, Andrew. *The Catholic Revolution*. Berkeley: University of California Press, 2004.

Henn, William. *The Hierarchy of Truths according to Yves Congar OP*. Rome Editrice Pontificia Università Gregoriana, 1987.

———. "Hierarchy of Truths and Christian Unity." *Ephemerides Theologicae Louvanienses* 66, no. 1.

Hoose, Bernard, ed. *Authority in the Roman Catholic Church: Theory and Practice*. Aldershot, UK: Ashgate, 2002.

Huizing, Peter, and Knut Walf. *Ecumenical Council: Its Significance in the Constitution of the Church*. Edinburgh: Concilium T. & T. Clark/New York: Seabury Press, 1983.

Ivereigh, Austen, ed. *Unfinished Journey: The Church Forty Years after Vatican II*. London: Continuum, 2003.

Jedin, Hubert. *Crisis and Closure of the Council of Trent: A Retrospective View from the Second Vatican Council.* London: Sheed & Ward, 1967.

Kelly, Kevin. *Fifty Years Receiving Vatican II.* Blackrock, Ireland: Columba, 2012.

Küng, Hans. *The Council and Reunion.* London: Sheed & Ward, 1961.

———. *The Living Church: Reflections on the Second Vatican Council.* London: Sheed & Ward, 1963.

Küng, Hans, and Leonard Swidler. *The Church in Anguish: Has the Vatican Betrayed Vatican II?* San Francisco: Harper & Row, 1987.

Lakeland, Paul. "*Lumen Gentium* Unfinished Business." *New Blackfriars* 90, no. 1026 (March 2009).

Lamb, Matthew L., and Matthew Levering. *Vatican II: Renewal within Tradition.* Oxford: Oxford University Press, 2008.

Lamberigts, Mathijs. *Vatican II and Its Legacy.* Leuven: University Press, 2002.

Lamberigts, Mathijs, ed. *The Belgian Contribution to Second Vatican Council.* Leuven: Peeters, 2008.

Lash, Nicholas. "Vatican II, O Happy Memory and Hope." In *Unfinished Journey: The Church Forty Years after Vatican II,* edited by Austen Ivereigh. London: Continuum, 2003.

———. "The Struggle for the Council." In Nicholas Lash, *Theology for Pilgrims.* London: Darton, Longman & Todd, 2008.

Leeming, Bernard, SJ. *The Vatican Council and Christian Unity.* London: Darton, Longman & Todd, 1966.

Legrand, Hervé. "Forty Years Later: What Has Become of the Ecclesiological Reforms Envisaged by Vatican II?" *Concilium* 4 (2005).

Lindbeck, George A. *The Future of Roman Catholic Theology.* London: SPCK, 1970.

———. "Reminiscenses of Vatican II." In *The Church in a Postliberal Age,* edited by James J. Buckley. London: SCM, 2002.

Madge, William. *Vatican II: Fifty Personal Stories.* Maryknoll, NY: Orbis, 2012.

Mannion, Gerard. *Ecclesiology and Postmodernity.* Collegeville, MN: Liturgical Press, 2007.

Manz, James. *Vatican II Renewal or Reform.* St. Louis/London: Concordia, 1966.

Marchetto, Agostino. *The Second Vatican Council: A Counterpoint for History of the Council.* Scranton, PA: Scranton University Press, 2010.

Massa, Mark S., SJ. *The American Catholic Revolution: How the Sixties Changed the Church for Ever.* Oxford: Oxford University Press, Scholarship on Line September 2010.

McAleese, Mary. *Quo Vadis? Collegiality in the Code of Canon Law.* Dublin: Columba, 2012.

McEnroy, Carmel. *Guests in Their Own House: The Women at Vatican II.* New York: Crossroad, 1996.

Melloni, Alberto, and Christoph Theobald. "Vatican II: A Forgotten Future." *Conclium* 4 (2005).

Mey, Peter de, Denaux Adelbert, et al. *The Ecumenical Legacy of Johannes Cardinal Willebrands, 1909-2006*. Leuven: Peeters, 2012.

Miller, John H., ed. *Vatican II: An Interfaith Appraisal*. Notre Dame and London: University of Notre Dame Press, 1966.

Mulligan, Suzanne. *Reaping the Harvest, 50 Years after Vatican II*. Blackrock, Ireland: Columba, 2012.

Noll, Mark, and Carolyn Nystrom. *Is the Reformation Over? An Evangelical Assessment of Contemporary Roman Catholicism*. Grand Rapids: Baker Academic, 2005.

Novak, Michael. *The Open Church: Vatican II, Act II*. London: Darton, Longman & Todd, 1964.

Oakley, Francis. *Council over Pope? Towards a Provisional Ecclesiology*. New York: Herder & Herder, 1969.

Oakley, Francis, and Bruce Russett, eds. *Governance, Accountability: The Future of the Catholic Church*. London: Continuum, 2004.

O'Brien, John. *Steps to Christian Unity* (Reports Based on Interviews with Observers and Others at Vatican II). London: Collins, 1964.

O'Mahony, T. P. *Why the Catholic Church Needs Vatican III*. Dublin: Columba, 2010.

O'Malley, John W. "Vatican II: Did Anything Happen?" *Theological Studies* 1 (March 2006).

———. *What Happened at Vatican II*. Cambridge, MA: Belknap Press, 2008.

Orsy, Ladislas. *Receiving the Council*. Collegeville, MN: Liturgical Press, 2009.

Outler, Albert C., and John Deschner, eds. *Our Common History as Christians*. New York: Oxford University Press, 1975.

Pawley, Bernard C. *Looking at the Vatican Council*. London: SCM, 1962.

———. *Observing Vatican II: The Confidential Reports of the Archbishop of Canterbury's Representative, Bernard Pawley, 1961-1964*. Edited by Andrew Chandler and Charlotte Hansen. Cambridge: Cambridge University Press, 2013.

Pawley, Bernard C., ed. *The Second Vatican Council: Studies by Eight Anglican Observers*. London: Oxford University Press, 1967.

Rahner, Karl. "The Sinful Church in the Decrees of Vatican II." In *Theological Investigations* VI. London: Darton, Longman & Todd, 1969.

Ratzinger, Joseph (Pope Benedict XVI). *Die erste Sitzungsperiode des Zweiten Vatikanischen Konzils.* Cologne: J. P. Bachem, 1963.

———. *Das Konzil auf dem Weg. Zweite Sitzungsperiode*. Cologne: J. P. Bachem, 1964.

———. *Ergebnisse und Probleme der Dritten Konzilsperiode*. Cologne: J. P. Bachem, 1965.

————. *Die Letze Sitzungsperiode des Konzils*. Cologne: J. P. Bachem, 1966.

————. *Theological Highlights of Vatican II*. 1966; revised edition, New York: Paulist Press, 2009.

Rynne, Xavier. *The Fourth Session: Debates and Decrees of Vatican II, September 14th–December 8th, 1965*. London: Faber & Faber, 1966.

Schelkens, Karen. "*Lumen Gentium's* 'Subsistit in' Revisited." *Theological Studies* 69, no. 4 (2008).

Schillebeeckx, Edward, OP. *Vatican II: The Real Achievement*. London: Sheed & Ward, 1967.

Schloesser, Stephen. "Against Forgetting: Memory, History, Vatican II." *Theological Studies* 67, no. 2 (2006).

Stacpoole, Alberic, ed. *Vatican II by Those Who Were There*. London: Geoffrey Chapman, 1986.

Suenens, Léon Joseph. *Co-Responsibility in the Church*. London: Burns & Oates, 1968.

Sullivan, Francis A., SJ. "The Meaning of Subsistit In." *Theological Studies* 69, no. 1 (2008).

Tanner, Norman P., SJ, and Giuseppe Alberigo, eds. *The Decrees of the Ecumenical Councils*, vols. 1 and 2. London: Sheed & Ward, 1990.

Tanner, Norman. *The Church in Council*. London: I. B. Tauris, 2011.

Vorgrimler, Herbert, ed. *Commentary on the Documents of Vatican II*, vols. 1-5. New York: Herder & Herder/London: Burns & Oates, 1968.

Wilde, Melissa. *Vatican II: A Sociological Analysis of Religious Change*. Princeton: Princeton University Press, 2007.

Wiltgen, Ralph. *The Rhine Flows into the Tiber*. Chumleigh, UK: Augustine Publishers, 2008.

World Council of Churches Documents and Publications

The following are some of the key texts consulted for this study:

Documents and Reports of Assemblies in Barth's Lifetime

The Universal Church in God's Design. London: SCM, 1948.

The First Assembly of the World Council of Churches 1948. London: SCM, 1949.

The Evanston Report, Second Assembly of WCC 1954. London: SCM, 1955.

The New Delhi Report, Third Assembly 1961. London: SCM, 1962.

The Uppsala 68 Report. Geneva: WCC, 1968.

Faith and Order Documents

Rodger, R. C., and Lukas Vischer, eds. *The Fourth World Conference on Faith and Order, Montreal 1963*. London: SCM, 1964.

Baptism, Eucharist and Ministry. Geneva: WCC, 1982.

Churches Respond to BEM, edited by Max Thurian, 6 vols. Geneva: WCC, 1986-88.

Report on the Process. Geneva: WCC, 1990.

BEM at Twenty-five. Geneva: WCC, 2007.

Reports on Dialogues at World Level

Meyer, Harding, and Lukas Vischer, eds. *Growth in Agreement*. New York: Paulist Press and Geneva: WCC, 1984.

Gros, Jeffrey, Harding Meyer, and William G. Rusch, eds. *Growth in Agreement II, 1982-1998*. Grand Rapids: Eerdmans and Geneva: WCC, 2000.

Gros, Jeffrey, Thomas F. Best, and Lorelei F. Fuchs, eds. *Growth in Agreement III, 1998-2005*. Grand Rapids: Eerdmans and Geneva: WCC, 2007.

Joint Working Group between the Roman Catholic Church and the World Council of Churches

The Group, established by Vatican II and the WCC, first met in 1965, even before the Council ended. Notable reports include *The Notion of "Hierarchy of Truths": An Ecumenical Interpretation*, and *The Church Local and Universal* (Geneva: WCC, 1990).

The JWG now helps prepare material for the Week of Prayer for Christian Unity, usually observed January 18-25 each year.

Ecumenical Prayer Cycle

For All God's People. Geneva: WCC, 1978.

With All God's People. Geneva: WCC, 1989.

In God's Hands: Common Prayer for the World. Geneva: WCC, 2006.

History of the Ecumenical Movement

Rouse, Ruth, and Stephen Charles Neill, eds. *History of the Ecumenical Movement*, vol. 1: *1517-1948*, 3rd edition. Geneva: WCC, 1986.

Fey, Harold, ed. *History of the Ecumenical Movement*, vol. 2: *1948-1968*, 2nd edition. Geneva: WCC, 1986.

Briggs, John, Mercy Amba Oduyoye, and George Tsetsis, eds. *History of the Ecumenical Movement*, vol. 3: 1968-2000. Geneva: WCC, 2004.

Dictionary

Lossky, Nicholas, José Bonino, et al., eds. *Dictionary of the Ecumenical Movement,* 2nd edition. Geneva: WCC, 2002.

Journals

WCC Journals published since 1948 include:

Ecumenical Review
International Review of Mission

General Topics

Alexander, Marc. *Church and Ministry in the Works of G. H. Tavard.* Leuven: Leuven University Press, 1994.

Allmen, Jean-Jacques von. *La Primauté de l'Église de Pierre et de Paul.* Paris: Cerf, 1977.

Alston, Wallace, and Michael Welker, eds. *Reformed Theology: Identity and Ecumenicity.* Grand Rapids: Eerdmans, 2003.

Anglican-Methodist. *Fresh Expressions in the Mission of the Church.* London: Church House, 2012.

Anglican-Reformed International Commission. *God's Reign and Our Unity.* Edinburgh: St. Andrew Press, 1984.

Anglican–Roman Catholic International Commission. *Mary, Grace and Hope in Christ.* London: Morehouse, 2005.

Aspden, Kester. *Fortress Church: English Roman Catholic Bishops and Politics, 1903-1963.* Leominster, MA: Gracewing, 2002.

Asprey, Christopher, and Francesca Murphy, eds. *Ecumenism Today.* Aldershot, UK: Ashgate, 2008.

Asprey, Christopher. *Eschatalogical Presence in Karl Barth's Göttingen Dogmatics.* Oxford: Oxford University Press, 2010.

Augustijn, G. "Ecclesiology of Erasmus." In *Scrinium Erastianum,* edited by J. Coppens. Leiden: E. J. Brill, 1969.

Avis, Paul. *Beyond the Reformation: Authority, Primacy and Unity in the Conciliar Tradition.* London: T. & T. Clark, 2006.

———. *Reshaping Ecumenical Theology.* London: T. & T. Clark, 2010.

Badcock, Gary D. *The House Where God Lives: Renewing the Doctrine of the Church for Today.* Grand Rapids: Eerdmans, 2009.

Balthasar, Hans Urs von. ET Andrée Emery, *Office of Peter and the Structure of the Church.* San Francisco: Ignatius Press, 1986.

————. ET Robert Nowell, *Mary for Today.* Slough, UK: St. Paul, 1987.

————. ET Edward T. Oakes, *Theology of Karl Barth.* San Francisco: Ignatius Press, 1992.

Bamforth, Nicholas. *Patriarchal Religion, Sexuality and Gender.* Cambridge: Cambridge University Press, 2008.

Barr, James. *Biblical Faith and Natural Theology.* Oxford: Clarendon, 1993.

Baum, Gregory. *Amazing Church: Catholic Theologian Remembers Half a Century of Change.* Maryknoll, NY: Orbis, 2005.

Beek, Huibert van. *Revisioning Christian Unity: Global Christian Forum.* Oxford: Regnum Books, 2009.

Bender, Kimlyn. *Karl Barth's Christological Ecclesiology.* Aldershot, UK: Ashgate, 2005.

Benedict, Philip. *Christ's Churches Purely Reformed: A Social History of Calvinism.* New Haven: Yale University Press, 2002.

Benedict, Philip, and Irena Backus. *Calvin and His Influence 1509-2009.* Oxford: Oxford University Press, 2011.

Bentley, Wessed. *The Notion of Mission in Karl Barth's Ecclesiology,* Newcastle and Cambridge: Scholars, 2010.

Berkouwer, G. C. ET Harry Boer, *The Triumph of Grace in Theology of Karl Barth.* London: Paternoster Press, 1956.

Bermejo, Luis M. *Infallibility on Trial.* Westminster, MD: Christian Classics, 1992.

Biggar, Nigel, ed. *Reckoning with Barth: Centenary Essays.* Oxford: Mowbray, 1988.

Biggar, Nigel. *The Hastening That Awaits: Karl Barth's Ethics.* Oxford: Clarendon, 1993.

Black, Antony. *Council and Commune: The Conciliar Movement and the Council of Basle.* London: Burns & Oates, 1979.

Bliss, Kathleen. *The Service and Status of Women in the Churches.* London: SCM, 1952.

Boegner, Marc. ET René Hague, *The Long Road to Unity.* London: Collins, 1970.

Boff, Leonardo. ET John Diercksmeier, *Church, Charism and Power: Liberation Theology and the Institutional Church.* London: SCM, 1985.

Bonhoeffer, Dietrich. ET R. H. Fuller and Imgard Booth, *The Cost of Discipleship.* London: SCM, 1959.

Bouteneff, Peter. *Sweeter Than Honey: Orthodox Thinking on Dogma and Truth.* Crestwood, NY: St. Vladimir's Seminary Press, 2006.

Bouwsma, William J. *John Calvin: A Sixteenth Century Portrait.* Oxford: Oxford University Press, 1988.

Bouyer, Louis. ET A. V. Littledale, *Spirit and Forms of Protestantism.* London: Collins Fontana, 1963.

Braaten, Carl E., and Robert W. Jenson, eds. *Catholicity of the Reformation.* Grand Rapids: Eerdmans, 1996.

Braaten, Carl E., and Robert W. Jenson, eds. *Church Unity and the Papal Office.* Grand Rapids: Eerdmans, 2001.

Braaten, Carl E., and Robert W. Jenson, eds. *In One Body Through the Cross: Princeton Proposal for Christian Unity.* Grand Rapids: Eerdmans, 2003.

Braaten, Carl E., and Robert W. Jenson, eds. *The Ecumenical Future: Background Papers for* In One Body Through the Cross. Grand Rapids: Eerdmans, 2004.

Bradbury, John P. *Perpetually Reforming: A Theology of Church Reform and Renewal.* London: T. & T. Clark, 2013.

Brock, Anne Graham. *Mary Magdalene: The First Apostle, the Struggle for Authority.* Cambridge, MA: Harvard University Press, 2003.

Brown, Raymond. *The Churches the Apostles Left Behind Them.* London: Geoffrey Chapman, 1984.

Brown, Robert McAfee. *Gustavo Gutiérrez: Introduction to Liberation Theology.* Maryknoll, NY: Orbis, 1990.

Buckley, Michael. *Papal Primacy and the Episcopate.* New York: Crossroad, 1998.

Bührig, Marga. *Woman Invisible: A Personal Odyssey in Christian Feminism.* London: Burns & Oates, 1993.

Burgess, Andrew. *The Ascension in Karl Barth.* Aldershot, UK: Ashgate, 2004.

Burnett, Amy. *Teaching the Reformation: Ministers and Their Message in Basle 1529-1629.* Oxford: Oxford University Press, 2006.

Burns, J. H., and Thomas Izbicki. *Conciliarism and Papalism.* Cambridge: Cambridge University Press, 1997.

Busch, Eberhard. ET John Bowden, *Karl Barth from Letters and Autobiographical Texts.* London: SCM, 1976.

———. *Unter dem Bogen Karl Barth und Die Juden 1933-1945.* Neukirchen: Neukirchener-Verlag, 1996.

———. ET Geoffrey Bromiley. *The Great Passion: Introduction to Karl Barth's Theology.* Grand Rapids: Eerdmans, 2004.

———. ET Daniel Bloesch, *Karl Barth and the Pietists: The Young Karl Barth's Critique of Pietism and Its Response.* Downers Grove, IL: InterVarsity Press, 2004.

———. ET Darrell and Judith Guder, *The Barmen Theses Then and Now.* Grand Rapids: Eerdmans, 2010.

———. *Meine Zeit mit Karl Barth, Tagebuch 1965-1968.* Göttingen: Vandenhoeck & Ruprecht, 2011.

Butler, Carolyn. *Basil Hume by His Friend.* London: Fount, 1999.

Byrne, Lavinia. *Woman at the Altar.* London: Mowbray, 1994.

Calvin, John. "Letter to Sadolet." Edited by J. K. S. Reid. *Calvin: Theological Treatises.* London: SCM, 1954.

————. *Institutes of the Christian Religion* (1559). Edited by John T. McNeill. Philadelphia: Westminster/London: SCM, 1960.

Casteel, Theodore. "Calvin and Trent," *Harvard Theological Review* 63 (1970).

Chinnici, Joseph. *When Values Collide: The Catholic Church, Sexual Abuse, and the Challenges of Leadership.* Maryknoll, NY: Orbis, 2010.

Chirico, Leonardo de. *Evangelical Perspectives on Post Vatican II Roman Catholicism.* Bern: Peter Lang, 2003.

Chung, Sung Wook. *Admiration and Challenge: Karl Barth's Theological Relationship with John Calvin.* Bern: Peter Lang, 2003.

Chung, Sung Wook, ed. *Karl Barth and Evangelical Theology.* Grand Rapids: Baker Academic, 2006.

Clements, Keith, ed. *The Moot Papers.* London: T. & T. Clark, 2010.

Clough, David. *Ethics in Crisis: Interpreting Barth's Ethics.* Aldershot, UK: Ashgate, 2005.

Collins, Paul. *From Inquisition to Freedom: Seven Prominent Catholics and Their Struggles with the Vatican.* London: Continuum, 2001.

————. *Trinitarian Theology, West and East: Karl Barth, Cappadocian Fathers and John Zizioulas.* Oxford: Oxford University Press, 2007.

Costigan, Richard F., SJ. *Consensus of the Church and Papal Infallibility.* Washington, DC: Catholic University of America Press, 2005.

Courvoisier, Jacques. *De la Réforme au Protestantisme.* Paris: Beauchesne, 1977.

Coventry, John, SJ. *Reconciling.* London: SCM, 1985.

Cox, Harvey. *The Silencing of Leonardo Boff: The Vatican and the Future of World Christianity.* Oak Park, IL: Meyer-Stone, 1988.

Cullmann, Oscar. *Catholics and Protestants: Plea for Christian Solidarity.* London: Lutterworth, 1959.

————. ET Floyd Filson, *Peter, Disciple, Apostle, Martyr,* 2nd edition. London: SCM, 1962.

————. *Unity Through Diversity.* Philadelphia: Fortress Press, 1988.

Curran, Charles. *Faithful Dissent.* London: Sheed & Ward, 1987.

————. *Loyal Dissent: Memoirs of a Catholic Theologian.* Washington, DC: Georgetown University Press, 2006.

Dahlke, Benjamin. *Die Katholische Rezeption Karl Barths.* Tübingen: Mohr-Siebeck, 2010.

————. *Karl Barth, Catholic Renewal and Vatican II.* London: T. & T. Clark, 2012.

Dick, John A. *Malines Conversations Revisited.* Leuven: Peeters, 1989.

Dorrien, Garry. *Barthian Revolt in Modern Theology.* Louisville: Westminster, 2000.

Douglas, Richard M. *Jacopo Sadoleto, Humanist and Reformer.* Grand Rapids: Baker, 1976.

Duffy, Eamon. *Saints and Sinners: History of the Popes*, 3rd edition. New Haven: Yale University Press, 2006.

Duffy, Eamon. *Fires of Faith: Catholic England under Mary Tudor*. New Haven: Yale University Press, 2009.

———. *Ten Popes Who Shook the World*. New Haven: Yale University Press, 2011.

Dulles, Avery. *Models of the Church*. Dublin: Gill & Macmillan, 1976.

———. *Catholicity of the Church*. Oxford: Oxford University Press, 1985.

———. *The Reshaping of Catholicism*. San Francisco: Harper & Row, 1988.

———. "Newman on Infallibility." *Theological Studies* 51, no. 3 (1990).

Dunn, James D. G. *The Parting of the Ways Between Christianity and Judaism*, 2nd edition. London: SCM, 2006.

———. *Unity and Diversity in the New Testament*, 3rd edition. London: SCM, 2006.

———. *Baptism in the Holy Spirit*, 2nd edition. London: SCM, 2010.

Duquoc, Christian. ET John Bowden, *Provisional Churches*. London: SCM, 1986.

Epp, Eldon Jay. *Junia: The First Woman Apostle*. Minneapolis: Fortress Press, 2005.

Evans, G. R. *The Church and the Churches*. Cambridge: Cambridge University Press, 1994.

———. *Method in Ecumenical Theology: The Lessons So Far*. Cambridge: Cambridge University Press, 1996.

Fiddes, Paul. "Status of Woman in the Thought of Karl Barth." In *After Eve*, edited by Janet Soskice. London: Collins, 1990.

Flett, John G. *The Witness of God the Trinity: Missio Dei, Karl Barth, and the Nature of Christian Community*. Grand Rapids: Eerdmans, 2010.

Foley, Gregor. "Catholic Critics of Karl Barth." *Scottish Journal of Theology* 14, no. 2 (1961).

Forsyth, Peter Taylor. *Rome, Reform and Reaction*. London: Hodder & Stoughton, 1899.

———. *Church and the Sacraments*. 1917; London: Independent Press, 1947.

Frawley-O'Dea, Mary Gail, and Virginia Goldner, eds. *Predator Priests, Silenced Victims*. London: Analytic Press, 2007.

Fries, Heinrich. *Kirche als Ereignis*. Düsseldorf: Patmos, 1958.

———. ET Leonard Swidler, *Bultmann-Barth and Catholic Theology*. Pittsburgh: Duquesne University Press, 1967.

———. ET Arlene and Leonard Swidler, *Suffering from the Church: Renewal or Restoration?* Collegeville, MN: Liturgical Press, 1995.

Fries, Heinrich, and Karl Rahner. ET Ruth and Eric Gritsch, *Unity of the Churches: An Actual Possibility*. Philadelphia: Fortress Press, 1985.

Fuchs, Lorelei, SA. *Koinonia and the Quest for an Ecumenical Ecclesiology*. Grand Rapids: Eerdmans, 2008.

Fuerth, Patrick. *Concept of Catholicity in the Documents of the World Council of Churches.* Rome: Editrice Anselmiana, 1974.

Gaál, Emery de. *Theology of Pope Benedict XVI: The Christocentric Shift.* New York: Palgrave Macmillan, 2010.

Ganoczy, Alexandre. *Ecclesia Ministrans.* Freiburg: Herder, 1968.

————. ET David Foxgrover and Wade Provo, *The Young Calvin.* Edinburgh: T. & T. Clark, 1988.

George, Timothy, ed. *John Calvin and the Church.* Louisville: Westminster, 1990.

Gerrish, Brian. *Continuing the Reformation.* Chicago: University of Chicago Press, 1993.

————. *Thinking with the Church.* Grand Rapids: Eerdmans, 2010.

Gibellini, Rosino. *The Liberation Theology Debate.* London: SCM, 1987.

Gockel, Mathias. *Barth and Schleiermacher on the Doctrine of Election.* Oxford: Oxford University Press, 2006.

Goodall, Norman. *The Ecumenical Movement.* Oxford: Oxford University Press, 1961.

————. *Ecumenical Progress, 1961-1971.* Oxford: Oxford University Press, 1972.

Gorringe, Timothy. *Karl Barth, Against Hegemony.* Oxford: Oxford University Press, 1999.

Granberg-Michaelson, Wesley. *From Times Square to Timbuktu.* Grand Rapids: Eerdmans, 2013.

Groupe des Dombes. *For the Conversion of the Churches.* Geneva: WCC, 1993.

————. *Mary in the Plan of God.* New York: Paulist Press, 1999.

————. *"One Teacher": Doctrinal Authority in the Church.* Grand Rapids: Eerdmans, 2010.

Gruchy, John de. *Liberating Reformed Theology: A South African Contribution to an Ecumenical Debate.* Grand Rapids: Eerdmans, 1991.

Gunton, Colin E. *Becoming and Being: The Doctrine of God in Charles Hartshorne and Karl Barth.* 1978; 2nd edition, London: SCM, 2001.

————. *Act and Being: Towards a Theology of the Divine Attributes.* London: SCM, 2002.

————. *The Barth Lectures.* Edited by P. H. Brazier. London: T. & T. Clark, 2007.

————. *Revelation and Reason.* Edited by P. H. Brazier. London: T. & T. Clark, 2008.

Guretski, David. *Karl Barth on the Filioque.* Aldershot, UK: Ashgate, 2009.

Gutiérrez, Gustavo. ET Caridad Inda and John Eagleson, *Theology of Liberation.* London: SCM, 1974.

Haight, Roger, SJ. *Christian Community in History: Comparative Ecclesiology.* London: Continuum, 2005.

Hall, Basil. "Colloquies between Catholics and Protestants, 1539-1541." In Basil Hall, *Humanists and Protestants 1500-1900.* Edinburgh: T. & T. Clark, 1990.

Halter, Deborah. *The Papal "No": A Comprehensive Guide to the Vatican's Rejection of Women's Ordination.* New York: Crossroad, 2004.

Hamer, Jérôme. *L'Occasionalisme Théologique de Karl Barth.* Paris: Desclée de Brouwer, 1949.

Hancock, Angela Dienart. *Karl Barth's Emergency Homiletic, 1932-1933.* Grand Rapids: Eerdmans, 2013.

Häring, Hermann. ET John Bowden, *Hans Küng: Breaking Through.* London: SCM, 1998.

Hart, John W. *Karl Barth Versus Emil Brunner.* Bern: Peter Lang, 2001.

Hart, Trevor. *Regarding Karl Barth.* Carlisle, UK: Paternoster, 1999.

Hartwell, Herbert. *The Theology of Karl Barth: An Introduction.* London: Duckworth, 1964.

Hauerwas, Stanley. *With the Grain of the Universe.* London: SCM, 2002.

Healey, Nicholas. "The Logic of Karl Barth's Ecclesiology." *Modern Theology* 10, no. 3 (1994).

———. *Church, World and the Christian Life: Practical-Prophetic Ecclesiology.* Cambridge: Cambridge University Press, 2000.

———. "Karl Barth's Ecclesiology Reconsidered." *Scottish Journal of Theology* 57, no. 3 (2004).

———. "Karl Barth, German-Language Theology and the Catholic Tradition." In *Trinity and Election in Contemporary Theology,* edited by Michael T. Dempsey. Grand Rapids: Eerdmans, 2011.

Hebblethwaite, Peter. *The Runaway Church,* revised edition. London: Collins-Fount, 1978.

———. *The New Inquisition? Schillebeeckx and Küng.* London: Collins, 1980.

———. *Paul VI, the First Modern Pope.* London: HarperCollins, 1993.

———. *John XXIII, Pope of the Century.* Revised edition edited by Margaret Hebblethwaite. London: Continuum, 1994.

———. *The Next Pope.* Revised edition edited by Margaret Hebblethwaite. London: HarperCollins, 2000.

Hengel, Martin. ET Thomas H. Trapp, *St. Peter: The Underestimated Apostle.* Grand Rapids: Eerdmans, 2010.

Henn, William. *The Hierarchy of Truths According to Congar.* Rome: Editrice Pontificia Università Gregoriana, 1987.

Herwig, Thomas. *Karl Barth und die Ökumenische Bewegung.* Neukirchen: Neukirchener-Verlag, 1998.

Highfield, Ron. *Barth and Rahner in Dialogue: Toward an Ecumenical Understanding of Sin and Evil.* Bern: Peter Lang, 1989.

Hill, Christopher. *Antichrist in Seventeenth Century England.* London: Verso, 1989.

Hinze, Bradford E. *Practices of Dialogue in the Roman Catholic Church.* London: Continuum, 2006.

————. "Ecclesial Impasse: What Can We Learn from Our Laments?" *Theological Studies* 72, no. 3 (September 2011).

Hirzel, Martin, and Martin Sallmann, eds. *John Calvin's Impact on Church and Society, 1509-2009.* Grand Rapids: Eerdmans, 2009.

Hogan, Linda. "Clerical Abuse Scandal." *Theological Studies* 72, no. 1 (March 2011).

Hoose, Bernard, ed. *Authority in the Roman Catholic Church.* Aldershot, UK: Ashgate, 2002.

Hromádka, Josef. ET Monica and Benjamin Page, *Thoughts of a Czech Pastor.* London: SCM, 1970.

————. *From the Reformation to Tomorrow.* Geneva: WARC, 1999.

Hühne, Werner. ET Robert W. Fenn, *A Man to Be Reckoned With: The Story of Reinhold von Thadden-Trieglaff, the Founder of the German Kirchentag.* London: SCM, 1962.

Hunsinger, George, ed. *Karl Barth and Radical Politics.* Philadelphia: Westminster, 1976.

————. *How to Read Karl Barth: The Shape of His Theology.* Oxford: Oxford University Press, 1991.

————. *Disruptive Grace: Studies in the Theology of Karl Barth.* Grand Rapids: Eerdmans, 2000.

————, ed. *For the Sake of the World: Karl Barth and the Future of Ecclesial Theology.* Grand Rapids: Eerdmans, 2004.

————, ed. *Torture Is a Moral Issue: Christians, Jews, Muslims and People of Conscience Speak Out.* Grand Rapids: Eerdmans, 2008.

————, ed. *Thy Word Is Truth: Barth on Scripture.* Grand Rapids: Eerdmans, 2012.

Hütter, Reinhard. "Karl Barth's Dialectical Catholicity." *Modern Theology* 16, no. 2 (April 2000).

————. *Suffering Divine Things: Theology as Church Practice.* Grand Rapids: Eerdmans, 2000.

————. *Bound to Be Free: Evangelical Catholic Engagements in Ecclesiology, Ethics, and Ecumenism.* Grand Rapids: Eerdmans, 2004.

Jackson, Eleanor, ed. *The Question of Woman: Collected Writings of Charlotte von Kirschbaum.* Grand Rapids: Eerdmans, 1996.

Jedin, Hubert. ET N. D. Smith, *Crisis and Closure of the Council of Trent: A Retrospective View from the Second Vatican Council.* London: Sheed & Ward, 1967.

Jehle, Frank. ET Richard and Martha Burnett, *Ever Against the Stream: The Politics of Karl Barth, 1906-1968.* Grand Rapids: Eerdmans, 2002.

Jenkins, Philip. *God's Continent.* Oxford: Oxford University Press, 2007.

————. *Next Christendom.* Oxford: Oxford University Press, 2007.

Jenson, Robert. *Unbaptized God: The Basic Flaw in Ecumenical Theology.* Minneapolis: Fortress Press, 1992.

————. "You Wonder Where the Spirit Went." *Pro Ecclesia* 2 (1993).

Johnson, Keith L. *Karl Barth and the Analogia Entis*. London: T. & T. Clark, 2010.

Jüngel, Eberhard. ET Garrett E. Paul, *Karl Barth: A Theological Legacy*. Philadelphia: Westminster, 1986.

Jüngel, Eberhard. ET John Webster, *God's Being Is in Becoming: The Trinitarian Being of God in the Theology of Karl Barth*. Edinburgh: T. & T. Clark, 2001.

————. ET Jeffrey Cayzer, *Justification: Heart of the Christian Faith*. Edinburgh: T. & T. Clark, 2001.

Kasper, Walter. *That They May All Be One: The Call to Unity Today*. London: Burns & Oates, 2004.

————. ET Brian McNeil, *Sacrament of Unity: The Eucharist and the Church*. New York: Herder & Herder, 2004.

————. *A Handbook of Spiritual Ecumenism*. New York: New City Press, 2006.

Kasper, Walter, ed. *The Petrine Ministry: Catholics and Orthodox in Dialogue*. New York: Newman Press, 2006.

Kehl, Medal. *Kirche als Institution*. Frankfurt am Main: Josef Knecht, 1976.

Keller, Adolf. *Karl Barth and Christian Unity*. London: Lutterworth, 1931.

Kelly, J. N. D. *Oxford: Dictionary of Popes*. Oxford: Oxford University Press, 2005.

Kenny, Anthony. *A Path from Rome: An Autobiography*. Oxford: Oxford University Press, 1986.

————. *A Life in Oxford*. London: John Murray, 1997.

Ker, Ian. *Newman on Vatican II*. Oxford: Oxford University Press, 2014.

Kerr, Fergus. *Theology after Wittgenstein*. Oxford: Basil Blackwell, 1986.

————. *Immortal Longings: Versions of Transcending Humanity*. London: SPCK, 1997.

————. "Barthiana." *New Blackfriars* 79, no. 934 (December 1998).

————. *Twentieth Century Catholic Theologians*. Oxford: Blackwell, 2007.

Kim, JinHyok. *The Spirit of God and the Christian Life: A Constructive Study of Karl Barth*. Unpublished Oxford DPhil Thesis, 2012.

Kraemer, Hendrik. *A Theology of the Laity*. London: Lutterworth, 1958.

Küng, Hans. ET *Justification: The Doctrine of Karl Barth and a Catholic Reflection*. 1964; London: Burns & Oates, 1981.

————. *Structures of the Church*. London: Burns & Oates, 1965.

————. *The Church*. London: Search Press, 1968.

————. *Infallible?* London: Collins Fontana, 1972.

————. *Why Priests?* London: Collins Fontana, 1972.

————. "Why I Remain a Catholic." In *The Church Maintained in Truth*. London: SCM, 1980.

————. *Theology for the Third Millennium: An Ecumenical View*. London: Harper, 1991.

————. *Judaism: The Religious Situation of Our Time*. London: SCM, 1992.

————. *My Struggle for Freedom: Memoirs*. London: Continuum, 2003.

————. *Disputed Truth: Memoirs II*. London: Continuum, 2008.

————. *Can We Save the Catholic Church?* London: William Collins, 2013.

Kurian, M. *Sarah Chakko: A Voice of Women in the Ecumenical Movement*. Thiruvalla, India: Christhava, 1998.

Lacey, Michael, and Francis Oakley, eds. *Crisis of Authority in Catholic Modernity*. Oxford: Oxford University Press, 2011.

Lakeland, Paul. *Liberation of the Laity*. New York: Continuum, 2003.

————. *Catholicism at the Crossroads: How the Laity Can Save the Church*. London: Continuum, 2007.

Lane, Anthony N. S. *Justification by Faith in Catholic Protestant Dialogue*. Edinburgh: T. & T. Clark, 2002.

Lash, Nicholas, ed. *Doctrinal Development and Christian Unity*. London: Sheed & Ward, 1967.

Lash, Nicholas. *Theology for Pilgrims*. London: Darton, Longman & Todd, 2008.

Lehmann, Karl, and Wolfhart Pannenberg. *The Condemnations of the Reformation Era: Do They Still Divide?* Minneapolis: Fortress Press, 1990.

Leuba, Jean-Louis. *L'institution et l'événement*. Neuchâtel: Delachaux, 1950.

Leys, Ad. *Ecclesiological Impacts of the Principle of Subsidiarity*. Kampen: Uiteverij Kok, 1995.

Loades, Ann. *Feminist Theology: A Reader*. London: SPCK, 1990.

Lochman, Jan Milic. "Human Rights: Ecumenical Identity in a Divided World." In Jan Milic Lochman, *Christ and Prometheus?* Geneva: WCC, 1988.

Lortz, Joseph. ET Otto Knab, *How the Reformation Came*. New York: Herder & Herder, 1964.

Louth, Andrew. *Mary and the Mystery of Incarnation: An Essay on the Mother of God in the Theology of Karl Barth*. 1977; Oxford: SLG Press, 2002.

Lubac, Henri de. ET Michael Mason, *The Splendour of the Church*. London: Sheed & Ward, 1955.

————. *Résistance Chrétienne à l'Antisémitisme: Souvenirs 1940-44*. Paris: Fayard, 1988.

Lutheran World Federation/Roman Catholic Church. *Joint Declaration on the Doctrine of Justification*. Geneva: WCC, 1999.

MacDonald, Neil B. *Calvin, Barth and Reformed Theology*. Milton Keynes, UK: Paternoster, 2008.

Macken, John, SJ. *Autonomy Theme in Church Dogmatics*. Cambridge: Cambridge University Press, 1990.

Mangina, Joseph. *Karl Barth Theologian of Christian Witness*. Aldershot, UK: Ashgate, 2004.

Marga, Amy. *Karl Barth's Dialogue with Catholicism in Göttingen and Münster*. Tübingen: Mohr Siebeck, 2010.

Martin, David. *Pentecostalism: The World Their Parish*. Oxford: Blackwell, 2002.

Massa, Mark S., SJ. *The American Catholic Revolution: How the Sixties Changed the Church for Ever*. Oxford: Oxford University Press, 2010.

Matheson, Peter. *Cardinal Contarini of Regensburg*. Oxford: Clarendon, 1972.

Maury, Pierre. *Predestination and Other Papers*. London: SCM, 1960.

McConnachie, John. *The Barthian Theology and the Man of Today*. London: Hodder, 1933.

McCord, Peter. *A Pope for All Christians*. London: SPCK, 1976.

McCormack, Bruce. *Karl Barth's Critically Realistic Dialectical Theology: Its Genesis and Development, 1909-1936*. Oxford: Clarendon, 1995.

———. *Orthodox and Modern Studies in the Theology of Karl Barth*. Grand Rapids: Baker Academic, 2008.

McCormack, Bruce, and Clifford Anderson, eds. *Karl Barth and American Evangelicalism*. Grand Rapids: Eerdmans, 2011.

McCormack, Bruce, and Thomas White OP, eds. *Thomas Aquinas and Karl Barth: An Unofficial Catholic Protestant Dialogue*. Grand Rapids: Eerdmans, 2013.

McCulloch, Diarmaid, "Calvin, Fifth Doctor of the Church." In Irena Backhus and Philip Benedict, *Calvin and His Influence*. Oxford: Oxford University Press, 2011.

McDonnell, Kilian. *John Calvin, the Church and the Eucharist*. Princeton: Princeton University Press, 1967.

McDowell, John. *Hope in Barth's Eschatology*. Aldershot, UK: Ashgate, 2000.

McDowell, John, and Mike Higton. *Conversing with Barth*. Aldershot, UK: Ashgate, 2004.

McKee, Anne, and Brian Armstrong, eds. *Probing the Reformed Tradition*. Philadelphia: Westminster John Knox, 1989.

McKenny, Gerald. *Analogy of Grace: Karl Barth's Moral Theology*. Oxford: Oxford University Press, 2010.

McKim, Donald. *Introducing the Reformed Faith*. Louisville: Westminster John Knox, 2001.

McKim, Donald, ed. *How Karl Barth Changed My Mind*. Grand Rapids: Eerdmans, 2006.

McNeill, John T. *Unitative Protestantism: The Ecumenical Spirit and Its Persistent Expression*. London: Epworth, 1964.

Migliore, Daniel. "Reforming the Theology and Practice of Baptism: The Challenge of Karl Barth." In *Toward the Future of Reformed Theology*, edited by David Willis and Michael Welker. Grand Rapids: Eerdmans, 1999.

Migliore, Daniel L., ed. *Commanding Grace: Studies in Karl Barth's Ethics*. Grand Rapids: Eerdmans, 2010.

Mikkelsen, Hans Vium. *Reconciling Humanity: Karl Barth in Dialogue*. Grand Rapids: Eerdmans, 2010.

Miller, Michael J. *Divine Right of the Papacy in Recent Ecumenical Thought.* Rome: Università Gregoriana.

Minear, Paul S. *Images of the Church in the New Testament.* Louisville: Westminster, 1960.

Molnar, Paul D. *Karl Barth and Theology of the Lord's Supper.* New York: Peter Lang, 1996.

Morgan, D. Densil. *Barth Reception in Britain.* London: T. & T. Clark, 2010.

Mortiau, Jacques, and Raymond Loonbeek. *Dom Lambert Beauduin: Visionaire et Précurseur 1873-1960.* Paris: Éditions de Chevetogne, 2005.

Moseley, Carys. *Nations and Nationalism in the Theology of Karl Barth.* Oxford: Oxford University Press, 2013.

Mudge, Lewis. *One Church: Catholic and Reformed.* London: Lutterworth, 1963.

Murray, Paul D., ed. *Receptive Ecumenism and Catholic Learning.* Oxford: Oxford University Press, 2008.

Murray, Paul D., and Gabriel Flynn, eds. *Ressourcement: Movement for Renewal in Twentieth Century Catholic Theology.* Oxford: Oxford University Press, 2012.

Newbigin, Lesslie. *The Household of God.* London: SCM, 1953.

————. *The Reunion of the Church: A Defence of the South India Scheme,* revised edition. Westport, CT: Greenwood Press, 1960.

————. *Unfinished Agenda: An Autobiography.* London: SPCK, 1985.

Nissiotis, Nicos. "Some Thoughts on Orthodoxy." In *Lambeth Essays on Unity,* edited by D. W. Allen et al. London: SPCK, 1969.

————. *Religion, Philosophy and Sport in Dialogue.* Athens: Aohnai, 1994.

Noll, Mark, and Carolyn Nystrom. *Is the Reformation Over?* Grand Rapids: Baker Academic, 2005.

Oberman, Heiko. *John Calvin and the Reformation of the Refugees.* Geneva: Droz, 2009.

O'Gara, Margaret. *Ecumenical Gift Exchange.* Collegeville, MN: Liturgical Press, 1998.

O'Grady, Colm, MSC. *The Church in the Theology of Karl Barth.* London: Geoffrey Chapman, 1970.

————. *The Church in Catholic Theology: Dialogue with Karl Barth.* London: Geoffrey Chapman, 1970.

Olin, John C. *John Calvin, Jacopo Sadoleto, Reformation Debate.* Grand Rapids: Baker, 1976.

O'Malley, John W. *Trent and All That.* Cambridge, MA: Harvard University Press, 2000.

Opočensky, Milan, and Paraic Reamonn, eds. *Justification and Sanctification in the Traditions of the Reformation.* Geneva: WARC, 1999.

Puglisi, James F., ed. *Petrine Ministry and the Unity of the Church.* Collegeville, MN: Liturgical Press, 1999.

Przywara, Erich. *Analogia Entis: Metaphysics, Original Structure, and Universal Rhythm.* Translated by John R. Betz and David Bentley Hart. Grand Rapids: Eerdmans, 2013.

Quinn, John R. "The Exercise of the Primacy and the Costly Call to Unity." In *The Exercise of the Primacy: Continuing the Dialogue,* edited by Phyllis Zagano and Terrance Tilley. New York: Crossroad, 1998.

Quinn, John R. *The Reform of the Papacy.* New York: Crossroad, 1999.

Radcliffe, Timothy, OP. *Taking the Plunge: Living Baptism and Confirmation.* London: Bloomsbury, 2012.

Rahner, Karl. "Immaculate Conception." In *Theological Investigations* I. ET London: Darton, Longman & Todd, 1961.

———. "Interpretation of the Dogma of the Assumption." In *Theological Investigations* I. ET London: Darton, Longman & Todd, 1961.

———. "Barth's Agreement with the Catholic Doctrine of Justification." In *Theological Investigations* IV. ET London: Darton, Longman & Todd, 1966.

———. "The Sinful Church in the Decrees of Vatican II." In *Theological Investigations* VI. ET London: Darton, Longman & Todd, 1969.

———. "The Teaching Office of the Church and the Present Day Crisis of Authority." In *Theological Investigations* XII. ET London: Darton, Longman & Todd, 1974.

———. "Is Church Union Dogmatically Possible?" In *Theological Investigations* XVII. ET London: Darton, Longman & Todd, 1981.

———. "Women and the Priesthood." In *Theological Investigations* XX. ET London: Darton, Longman & Todd, 1981.

Ramsey, Michael. *The Gospel and the Catholic Church.* London: Longman Green, 1936; London: SPCK, 1990.

Ramsey, Michael, and Leon-Joseph Suenens, *Future of the Christian Church.* London: SCM, 1971.

Ratzinger, Joseph. ET Robert Nowell, *Church, Ecumenism and Politics.* New York: Crossroad, 1988.

Resch, Dustin. *Barth's Interpretation of the Virgin Birth.* Farnham, UK: Ashgate, 2013.

Reymond, Bernard. *Théologien ou Prophète: Les Francophones et Barth avant 1945.* Lausanne: Éditions d'Homme, 1985.

Rogers, Eugene. *Thomas Aquinas and Karl Barth.* Notre Dame: University of Notre Dame Press, 1995.

Rose, Matthew. *Ethics with Barth: God, Metaphysics and Morals.* Farnham, UK: Ashgate, 2010.

Rusch, William G. *Ecumenical Reception: Its Challenge and Opportunity.* Grand Rapids: Eerdmans, 2007.

———, ed. *Justification and the Future of the Ecumenical Movement.* Collegeville, MN: Liturgical Press, 2003.

————. *Pontificate of Benedict XVI.* Grand Rapids: Eerdmans, 2009.

Schmidt, Stjepan, SJ. *Augustin Bea: Cardinal of Unity.* New York: New City Press, 1992.

Scholder, Klaus. ET John Bowden, *The Churches and the Third Reich, Volume Two: The Year of Disillusionment 1934, Barmen and Rome.* London: SCM, 1988.

————. "Eugenio Pacelli and Karl Barth." In *Requiem for Hitler.* London: SCM, 1989.

Scholl, Hans. *Calvinus Catholicus.* Freiburg: Herder, 1974.

Schüssler Fiorenza, Elisabeth. *In Memory of Her.* London: SCM, 1983.

————. *Discipleship of Equals: A Critical Feminist Ekklesia-logy of Liberation.* London: SCM, 1993.

Schüssler Fiorenza, Elisabeth, and Herman Häring. *The Non Ordination of Women and the Politics of Power.* London: SCM/Maryknoll, NY: Orbis Concilium, 1999.

Schweizer, Eduard. ET Frank Clarke, *Church Order in New Testament.* London: SCM, 1961.

Senarclens, Jacques de. ET Geoffrey Bromiley, *Heirs of Reformation.* London: SCM, 1963.

Sheeran, Michael J., SJ. *Beyond Majority Rule: Voteless Decisions in the Religious Society of Friends.* Philadelphia: Yearly Meeting, 1983.

Sonderegger, Katherine. *That Jesus Christ Was Born a Jew: Karl Barth's "Doctrine of Israel."* University Park: Pennsylvania State University Press, 1992.

Spencer, Archibald. *Clearing a Space for Human Action: Towards an Ethical Ontology in the Early Theology of Karl Barth.* Oxford: Peter Lang, 2003.

Stumme, Wayne C., ed. *The Gospel of Justification in Christ: Where Does the Church Stand Today?* Grand Rapids: Eerdmans, 2006.

Subilia, Vittorio. ET Reginald Kissak, *Problem of Catholicism.* London: SCM, 1964.

Swanson, R. N., ed. *The Church and Mary.* Woodbridge, UK: Boydell Press, 2004.

Sykes, Stephen, ed. *Karl Barth: Studies of His Theological Methods.* Oxford: Clarendon, 1979.

Sykes, Stephen, ed. *Karl Barth Centenary Essays.* Cambridge: Cambridge University Press, 1989.

Tabart, Jill. *Coming to Consensus: A Case Study for the Churches.* Geneva: WCC, 1993.

Tanner, Norman, SJ, ed. *Decrees of the Ecumenical Councils,* vol. 1: *Nicaea I to Lateran V.* Washington, DC: Sheed & Ward, 1990.

————, ed. *Decrees of the Ecumenical Councils,* vol. 2: *Trent to Vatican II.* Washington, DC: Sheed & Ward, 1990.

————. *The Church in Council.* London: I. B. Tauris, 2011.

Tavard, George. *The Church Tomorrow.* London: Darton, Longman & Todd, 1965.

————. *A Review of Anglican Orders: The Problem and the Solution.* Collegeville, MN: Liturgical Press, 1990.

————. *The Thousand Faces of the Virgin Mary.* Collegeville, MN: Liturgical Press, 1996.

————. *The Starting Point of Calvin's Theology.* Grand Rapids: Eerdmans, 2000.

Thompson, John, ed. *Theology Beyond Christendom: Essays on Centenary of Birth of Karl Barth.* Eugene, OR: Pickwick, 1986.

Tierney, Brian. *Origins of Papal Infallibility 1150-1350.* Leiden: Brill, 1988.

————. *The Idea of Natural Rights.* Atlanta: Scholars, 1997.

Tillard, J.-M. R. ET John de Satgé, *The Bishop of Rome.* London: SPCK, 1983.

————. *Église d'Églises: L'ecclésiologie de communion.* Paris: Cerf, 1987.

Tillich, Paul. *The Protestant Era.* London: Nisbet, 1951.

Tomkins, Oliver. "Roman Catholic Church and the Ecumenical Movement 1910-1948." In *History of the Ecumenical Movement,* vol. 1, 3rd edition, edited by Ruth Rouse and Stephen Neill. Geneva: WCC, 1986.

Torrance, Thomas. *Conflict and Agreement in the Church.* London: Lutterworth, 1959.

————. *Karl Barth: Introduction to His Early Theology 1910-1931.* Edinburgh: T. & T. Clark, 1962.

————. *Theology in Reconciliation: Essays Toward Evangelical and Catholic Unity in East and West.* London: Geoffrey Chapman, 1976.

————. *Karl Barth: Biblical & Evangelical Theologian.* Edinburgh: T. & T. Clark, 1990.

————. *Trinitarian Perspectives.* Edinburgh: T. & T. Clark, 1994.

Trost, Theodore. *Douglas Horton and the Ecumenical Impulse in American Religion.* Cambridge, MA: Harvard University Press, 2002.

Vallely, Paul. *Pope Francis: Untying the Knots.* London: Bloomsbury, 2013.

Valliere, Paul. *Conciliarism: A History of Decision Making in the Church.* Cambridge: Cambridge University Press, 2012.

Vereb, Jerome-Michael, CP. *Because He Was a German! Cardinal Bea and the Origins of Roman Catholic Engagement in the Ecumenical Movement.* Grand Rapids: Eerdmans, 2006.

Villa-Vicencio, Charles. *On Reading Karl Barth in South Africa.* Grand Rapids: Eerdmans, 1988.

Vischer, Lukas. *Spirit of God, Spirit of Christ: Ecumenical Reflections on the Filioque Controversy.* Geneva: WCC/London: SPCK, 1981.

————. "The Ministry of Unity and the Common Witness of the Churches." In *Petrine Ministry and the Unity of the Church,* edited by James Puglisi. Collegeville, MN: Liturgical Press, 1999.

————. *Pia Conspiratio: Calvin on Unity of Christ's Church.* Geneva: John Knox Centre, 2000.

————, ed. *The Church in Reformed Perspective: A European Reflection.* Geneva: John Knox Centre, 2002.

————, ed. *Christian Worship in Reformed Churches, Past and Present.* Grand Rapids: Eerdmans, 2003.

————. "The Council as an Event in the Ecumenical Movement." In *History of Vatican II*, vols. 1-5, edited by Giuseppe Alberigo and Joseph A. Komonchak. Maryknoll, NY: Leuven: Peeters, 2006.

Vischer, Lukas, and Jean-Jacques Bauswein. *The Reformed Family Worldwide: A Survey.* Grand Rapids: Eerdmans, 1999.

Visser 't Hooft, W. A. *The Meaning of Ecumenical.* London: SCM, 1953.

————. *Memoirs* (1973), 2nd edition. Geneva: WCC, 1987.

————. *Barth's Ethics of Reconciliation.* Cambridge: Cambridge University Press, 1995.

————. *Barth's Moral Theology: Human Action in Barth's Thought.* Edinburgh: T. & T. Clark, 1998.

————. *Barth.* London: Continuum, 2000.

————, ed. *Cambridge Companion to Karl Barth.* Cambridge: Cambridge University Press, 2000.

————. *Teachers and Teaching Authorities.* Geneva: WCC, 2000.

————. *Barth's Earlier Theology: Four Studies.* London: T. & T. Clark, 2005.

Weinrich, Michael, and John Burgess, eds. *What Is Justification About? Reformed Contributions to an Ecumenical Theme.* Grand Rapids: Eerdmans, 2009.

White, Thomas Joseph, OP, ed. *The Analogy of Being: Invention of the Antichrist or Wisdom of God?* Grand Rapids: Eerdmans, 2011.

Wigley, Stephen. *Karl Barth and Hans Urs von Balthasar: A Critical Engagement.* London: T. & T. Clark, 2007.

Willis, David, and Michael Welker. *Toward the Future of Reformed Theology.* Grand Rapids: Eerdmans, 1999.

Wills, Gary. *Papal Sin.* New York: Doubleday, 2000.

Wood, Donald. *Barth's Theology of Interpretation.* Aldershot, UK: Ashgate, 2007.

Wyschogrod, Michael. "A Jewish Perspective on Karl Barth." In *How Karl Barth Changed My Mind*, edited by Donald McKim. Grand Rapids: Eerdmans, 1986.

————. *Abraham's Promise: Judaism and Jewish Christian Relations.* Grand Rapids: Eerdmans, 2004/London: SCM, 2006.

Yarnold, Edward. *They Are in Earnest: Christian Unity in the Statements of Paul VI, John Paul I and John Paul II.* Slough, UK: St. Paul Publications, 1982.

————. *In Search of Unity: Ecumenical Principles and Prospects.* Slough, UK: St. Paul Publications, 1989.

Yocum, John. *Ecclesial Mediation in Karl Barth.* Aldershot, UK: Ashgate, 2004.

Zachman, Randall. *John Calvin and Roman Catholicism.* Grand Rapids: Baker, 2008.

Index of Names

Aquinas, Thomas, 29, 123, 144; *analogia entis,* 179; comparisons with Barth, 11; comparisons with Tillich, 13

Avis, Paul, 205

Balthasar, Hans Urs von, 12, 16, 166, 221; Barth as "catholic theologian," 122-24; partner in dialogue, 14

Barth, Markus: sacraments, 129-30; "vicar of Christ," 77

Baxter, Richard: unity, 195

Bea, Augustin, 45, 51, 199; on the Jews, 228-29

Beauduin, Dom Lambert, 23, 34, 123

Beauvoir, Simone de, 150

Boegner, Marc: help for Jews, 224; observers, 50-51

Bonhoeffer, Dietrich: cost of discipleship, 173-74; the Jews, 224-25; wives and husbands, 156, 162

Bonino, José Míguez, 215

Boulding, Cecily, 164

Bouyer, Louis, 5, 121

Brown, Raymond, 21, 48

Brown, Robert McAfee, 21, 48; Barth, 117; observers, 89-91, 215

Bührig, Marga, 162

Busch, Eberhard: *analogia entis,* 178; Barmen, 116, 178; Barth and Jews, 224

Butler, Christopher, 86, 121

Byrne, Lavinia, 156

Caird, George, 40, 45; magisterium, 105; Mariology, 189-91

Calvin, John: Barth on Calvin, 29, 35-38; Calvin and Sadolet, 30-33; "catholic" and Reformed collegiality, 90; Geneva, 231; Jews, 226; Mary, 183; as "pope" in Geneva, 66

Chakko, Sarah, 153, 155-56, 158

Congar, Yves: Barth, respect for and criticism of, 28, 137; biographical, 122-23; filioque and councils, 145; laity, 114, 155; reform, 6, 7, 11, 23, 26-28; tradition, 69; Vatican II journal, 39, 43, 163-64; Vatican II *peritus,* 24, 42-43; vocation to unity, 27-28, 32-33, 38; World Council of Churches, 49-50

Contarini, Caspar, 30, 38

Courtney Murray, John: religious freedom, 41, 123, 215

Cullmann, Oscar, 10, 58, 195, 208, 215; on Peter, 98

Dahlke, Benjamin, 18

Daly, Mary: misogyny, 150

Dulles, Avery: images of the church, 72; infallibility, 96; Protestant background, 121

Dunn, James D. G., 6, 163

Duquoc, Christian, 126-27

Faggioli, Massimo, 60
Fiddes, Paul, 161
Forsyth, P. T., 81
Francis I: criticisms of, 92n26; global
  pope, 3; popularity and respect, 231
Fries, Heinrich, 59, 141

Gorringe, Timothy J.: hegemony, 105,
  160
Granberg-Michaelson, Wesley, 2-3
Green, Clifford: Barth and feminism,
  158, 161
Grosche, Robert, 13, 18, 33
Gunton, Colin, 14-15

Halter, Deborah, 154-55
Hamer, Jérôme, 13; church as event, 141;
  Joint Working Group, 217
Hancock, Angela, 62, 225
Hardy, Daniel, 203, 215
Hastings, Adrian, 96
Hauerwas, Stanley, 118
Hebblethwaite, Peter, 9, 78, 89, 90, 93, 191
Hinze, Bradford, 78, 82
Horton, Douglas: observers, 18; women
  observers, 147-48; worship at Vati-
  can II, 206-7
Hromádka, Josef, 54-55
Hume, Basil: Swanwick Conference and
  praying together, 203, 207
Hunsinger, George, 132
Hütter, Reinhard: abstract and catholic
  ecclesiology, 80, 143

Isaac, Jules: Jews, 228-29

Jenkins, Philip, 2
Jenson, Robert W., 4-5, 125
John XXIII: Congar and reform, 27;
  decision to call Council, 7, 39, 57; Jews,
  227; vision of Council, 200-202
John Paul II, 7, 24. *See also Ut Unum Sint*
Jüngel, Eberhard: Barth on baptism, 132;
  justification, 171-72

Kasper, Walter: church, local and universal, 81; Kasper-Ratzinger debate,
  98-99, 146
Kerr, Fergus, 121; cooperation in salvation, 135; von Balthasar, 123
Kirschbaum, Charlotte von: Barth's assistant and "helpmeet," 157; question of
  woman, 125, 149-52, 159
Kraemer, Hendrik: laity, 155
Küng, Hans: Barth, friendship with, 22,
  23, 35; Barth's invitation to Council,
  57-58, 60-61; church and incarnation,
  76; church as event, 142; election of
  bishop in Basel, 220-21; infallibility,
  95-97; official rejection as a Roman
  Catholic theologian, 23, 123

Lakeland, Paul, 9-10, 114
Lamb, Matthew, 59
Lapide, Pinchas: Barmen, 225
Lash, Nicholas: celibacy, 8-9; *Dominus
  Jesus*, 79n75; ordination of women,
  8; Rome too centralized, 218-19, 221;
  Vatican II, 218-19
Lichtenberg, Bernhard, 223
Lindbeck, George, 193
Lubac, Henri de, 41, 51, 123; friendship
  with Boegner and help for Jews, 224
Luther, Martin: Barth in Lutheran
  Göttingen, 29; Congar's criticisms, 34;
  Jews, 226; justification, Barth's queries
  about, 172-73; Mariology, 183; Pneu-
  matology, 144; Reformation, 6-7

Macken, John, 137-38
Marchetto, Agostino, 60
McCormack, Bruce L.: Barth and the
  analogia entis, 179-81
McEnroy, Carmel: women at Vatican II,
  148
Micklem, Nathaniel, 203
Minear, Paul: Christ as head of the
  Church, 77; New Testament images of
  Church, 72-73
Moorman, John R. H.: observers, 42,
  44, 86

Murray, Paul D., 26, 50; receptive ecumenism, 212

Newbigin, Lesslie: Barth and ecumenism, 17-18, 24; Collegial Theology, 116; criticism of Barth's event ecclesiology, 139-40; New Delhi Unity Statement, 198
Newman, John Henry: development of doctrine, 39, 176
Nissiotis, Nikos, 63, 140-41

O'Gara, Margaret: gift exchange, 213; minority at Vatican I, 221
O'Grady, Colm: church as event and institution, 139; universal church, 125, 145-46
O'Malley, John W., 30, 59, 171
Orsy, Ladislas, 214-15
Ottaviani, Alfredo, 41, 44

Paul VI: authority and *Humanae Vitae*, 88; Mary "Mother of the Church," 182, 190-92; meetings with observers, 39; mutual respect between Barth and Pope, 11-12, 24, 92-93; papacy as the ecumenical problem, 89; United Nations address, 93
Pius IX, 58
Pius XI: Jews, 227-28
Pius XII: Barth, 11, 24; Council, 57; Jews, 203, 224, 227
Przywara, Erich: *analogia entis,* 177-82; colleague of Barth, 13, 33, 117, 122

Radcliffe, Timothy: baptism, 133
Rahner, Karl: justification, 175; *peritus* at Council, 45, 121; sacraments, 134; unity, 141, 176, 195; women and ordination, 8, 45, 121, 152; world church, 216
Ramsey, Michael: reunion with Rome, 197
Ratzinger, Joseph (Benedict XVI): *analogia entis,* 181; appreciation of Barth, 47; Benedict XVI, 89; commentaries

on Vatican II, 60; critic of Preparatory Commission for Council, 40; Mary, 134, 186; universal church, 98-99, 146
Rogers, Eugene F., 144-45
Rosato, Philip J.: Holy Spirit, 125; mediation, 128
Rusch, William G.: Barth's "classic," 17, 28; Benedict XVI, 89; ecumenical reception, 40

Sadolet, Jacopo, 30-32
Schillebeeckx, Edward: charism and institution, 115; *peritus,* 45, 123
Schleiermacher, Friedrich: our contemporary, 14-15; Reformation, 118; Vatican I, 222
Schüssler Fiorenza, Elisabeth, 159-60, 162
Söhngen, Gottlieb, 181
Sonderegger, Katherine, 173
Soskice, Janet Martin, 121
Suenens, Léon Joseph: Mary, "Mother of the Church," 191; people before hierarchy, 48, 73; progressive Belgians, 41, 44
Sullivan, Francis A.: *"subsistit in,"* 78-79
Sykes, Stephen, 86

Tavard, George: Calvin, 35-36; Council and ordination of women, 154; experience and unity, 199
Thurian, Max, 4
Thurneysen, Eduard, 120
Tierney, Brian: infallibility, 96-97
Tillich, Paul, 5, 13
Torrance, Thomas F.: Barth as catholic theologian, 14; ordination of women, 160-61; sacraments, 132

Van der Meer, Haye, 149
Vischer, Lukas: observers, 49, 125-26
Visser 't Hooft, Henriette: arguments with Barth, 152, 155, 158
Visser 't Hooft, Willem: Barth and ecumenical movement, 19-20; observers, 52; Rome, 49-51; teachers and authority, 215; women, 155

Webster, John, 132, 135; criticism of Congar, 48
Wendel-Moltmann, Elisabeth: Barth and women, 156, 158
Wijngaards, John: women's ordination, 162
Willebrands, Johannes: friendship with Visser 't Hooft, 51; Jews and ecumenism, 229; women, 148

Wolf, Erik: christocratic community, 104
Wyschogrod, Michael: Jews, 200

Yeago, David: justification, 175
Yocum, John: mediation, 126, 128

Zwingli, Huldrych: Barth lectures on, 16, 29, 33; celebration of Mary, 184

Index of Subjects

analogia entis, 177-82
Anglican Roman Catholic International
    Commission (ARCIC): on Mary,
    188-89
Antichrist, 91-92, 177-78
authority, 86-88, 210-11

Baptism, Eucharist and Ministry, 110, 129
Barmen Declaration, 17, 19, 66, 83-84,
    115-16, 135-36, 205, 225

celibacy, 8-9, 17, 96
church order, 104-6
collegiality, 89-90, 115-16, 218
Communism, 54-55
consensus, 220-22
councils, conciliarism, 7, 35, 39, 41, 87,
    199, 218-19

democracy in the church, 77-78
dialogue, 118-19
dogma, irreformable, 99-102
Dombes, Groupe des: conversion of
    churches, 7; dialogue, 119; Mary,
    184-88
Dominus Jesus, 79

ecumenical gift exchange, 213-15
event/institution ecclesiology, 74-75, 138-
    43; Vatican II as event, 75, 202-3

filioque, 145

Global Christian Forum, 218

hierarchy, 102-3, 106-9; apostolic succes-
    sion, 135; laity, 114
hierarchy of truths, 65, 192-96
Humanae Vitae, 87-88
human cooperation in salvation, 135-38
human rights and religious freedom, 53

Jews and Israel: Barth and Kasper on "Is-
    rael church," 77; ecumenical issue, 71;
    "Hope of Israel," 19; Vatican II, 222-30
Joint Working Group: catholicity, 217;
    hierarchy of truths, 65, 194; mystery of
    Christ, 196
justification, 101, 167-76

laity, 9-10, 108-9, 114
local church/universal church, 81-82,
    98-99, 146

Mariology, 34, 47, 50, 182-92; Barth and
    Paul VI, 182-83; Co-Redeemer/Me-
    diatrix, 55, 65, 135-36; "Mother of the
    Church," 55, 191
ministry of the community, 110-13
mission, 70-71

Montreal Faith and Order Conference, 47, 68
Mortalium Animos, 27, 49, 64-65
Mystici Corporis: Barth's criticism, 76; Fries's criticism, 141

New Delhi Assembly: "All in each place," 198; Jews, 229

Observers at Vatican II: heirs of Reformation, 42; influence, 44-46

papacy: Barth's desire to be pope for a day, 90; Calvin as "pope" in Geneva, 66; infallibility, 34, 41, 95-97; Paul VI and Barth, 91-93; "Pope for all Christians," 88-89; successors of Peter, 97-99; United Nations and Peace, 93-94. *See also Ut Unum Sint*
Pentecostalism, 4
provisional ecclesiology, 126-27

reception, 40, 68
Receptive Ecumenism, 211-13
Reformers, 3, 6, 12, 29, 33, 35-36, 39, 41
return to Rome, 52; reunion with Rome, 197

sacraments, 111, 128-34, 176
Scripture: Barth's impact on *Dei Verbum,* 47, 86; Barth's lecture on Bible, 16, 85, 97, 136; biblical preaching, 41, 62, 80; Common Lectionary, 165; *Dei Verbum,* 61-69; observers' influence, 44-46; Scripture and tradition, 47-48, 64-65
semper reformanda, 7, 55, 102
sexual abuse scandal, 9-10, 176
subsidiarity, 89, 219
subsistit in, 78-80, 120

Toronto Statement, 83
Trent, 30, 34, 42; anathemas, 101; Calvin on Trent, 37-39, 42; invitation to Protestants, 167; justification, 174-75; tradition, 67

United Nations, 3, 93-94; Paul VI, 93; Secretary General as "secular pope," 91
United Reformed Church, 3-4, 106, 211, 218
Ut Unum Sint, 7, 86, 88-89, 94; ecumenical responses, 98, 120

Vatican I, 86-87, 95-96, 99, 221-22
Vatican II, documents (English titles as in Norman Tanner, *Ecumenical Councils*): *Ad Gentes* (Missionary Activity), 70-71, 113; *Apostolicam Actuositatem* (Laity), 61, 72, 113, 146-49, 190; *Dei Verbum* (Revelation), 41, 44-45, 47, 61, 62-69, 73, 136, 208, 220; *Dignitatis Humanae* (Religious Freedom), 53-54, 60-61, 223, 229; *Gaudium et Spes* (Church in World), 54, 93, 147, 232; *Lumen Gentium* (Church), 47-48, 55, 60-61, 70-84, 109-10, 113-14, 120, 126-27, 136, 143, 189-92, 208, 213, 220; *Nostra Aetate* (Non-Christian Religions), 77, 200, 222, 225-27, 228; *Sacrosanctum Concilium* (Liturgy), 41, 80, 128-29, 208-9; *Unitatis Redintegratio* (Ecumenism), 7, 46-48, 52, 53, 65, 71-72, 102, 120, 192-93, 198-200, 206, 208, 209, 210-11, 212, 213, 215, 229

Women, 11-12, 146-54, 156, 157; ordination of women, 154-56, 160-63; women bishops, 164n160
World Council of Churches, 2, 3, 4, 17, 21, 25-26, 49, 74, 91, 104-5, 136, 156, 198, 202, 212, 216-17, 227, 229